Handbook of Postmodern Biblical Interpretation

Also by Chalice Press:

Postmodern Interpretations of the Bible—A Reader
A. K. M. Adam, editor

Handbook of Postmodern Biblical Interpretation

A. K. M. ADAM
Editor

Chalice Press.
St. Louis, Missouri

Biblical quotations, unless otherwise noted, are author's translations. Those marked NRSV are from the *New Revised Standard Version Bible,* copyright 1989, Division of Christian Education of the National Council of Churches of Christ in the United States of America. Used by permission. All rights reserved.

Biblical quotations marked REB are from *The Revised English Bible* copyright © Oxford University Press and Cambridge University Press 1989. *The Revised English Bible with the Apocrypha* first published 1989. *The Revised English Bible* is a revision of *The New English Bible; The New English Bible New Testament* was first published by the Oxford and Cambridge University Presses in 1961, and the complete Bible in 1970.

Cover design: Mike Foley
Cover art: Bob Watkins
Interior design: Elizabeth Wright
Index: Margaret Adam
Art direction: Michael Domínguez

This book is printed on acid-free, recycled paper.

Visit Chalice Press on the World Wide Web at
www.chalicepress.com

10 9 8 7 6 5 4 3 2 1   00 01 02 03

Library of Congress Cataloging–in–Publication Data
Handbook of postmodern biblical interpretation / edited by A. K. M. Adam.
     p.   cm.
Includes bibliographical references.
ISBN 0-8272-2971-2
1. Bible–Hermeneutics. 2. Postmodernism. I. Adam, A. K. M. (Andrew Keith Malcolm), 1957-
  BS476 .H24 2000
  220.6' 01–dc21
                             00–010043

Printed in the United States of America

contents

preface

Innovations in the field of biblical studies follow a fairly predictable course. A few venturesome souls read papers at regional and national meetings and perhaps publish a few essays (often beginning in the journal *Semeia*). These preliminary forays usually draw on modes or methods that have flourished outside the biblical-interpretation industry, whether in departments of anthropology, comparative literature, or philosophy—though the versions that appear in biblical studies tend to arrive after a delay of from five to twenty years. The new-fangled interpretations meet an indifferent reception among the vast preponderance of biblical scholars, who already *know* how the Bible ought properly to be interpreted. These well-established, sensible souls either ignore or resist challenges to the guild's conventional wisdom—but after a while the would-be innovators build a core group of like-minded interpreters. They start their own groups at the professional meetings, apply their new mode of reading to every text possible, and attract the attention of an increasing audience. Some of their interpretations are forced, labored, or unconvincing, but others scintillate with unpredicted brilliance. On the strength of these exemplary interpretations, the new method elbows its way into "mainstream" interpretive venues: papers in the large-membership "sections" of the professional meeting, publication in the official academic journals, a spate of books (rushing to take advantage of the void of New-Interpretive-Method studies of every book of the biblical canon). After an academic generation or so, the once-new method has established itself as yet another mainstream approach to biblical interpretation; not everyone will be conversant with the method or its literature, but they've grown accustomed to its place in the Society of Biblical Literature's Annual Meeting program. At this point, it is time for another New Method to move into the hallowed ground of the biblical disciplines and for the cycle of resistance and acceptance to begin again.

How long ago did that cycle begin for "postmodernism" in biblical studies? Much depends on which definition of "postmodernism" one relies on, but to adopt one arbitrary criterion—"engagement with the work of Jacques Derrida"— we may estimate that the discipline of biblical studies intersected "postmodernism" *roughly* twenty years ago. Of course, there are many more subtle and profound barometers we might use, and we might allow that postmodernism—as the bad conscience of modernism—has been haunting the biblical academy more than a hundred years. Such disputes illustrate the futility of trying to pin down any fixed stars of postmodern discourse at the same time that they buttress the very modern effort to identify epochs and eras, decades and origins. We have never been immune to the problems and temptations of postmodern sorts of reasoning; at the same time, the biblical academy has been talking and writing self-consciously about postmodern matters for only a relatively short while.

Or perhaps we have been postmodern for a long while, a long enough while to generate manifestos and introductions, to authorize the production of doctoral dissertations (still rather few) and books and symposia (increasing in number) that approach biblical interpretation with explicit recourse to discourses entwined in the "postmodern." Inasmuch as many, therefore, have taken it in hand to produce postmodern interpretations of the texts that have been interpreted among us, just as they were handed on to us from those who were servants of the word, we too decided, after examining everything carefully, that the time had come to compile an enchiridion of the multifarious names and approaches and phenomena that are widely associated with the designation "postmodernism." This can be read as a sign that "postmodern" biblical studies have come into their own (though their own may know them not), that this is indeed the postmodern era of biblical studies, that "one must absolutely be postmodern" (to paraphrase Rimbaud). This endeavor does embrace the work of dozens of interested scholars, perhaps a cadre of leaders to bring their nomadic generation into a pomo promised land. It is incomplete (where is Baudrillard? where is "New Historicism"?), but humbly and perhaps necessarily so; we make no pretension to a comprehensive survey, but are pleased to have attained a relatively broad constituency of women and men, of varying academic generations, with varying (sometimes opposing) interpretations of their topics, all to come together for a few pages in a carnival of meanings.

At the same time, one might equally construe the appearance of so ambitious a monument as a sign that the provocative energies of the postmodern intervention in biblical studies have exhausted themselves. No longer only the scruffy grad students who scrambled to get their theses past hostile examiners, many of today's postmodern interpreters hold tenure, and some occupy named academic chairs. No longer can senior advisers shake their heads solemnly and advise younger colleagues that it would be vocational suicide to be associated with postmodernism. Though many critics still regard postmodernism as a dangerous threat, each passing year suggests that the dire warnings may be more the fearful projections of an uncomprehending *derriere-garde* than a plausible warning of a looming cultural catastrophe.

At such a moment, this compendium may serve any of a number of useful functions. It may help readers who are just now beginning their excursions into postmodern discourses to find their way more readily, by describing for them particular landmarks and points of orientation–though, of course, the characterizations of such landmarks and orientation points are not dispassionate, fixed, immutable identifications, but are their authors' ineluctably partial reflections. For such readers, this handbook may ease the transition into the primary sources by acquainting them with terms, names, and tactics that might seem daunting at first glance. It was with such readers in mind that this handbook was first proposed; in inviting contributors, we asked authors to imagine a colleague down the hall who had not yet quite climbed aboard the train, who might want to know what this Derrida fellow was up to. It also provides initial responses to dubious readers who may wonder what a postmodern theoretician might be able to say in reply to challenges from opponents to postmodern thought, to sensible souls who know that postmodern thinkers cannot possibly care about the truth, to anxious readers who fear that a postmodern discourse is a discourse systematically insulated from ethical evaluation.

This book may also serve those who are already acclimated to postmodern discursive climates to branch out, to learn more about different topics or figures. The field is vast and the laborers are still few, and even the major impulses in postmodern thought have still had only limited impact in biblical studies. Moreover, such impact as these discourses have made may not be uniformly profound or well-informed; the fact that an article under the heading "A Lacanian Reading of the Psalms" has been published does not make that article sound. By broadening horizons, and by offering opportunities to deepen readers' engagement with postmodern studies, this book may help clear some foggy air and may help critics recognize how obscure certain misty patches are.

For readers who are quite well versed in postmodern theory, this book may provide them with a source for capsule summaries (perhaps one should be honest and say "capsule distortions") of prominent features of the postmodern landscape. Such readers may conveniently find in these pages useful stock figures for the netherworld of footnoted explication, or in conversation they may suggest that their uncertain students, friends, or teachers consult these pages.

Finally, for those who are sure that the end of the ages has come upon us—barbarians at the gates, beast from the abyss about to rise from the waters—this handbook may provide all the evidence they need that 666, the ten horns, and the seventh seal are all subtly coded references to Levinas, postcolonialism, and trauma. Such readers should publicize their conclusions widely, cite page number and author, and encourage all interested parties to purchase several copies of the book for closer consultation.

It would not be reasonable to offer a single dedication for a work of so many participants. At the same time, I propose a purpose to this handbook that goes beyond pragmatic market considerations. Many of the authors represented in this volume will have incorporated postmodern theory into their intellectual repertoire less as a requirement imposed by pedagogical authorities and more as a joyous exploration of forbidden, or at least highly guarded, intellectual terrain. I invite our readers to consider this volume a thank-offering to those who encouraged us to keep reading, who slipped us photocopied articles or guided us to hitherto unknown resources, and especially now to the students who come after us, whose interests we (in our turn) will probably try to constrain and circumscribe, in the hope that none of us will cease from learning, working, thinking something different from what we have thought before.

A. K. M. Adam
May 2000

list of contributors

A. K. M. Adam–Seabury-Western Theological Seminary, Evanston, Illinois

George Aichele–Adrian College, Adrian, Michigan

Timothy K. Beal–Case Western Reserve University, Cleveland, Ohio

William A. Beardslee–Claremont, California

Roland Boer–Monash University, Victoria, Autstralia

Daniel Boyarin–University of California, Berkeley, California

Susan Brayford–Centenary College, Shreveport, Louisiana

Fred W. Burnett–Anderson University, Anderson, Indiana

David S. Cunningham–Seabury-Western Theological Seminary, Evanston, Illinois

James W. Flanagan–Case Western Reserve University, Cleveland, Ohio

Mary McClintock Fulkerson–Duke University, Durham, North Carolina

Jay Geller–Vanderbilt University, Nashville, Tennessee

Mark K. George–Iliff School of Theology, Denver, Colorado

Barry Harvey–Baylor University, Waco, Texas

Faith Kirkham Hawkins–Gustavus Adolphus College, Saint Peter, Minnesota

Gina Hens-Piazza–Jesuit School of Theology at Berkeley, Berkeley, California

Shawn Kelley–Daemen College, Amherst, New York

Philip D. Kenneson–Milligan College, Johnson City, Tennessee

Tod Linafelt–Georgetown University, Washington, D.C.

Burke O. Long–Bowdoin College, Brunswick, Maine

Francisco Lozada, Jr.–University of the Incarnate Word, San Antonio, Texas

Vincent J. Miller–Georgetown University, Washington, D.C.

Stephen D. Moore–Drew University Theological School, Madison, New Jersey

Carol A. Newsom–Emory University, Atlanta, Georgia

David W. Odell-Scott–Kent State University, Kent, Ohio

Gary A. Phillips–University of the South, Sewanee, Tennessee

Tina Pippin–Agnes Scott College, Atlanta, Georgia

S. Brent Plate–University of Vermont, Burlington, Vermont

Ilona Rashkow–State University of New York, Stony Brook, New York

Laurel C. Schneider–Chicago Theological Seminary, Chicago, Illinois

Yvonne Sherwood–University of Glasgow, Glasgow, Scotland

Jeffrey L. Staley–Pacific Lutheran University, Seattle, Washington

Ken Stone–Chicago Theological Seminary, Chicago, Illinois

Beverly J. Stratton–Augsburg College, Minneapolis, Minnesota

Kenneth Surin–Duke University, Durham, North Carolina

Jan Tarlin–Emory University, Atlanta, Georgia

Eric Thurman–Drew University, Madison, New Jersey

Mary Ann Tolbert–Pacific School of Religion, Berkeley, California

Andrew Wilson–University of Sheffield, Sheffield, England

Frank M. Yamada–Seabury-Western Theological Seminary, Evanston, Illinois

anti-postmodernism
Barry Harvey

As it has in virtually every other field of study, the specter of "postmodernism" has made its way into the world of biblical scholarship, setting off a heated debate over the basic assumptions that have underwritten the academic study of the Jewish and Christian scriptures for the better part of two centuries. During this time these suppositions gained axiomatic status within the guild, and the few scholars who did not accept the methods of interpretation based on them found themselves on the outside looking in. In recent years, however, these assumptions have come under attack by increasing numbers of those within the world of religious studies who either claim or have been saddled with the label of postmodern. This dispute has led some to draw a proverbial line in the sand to safeguard what they regard as the foundational assumptions of their craft.

The idea of postmodernism conjures up haunting images of nihilism, relativism, and linguistic idealism (the contention that there is nothing in the world other than writing). There are, to be sure, holophobic cults of ambiguity and indeterminacy–gathered together in cultural enclaves dedicated to the celebration of otherness, mobility, marginality, and disruption–that do their best to reinforce this impression at every opportunity (Eagleton, 1996: 4f.). They claim that the world is a never-ending (and often brutal) play of difference and non-identity and emphasize at every opportunity the death of God, the primordiality of violence and opposition, and the endless flux of existence. History is but a mere succession of happenings without connection, purpose, or goal other than the values we impose on each other and the world about us, and the arbitrary nature of these impositions only serves to mock us with the capriciousness of our existence.

In actuality there is no consensus about what constitutes postmodernism, save possibly for the rather trivial observation that it represents some kind of reaction to modernity (which is itself a contested term). It would be impossible even to draw up a list of writers whom everyone would recognize as postmodern. Should we limit the term to post-structuralists, or should it include pragmatists and reader-response theorists? How do feminist and womanist authors relate to postmodern motifs? Where in the postmodern mélange does the revival of interest in Aristotelian, Augustinian, and Thomist philosophies and other forms of classical thought fit? How should we regard the resurgence of traditional Jewish modes of reasoning? Jeffrey Wasserstrom observes that

1

the linguistic career of the idea of postmodernism resembles that of a kitchen sponge. At first the sponge is kept next to the sink and reserved for one or two particular tasks (washing the dishes and maybe wiping off the counters), but eventually the family starts to use it for a variety of jobs, and it makes its way throughout the house. In the process it becomes virtually worthless for the tasks for which it was originally intended (Wasserstrom: B4).

It is possible, however, to identify traits that are common to most candidates for the title of postmodern. Terry Eagleton, for example, describes postmodernity as "a style of thought which is suspicious of classical notions of truth, reason, identity and objectivity, of the idea of universal progress or emancipation, of single frameworks, grand narratives or ultimate grounds of explanation" (1996: vii). Postmodern writers in general resist habits of thinking privileged by the modern world. These habits include the assumption that there exists in or for the unfettered mind a single substantive conception of rationality that provides standards and methods leading to an exhaustive scientific conception of the whole of reality, which in turn replicates the fundamental structure of the universe. These habits are themselves part of a history of inevitable progress as judged by an idea of progress that is a product of this history (MacIntyre, 1990: 23f.). Modern habits of mind foster ever more discrete spheres of knowledge–science, morality, art, religion–over which highly trained experts have obtained exclusive mastery. Modern biblical interpretation, for example, has become its own specialized province with its own methodology, separate from theological inquiry (a position that Krister Stendahl simply takes for granted in his famous essay on biblical theology). Postmodern authors have put these and other ideas and dispositions into question, though the conclusions they draw from their analyses vary widely.

As one would expect, a variety of responses to the challenges posed by these critiques have emerged in the field of religious studies. A few wear the name of postmodernity as a badge of honor; many others regard it as a sure way to finish off all religious pretensions; still others see it as a way to reinvigorate theological inquiry. All these responses have secured a place in the *agon* of academic inquiry. In the last few years, however, a number of scholars have appeared on the scene whose opposition to what they regard as postmodernism exhibits a character not unlike that of a religious obligation or holy quest. Indeed, there are those who appear to tie the future of religious faith and/or rationality to defeating the postmodern beast.

There is no easy way to characterize these "anti-postmodernists." No two people will agree on who deserves this title. Disagreeing with most or all of what postmodernism purportedly stands for does not automatically make one an anti-postmodernist. There are good reasons to question much of what travels under the banner of postmodernism. Rather, it would seem that a specific type of opposition to the rejection of modern habits of mind and Enlightenment sensibilities defines anti-postmodernism. When faced with the implications of postmodernism for their disciplines, a group of scholars has risen to the defense of modern suppositions and the methods that in their estimation have served them well for so long.

In the field of biblical studies this defense of modern ideas frequently takes the form of the claim that biblical texts have a single determinate meaning created by their authors and accessible to later generations through the use of scholarly interpretive models. Luther and Calvin set the stage for this claim when they rejected the multiple levels of meaning in biblical texts recognized by patristic and medieval forms of exegesis and argued instead for the priority and sufficiency of the literal sense of scripture as disclosed by grammatical-historical interpretation. In the eighteenth and nineteenth centuries, however, new methods for uncovering these grammatical and historical meanings began to emerge that divorced the interpretation of scripture from the ecclesial setting that was as sacrosanct to the Reformers as it was to their Catholic forebears (Freeman). While some were slow to embrace these new methods and techniques, the majority of biblical scholars were eventually won over. Through the first half of the twentieth century the "historical-critical method" exercised a virtual monopoly over the field, and for a time it appeared as though its dominance would remain unchallenged for decades to come.

The suppositions that drove the modern approach to scripture were clearly articulated more than a century ago in a well-known essay by Benjamin Jowett. According to Jowett, "Scripture has one meaning—the meaning which it had in the mind of the Prophet or Evangelist who first uttered or wrote, to the hearers or readers who first received it." He went so far as to claim that the aim of biblical interpretation was to get rid of it, that is, to set aside everything that had accumulated around this text during the intervening years "and leave us alone in company with the author." Jowett was supremely confident that, when provided with the proper linguistic and historical tools, the interpreter of the biblical text would be able to distill the timeless and universal meaning of these texts from "the accidents of time and place" (Jowett).

Many anti-postmodernist scholars have responded to recent claims about the radical undecidability of meaning by asserting that Jowett's viewpoint is a non-negotiable sine qua non of biblical interpretation. For example, one author contends that "a Christian faith concerned to retain its own coherence cannot for a moment accept that the biblical texts (individually and as a whole) lack a single, determinate meaning, that their meanings are created by their readers, or that theological interpretations must see themselves as non-privileged participants in an open-ended, pluralistic conversation" (Watson, 1997: 97). But we should not assume that only scholars with some sort of explicit theological agenda share this understanding of how meaning and texts are related. Biblical scholars of various ideological stripes consider it essential that we view texts as "objective, stable 'givens,' available as self-subsistent entities for us to interpret" (Noble: 419). Only if we follow this theory of meaning, says Paul Hanson, can "the text offer any assistance in sorting out fitting interpretations from unsuitable ones." (Actually, Hanson fudges on his preference for the priority of "non-subjective" forms of interpretation when he admits that there could be multiple historical settings for a text and thus multiple meanings: 10).

According to Jowett's viewpoint, the biblical text has a meaning, as though it were a container filled with some kind of substance. As Stephen Fowl points out, this is more than simply a claim about the basic intelligibility or meaningfulness of biblical texts. In this model,

> meaning is conceived (at least implicitly) as a sort of property with which the text has been endued. Further, such meaning can be uncovered through the application of some set of interpretive procedures. In this view, the biblical text is seen as a relatively stable element in which an author inserts, hides, or dissolves (choose your metaphor) meaning. The task of the interpreter, whether lay, clerical, or professional, is to dig out, uncover, or distill the meaning of the text." (Fowl, 1998: 33f.)

In their dispute with postmodernity, anti-postmodernists contend that without a determinate view of textual meaning, intellectual and moral anarchy will inevitably ensue at some point. But does this argument hold up under close examination?

In fact, it fails on several counts. First, it is not really an argument at all, but, as Fowl points out, a cluster of metaphors that prescribe how one should relate to texts in general, and the Bible in particular. As such it doubtlessly offers comfort to some whose faith in truth, goodness, and beauty has been badly shaken, and it may well provide a thesis to be argued, but as an argument it begs the question because it assumes the very image of textual meaning that is in dispute. Perhaps it is the case that a single, stable, and accessible property called meaning somehow resides in a text, but this is by no means a matter of common sense or consent, and not just to postmodern habits of mind. Patristic and medieval Christian thought recognized multiple levels of meaning in their readings of the biblical texts. No doubt some spiritual readings of scripture were outlandish, but important figures within this tradition of interpretation helped to put a check on such readings (Fowl, 1998: 36–40; Freeman: 21f.). Jewish interpreters of the Bible also worked with more than one sense of textual meaning, though they did so in substantially different ways from their Christian counterparts (Halivni).

Second, the contention that without a determinate view of textual meaning, intellectual and moral anarchy will necessarily follow, is logically flawed. The argument runs something like this: Unless there is a single meaning created by their authors and accessible to later generations through objective methods of study, biblical texts (individually and as a whole) have no stable sense or significance; consequently, these texts must have a single, determinate meaning. Unfortunately, wanting and having are not the same thing. People may intuitively feel that without God we could not stand life, but by itself such a feeling does not certify that God might be anything more than a comforting illusion. In like fashion, a single meaning deposited into the linguistic symbols of a text and recoverable by objective methods of interpretation may intuitively seem to some an absolute necessity, but the appeal to intuition is almost always a clear indication that something has gone badly wrong with an argument (MacIntyre, 1984: 69).

Third, modern methods of textual interpretation are nowhere near as reliable or as theologically efficacious as once advertised. In particular, the so-called historical-critical method simply does not exist "in the singular form that is normally envisaged. What does exist is a shifting set of conventions, never clearly defined and constantly under negotiation, about questions that it is proper to address to the biblical texts and the answers that it is proper to expect from them" (Watson, 1995: 518). Moreover, the assumption that questions of religious doctrine and practice can be settled by an objective appeal to the meaning "deposited" in scripture is unwarranted, for as Fowl observes, "one will find in both ecclesial and academic communities that those committed to a determinate account of biblical interpretation will still disagree sharply on the implications or applications of a biblical text on whose meaning they all agree" (Fowl, 1998: 34).

Anti-postmodernist critiques also often fail to account for differences between, on the one hand, the wide variety of "postmodern" philosophies, theologies, and modes of literary criticism that exist, and on the other, postmodernism as a peculiar style of contemporary culture. In particular, the contention that a methodological slippery slope leads inevitably from the rejection of modern conceptions of truth, reason, identity, and objective facts to relativism and nihilism is unwarranted. Mieke Bal, Zygmunt Bauman, Michel de Certeau, Jacques Derrida, Stanley Fish, Michel Foucault, Donna Haraway, Luce Irigaray, Alasdair MacIntyre, Jean-Luc Marion, Richard Rorty, and Cornel West all find the staples of Enlightenment thought seriously lacking, but they do so from a wide variety of standpoints, with very different epistemic, moral, and social conclusions.

The absolute relativism and romantic nihilism that often characterize postmodernism as a cultural style should be viewed as inverted images of modern culture's arrogant longing for godlike powers (Harvey, 1999: 95–134). Devotees of this cult(ure) despair of all coherence and intelligibility, not only for themselves but for all traditions of inquiry, now that it is clear that the procedures and habits, ends and relations of modernity cannot transcend their own brands of contingency. Indeed, much of what passes for postmodern culture and thought is parasitic, requiring the pathology of that which it rejects for its own coherence and intelligibility. Postmodern critiques are frequently "symbiotic with their very object of criticism: that is, they remain alive only as long as they give life to their enemy. In short, deconstructionist assaults must breathe life into metaphysical, epistemological, and ethical discourses if their critiques are to render these discourses lifeless" (West, 1986: 139).

Many self-styled postmodernists thus find themselves hopelessly entangled in the binary oppositions that they labor so diligently to undermine. William Poteat sums up their dilemma nicely when he notes that after the chimera of an eternal, ahistorical truth has been unmasked, they "still perceive and evaluate the realm of the pretensions and retrotensions of time as from the perspective of eternity—static and changeless as the printed word is when compared with the spoken." Thus, they come to think that they are "left with 'only' the realities and Being that are disclosed in time, and left 'only' with history" (Poteat: 65). The modern longing for a definitive edition of the universe, on the basis of which the particularities of time and space can be mastered, and the postmodernist's claim that texts escape Enlightenment standards of truth and intelligibility, and thus everyone is free (or is it condemned?) to play outside the arbitrary lines of mere convention, are products of the same intellectual gene pool.

There is thus a good deal to examine with a critical eye in postmodern culture and theory. But the strategy of combating postmodernism by defending the Enlightenment dream of a universal humanity living according to a single reason and a single morality, with its peculiar conceptions of truth, reason, identity, rationality, and progress, only perpetuates the binary oppositions that postmodern authors cannot seem to shake. For example, in a critique of Hans Frei's description of the authoritative rules that govern the literal reading of scripture within the Christian community, Francis Watson wonders whence such rules come: "Are they authoritative for the community because the texts themselves require to be understood along these lines, or are they authoritative because the community has 'arbitrarily' decided to read the text in certain ways and to exclude other readings that might appear to be equally plausible in themselves?" (Watson, 1997: 125 n. 11). It is not at all clear, however, that the only two viable alternatives are to regard meaning as either an active quality somehow implanted by the author in paper and ink or the arbitrary imposition of a community.

It is simply not the case that in the hands of non-determinate methods of interpretation anything can mean anything else, such that "texts become victims of the reading communities and every possibility that texts might change readers and reading communities is denied" (Jeanrond: 112). John Milbank notes, for example, that the act of narrating does not assume punctilinear facts or discrete meanings, nor is it concerned with universal laws or truths of the spirit: "Yet it is not arbitrary in the sense that one can repeat a text in just any fashion, although one can indeed do so in any number of fashions" (Milbank: 267). Moreover, one need not believe that there is a realm of objective facts independent of human description and judgment to affirm that the world "is at least real enough to be acted upon and altered," that most of the time it is dense and autonomous enough to resist our designs upon it (Eagleton, 1996: 13). Our engagements with the world are always mediated by the interchange of sign and signified, but neither can be reduced to the other. It is ironic that the defense of modern notions of truth, reason, identity, and history in opposition to postmodernism virtually abandons the rhetoric of frankness that is an enduring mark of the Enlightenment (Rosen, 1987: 27–32). Indeed, the unwillingness to deal seriously with the claims of postmodern thought lends credence to them. In contrast, those who confront these claims head-on not only break through some of the esotericism that frequently attends postmodern conversations, but in the process develop insights that they might not otherwise have had. George Grant is no fan of Friedrich Nietzsche, stating repeatedly that he does not regard Nietzsche's thought as the best or most profound word about what is. Nevertheless, he recognizes that "Nietzsche's words raise to an intensely full light of explicitness what it is to live in this era. He articulates what it is to have inherited existence as a present member of Western history. His thought does not invent the situation of our contemporary existing; it unfolds it" (Grant: 34).

Another irony that attends anti-postmodern defenses of modernity, particularly on the part of those who undertake the interpretive task out of their commitment to Christianity, concerns its choice of allies. As J. Bottum observes, the history of modernity is in many respects nothing other than a three-hundred-year attempt to undermine the Christian tradition. The pioneers of the modern age sought to replace the authority of the scriptures with a construct of science and morality based solely on what has been shown to be a contingent conception of human rationality. Now that modernity is under assault from many quarters, its axioms and formulae already regarded by many as unfounded, it seems unwise for believers to spend precious intellectual capital in the effort to shore up its crumbling architecture (Bottum: 31).

We should remember that lived history is the only venue human beings have in which to test the social and moral consequences of thought. In the final analysis, the debate over postmodernism is not a battle over a set of disembodied ideas, waged by academics whose lives and livelihoods are seldom at stake. Wherever people are confronted with questions of prescription and proscription, they invariably find themselves entangled in issues of power. Both the devotee of postmodernity, who contends that the world is a ceaseless flux of difference and non-identity, without goal or purpose, and the anti-postmodernist, who tries to refute that contention by reclaiming the confidence and explanatory power of modern ideas, are making strong political bids. And as with all such bids, the outcome of this contest will no doubt be both unpredictable and untidy.

author
A. K. M. Adam

To the extent that postmodern theory has impressed itself upon contemporary readers, they probably are confident that postmodernism proclaims The Death of the Author. They reckon that the putative absence of the Author constitutes a license to make of texts whatever one will, and they chortle with glee when postmodern writers still claim copyrights and argue that they have been misinterpreted.

As much as the reports of the Author's death have been greatly exaggerated, the facile assumption that postmodern interrogations of notions like "the author" entail a great liberation from textual authority or the penultimate phase in the decline of Western civilization are equally misguided. Yes, Roland Barthes announced the death of the author in his 1968 article, "The Death of the Author." But no, the author hasn't gone away; people still write, and readers care, justifiably, about the authors of the texts they read.

The background for this brouhaha about "the author" involves more than just postmodern theory. As far back as the fifties, American New Critics Monroe Beardsley and William Wimsatt argued that a literary text is an autonomous entity that should be interpreted without reference to an author's intent in writing it. Their article "The Intentional Fallacy" (1954) generated a controversy that still persists even where the theoretical lights of Paris have never shone. While Beardsley and Wimsatt did not necessarily win the day, they opened the possibility that respectable critics might be able to produce legitimate interpretations without reference to the author.

Part of the resistance to Wimsatt and Beardsley's position derives from common practice; one so readily imagines asking an author "what did you mean?" that one forgets that authors are often unavailable for consultation, that a certain amount of critical interpretation necessarily goes beyond an author's deliberate intentions, and that the entire question of "meaning" may be more complicated than the question allows. It is one thing to ask one's mate, "What did you mean by *this*?" while pointing to an illegible smear on the grocery list; it is another thing to ask T. S. Eliot, "When you wrote 'three white leopards sat under a juniper-tree / In the cool of the day,' what did you mean?"–the question to which Eliot reputedly answered, "When I wrote 'three white leopards sat under a juniper-tree / In the cool of the day,' I meant 'three white leopards sat under a juniper-tree / In the cool of the day.'"

Readers who affirm their faith in the necessity of interpreting texts by determining an author's intention need also to go further and clarify what they mean by "intention" and "meaning," each a term whose apparent simplicity cloaks a multitude of conceptual problems. Does "intention" include only *deliberate* intention, or shall we also categorize as "intentional" the traces of subconscious or unconscious authorial activity? Must an authorial intention be sustained throughout the entire process of composing a literary work, or shall we count an intention held at the beginning but discarded halfway through (or an intention realized only when a work is partly completed)? Is an author permitted, in other words, to change intentions in midstream? Is it possible that a literary work can be greater than its author intended—can one ascribe excellence to a novel whose author scribbled it hurriedly simply to pay for some food? The complications surrounding the term "meaning" are even more daunting; one can hardly blame an interpreter who decides that the difficulties in using "intention" outweigh its benefits.

Another background difficulty concerns the critic's prerogative to pronounce some interpretations legitimate, valid, or good (on one hand) or illegitimate, invalid, or bad (on the other). Defenders of the importance of "the author" frequently couch their arguments as an ethical claim that readers owe "the author" their best efforts to interpret a text as the author would have intended.

At other times, the author's partisans suggest that insufficient attention to "the author" marks a fatal stage in the decline of the West. What if *no one* paid attention to authors' intentions? If school bus drivers ignored stop signs, if banks honored checks with sums that were only whimsically associated with the amounts specified on them, the entire edifice of social organization might crumble. Such apocalyptic prophecies neglect the fact that reading-for-intention is a relatively recent, local development. Such interpretive practices as midrash and allegorical interpretation—which manage very well without analysis of a specific writer's intent—can boast long periods of cultural prominence, coincident with the ascendancy of the West.

Much of this hand-wringing misses a number of points. Were the adversaries of postmodern analysis paying careful attention, they would note that postmodern theorists can't be *simply* proposing that there is no more "author," that one can attribute any meaning one wants to a text; the postmoderns themselves debate how this or that text should be construed, and they regularly analyze one another's critical interventions with a rigor that would gratify even the most orthodox modern critic. Where hostile critics interpret this as a performative contradiction—"those who claim that there is no author, do they not themselves write?"—they might more productively recognize a sign that they have oversimplified the ways postmodern theorists attend to the phenomenon of authorship.

Roland Barthes proposed the death of the author in the culturally momentous year 1968 as one implication of the history of literature and of linguistics. As literature had gradually shed the trappings of personal genius as the source of writing, so linguistics had demonstrated that language functions perfectly without an enunciator standing behind the enunciation. Barthes points out that the author simply disappears in specifically modern writing (1977: 145), but once the (modern) author disappears, that absence makes it evident that all authors are dispensable. "To give a text an Author is to impose a limit on that text, to furnish it with a final signified, to close the writing. Such a conception suits criticism very well, the latter then allotting itself the important task of discovering the Author (or its hypostases: society, history, psyché, liberty) beneath the work. When the author is found, the text is 'explained'– victory to the critic" (1977: 147). Barthes views his antithetical reversal as a gesture toward liberation: "To refuse to fix meaning is, in the end, to refuse God" (1977: 147). Powers of domination had anointed a surrogate, an "author," to constrain readers; but according to Barthes, the author is dead–long live the reader!

A quick rebuttal to Barthes's essay came from a quarter that would surprise the cultured defenders of the author. Michel Foucault offered several postmodern ripostes to Barthes's claims. He argued that the author is not dead, can never die, inasmuch as the author is not solely a principle of domination by which interpretations are restricted, but more fundamentally constitutes one inescapable element in the complex process of interpretation. In important senses, "a work" is unthinkable without "an author"; the two are correlative concepts. That which is without author defies interpretation; it is a naked phenomenon, with no further signification. In order to ascribe "meaning" to anything, one must treat it as though it had been composed by an author. Likewise, the identity of an author is decisively shaped by the works he or she presumably wrote: Were we satisfied that Shakespeare had written all the works commonly ascribed to Francis Bacon, that conclusion would transform our sense of both "Shakespeare" and "Bacon" (1979: 146).

Foucault identifies authorship not only with writing–as though just any written text had an "author"–but with a social complex that isolates writers and ascribes to them particular qualities. (Foucault treats these complexes of enacted theory, or theorized practice, as *discourses*.) We do not treat everyone who writes something as an "author"; we ascribe to authors qualities of origination, of responsibility, of *difference* from the transcribers of humdrum everyday texts such as personal letters, contracts, laundry lists, graffiti. The practices and ideologies that assign special significance to particular sorts of writing and writers vary depending on the cultural circumstances, and the importance of an author depends to a great extent on the pertinent social forces. As Foucault points out, the author can serve as a basis for authentication of truth-claims, as when the Pythagoreans verified their maxims by binding them to the name of Pythagoras with *ipse dixit* ("He himself said…"). The author can serve as an index of continuity, so that a work fits into a historical context, a corpus of other works, and a spectrum of canonical value. The author can appear as an oracle of transcendent truth, the creative individual genius of romanticism; or the author can disappear, as in the high-modern literary sphere of which Barthes was theorizing. Above all, in certain cases the author can inaugurate a new complex of discursive practice; Foucault cites the examples of Freud and Marx, whose significance as authors extends beyond their actual production of texts to their production of fields of knowledge and practice.

When one situates the author in this multidimensional social space, the question of "the death of the author" takes on a different cast. Even the high-modern Barthesian author has not precisely *died*, but plays a specific, reticent role in the critic's construction of textual meaning. Such a reticence is not necessary, however; Foucault himself illustrates a variety of roles for authors. He thus differentiates the constrictive "author," the censor of interpretative legitimacy, from the inevitable "author" whose (hypothetical) existence alone constitutes the object of interpretation as "text." Such a postmodern sense of the author–the "author-function" (1979: 148–53)–recognizes that the author always plays a role in the limitation of interpretation, but allows the ways in which the author constrains interpretation to modulate with the genre of a text, with specific features of the text, with the social setting. The author is thus neither modern and dead nor romantic and fecund, but is always instrumental in the function of discourses that produce and exclude meanings.

Foucault's argument that the author–far from being dead–is *necessary* to the production of interpretation seems to fly in the face of not only Barthes's wake for the late author, but also Derrida's argument ("Signature Event Context" in 1988) that writing, in its very existence, must be able to function in the radical absence of any specific reader, indeed, in the absence of the author (1988: 8–9). The author is part of the context of a writing, but that context is always removed from the writing; the author, necessarily dispensable, is thus, in effect, *already* absent from the writing. At the same time, however, Derrida points out that because the same writing that must be separable from the specific context of a receiver and an author can never be separated from context-in-general, contextuality is inescapable, recipients are inescapable, and even–in some sense–authors are inescapable.

Stanley Fish embraces the claim that authors are necessary (in a certain way) and presses even further by insisting that interpretation requires not merely an author but more specifically an authorial *intention*. All textual interpretation depends on the assumption that the text represents the product of intentional agency; stimuli that seem to bear no relation whatever to intentional production we dismiss, and things that seem textual we interpret by ascribing them to at least a hypothetical intentional agent. Fish reminds his readers that his position does not itself constrain interpretations; he leaves open the questions of who the intentional agent might be and of what counts as evidence of intention, allowing (for instance) for the possibility that "my hand held the pen but it was the spirit of the Lord that moved me" (1994:

300). At the same time, he refuses–as does Derrida (explicitly, in "Limited Inc a b c…" and "Afterword: Toward an Ethic of Discussion," in *Limited Inc*)–to exclude intention from interpretation. "One cannot read *or* reread independently of intention, that is, of the assumption that one is dealing with marks or sounds produced by an intentional being, a being situated in some enterprise in relation to which he has a purpose or a point of view" (1989: 99–100).

There are, no doubt, postmodern theorists who resist such claims. Readers should bear in mind, however, that the necessity of imagining an intentional author of some sort does not entail the methodological or ethical obligation to defer to the intention of the original author or "the historical author" or any particular stand-in. The point of these essays is that all interpretation, however fanciful, however academically serious, involves treating texts as artifacts characterized by intention. As Fish would point out, however, nothing whatever follows from that axiom.

Fish himself invokes the possibility that the pertinent intention derives not from human agency, but from the Spirit of God. Such a possibility has a long and honorable history in the field of biblical interpretation. Otherwise, one may interpret a text by the guideline "This is what *I* would have meant if *I* had written these words." Or one may search for guiding intentions in a text that many thoughtful readers deem composite (say, the Book of Genesis or the *Iliad*): "If there were but one author to this work, what intention best accounts for the resulting composition?"

One motivation for advancing the sole legitimacy of interpreting the text according to the (reconstructed) intention of the actual author lies in the possibility that actual intentions may provide an impartial criterion for adjudicating interpretive conflicts. Alas, such a hope comes a cropper on the complexity of ascertaining what the actual intention might have been; claims about the actual intention of Paul in Romans 1 are no less controverted than are claims about how best to interpret Romans 1. The posited moral or intellectual obligation to find out the actual author's intention simply displaces most arguments over interpretation from the text–on the constitution of which there is frequently consensual agreement and for which there is usually material evidence–to a fictive authorial intention, about which there is little agreement and for which the evidential value of the only material evidence has occasioned the interpretive question.

This points to Derrida's argument in "Signature Event Context" that although interpretation always involves attention to intention, such intention constitutes one among many elements of the intepretive context. In that array of elements, "intention" cannot hold a privileged position unless someone or some body of interpreters decree that "among *us*, the historical author's actual literary intention will be paramount." The force of that determination will remain limited to those readers who avow allegiance to the intentionalist camp, and–as Fish would remind us–their allegiance will not affect the tenor of their interpretations, but manifestos and vows of allegiance need not change their adherents' behavior to have a useful effect. Other interpreters may adopt alternative party platforms, and still others may eschew programmatic creeds in favor of attention to the specific hermeneutical circumstances with which they're dealing (and all manner of mediating variations on these themes will likewise flourish).

In all of these approaches to interpretation, however, a postmodern reader can discern the role of the author-function, the trace of an origin that need not subsist in order to be interpreted. Such a return will not console some worried critics, nor will it exhilarate adventuresome reader-oriented interpreters. Still, the author provides an avenue for interpretive inquiry that neither begs hermeneutical and metaphysical questions nor throws ordered discourse to the winds. The postmodern question of the author will thus not be "Is the author dead or alive?" but "How do you imagine the author, and why?"– which question gives ample scope for debate, for agreement, and for further exploration.

autobiography
Jeffrey L. Staley

The Invention of a Genre

The word *autobiography* is a fairly recent invention, appearing first in the preface to the 1786 edition of Ann Yearsley's *Poems*. But by 1830 in England there was an institutional recognition of the term and the genre, and a growing canon of recognizable autobiographical literature. However, there was very little theorizing about the genre until the mid-twentieth century.

Since the early 1980s theoretical studies of autobiography in the United States have increased exponentially. This is due in part to the rise of feminist literary criticism, which has been interested in uncovering the little-known works of so-called nonliterary and noncanonical women authors—people whose personal writings had rarely been published. The increase in theoretical studies is also due in part to the textualized, disappearing self of poststructuralist thought, which problematized earlier romantic notions of the inscribed persona. More recently, autobiographical interests have found their way into biblical studies as scholars have begun to think and write about the social and ideological constraints that have formed them as real readers of the Bible.

Many contemporary studies in autobiography look to Roy Paschal's *Design and Truth in Autobiography* as the turning point in the modern investigation of the genre. This is because Paschal's theoretical approach functions as a formalist bridge linking the strictly historical delineation of autobiographical studies in the 1920s–1940s to the anti-formalist theories of the 1970s and beyond.

Paschal began his 1960 study with an attempt to clarify autobiography as a genre, comparing it with diaries, memoirs, autobiographical writings, and philosophical reflections on the self. For Paschal, autobiography is a genre that seeks to represent the self in and through its relations with the outer world and is historical in its method. In other words, autobiography "involves the reconstruction of the movement of a life, or part of a life, in the actual circumstances in which it was lived" (9) and "is...an interplay, a collusion between past and present" (10). Thus, the significance of autobiography as a genre lies more in its revelation of the present situation than in the uncovering of the author's past.

Paschal's study had three essential foci: (1) the history of autobiography as a literary genre, (2) the structure of autobiography and its various sub-types, and (3) the issue of truth in autobiography. For Paschal and most other theorists working in the 1960s–1970s, Augustine's *Confessions* represented the historical origins of an essentially European genre. Thus, for most theorists prior to 1980, autobiography was a "distinctive product of Western, post-Roman civilisation, [which] only in modern times has…spread to other civilisations" (180). This description is convincing, however, only insofar as autobiography is defined specifically in terms of "a preoccupation with the self [that]…holds the balance between the self and the world, the subjective and the objective, [and]…is inspired by a reverence for the self…in its delicate uniqueness" (180–81). Many women and Third World autobiographers are automatically excluded from this definition, for they often blur that "balanced" distinction between the self and the world and show little interest in the "delicate uniqueness" of the self (recently, see van Herk, 1991, 1992; Kerr and Nettelbeck.)

For Paschal and other critics writing before 1980, the sixteenth-century Renaissance marked the beginning of a period of "extraordinary psychological insight" that distinguishes truly great autobiography (30). And the classical age of autobiography is primarily represented by the late eighteenth- and early nineteenth-century works of Rousseau, Goethe, and Wordsworth, who "were inwardly turned, deeply concerned with their sensibility and imagination" (36).

In terms of the structure of autobiography and its various sub-types, Paschal was careful to distinguish four categories: "autobiography as the story of a man's theoretical understanding of the world," the "essayist autobiography," the "autobiography which restricts itself to childhood," and "innovations of method" (56). Finally, Paschal described autobiographical truth in terms of an internal narrative consistency where "that unique truth of life…is seen from inside" (195). For him and most other theorists of the period, "truth lies in the building up of a personality through the images it makes of itself, that embody its mode of absorbing and reacting to the outer world, and that are profoundly related to one another at each moment and in the succession from past to present" (188).

Over the past twenty years, the three foci of Pascal's work—the history of the genre, the structure of autobiography, and the issue of truth—have remained important to theoretical discussions of autobiography. But each focal point has been scrutinized and strongly critiqued. In a general sense, the original elements of the term *auto/bio/graphy* have provided a helpful framework for contemporary theorizing about the genre. For example, during the first half of the twentieth century, ending with Paschal's work, the emphasis in autobiographical literary criticism was on the *bio* of the author. Writing of this early period of theory, James Olney describes

> a rather naive threefold assumption about the writing of autobiography: first that the *bios* of autobiography could only signify "the course of a lifetime"…second that the autobiographer could

narrate his life in a manner at least approaching the objective historical account…;and third, that there was nothing problematical about the *autos,* no agonizing questions of identity, self-definition, or self-deception—at least none the reader need attend to. (20)

However, beginning with Paschal, the subsequent generation of twentieth-century critics began to agonize over questions inherent in self-representation. Thus, interest shifted away from the *bio,* or "life," elements of autobiography to the *auto,* or the "self," and its many fictive constructions. By the late 1960s, truthfulness had become a much more complex and problematic phenomenon for literary theorists working with autobiography, and the psychological dimensions of truth began to take precedence over those of fact or morality.

Finally, a third phase of autobiographical theory can be discerned in the contemporary scene where "*graphy,*" or the concentration on inscripted selves and readers, has taken over center stage. Here, an emphasis on the death of the unified self has led to a concern for the rhetorical, linguistic function of "selves" and "readers," with a "careful teasing out of warring forces of signification within the text itself" (S. Smith: 6). Not surprisingly, writing epitaphs for the self-polluting *auto* have been the norm in poststructuralist autobiographical studies from the late 1970s to the present. Nicole Jouve's internal monologue describing the demise of the self is not atypical of the topos:

> Contemporary theory has problematized the subject in manifold ways that preclude the search for the self that you propose. Psychoanalysis would demonstrate to you, through Lacan in particular, that "I" is always another, first grasped as an imago. And what about the unconscious, the divided self and all that? Self-knowledge is a mirage, a hangover oasis from the Greeks. And you speak about the autobiographical voice as if there was such a thing, as if the prodigious wealth of recent studies on autobiography, first male then female, hadn't endlessly questioned its existence as a genre. (9–10)

Despite such epitaphs, scholarly interest in cross-cultural and bicultural autobiography has continued to grow. As a result there has been an increasing need to readdress the confessional, "autobiographical voice" mode of representation exhibited by much of marginalized self-writing. From the perspective of ideological criticism, Leigh Gilmore asks the crucial questions:

> Has the claim of representativeness, which characterized auto-biography as practiced by an elite group, become passé and naive because the poststructuralist critique of such a grounding has been overwhelmingly persuasive? Or has representativeness been marginalized with the effect of forcing those who now claim it to the "margin" of representation? Why does the coincidence of post-structuralist skepticism and "truth telling" produce a judgment of naiveté when representative identity is self-claimed by a non-"representative" person (in terms of the dominant culture)? (228)

Challenges from feminist and Third World, postcolonial critics to poststructuralist understandings of writing and representation have not yet been fully integrated into a postmodern understanding of autobiography. Nevertheless, feminist and Third World, postcolonial critics are surely right to reject Paschal's definition of the autobiographical genre and its history for its male, European bias, and its narrow structure for its Western emphasis on the ideology of the individual and internal change. What this has meant for feminist and Third World, postcolonial theorists is that autobiography is now being shaped by "nonessentialist aesthetics [that are] tied to the emergence of occluded oral cultures; to the articulation of a reality that emphasizes relational patterns over autonomous ones, interconnectedness over independence, isomorphic analogies over unifying totalities, and opacity over transparency" (Lionnet: 245).

The Invention of a Hermeneutical Approach

At the same time that theoretical approaches to autobiography were multiplying, reader-response critics and feminist literary critics were beginning to experiment with autobiographical modes of scholarly writing. The impetus for this experimentation had its roots in feminist, ideological, and postmodern critiques of formalist reader response criticism. Here, formalist notions of "readers-in-the-text" such as "implied," "inscribed," or "encoded" readers raised questions about the social, gendered, and ideological locations of the masked interpreters who so solicitously extracted "implied readers" from texts. Real readers, critics, and authors felt compelled by their academic peers and by their own theoretical positions to "'fess up" to the interested nature of their critical moves.

Jane P. Tompkins, former professor of English at Duke University and editor of one of the earliest collections of reader-oriented approaches to literature (*Reader-Response Criticism*), marked the transition to this new genre of criticism with her strikingly personal essay "Me and My Shadow" (1988). Nancy Miller's *Getting Personal* (1991) and Nicole Ward Jouve's *White Woman Speaks with Forked Tongue* (1991) soon followed, and thus autobiographical literary criticism was born. Linda Kaufman's "The Long Goodbye" and *The Intimate Critique,* edited by Diane P. Freedman, Olivia Frey, and Francis Murphy Zauhar, both appeared in 1993 and were evidence that the autobiographical approach would survive the trauma of childhood. In 1994, Alicia Suskin Ostriker experimented with autobiographical criticism in her *The Nakedness of the Fathers,* a feminist, midrash-like retelling of the biblical patriarchal narratives. And by 1995 biblical critics were seriously engaged in the autobiographical discussion (Staley, *Reading with a Passion;* Segovia and Tolbert, *Reading from this Place*). In 1996, H. Aram Veeser edited a collection of essays titled *Confessions of the Critics,* and autobiographical, literary-critical journal articles have continued to appear (Miller, 1997; Kilcup). In the field of biblical studies, additional important works in autobiographical biblical criticism have appeared: Janice Capel Anderson and Jeffrey L. Staley's *Taking*

It Personally (Semeia 72) and Igrid Rosa Kitzberger's *The Personal Voice in Biblical Interpretation* (1999).

Autobiographical literary criticism is similar to reader-response criticism of the 1970s and early 1980s in that it focuses on readers and readers' responses to texts. However, in autobiographical literary criticism, attention is weighted toward the individual, contemporary reader-critic's responses to texts rather than toward implied readers or real readers at earlier historical periods. Thus, for some biblical scholars, autobiographical criticism shamelessly abandons the hard-won breastworks of historical and literary scholarship for adolescent, narcissistic play. Yet as Linda Alcoff notes, uncritical autobiographical acts

> serve no good end when [they are] used as disclaimers against...
> ignorance or errors and [are] made without critical interrogation of
> the bearing of such...autobiograph[ies] on what is about to be said.
> [They] leave for the listeners all the real work that needs to be done.
> For example, if a middle-class white man were to begin a speech by
> sharing with us this autobiographical information and then using it
> as a kind of apologetics for any limitations of his speech, this would
> leave those of us in the audience who do not share his social location
> to do the work by ourselves of translating his terms into our own,
> appraising the applicability of his analysis to our diverse situation,
> and determining the substantive relevance of his location on his claims.
> (25)

From Alcoff's perspective, autobiographical criticism can be useful if it functions as a heuristic tool for forming an ethics of reading (see also Harding). Under such constraints, critically constructed autobiography becomes a means to explore the individual reader's changing commitments to texts (Kilcup), or it becomes a means to illuminate and evaluate the political and social aspects of contemporary interpretation at large (Suleri).

But autobiographical literary criticism also shares with feminism an abiding interest in authorial voice and gender constructions. Both are informed by multicultural studies that often stretch the boundaries of the literary canon and the genre of literary criticism. From a rhetorical perspective, then, autobiographical literary criticism may appear to be more interested in voice than in argumentation, performance rather than coherence. For some it simply values style over substance. This perception is due, in part, to the fact that voice or style is usually what strikes the reader's senses first in autobio-critical essays. However, by raising autobiography to the level of professional discourse, autobiographical literary criticism challenges the implicit rules and boundaries of academic argumentation.

Autobiographical literary criticism is particularly attuned to the problematics of self and distance in narrative or those rhetorical tropes whereby writers define the narrating self and then separate that self from the argumentative situation of professional discourse. At this juncture the problematics of self and distance reflected in the critic's/autobiographer's "I" can be connected with process philosophy, quantum theory, or biology. For example, Donna Haraway has argued that

> in the early 1970s, the Nobel Prize winning immunologist, Niels Jerne, proposed a theory of immune system self-regulation, called the network theory. [In Jerne's theory] there could be no *exterior* antigenic structure, no "invader," that the immune system had not already "seen" and mirrored internally. [Thus,] "self" and "other" lose their oppositional quality and become subtle plays of partially mirrored readings and responses. (218, emphasis hers)

Using this theory of the immune system—or using quantum theory or process philosophy—one can argue for the value of a postmodern, autobiographical turn in biblical criticism whereby "[t]he internal, structured activity of the system is the crucial issue, not formal representations of the 'outer' [read 'objective'] world within the 'inner' [read 'subjective'] world of the communications system that is the [human] organism" (219).

Frederick Buechner once wrote that

> most theology, like most fiction, is essentially autobiography. Aquinas, Calvin, Barth, Tillich [where is Augustine, where are the women theologians?], working out their systems in their own ways and in their own language, are telling us stories of their lives, and if you press them far enough, even at the most cerebral and forbidding, you find an experience of flesh and blood, a human face smiling or frowning or weeping or covering its eyes before something that happened once. [It made] a difference which no theology can ever entirely convey or entirely conceal. (3)

It is not at all unusual to find biblical scholars, at the turn of the millennium, returning in vigorous and critical ways to the autobiographical foundations of their hermeneutical enterprise.

bakhtin
Carol A. Newsom

Mikhail Mikhailovich Bakhtin (1895–1975) was born in Orel, Russia, to an educated and liberal family who belonged to the minor nobility (but see Hirschkop, 111). He was trained in philology and classics at the University of Petrograd during the war years and the time of the Russian revolution (1914–1918). In the ensuing years of the Civil War he taught school and lectured, first in the town of Nevel in western Russia and later in Vitebsk, where his intellectual circle included Valentin Voloshinov and Pavel Medvedev, whose work was destined to be closely linked with Bakhtin's own. Bakhtin's first significant writings were composed during this time, including *Toward a Philosophy of the Act,* the essays later published in *Art and Answerability,* and a draft of what was to become his book on Dostoevsky. In Vitebsk, Bakhtin married Elena Aleksandrovna, on whom he became deeply dependent, and also began to suffer from the acute osteomyelitis that was to plague him for the rest of his life. Bakhtin moved to Leningrad in 1924, where his alleged participation in activities in the underground Russian Orthodox Church led to his arrest in 1929, the year his Dostoevsky book was published. Although he was initially sentenced to a Siberian labor camp, intervention by influential friends and concern for Bakhtin's fragile health caused the sentence to be changed to six years' internal exile in Kazakhstan. There, while working as a bookkeeper, Bakhtin composed "Discourse in the Novel." Following his exile, Bakhtin taught briefly at the Mordovia Pedagogical Institute in Saransk (1936–1937) and lived for a time in Savelovo. Largely unemployed until 1941, he wrote several of his important essays on the novel, as well as his book on Rabelais, for which he was eventually awarded a degree by the Gorky Institute of World Literature (1952). During the war Bakhtin taught in Savelovo, returning to his post at the Mordovia Pedagogical Institute in 1945, where he taught until his retirement in 1961. During the late 1950s Bakhtin's work began to be rediscovered and discussed by students of literature in Moscow. Through their intervention a revised version of Bakhtin's book on Doestoevsky was published in 1963 and the manuscript on Rabelais in 1965. With both Bakhtin and his wife in ill health, friends arranged for them to be moved to Moscow in 1969. From then until 1975, when he died, Bakhtin continued to write and revise earlier drafts of essays.

The introduction of Bakhtin's work to the West is largely credited to Julia Kristeva's discussion of his ideas in the late 1960s and early 1970s. The attempt to take account of Bakhtin and his intellectual significance in the English-speaking West has been complicated by the sequence in which his works have been translated, the debate about Bakhtin's possible authorship of certain books published by Medvedev and Voloshinov, and finally by Bakhtin's own unsystematic turn of mind. *Rabelais and His World,* perhaps the least characteristic and most problematic of Bakhtin's works, was the first translated (1968). His essays on the novel (*The Dialogic Imagination,* 1981), on *Problems of Doestoevsky's Poetics* (1984), and a collection of some of his later essays (*Speech Genres & Other Late Essays,* 1986) followed in the 1980s. Thus, early reception of Bakhtin has focused on these works and their concern with carnival, dialogue, genre, and the novel. More recently, however, Bakhtin's early philosophical essays have been translated and published as *Art and Answerability* (1990) and *Toward a Philosophy of the Act* (1993), spurring interest in the ethical issues that first engaged Bakhtin.

In 1970 the Soviet linguist Vyacheslav Ivanov asserted that Bakhtin had in fact written several works attributed to Voloshinov (*Marxism and the Philosophy of Language, Freudianism: A Critical Sketch*) and Medvedev (*The Formal Method in Literary Scholarship: A Critical Introduction to Sociological Poetics*). This position was accepted by Clark and Holquist in their influential 1984 biography of Bakhtin but has since been decisively refuted by Morson and Emerson. Although the issues of authorship have been clarified, the role of these books for understanding Bakhtin's own thought remains significant, since all three were close intellectual companions in the formative decade of the 1920s, and many related ideas find expression in the works of each.

While some interpreters have attempted to present Bakhtin's thought in more or less sytematic terms (see Todorov, Holquist), changes in his categories, foci, and even style of writing make this approach problematic, as does Bakhtin's own resistance to the notion of system. More helpful is a chronological account of Bakhtin's thought (Clark and Holquist, Morson and Emerson), though Bakhtin's habit of revising earlier manuscripts after several decades complicates a strictly chronological approach. Moreover, Bakhtin's thought does not reflect any clear pattern of development so much as it reveals certain recurrent issues that were pursued at different times of his life by means of different organizing concepts. For convenience, this essay will follow Morson and Emerson's division of Bakhtin's work into roughly four periods of thought:

1. 1919–1924. Focus on philosophical issues, including the relationship of the ethical and the aesthetic. Writings include *Toward a Philosophy of the Act* and "Author and Hero in Aesthetic Activity."

2. 1924–1930. Characterized by the shift to language rather than the act as the priviliged category. Development of the understanding of the dialogic nature of language. Primary writing, *Problems of Dostoevsky's Poetics* (1929 edition).

3. 1930s–1950s. Development of thought concerning genre, the novel, concept of heteroglossia. Writings include "Discourse in the Novel"

and "Forms of Time and Chronotope in the Novel." Toward the end of this period Bakhtin emphasized the liberating character of parody and idealized the antinomian aspects of carnival in *Rabelais and His World.*

4. 1950s–1975. Return to some of the early philosophical and ethical issues (e.g., responsibility, creativity), now rethought in light of the categories associated with dialogue. Retreat from the radical unfinalizability celebrated in the Rabelais book. Essays collected in *Speech Genres and Other Late Essays.*

The essays representing Bakhtin's first period of work present many difficulties, since they were unpolished and sometimes incomplete drafts that were edited and published only after Bakhtin's death. In them, however, one can see the relationship between philosophical and aesthetic categories that was characteristic of Bakhtin's work as a whole. *Toward a Philosophy of the Act* engages a problem in Kantian ethics: how to understand the relation between the immediacy of an act and its significance. Bakhtin opposed what he described as the "theoretism" of systems of ethics, which assume that the ethical situation can be comprehended in terms of rules. What is lost in such an analysis is the quality of the particular, the quality of "eventness." In seeking a more adequate vocabulary for describing the ethical significance of acts, Bakhtin speaks of obligation as a matter of "oughtness," not of norms. To take responsibility for an act is to give it one's "signature." Or as Bakhtin memorably phrases it, there is "no alibi for being." In terms of relations with others, Bakhtin rejects the category of "empathy" for its (futile and unhelpful) attempt to fuse oneself into the feelings or perceptions of another. Equally wrong is the attempt to live "aesthetically," creating a sort of character who participates, while the self remains essentially and irresponsibly separate from life. In contrast, the appropriate mode is that of "live entering," that is, entering into another's place without leaving one's own. This maintains one's "outsideness," a perspective that does not completely dissolve into the other and that makes it possible to be of genuine aid to another. Although Bakhtin intended to write a section dealing with the theological implications of his insight, it was never composed. He does, however, use as an example of "live entering" the incarnation of Christ.

In a slightly later work from this first period, "Author and Hero in Aesthetic Activity," Bakhtin explores the ways in which a self is formed in the interaction with others. It is never possible for an individual to see herself adequately, for how I seem to myself is not how I seem to others who stand outside me and possess a surplus of vision with respect to me. They see me against a background, within an environment, that I myself cannot see. Bakhtin understands this process of the other's vision as an aesthetic act, very much like the relation between author and character. An author projects a character against an environment, giving the character a provisional stability or "finalized" quality. Although Bakhtin later explores some of the negative aspects of such a relationship, in "Author and Hero" he speaks in terms of the conveying of a gift. The "I as I appear to myself" is unfinalized, non-coincident, always under construction, always with a loophole. Thus, it cannot be the hero of a story or carry a story line. The finalizing closure given to me by the way others perceive me against a background is what offers a degree of stability that the self can provisionally incorporate. What is conveyed to the self is a rhythm, the capacity to be a hero in a story. Obviously, an excess of such finalization by others would mean the loss of freedom and the capacity for ethical action. But at this stage in his thought Bakhtin considered the interaction between loophole and rhythm, finalized and unfinalized, self and other as essential to the formation of a self and the process to be a fundamentally aesthetic one.

The major work of Bakhtin's second period is the 1929 version of the Dostoevsky book (*Problems of Doestoevsky's Poetics*), which was later significantly revised and published in a second edition in 1963. With this work Bakhtin shifts decisively from a focus on the act to a focus on language, specifically language as utterance. He is strongly critical of Saussurean linguistics, which had no way of conceptualizing and studying the utterance and the dialogic relationship in which persons actually speak to one another. The phenomena that interested Bakhtin thus could not be the subject of a linguistics but of a metalinguistics. Although it is no longer accepted that Bakhtin "wrote" the books by Medvedev and Voloshinov, their works, especially Voloshinov's exploration of the dialogic nature of language and the development of a psychology that understands the psyche as constituted by inner speech, are crucial for understanding the context of Bakhtin's thought.

In the Doestoevsky book Bakhtin develops his understanding of three important topics: (1) the complex voicing of speech, (2) the contrast between monologic and dialogic truth, and (3) polyphony. In analyzing speech, Bakhtin distinguished between three types of discourse. The first he called "single-voiced." It characterizes speech in which a person unselfconsciously directs remarks toward a referential object. Though one could easily find in such speech the traces of the words of others, the speaker is not intentionally or for rhetorical effect making the speech of others evident in his own words. Nevertheless, though the speaker may not be aware of it or intending to exploit the fact, he may be speaking in a distinctly stylized manner, for instance, in the jargon of a particular social or professional class. Thus, the speech will be objectified, recognizable as speech of a characteristic type. Still, insofar as the speaker is not aware of the relation between his own words and a jargon or social dialect, Bakhtin understands the utterance as "single-voiced."

If, however, the speaker is aware of or intends listeners to hear the stylized or objectified speech of a class or a group or a tradition ringing through his own words, then one has an instance of "double-voiced" speech. Although the purposes for which such double voicing are used can vary, it often serves the purpose of asserting identity with the language thus stylized or invoking the authority of the other voice in support of one's own. The relationship between the two voices or speech centers is dialogic, specifically the dialogic of agreement. This differs from another type of double-voiced speech in which the speaker's intention is directly opposed to the discourse he takes into his speech (e.g., parody). Finally, Bakhtin distinguishes the double-voicing characteristic of hidden polemic, what he calls "the word with a sideward glance at someone else's hostile word" (1984: 196), as when one simultaneously acknowledges and resists another's criticism by using falsely self-deprecating speech ("readers must forgive this 'poor excuse for analysis,' but…").

Although Bakhtin used the terms *dialogue* and *dialogic* in several different ways in his works, his distinction between dialogic and monologic conceptions of truth is most important. Monologic truth is based on propositional statements that do not depend on the identity of the speaker for their truth value and that are congenial to being organized into a system (e.g., the kind of truth characteristic of critical thought, philosophy, systematic theology, and much literature). Even if such propositions or systems of thought are actually the product of many minds, they can be represented as capable of being spoken by a single voice or comprehended by a single consciousness. Not so dialogic truth. It exists at the point of intersection of several unmerged voices and "requires a plurality of consciousnesses…[that] in principle cannot be fitted within the bounds of a single consciousness" (1984: 81). Instead of the unity of a system, dialogic truth has the unity of an "event," such as a conversation. To summarize a conversation is to reduce it to the unity of a proposition and so to lose the dynamic structure of its dialogic nature. Moreover, in contrast to the abstract quality of monologic truth, dialogic truth has an embodied, personal quality. For dialogic truth, "the ultimate indivisible unit is not the assertion, but rather the integral point of view, the integral position of a personality" (1984: 93), what Bakhtin calls a "voice-idea." Thus, dialogic truth is by nature always open, "unfinalizable." One can see here Bakhtin's continuing concern with the ethical dimensions of speech. Whereas in "Author and Hero in Aesthetic Activity" Bakhtin had valued "finalization" as a gift that makes selfhood possible, in the Dostoevsky book Bakhtin's position has shifted, and he is wary that an excess of finalization—characteristic of monologic discourse—makes it too easy to "sum up" a person. But a dialogic orientation recognizes that a person has never spoken her final word and thus remains open and free.

The relationship between the ethical and the aesthetic also appears in Bakhtin's notion of polyphony. Most literature, including novels, is monologic, in that the author controls all of the voices, subordinating all but the one that expresses the author's own position. But it is possible to conceive of a form of writing, Bakhtin believed, that allows the various voices in a work to function as though they are independent consciousnesses, engaging one another and the author in a polyphonic discourse that is truly dialogic and open. Indeed, Bakhtin thought that Doestoevsky had achieved such a form of writing. Polyphonic composition requires changes in the position of the author, the role of the reader, the status of the plot, and the nature of the ending. The author retains a perspective and a voice, but it is no longer the controlling voice. Bakhtin's analogy was that the author creates free characters much as God creates human beings as morally free agents (1984: 285). Thus, in a polyphonic work the play of ideas is central, and it is this that drives the plot. The reader's task is consequently not so much to analyze plot and characters but to become a kind of participant in the dialogue itself, like a bystander who has become involved in a quarrel. Endings present particular problems for polyphonic works. They should not end with closure, since dialogue is by its nature unfinalizable, but should rather end in a way that invites the reader "to draw dotted lines to a future, unresolved continuation" (Morson and Emerson, 253).

Bakhtin's third period (1930s to 1950s) is characterized by his development of ideas first put forward in the Dostoevsky book. Morson and Emerson appropriately distinguish two phases. In the first, reflected in the seminal essays "Discourse in the Novel" and "Forms of Time and Chronotope in the Novel," Bakhtin heroizes the novel as a genre. He sees in the novel a form of consciousness that alone does justice to the complex voicing of human speech (*heteroglossia*, the internal dialogization of the word) and to the representation of time and space (*chronotope*). By the internal dialogization of the word, Bakhtin refers to the fact that every utterance, every word that is spoken, enters into a world that is already spoken about. Thus, since Adam, no word relates to its object in a simple or virginal way, but always also in relation to what has previously been said and indeed what might yet be said. Therefore, even when not intentionally double-voiced, a word cannot escape the dialogism that comes with the essentially historical and social nature of language.

These features of language are also highlighted by Bakhtin's concept of heteroglossia, that is, the characteristic vocabulary, syntax, intonation, or other features by which a national language is stratified into social dialects. These social dialects may belong to a class, a profession, a region, a cultural subgroup, or simply a fashion of the day. Although such dialects may be individually present in many types of written and oral speech, only in the novel are they self-consciously represented in all their social diversity. Bakhtin also uses these insights in developing a new understanding of the nature of the self as formed in large measure through the orientation of one's own words to the words of others. The appropriation of the discourse of others as an "internally persuasive" word and the complex negotiation among several different internally persuasive discourses is the key to the ideological formation of a person. Thus, for Bakhtin the human consciousness is both resolutely linguistic and thoroughly social in its structure.

Though the ethical implications are not as clearly drawn out, in his study of the chronotope Bakhtin observed that each narrative genre that developed in the history of Western literature (e.g., the Greek romance, ancient biography, the chivalric romance, the early picaresque novel, the idyll, the modern novel) has a characteristic way of representing actions and persons in terms of time and space. Although the chronotope is simply one of the conventions of a particular genre, it is nevertheless a means of understanding and rendering experience. Thus, issues fundamental to ethics are implicit in such representations. Are events the result of chance or causality? To what extent is human initiative a factor? Do persons change through time, by means of experiences, or are they static? Is time rich with possibility or already scripted? Are actions repeatable, reversible, or unique? What kinds of ethical actions are possible within a particular construction of reality? What is the image of the person offered by each chronotope (see Morson and Emerson: 369)? Even though chronotopes may be linked to particular genres, like words or dialects they can also interact in a dialogic fashion.

In Bakhtin's earlier writings one can observe variation in the way he evaluates certain concepts, most notably those having to do with the role of things that "finalize" or are "unfinalizable," for example, the role of others' perceptions and words in relation to the formation of the self and its freedom, the relationship between genres and parodic speech, centripetal and centrifugal dynamics in human speech, the functions of laughter. In some of the writings of his third period, however, Bakhtin carries to an extreme his valorization of the unfinalizable, most notably in *Rabelais and His World.* Carnival becomes the privileged figure for this value of utter openness, for that which mocks closed structures and attitudes, hierarchies and fixed values. Carnival laughter is free of fear and piety, loosed from memory and tradition. The carnival body is the grotesque body, the place of orifices that ingest and defecate, that is never finished. The messiness of the carnival body that is celebrated in the Rabelais book is an elaborated and exaggerated counterpart to Bakhtin's earlier appreciation of the novel's capacity, in contrast to other genres, to represent something of the messiness of life. And in this period Bakhtin increasingly assimilated his understanding of the novel's function in literature to the social function of carnival as he understood it. Social historians have severely criticized Bakhtin's understanding of carnival as historically inaccurate, and critics have become wary of the antinomian and anarchistic excesses of *Rabelais and His World.* Yet it has also been noted that this work needs be considered in relation to its time, in particular as a response to the closed and oppressive culture of Stalinist Russia (Clark and Holquist: 305–14; Hirschkop: 272–74).

In the writings of his fourth period, Bakhtin retreated from the more extreme representations of carnival and its unqualified valorization of unfinalizability, though in his 1963 revision of the Dostoevsky book he incorporated a long discussion of Menippean satire and carnival. But in later essays, especially in "The Problem of Speech Genres," his work reflects a return to the more nuanced appreciation of the constructive role played by certain types of finalization in making speech and dialogue possible. Ethical issues related to dialogue also received renewed attention, as Bakhtin explored the nature of the addressee and response to speech ("The Problem of the Text") and the nature of self and other as mediated through dialogue ("From Notes Made in 1970–71").

Given Bakhtin's focus on the novel, it is not surprising that his influence has been strongest in literary studies, where there was something of a cult of Bakhtin in the 1980s and early 1990s. The wide-ranging and interdisciplinary quality of much of Bakhtin's work, however, has facilitated his engagement by various fields, including cultural studies, rhetoric, feminism, sociology (Bell and Gardiner), psychology, ethics, theology, and biblical studies (Green).

Web Site

For a comprehensive listing of resources related to Bakhtin, see the Bakhtin Centre Web page: http://www.shef.ac.uk/uni/academic/A-C/bakh/bakhtin.html

bataille
Timothy K. Beal and Tod Linafelt

Life and Work

Georges Bataille (1897–1962) is perhaps known more for those he has profoundly influenced (e.g., Jean Baudrillard, Maurice Blanchot, Norman O. Brown, Jacques Derrida, Michel Foucault, Jane Gallop, Jean-François Lyotard, Jean-Luc Nancy) than for his own work. As a writer, he was and remains notoriously beyond classification: numismatist, erotic fiction writer, erotic nonfiction writer, autobiographer, commentator, political critic, literary critic, philosopher, sociologist, aphorist, pamphleteer. Likewise, his other activities are widely varied, reflecting a great deal of career continuity, on the one hand, and a dramatic dynamism of thought and action, on the other: Trained in paleography and library science, he worked for twenty years at Bibliothèque nationale, and in 1951 was named conservator at Bibliothèque municipale at Orléans; raised without any religious education, he converted to Catholicism as a teenager in 1914, but in 1920 "suddenly loses his faith because his Catholicism has caused a woman he has loved to shed tears" (1986a: 107; in Botting, 1997: 113), nonetheless remaining deeply interested in religion, including Catholic traditions of mysticism; he was involved in a number of short-lived, radical leftist, anti-fascist groups, including the surrealist movement (which denounced him in its Second Surrealist Manifesto in 1929) and the Democratic Communist Circle, with its short-lived journal *La Critique Sociale* (1931–1934); he also organized a group called Countre-Attaque (1935–36); soon after that he was one of the founders of a "'secret society' which, turning its back on politics, would pursue goals that would be solely religious (but anti-Christian, essentially Nietzschean)" (1986a: 109; in Botting, 1997: 115), and whose public face was the Collège de sociologie and the journal *Acéphale* ("headless"; 1936–39). Toward the end of his "autobiographical note," dated "1958?," Bataille sums up this dizzying disparity of engagement and reflection as follows: "If thought and expression have become his main area of activity, this has not been without repeated attempts, within the limits of his means, at experiences lacking apparent coherence, but whose very incoherence signifies an effort to comprehend the totality of possibility, or to put it more precisely, to reject, untiringly, any possibility exclusive of others. Bataille's aspiration is

28

that of a sovereign existence" (1986a; in Botting, 1997). Or as Denis Hollier puts it, "to bring into play a crack that frustrates plans and shatters monuments" (1989: 3).

Consistent with this inevitably failed desire for a sovereignty of experience that could not be objectified or *made useful* is Bataille's interest in religion. Most simply, Bataille was steadfastly interested in the ambiguity inherent in social constructions of the sacred as both attractive and repulsive, that is, in the sacred as that which cannot be reduced to the values of utility or moral goodness, that which is beyond accommodation by instrumental reason. Indeed, throughout his numerous writings, which span about four decades, Bataille's interest in religion was profound and abiding. Here we focus primarily on three important texts: first, an early manuscript, written between 1927 and 1930, that outlines his notion of heterology "as the study of that which is other" in relation to the sacred and religion; second, the volume *Erotism* from 1957 (Eng. 1986), in which he lays out his theory of sexuality and its relation to death; and third, his formal *Theory of Religion,* written in 1948 (published in 1973; Eng. 1989a).

Heterology

In his early manuscript "The Use-Value of D. A. F. de Sade (An Open Letter to My Current Comrades)," Bataille proposed an outline for a radical program of study that he called "practical and theoretical *heterology*" and that he defined as follows: "The science of what is completely other. The term *agiology* would perhaps be more precise, but one would have to catch the double meaning of *agio* (analogous to the double meaning of *sacer* [sacred]), *soiled* as well as *holy*" (1985: n. 2). He writes further, "Heterology is restricted to taking up again, consciously and resolutely, this terminal process which up until now has been seen as the abortion and shame of human thought" (1985: 97). Bataille's heterology attends to that which is other, excessive, wasteful, useless, that which is unassimilable, inappropriate within and according to the ideals of homogeneous society (which in a related article he identifies with fascism). As his basic definition makes clear, moreover, the heterologous is closely identified with the sacred or wholly other (elsewhere in the essay the heterogeneous is equated with a series of related terms, including the numenous, *das ganz Anderes*, the unknowable, the sacramental, and the religious). Bataille even considers whether his program should be called simply religion rather than heterology, but is concerned that "religion" in modern Western society is too closely associated with institutions that regulate and prohibit access to the sacred. And neither is religion quite deserving of the status of science. Heterology is to religion as chemistry is to alchemy.

But as the alchemy/chemistry analogy suggests, the difference between religion and heterology for Bataille can only be one of degree rather than kind. Like religion, heterology has no alternative but to do its work *within* the order of things; one attends to the heterological, the other, within the logic of the same, feeling one's way along the cracked and suppurating edges for the points of rupture that might open to the necessarily violent inbreaking of that which exceeds the order of things: that which is useless in a world driven by use-value, that which is wasteful in a world driven by production, that which is pronounced evil in a world that reduces the sacred to moral goodness—that is, the accursed share.

Heterology, as presented in this early open letter and others, is a fitting description of Bataille's entire subsequent literary corpus. And throughout his writing he attended to religion as a potential locus of heterological rupture.

Erotism

Bataille is also well known for his deep and abiding interest in eroticism, which he also identifies as a point of heterological rupture. For Bataille, desire begins when one is torn out of contentment, and it reaches its end with a return to that contentment. Eros exists, then, only as a denial of its beginning and as a deferral of its end. That is, if Eros ensues from separation, lack, a felt absence, then union, plenitude, and presence represent its *telos*. This is, of course, a *telos* (or "end") in both senses of that word: *telos* as the goal or objective, that which is sought; and *telos* as cessation or termination, the quitting of seeking. Recognizing the threat that contentment harbors for desire, Bataille writes that "happiness is the most demanding test of all for lovers" (1997a: 95). And though one may learn this seeming truism by watching any soap opera, where as soon as a couple appears happy we know they are headed for trouble, Bataille has explored its implications and paradoxes in a striking way. He writes, "Compared to the person I love, the universe seems poor and empty. This universe isn't 'risked' since it's not 'perishable'...Carnal love, because not 'sheltered from thieves' or vicissitudes, is thus greater than divine love. It 'risks' me and the one I love" (1997a: 95).

Affirming that it is the very precariousness of desire—the fact that it is not sheltered—that constitutes its desirability, Bataille nevertheless complicates the truism by introducing two other propositions: first, that carnal love not only is at risk itself but also puts those in its thrall at risk; and second, that precisely this double-edged risk makes carnal love superior to divine love.

The first of these propositions may once again seem to repeat what any melodrama or soap opera knows about desire—"star-crossed lovers" and all that—but Bataille pursues it in unexpected ways. In the volume *Erotism* (1986b [1957]), he begins by emphasizing that we exist as "discontinuous beings." While individuals may interact, affect each other, and even experience an intense solidarity with each other, each being is nonetheless separate and distinct from all others. "Between one being and another," Bataille writes, "there is a gulf, a discontinuity" (1986b: 12). Birth is the starting point for this discontinuity, as *a* being emerges out of the continuity of *being-in-general* and into a self-contained existence. Death is the return to continuity, a dissolution of individual existence back into being-in-general. Eroticism arises when "we yearn for lost continuity." The promise of Eros is the promise of "a total blending of two beings, a continuity between discontinuous beings" (1986b: 20). Bataille himself cannot seem to decide whether or not the promise is ever kept, if desire is simply a quest for the impossible or if there is in carnal love a moment– "precarious yet profound"–of genuine dissolution of individual existence. In any case, it is this promise of continuity by which Bataille links sexuality to death: Both represent ways of overcoming the discontinuity of being–an overcoming that is, in each case, both promise and threat.

The second of these propositions–that carnal love is superior to divine love–is based on Bataille's insistence that "God by definition isn't risked." "However far the lovers of God go with their passion," he writes, "they conceive of it as outside the play of risk…In carnal love we ought to love excesses of suffering. Without them no risk would exist. In divine love the limitation of suffering is given in divine perfection" (1997a: 95–96). Returning to the etymological roots of "passion" (coming as it does from the Latin *passus*), one is reminded that the meaning of the word has progressed from "suffering" to "the state of being affected by an external agent" to "desire." It would seem that for Bataille, these three meanings are bound up with one another still. Passion in relation to an external agent exists as suffering both because the promise of unity may well turn out to be a fraud and because of the threat that this promise may *not* be a fraud. That is, to experience, even for the briefest of moments, continuity with another is to experience what Bataille calls "the abrupt wrench[ing] out of discontinuity." To take seriously the fact that we exist as discontinuous beings is to take equally seriously the fact that "the domain of eroticism is the domain of violence" (1986b: 16). The commingling of selves exists only in the violation of borders, only in the state of being affected by an external agent, which, though we may know such violation as an experience of ecstasy, is no less an experience of anguish.

There is something curious, however, about Bataille's insistence that the lovers of God perceive themselves to be outside the risk associated with the erotic. There is in fact a strong tradition, seen already with the biblical prophets and extending through medieval Jewish and Christian mystical writers and beyond, of understanding the divine-human relationship in terms of a risky and often surprisingly violent erotic attraction. A classic expression of this tradition may be found in the twelfth-century sermons on the Song of Songs by Bernard of Clairvaux. For Bernard, to be drawn into an erotic affair with God is a violent act against the resistance of our fallen nature (see Kristeva, 1987a). One does not naturally and peacefully experience union with God, but only through "tears, sighs, and moans." In many of Bernard's sermons we are not so far from Bataille, who writes that "intimacy is violence, and it is destruction, because it is not compatible with the positing of the separate individual" (1997a: 214). The violation of borders and the threat such violation represents for human lovers does not simply evaporate with lovers of God. The risk exists not in the *carnality* of love, but rather in the *erotic nature* of love–the two are intimately related but not coterminous; eroticism may begin with the carnal fact of sexuality, but it does not end there.

Yet even if lovers of God are at risk, does this mean that God is also thought to be at risk? Bataille would seem to be on firmer ground here, as both Jewish and Christian mystics have tended to downplay the effects of desire on God (see Turner, 1995: 143–44). That is, while divine Eros is said to be the cause of human desire for God, the reverse is rarely considered. But the effort seems ultimately in vain; once the divine is introduced into the vicissitudes of erotic existence, God is no longer "by definition" un-risked. Again, one sees this clearly in the biblical prophets (especially Hosea and Jeremiah), but even Bernard admits, "God desires us not only on account of his infinite love (as his only son who is in the Father's bosom tells us, 'My Father loves you'), but also for himself (as the prophet says, 'I shall do this not for you but for myself')" (in Kristeva, 1987a: 160).

Theory of Religion

Discussions and explorations of religion emerge throughout Bataille's writing, his early "Use-Value" article being but one example. But a theory of religion is most fully developed in his book *Theory of Religion* (1973b; 1989a), which is closely related to his more well known three-volume *The Accursed Share* (1988a; 1991). At the heart of Bataille's *Theory of Religion* are two radically opposed regions or "worlds": on the one hand, the order of things, which he also calls the profane or ordinary world, and on the other hand, the sacred world of intimacy, or immanence, which is incommensurable, that is, wholly other, to the order of things. Within this schema, religion functions according to the demands of an impossible necessity: As part of the order of things (society, consciousness, knowledge), religion is that which tries and necessarily fails to access the wholly other, incommensurable realm of sacred intimacy. Religion is in this world but not of it (see also 1991: 213–15).

The sacred world of intimacy in Bataille's theory is the realm of pre–self-conscious, prelinguistic, pre-objective continuity, the "opaque aggregate" (1989a: 36) in which there can be no distinct objects or individuals (reminiscent of the primordial chaos in many creation mythologies, also reminiscent of Lacan's imaginary). Bataille associates this order of intimacy with the idea of animality: "Every animal," Bataille writes, "is *in the world like water in water...* the animal, like the plant, has no autonomy in relation to the rest of the world" (1989a: 19). In intimacy, then, there is no self-consciousness of oneself as an individual in relation to other individuals and objects.

The order of things, on the other hand, is the order of discontinuity, of individuation, of division and subdivision into subjects and objects. Like many other thinkers of his time, Bataille hypothesizes that an early step into the order of things from the primordial animal intimacy is found in the use of tools. A tool is something outside oneself that one posits as an object, thereby positing oneself as a subject. The tool object and the tool-using subject are thus removed from the water-in-water continuity of intimacy and become "things." The subject uses this tool, moreover, with a larger objective in view, namely, the manipulation of other objects.

Such objectification (through tools, language, etc.) "has a meaning that breaks the undifferentiated continuity, that stands opposed to immanence or to the flow of all that is–[the intimacy] which it transcends" (1989a: 29). This process of object distinction leads us from the wilderness of the intimate order into the order of things and leads ultimately to self-objectification, to the positing of oneself as an object in a world of other objects. In language that is reminiscent of Lacan's mirror stage, which involves an experience of self-objectification that is necessary in order to become a subject within the social-symbolic order, Bataille writes, "We do not know ourselves distinctly and clearly until the day we see ourselves from the outside as another" (1989a: 31).

One experiences the order of things, the "world of things and bodies," as the profane, ordinary world, over against a "holy and mythical world" of intimacy. There is no reconciliation possible between these two worlds—no assimilation of or return to intimacy. "Nothing, as a matter of fact, is more closed to us than this animal life from which we are descended" (1989a: 20). Thus, the order of intimacy, which is lost to us, becomes "this world's" wholly other—sacred in its full, paradoxical-heterological sense, as both revered and accursed. As such, it elicits an irreducible experience of desire and fear, fascination and repulsion. Bataille describes intimacy as "vertiginously dangerous for that clear and profane world where [hu]mankind situates its privileged domain" (1989a: 36).

Bataille's emphasis on the paradoxical character of the "sacred world" as both attractive and repulsive, fearful and alluring, resonates with Rudolph Otto's characterization of religious experience as an encounter with *Mysterium tremendum et fascinans,* that is, with a radically unknowable other that is both terrifying and fascinating, repulsive and attractive. In his second volume of *The Accursed Share* (on the history of eroticism), Bataille writes, "It is obviously the combination of abhorrence and desire that gives the sacred world a paradoxical character, holding one who considers it without cheating in a state of anxious fascination....every horror conceals a possibility of enticement" (1991: 95).

As is the case with Otto, moreover, it should be noted that Bataille's interest in and characterization of the sacred in terms of an incomprehensible mystery that elicits both fear and desire is evidence of the influence of romantic and gothic notions of the sublime on his thought.

In his attendance to abject and repulsive dimensions of the sacred, Bataille pushes beyond religion within the limits of reason alone and attends to the sacred world that is revealed when reason doses, which it must inevitably do. This world, which is associated with the "order of intimacy," can break into our present "order of things," which excludes and opposes it, only by violence. Such inbreakings reveal heterological, excessive aspects of the sacred that are beyond conceptions of religion as morality, sovereign goodness, and reserved divine benevolence—beyond, as Bataille himself puts it, God as "simple paternal sign of universal homogeneity" (1997b: 138).

> [Humankind] is afraid of the intimate order that is not reconcilable with the order of things...intimacy, in the trembling of the individual, is holy, sacred, and suffused with anguish...The sacred is that prodigious effervescence of life that, for the sake of duration, the order

of things holds in check and that this holding changes into a breaking loose, that is, into violence. It constantly threatens to break the dikes, to confront productive activity with the precipitate and contagious movement of a purely glorious consumption. (1989a: 52–53)

What, then, is religion, whose object is this heterological/fascinating or terrifying/sacred? Bataille defines religion—with obvious parallels to his understanding of the erotic—as essentially "the search for lost intimacy" (1989a: 57). It is that which operates according to the impossible necessity of contacting the wholly other sacred world of intimacy while remaining part of the order of things. Religion is the anguished negotiation of incommensurable worlds, a series of necessarily failed departures from the order of things.

The quintessential expression of this longing in religious practice is sacrifice. For Bataille, sacrifice is religion's quintessential failed effort at departure. Sacrifice (*sacer-facere*): making sacred, removing a useful, domestic body or thing (animal, person, bushel of grain, spice) from the order of things and passing it over to the order of intimacy through wasteful consumption. This, for Bataille, is also why the object of sacrifice is usually domestic rather than wild. A wild animal would presumably be perceived as part of the order of intimacy, unassimilated into the order of things.

Sacrifice, as expression of the search for lost intimacy, is about the need to lose, to waste, to give away, the need, in other words, for ruin (Brown, 1991: 187). Sacrifice is ruin that makes sacred; it is worthless expenditure. In this light, festival, carnival, and potlatch are essentially sacrificial; they are about "killing wealth," removing it from the order of things, destroying its use-value by wasting it in the burning heat of the moment. In this light, too, the religious violence of sacrifice would be distinguished from other kinds of violence, such as the violence of war. In war the things and bodies that are spent are either foreign (enemy, other to our social homogeneity), or they are our own bodies spent usefully toward some larger goal of the empire, such as increase of power/territory/knowledge.

Religion, then, for Bataille, is deeply and fundamentally conflicted, an anguished negotiation between two "incompatible necessities"—to be in the world but not of it. As part of the order of things, the passion of saints, the bleating and bleeding of the sacrificial lamb, the outrageous excess of the carnival, all give witness to the impossible necessity of reuniting with a sacred world that is wholly other. Here, ecstasy (e.g., in one of his favorite images, Bernini's *The Ecstacy of St. Theresa*) is reconceived as anguish: Theresa's face is not the face of one achieving transcendence or mystical union with the sacred, but the face of one terribly close to the impossibility of such union. Religion for Bataille expresses a hopeless yet necessary search for lost intimacy, a desire that cannot be satisfied.

blanchot

S. Brent Plate

Unlike many founding "postmodernists," Blanchot is still alive (at least at the time of this writing he is–he was born in 1907). This is significant for a couple of reasons. First, the fact that most of the leading postmodern theorists are now dead should strike something odd in the minds of those who are still imagining postmodernism to be "trendy." The critique of logocentrism, the end of metanarratives, the dismantling of binary structures, the rethinking of the status of representation, and other postmodern impulses, began around thirty-five years ago. If postmodernism is (or was) simply a trend, then, it must be said, so was Modernism, Romanticism, the Baroque, and so forth.

More significantly and more to the point of this article, the status of Blanchot as one living while so many other postmodernists (many his friends) have died brings us to a starting point for understanding Blanchot's theories of reading and writing. Throughout Blanchot's fictional and theoretical writings, from the 1940s to the 1990s, the theme of death is prominent. Death, like language, suggests a limit, a border that divides. Death is divided from, yet borders, life. At the same time, death is not simply the dialectical opposite of life. Instead, death resides at the heart of life itself–like lava under the seemingly stable surface of the earth, keeping the unity and surety of life from establishing itself once and for all. Death always threatens to erupt into life. In the same way, language (particularly literary, poetic language) always contains the seeds of its own contestation within itself. There is always something in a literary text that escapes meaning or makes meaning ambivalent. This "something" is what Blanchot seeks as the "groundless ground" of his literary theory, as we will see, and to experience this abysmal (non)place is to experience a certain limit, between writer and reader, between death and life.

Indeed, it is along the lines of this "limit-experience" that i (I self-consciously use the lowercase "i" for the first person pronoun throughout this article–as i hope to make clear, it stands as a rhetorical figure that displays several of Blanchot's theories of writing and reading) wanted to subtitle this article "Inventing Reading." The word "invent" comes from the Latin *in venir,* which might literally be translated "in coming." A reading that is "inventing" suggests that there is something "coming in" from outside. When the reader opens a book, she or he may be trying to perform an exegesis and give a definitive reading by being in control of the text, but there is something that resides within the space of language that constantly foils any final, conclusive interpretation. Meaning may be made, but Blanchot's theoretical pursuit is to point toward the places where meaning becomes impossible, where the reader experiences a radical Otherness, where the Other "comes in" from outside. Here, death breaks into life just as ambivalent, poetic language breaks into ordinary communication.

Blanchot and Biography

Writing anything like a biographical sketch of Blanchot amounts to a work of failure. Just as life remains incomplete and is continuously undone by death, so would a biography or autobiography be doomed from the outset. There is no final word on a life. Blanchot, obscurely and perhaps strategically, resists making some story into his story, into a final product by which readers might finally understand who he is.

Regardless, there is a body living in France today, identified to the government and others by the name Maurice Blanchot, who began his writing career in the 1930s as a journalist. During this time he wrote for extremist, right-wing periodicals, and his own political stances tended toward fascism and nationalism (though he was not in support of Hitler and the Nazis). Yet, unlike other intellectuals implicated with right-wing groups at the outset of World War II (e.g., Heidegger and Paul de Man), Blanchot radically altered his political stances by the early 1940s and has since refused silence about the Holocaust—indeed, since 1971 all his writings have explicitly dealt with the catastrophe of the Holocaust. His retreat from right-wing politics coincided with a retreat from public life and from journalism, and since the early 1940s he has rarely been photographed or seen in public. The fictional writing that he took up in his reclusion of the 1940s and 1950s gave way to literary-theoretical work in the 1950s through the present. At the same time, all of his writing genres—journalism, fiction, theory, philosophy—commingle with one another, and, as Foucault has stated, "the distinction between 'novels,' 'narratives,' and 'criticism' is progressively weakened in Blanchot" (Foucault, 1987: 26). In other words, Blanchot is constantly transgressing boundaries. (More information on Blanchot's biography can be found in Hill, 1997; for primary sources, Blanchot's most important "fictional" works now available in English are perhaps *Thomas the Obscure* [1950], *Death Sentence* [1948], and *Awaiting Oblivion* [1962], while important "theoretical" works are *The Space of Literature* [1955], *The Infinite Conversation* [1969], and *The Writing of the Disaster* [1980].)

Death and Language

Following the writings of Hegel and Heidegger, Blanchot suggests that death stands at the extreme limit of *being* (human or other); death marks the final and ultimate possibility of existence. Existence itself is meaningless without nonexistence (if we could not die, we would not understand "life"). In a similar way, the linguistic sign only produces meaning out of the difference between the two parts that compose it: the signifier (the linguistic word or "name" for an object) and the referent (the object itself). Because there is a difference between the word and the object to which the word refers, we can talk about something that is absent or about someone who is dead. Indeed, consciousness, and therefore also writing, is self-reflexive, relying on a certain split within one's own self. When i type the character "I" on the keyboard, i have created a rift within myself, and this becomes particularly true as the paper on which i am writing is sent to the printers and multiplied and published in a book. "I" am separated from myself, and language performs the separation. What is more is that the "I" that "originally" wrote this article no longer exists. So we continue to make meaning through language in our writing and reading, speaking and listening, in spite of the absence of the object or subject itself. The object written about, or the writer writing about something, may be absent, yet through language we continue in meaningful ways to speak of the other who has died. In language, the other who is absent is re-*present*-ed.

Death, however, brings with it more than the possibility of meaning. Death also brings with it, paradoxically, the annihilation of meaning. While death marks the final possibility for being, it is also an impossible limit. That is, no single being can enter into death as a being. Entering into death—even if by choice, as in a suicide—a being's consciousness is dissipated. At a certain point, the meaning-making being is no longer able to make meaning. At this point, beings lose control; they no longer possess a consciousness that has the power to speak and to name. This death is radically Other. This version of death does not enter into the dialectic of meaning (the split between signifier and referent), but submerges both sides in a (non)space beyond dialectic.

Thus, there are two sides to death, though they are not in a dialectical opposition with each other. The one side of death stands opposed to life, generating meaning through an oscillation between absence and presence. The thing spoken of may be missing or dead, yet it can be re-presented through language. This is how beings make meaning. On the other side of death (which is ultimately impossible to differentiate from the first side), all dialectical oppositions become impossible. Blanchot's friend Levinas calls this radically Other aspect the "there is" (French: *Il y a*). The "there is" cannot be understood or explained in language, for it is beyond language, and beyond life and death. This is not the death of the individual being, which can still be named; this is a much more primary and radical "death," which undoes all naming. Levinas claims it is impersonal, anonymous, a murmur at the heart of being: "*There is* transcends inwardness as well as exteriority; it does not even make it possible to distinguish these. The anonymous current of being invades, submerges every subject, person or thing" (Levinas, 1978: 57–58; there are also strong correlations here to the writings of Blanchot's other great friend, Georges Bataille, particularly Bataille's notions of "eroticism" in Bataille, 1986b and "inner experience" in Bataille, 1988c). Blanchot calls this "Other death" many things through his writings, most notably the "neuter," the "outside," or the "catastrophe." By whatever (non)name, this radically Other element is beyond dialectic, beyond consciousness, and beyond interpretation. Death slips from the meaning-making side of death to the catastrophic side of death without a warning.

Drawing an analogy between death and language, Blanchot suggests that there are two types of language: "ordinary" and "poetic." Ordinary language has communication as its goal—a message passes from a sender to a receiver, and as the receiver understands the meaning of the message, the message itself "dies" as it gives way to the deeper concept behind the message. On this view of ordinary language, words are simply messengers that the receiver disposes of once the true meaning is grasped, even though communication relies on these very words. Similarly, the novelist utilizes this kind of language to remake the world in her or his own image through the novel. The world is reproduced in the novel: "A novelist writes in the most transparent prose, he describes men we could have met ourselves and actions we could have performed; he says his aim is to express the reality of the human world the way Flaubert did" (Blanchot, 1995: 333–34). Ordinary language (the language of the novelist) is *transparent;* its material elements recede as the immaterial idea comes into view by the reader. Ordinary language depends on words, but also on their ultimate demise.

To the contrary, in Blanchot's poetics something radically different is sought. Reappropriating some of Mallarmé's theories of poetry, Blanchot sees in poetry a mixture of material language and the ideas "behind" the language. Material words inevitably lead to immaterial ideas, but Blanchot states,

> My hope lies in the materiality of language, in the fact that words are things too, are a kind of nature…A name ceases to be the ephemeral passing of nonexistence and becomes a concrete ball, a solid mass of existence; language, abandoning the sense, the meaning which was all it wanted to be, tries to become senseless. Everything physical takes precedence: rhythm, weight, mass, shape, and then the paper on which one writes, the trail of ink, the book. (327)

In strict contradistinction to someone like Habermas, Blanchot stresses the material, concrete, non-transparent language. He seeks out the most opaque places of language, the places where the printed characters are black holes placed on white paper—ink becomes dense, impenetrable matter. This poetic language cannot die, yet neither can it be said to live.

In stressing the materiality of language, Blanchot is saying something other than McLuhan's aphorism, "The medium is the message." McLuhan's view (however hyperbolic) is that the medium takes precedence over the message and recasts the communication into something it was not intended to be; nonetheless, something is communicated. Blanchot's view has similarities to this, but in distinction Blanchot posits an "other" side of language, a side that *does not communicate.* Somewhere in the experience of poetry one stumbles, trips over words that cannot be simply transformed into ideas that the reader can appropriate in her or his mind. Blanchot is not interested in clarifying matters but in materializing clarity itself, seeking out the opaque in language. His own writings are perhaps the truest testimony to this desire—words follow words and the grammar structure is accurate, but the reader arrives at the end of the sentence and becomes dumbfounded. Frantically, the reader will go back and start over, thinking he or she has missed something, but again, nothing. Blanchot's writing is such that it coaxes the reader to continue to read because it seems so clear on the level of the words or phrases, but there is a rapid tumbling into obscurity that marks all his writing.

The writer of such poetic texts (e.g., Kafka, Rilke, Hölderlin, Char), in Blanchot's view, "belongs to a language which no one speaks, which is addressed to no one, which has no center, and which reveals nothing" (1982: 26). Literary language is not merely a tool for communication, it is also that which makes communication impossible. To be a good poet, of course, one must be able to use language, to re-present that which is absent. But at a certain point, something in language itself takes over the process. Something outside "comes in," inventing the writer. To experience the impossibility of communication is, for the writer, the "essential solitude." "Essential solitude" is the name that Blanchot gives to the experience of the "neuter," the "outside," within writing itself. Here the writer loses control, encounters the "there is," where subjects cannot be distinguished from objects. This essential solitude erases the writer's own subjectivity so that she or he cannot "express" her- or himself. The author loses author-ity; the writer "loses the power to say 'I'" (27; see also K. Hart, 1996). This point, as with Levinas' figure of the face-to-face with the Other, becomes the point of responsibility. Levinas considers that the only thing possible to utter in this overwhelming experience is the passive "here I am," clearly echoing Moses' response in Exodus 3 (Levinas, 1991a: 141–42). The "in coming" of this radical Otherness leaves one at a loss, without a voice of one's own, wandering in the wilderness. The essential solitude of the writer is akin to that of the prophet: No one chooses to be a prophet; one is chosen, and one lives in the wilderness where one cries out words not one's own.

On the other side of this writing, of course, is reading. The history of modern Western philosophy and science has been a movement toward greater and greater objectification, and correlatively, subjectification. That is, modern science seeks a detached, objective view of the world, leading to an ultimate Revelation and Truth of how things really are. Modern biblical criticism has followed the same path, offering new clues for the (objective) interpretation of scripture through archaeology, linguistic research, and new historical hermeneutics. Speculating on this in light of Blanchot, we might say that Blanchot is first and foremost incredulous toward any such project of "higher criticism," much as Lyotard suggests that postmodernism is marked by an "incredulity toward metanarratives." Blanchot does not offer a general theory of interpretation or a new hermeneutical tool that would allow the subjective reader to exercise her or his exegetical powers and finally unlock the key to difficult passages. In a certain way, Blanchot's thought is useless for literary/ biblical interpretation. He states, "Reading is ignorant.…It is receiving and hearing, not the power to decipher and analyze, to go beyond by developing or to go back before by laying bare; it does not comprehend (strictly speaking), it attends. A marvelous innocence" (1993: 320). Reading is passive: It attends; it awaits the "in coming" of that which is beyond the subjective realm of the reader.

At this point, there is a difference that must be noted between the death of a being and the kind of death marked by language, and here the analogy breaks down. Beings do indeed die, thus crossing from life into death, and cannot go back the other way. Beings lose the power to come back. But language as literature survives, lives on, even when its original author is dead. Literature remains suspended indefinitely in this liminal place between life and death. So we might be able to see why the processes of reading and writing are so important to Blanchot, for somewhere in the experience of writing and reading–particularly when they come close to the dense, material, non-dialectical aspect of language–readers and writers catch a glimpse of that liminal, non-existent "world" that erupts in between death and life.

This is why, for Blanchot, the biblical figure of Lazarus comes to stand as a figure for reading. Lazarus is one who has passed both ways, who stands in the liminal place between death and life. Jesus, like the reader of texts, stands at the tomb and proclaims *Lazarus, veni foras*, "Lazarus, come forth." The resurrection of Lazarus is an "in coming," an in-vention. Jesus, the crowd, and the reader all patiently await what comes in from beyond death.

While the analogy of language and death breaks down at a certain point, the "passive action" (paradoxical as it is) of the reader might be said to revive the relation, to bring death back. To do so, the reader must become vigilant, attending to the call of the *work* buried in the *book*. The book, like ordinary language, "always indicates an order that submits to a *unity*, a system of notions in which are affirmed the primacy of speech over writing, of thought over language, and the promise of a communication that would one day be immediate and transparent" (xii). The work, to the contrary, lies as the "groundless ground" to this system of language and lies hidden in the book's ordered system. The work is that which–when the reader is taken over by language–constantly threatens to unravel the systematic coherence of the book. It is "that which is when there is no more world, when there is no world yet" (1982: 33). The work, we might suggest, is the *tohu vabohu* (formlessness and void) of Genesis 1, that which was before creation, before distinctions between light and day, earth and sky. The work is revived when the threatening *tohu vabohu* erupts into the fine lines of creation; chaos comes into cosmos.

Here the tome (book) is the tomb, waiting to be called out, waiting for what i have called a "religious reading," a re-opening of the book and a re-reading of the work within the book (Plate).

> The book is there, then, but the work is still hidden. It is absent, perhaps radically so; in any case it is concealed, obfuscated by the evident presence of the book, behind which it awaits the liberating decision, the "Lazare, veni foras." (Blanchot, 1982: 195)

Yet it must be made clear that the reader might be surprised by what "comes in" from out of the tome/tomb, as Blanchot suggests Jesus must have been. On one hand we get the unity of the revived body, coming in from out of the tomb, wrapped in cloth; death returns into life. On the other hand we get the decaying, stinking carcass of a body that has been dead and is in a state of decomposition. To read, for Blanchot, means that we cannot have one without the other. To have the other re-presented, to be in the presence of one who was dead, is to also breathe in the unexpected and unpleasant odors from beyond.

For an extensive bibliography of texts by Blanchot see Leslie Hill, *Blanchot: Extreme Contemporary*. For extensive primary and secondary texts on Blanchot see the Web site maintained by Reg Lilly: http://lists.village.virginia.edu/~spoons/blanchot/blanchot_mainpage.htm

certeau
Vincent J. Miller

And after the fire, a light murmuring sound.
(1 Kings 19:13, New Jerusalem Bible)

Scholar of mysticism and demonic possession, urban planning and consumption, the French Revolution and popular culture; Jesuit priest; founding member of Lacan's *Ecole Freudienne;* and one of the most insightful critics of Foucault–this unlikely set of interests and orientations belongs to Michel de Certeau, S. J. (1925–1986), a scholar whom Julia Kristeva eulogized as "one of the boldest, the most secret and the most sensitive minds of our time" (1986: 22–23). Certeau's intellectual project was vast, ranging across the disciplinary reserves of anthropology, economics, history, linguistics, philosophy, psychology, and theology. His training in theology and study of early modern religion should make him among the most interesting of postmodern theorists for scholars of religion. Yet his reception in these disciplines lags behind others, where his theological concerns are either ignored or unknown; for instance, Michèle Lamont's review of *The Practice of Everyday Life,* reprinted on the book's back cover, incorrectly describes him as a "former" Jesuit (Certeau never left the order and is buried in a Jesuit Cemetery), and the translation of his theological writings lags behind his other works (on Certeau's complicity in the elision of his theological concerns see Bauerschmidt, 1996).

Certeau provides a number of provocative contributions to the practice of biblical interpretation. After an outline of the general orientation of his thought, this chapter will explore Certeau's sketch of the agency of consumption, which provides insights into the complex and unpredictable ways in which biblical texts are employed by those who revere and practice them; his notion of textual operations, which provides a focus for textual research somewhat different from philological and hermeneutic methods; and his understanding of the politics of the scholarly enterprise, which provides a set of cautions and opportunities for those engaged in the study of biblical texts.

Heterology

Certeau's intellectual project resists easy categorization. He intentionally avoided articulating a closed system of thought, preferring to work at the boundaries of disciplines and knowledges. Wrestling with the ossifications inherent in any system of knowledge, his thought was always, in Jeremy Ahearne's words, "on the move," seeking to disrupt seeming certainties with those things they inevitably overlook and repress. His work has been described by himself and others as "heterology"—a discourse on alterity or otherness. This term provides a compact way to sketch his scholarly project. His manifold works wrestle with alterity in one form or another. Although "otherness" has a range of meanings in his works, two predominate. The first of these, which Ahearne has termed "implicit alterity," can be associated with Foucault (Ahearne, 1996: 4). This concerns the formation of knowledge in language, culture, power, and institutions. Our knowledge is always historically constructed, but we are seldom conscious of this debt. With Foucault, Certeau sought to unearth these implicit structurings of thought; to bring to light the interests that guide it, the violences upon which it is founded, and the construction of the real that it presumes. "Alterity always reappears, and in a fundamental way, is the very nature of language. A truth is spoken by the organization of a culture, but it escapes its own collaborators. Certain relations predetermine subjects and cause them to signify something other than what they think they say or can say" (1986a: 181). By highlighting their particularities and limits, Certeau desired to show how such intellectual spaces are dependent on what they exclude as outside, or in a favored term, "ob-scene." Note that he is not speaking of "interdisciplinary knowledge," which too easily suggests an object in itself, outside construction in particular disciplines. Founding a more comprehensive field of knowledge would fall prey to the same dynamic. Rather, he engaged in a series of tactical disruptions of the borders of established knowledges, thematizing their boundaries so that they might be transgressed.

If the first meaning of alterity in Certeau's work is Foucaultian, the second can be associated with Levinas—ethical concern for the intellectual and physical repression of human others. Again, Certeau avoided representations of the "other" (although essentializing language is not absent from his writings) but undertook a series of heterological diversions of existing accounts to highlight the alternatives that dwell within and between them. This concern for otherness is linked to the first. He sought to expose the hierarchy of knowledge presumed in much academic discourse. This hierarchy censors (rather than silences) alternate voices, for through a variety of methods, for example quotation and turns to "popular culture," it employs them. Certeau offered repeated accounts of this "ethnographic method," which posited meaning in non-learned discourse that could only be unearthed by academic exegesis—exploiting them as natural resources for scholarly production in a capitalistic mode.

The Practices of Everyday Life

In his various studies of "everyday life," Certeau attempted to elucidate the rationality of non-erudite thought forms. Of this work, his analyses of the agency of cultural consumers rank among his most distinctive contributions.

Here he is thoroughly post-structuralist, having no recourse to a sovereign subject as a ground for agency. At the same time, he avoids the deterministic tendencies of structuralism. A comparison with Foucault is illuminative. Although he frequently expressed a desire to explore not only the ways in which power produces human culture but also the bases of manifold local resistances to power structures, Foucault so stressed the hegemonic function of discursive regimes that actual resistance became hard to conceive. Certeau, on the other hand, spoke of cultural production both in terms of the productive apparatus of the dominant discursive regime and as a productive appropriation through which individuals and groups engage and employ these structures. Cultural consumers are "unrecognized producers, poets of their own acts, silent discoverers of their own paths in the jungle of functionalist rationality." Their productions "trace out the ruses of other interests and desires that are neither determined nor captured by the system in which they develop" (1984: xviii). To derive a metaphor from the second volume of *The Practice of Everyday Life,* consumption is not mindlessly swallowing what one is handed; it is cooking, constituting a cuisine from the limited offerings of the local supermarket.

The nature of these actions must be carefully defined. It is tempting to describe them in terms of the Saussurean distinction between *langue* and *parole:* Cultural agents actualize the possibilities of their discursive formations (*langue*) in their utterances and practices (*parole*). These operations, however, are not simple actualizations but plays on the boundaries and absences of discursive formations. They are turnings, ruptures, and transgressions that bring new possibilities into play. For that reason they are not, strictly speaking, sayable. Such actions are marked by silence because they are disruptions of the conditions of utterance itself. Carried out in language, they are never fully expressed in it. Thus, for example, narrative is interesting not only for what it says but also as a *practice* of appropriation. An example of Certeau's ability to sense such capillary actions in all sorts of everyday practices can be found in his influential essay "Walking in the City" (1984: 91–110), which contrasts the limpid, transparent, frozen view from the top of the World Trade Center–a gaze that surveys a city carefully planned and knowable (symbolizing the panoptic ideal of modern Western knowledge and perhaps even the mythic ideal of the ordered, written page)–with the murmuring below where the innumerable, temporal-itineraries (narratives of space) of city dwellers act out significances and uses opaque to the comprehension and planning of urban administrators: The Euclidean plane beneath a dour Bauhaus tower is appropriated for skateboarding; a traffic island at a busy intersection supports vendors of immigrant foods.

This agency has the mode of a "tactic," which Certeau contrasts with "strategies." The latter are exercised by subjects with their own proper (*propre*) space, akin to a fortification, from which operations can be carried out on what lies outside (the mode of operation of academic disciplines). Tactics, on the other hand, are "the art of the weak," who dwell within foreign territory, making do and getting by in terrains and cultures not of their own design and beyond their control (1984: 36–37). Myriad examples of tactics abound in his writings, from the diversion of productive resources by factory employees to the creative activity of readers reading ("poaching") a text. In all these he repeatedly demonstrates that "we must not take people for fools" (1984: 176). Certeau helps restore the Brownian complexity to our understanding of culture and history, overlooked by structuralism and other thought forms that reduce culture to the frozen frame of the synchronic. This fundamentally hopeful element of his thought perdured throughout his career.

This distinction between strategies and tactics has been challenged for harboring a polar conception of power that essentializes the masses as an organic, unified resistance. Certainly, tactics and strategies are not dichotomized in war. They are two aspects of the same struggle. Certeau provides a helpful analysis of resistance but is less useful for envisioning the complexities and conflicts of plural power structures. In this regard, there was much that he did not learn from Foucault's account of power. Furthermore, his tendency to moralize the distinction renders strategic exercises of power suspect. John Frow argues that Certeau's portrayal of resistance overlooks the possibility of the oppressed having a strategic structural impact on the system of domination (1991: 58). Unfortunately, this polar model of power all too often corresponds with the concrete power dynamics in cultures. Tony Shirato (1993) has countered that Frow's analysis misses the tactical nature of Certeau's theoretical work and, for this reason, expects of his discourse the very dynamics its seeks to subvert.

Textual Operations

As the previous sketch would suggest, in his textual analyses Certeau did not engage in interpretation of the meanings born by texts but in an analysis of the operations they undertook within their discursive formations–that is, how they manipulated the language at their disposal and the effects that these manipulations brought about. This analysis privileges form over content. This is evident in his use of the term "articulation"–meaning not an expression of experience but the linking together of elements of the cultural/linguistic field in order to create new possibilities. While this method has affinity with classical philology and historical critical methods, he was suspicious of their constructions of an original or "proper" meaning. He was equally suspicious of hermeneutic methods that attempt to extract contemporary meanings from texts. He feared that all of these approaches too easily domesticated the strange voices that confront us in historical traces, glossing over the eccentric manipulations they undertake, reducing them and the tradition that maintains them to a glorious cemetery and museum (1971: 344).

His treatment of mystical texts is exemplary in this regard (1963, 1966, 1970, 1992). We are tempted to categorize these as expressions of an experience of the divine, to posit "behind the documents, the presence of a what-ever, an ineffability that could be twisted to any end" (1986a: 83). This presumes that we comprehend that which provoked their composition. Rather, we should "attempt to repeat [the text's] movements ourselves, to follow though at a distance, in the footsteps of its workings…refusing to equate this thing, which transformed graphs into hieroglyphs as it passed, with an object of knowledge" (1986a: 83). The distinguishing characteristic of mystic speech for Certeau is its ability to "induce a departure," to twist the language at its disposal (its theological certainties having been thrown into question) in such a way as to open it to what it could no longer render present. Mystic speech "testifies to a performance, a tactic in which the dominating discourse is undermined, confused, or played against itself so that another voice is heard. It is the voice of 'social inquietude,' it is the voice of the forgotten Other, the inaudible voice of God." This should not be confused with a claim for presence. "Because it is always less than what comes through it, it allows a genesis, the mystic poem is connected to the nothing which opens the future, the time to come, and more precisely, to that single work 'Yahweh,' which forever makes possible the self naming of that which induced departure" (1986a: 100; consult also Ward, 1996).

This attention to the operations within texts and their political power, their ability to create new spaces, provides a valuable tool for the analysis of biblical texts. Certeau applied this analysis to the Christian Scriptures. He approached the practice of Jesus not as a presence to be recovered but as a founding rupture (*la rupture instauratrice*), which made new experiences possible. "The event is 'historical' not because of its preservation outside time owing to a knowledge of it that supposedly has remained intact, but because of its introduction into time with various discoveries about it for which it '*makes room*.'" Jesus did not institute a new religious system but performed an articulation, "turned" the language of his tradition in another direction through his actions. The New Testament texts express "not the event itself, but that which the event made possible for the first believers" (1971: 336). Thus, fidelity consists not in reproducing the content of his language but in executing similar operations in cultures foreign to Christianity. "The process of the death (the absence) and the survival (the presence) of Jesus continues in each Christian experience: what the event makes possible is different each time, as a new remoteness from the event and a new way of erasing it" (1971: 337). He finds a resonance of this kenosis of content in the death of Jesus and his "resurrection within a multiplicity of Christian languages" (1971: 345). "There is a close bond between the absence of Jesus (dead and not present) and the birth of the christian language (objective and faithful testimony of his survival)" (1971: 336).

Jesus' articulation was a "work on limits," an action that involved recognizing the boundaries of the religious culture and crossing them–a "place and a departure." Thus, the fundamental form of Christian practice is making space for the other. Herein lies a brilliant riff on particularity. In contrast to liberalism, which seeks to gloss over particularity in pursuit of unity, limits have a "permissive function" for Certeau. They enable the "differentiation which constantly restores a Christian relationship with the other as necessary, but ungraspable." (1971: 340) Universalism resides only in idealist abstraction, harboring a denial of one's own limits and an unwillingness to enter into "articulation with others" (1971: 341). He cultivated a constant awareness of these limits and an active practice of their displacement. Repeating past truths provides no certainty. Continuity is found in rupture; stability in Abrahamic wandering. "Only new departures manifest...Christianity as still *alive*" (1971: 345).

The Politics of Scholarship

This analysis of textual operations within early Christian texts (which is equally a theology of tradition) has important consequences for the practice of biblical studies. It calls into question any method that is concerned primarily with establishing a "proper" reading of a text. Such authorized readings are "always guilty of infidelity to the riches" of the text and are "overprinted by a relationship of forces," which reduce the plurality of the text to a "literal private hunting reserve, open only to meanings given by socially authorized professionals" (1984: 171). Such readings of the Bible seem to be in danger of bringing the ongoing departures of the Christian tradition to a halt. More likely however, they simply miss the ongoing dynamism of the tradition carried out in innumerable contemporary readings.

Certeau offered further reflections on the politics of scholarship in his writings on historiography—a discipline at least cognate to biblical studies. Constituted in relationship to the absence of its object of study, historical inquiry is particularly sensitive to the political locus of its production. Traces of the past are never available outside their contemporary institutional organization—the separation of a particular profession (history), which circumscribes a particular object (the past) and sets aside particular objects for its inquiries (archives, texts, monuments; 1986a: 204; 1988: 73). Certeau emphasized the historiographical operation—*The Writing of History*—in order to bring these contemporary practices to the foreground. He was fascinated with what Roland Barthes termed the "reality effect" of historiography (Barthes, 1986). A contemporary writing, working according to circumscribed disciplinary norms, claims to make present an absent past, cloaking its own interests in realistic narrative. His aim was not negative—to eliminate truth claims in historiography—but positive—to thematize its fictional elements, to admit that its accounts of the past are just that. This implicates the producer, drawing her or him from behind the veil of supposed neutrality. When it acknowledges its entanglement in history, historiography provides a critique of the modern myth of objectivity and can play a key role in the "re-politicization" of the sciences. Time erodes the strategic certainties of place, disrupting detached academic observation of mute objects, tossing the historian into encounters with "interlocutors, who even if they are not specialists, are themselves subject-producers of histories and partners in a shared discourse" (1986a: 217). Historiography becomes a heterological and "ethical" undertaking that acknowledges the distance between what is and what ought to be, between the murmurs of the past and our ability to understand them on their own terms.

As is the case with any seminal thinker, a brief sketch cannot do justice to the breadth of Certeau's enterprise. These three elements of his heterological project–his understanding of creative reception, textual operations, and the politics of historiography–offer provocative suggestions for the practice of biblical studies. Located between a broad and multifarious community, which practices the texts in myriad ways, and the historical traces of the texts themselves, which are as strange as they are familiar, biblical studies has much in common with the heterologies of Michel de Certeau. In the end, this is not surprising, as his project grew out of a practice of these very texts.

culture/cultural criticism
Kenneth Surin

Raymond Williams once wrote that "culture is one of the two or three most complicated words in the English language" (Williams, 1983: 87). According to Williams, its "root" word, the Latin *colere,* had several distinct meanings that eventually separated over time, even if some continued to overlap: inhabit (from the Latin *colonus*) became *colony;* "honour with worship" (from the Latin *cultus*) became *cult;* and *cultura* had as its primary meaning *cultivation* or *husbandry,* that is, the tending of crops or animals. In the early sixteenth century this sense of caring for animals and plants was extended to the domain of human growth and development, but it was only in the late eighteenth century that *culture* came to designate "an abstract process or the product of such a process" (88). In French (*culture*) and German (*Kultur,* nineteenth century), "culture" functioned mainly as a synonym for *civilization.* Here, and there was a parallel development in English, it became harnessed to narratives of human development that charted our "progress" in the form of a universal history that saw Homo sapiens emerging from savagery or primitiveness through domestication before undergoing a "sentimental education" that ensued in a "race" of free beings (the German *Bildung*). At this stage, *culture* had three general meanings:

(i) "a general process of intellectual, spiritual, and aesthetic development";

(ii) "a particular way of life, whether of a people, a period, a group, or humanity in general"; and

(iii) "the works and practices of intellectual and especially artistic activity." (90)

These primary senses of *culture* have more or less prevailed to the present time. Different intellectual fields have, however, placed contrasting emphases on the different dimensions of culture and cultural production: Archaeology and cultural anthropology highlight *material* production, while cultural studies and history tend to focus on *symbolic* or *signifying* systems (91). Much of Williams' own work can be seen as an attempt to bring together these material and symbolic dimensions of cultural production. Two features of this brief genealogy of *culture* stand out.

The first is that the notion of *culture* in the senses important for us (i.e., the denizens of modern industrial societies) is of relatively recent provenance: It is only in the last two hundred years or so that culture has functioned, whether

49

explicitly or implicitly, as an intellectual instrument for organizing our convictions about progress, the good life, and so forth. In other times and places (even today in some cases), such notions as *umran* (plenitude, fullness), "divine election," "cosmic harmony," "providence," and so forth served the intellectual and practical functions associated today with the category of *culture,* and neither Thomas Aquinas nor Ibn Khaldun, for instance, would have been able to delineate their notions of the *summum bonum* in terms of this category and its cognates in the way that subsequently became possible for a Matthew Arnold or a Johann Gottfried von Herder.

The second feature brought to light by this genealogy has already been adverted to, namely, that the notion of *culture* is seemingly bound up with conceptions of progress and development, that is, with a certain narrative of the emergence and consolidation of modernity as a historical project, in the sense made well known by Kant in his essay on the Enlightenment and taken up more recently by Habermas as part of his critique of the French "neo-Nietzschean irrationalists." This feature is crucial for any understanding of the intellectual practices that come under the rubric of *cultural criticism,* because the cultural critic, on this account, is someone who works under the auspices of a story about the emergence of a better and more rational world. This story, or "grand narrative," posits a decisive break between a past that is deemed to be immured in "ignorance" and "superstition," and a present, the time of modernity, distinctively marked by the rule of reason. The cultural critic's fundamental task is thus to police the demarcations between these two discrepant times and their associated mores. However, since all versions of cultural criticism are constituted at their core by an ensemble of intellectual practices, it is the case that these practices may be sanctioned in this or that social formation or historical epoch even when the lexeme *culture* (or its cognates) is not semantically available to the formation or epoch in question. Thus, Augustine's *City of God* can be viewed as a powerful and remarkable exercise in cultural criticism, even though Augustine was not, of course, in a position to designate himself as the practitioner of a "cultural criticism" that went by that name. Where "culture" is concerned, Augustine, it could be said, had at his disposal, albeit only tacitly, its (mere) concept, but not its manifestation as a lexeme or theoretical category (though "lexeme" and "theoretical category" are not on this account to be conflated, since clearly not all lexemes can function as theoretical categories). A similar claim can be made on behalf of Machiavelli and such central figures of the Enlightenment as Hume and Kant: What the former undertook in his theory of princely power and "statecraft," and Hume as part of his critique of "false philosophy" and Kant in his "philosophical anthropology," can appropriately be viewed as a kind of cultural criticism. The availability of the concepts *culture* and *cultural criticism* to an epoch or society, such as Augustine's or Machiavelli's, which at the same time lacks these concepts' lexically visible modes of expression (these being later productions, so to speak), indicates that *culture* and *cultural criticism* are always evolving historical artifacts, and this in turn suggests the possibility of a cultural criticism whose codifications are *not* typically linked to eighteenth- and nineteenth-century narratives of progress and development.

While our intellectual ancestors may have engaged in what we today call "cultural criticism" under the rubrics of what they regarded as a philosophical anthropology, theological history, political history, and so forth, it is usual nowadays to assign this critical enterprise to the disciplinary field of *cultural studies* (though cultural anthropology, history, art history, and some forms of theoretical sociology and political economy do also serve as present-day vehicles of cultural criticism). How cultural studies serves as the embodiment of several if not all of the protean varieties of cultural criticism depends crucially on the version of cultural studies being sponsored, and especially on that version's particular and distinctive constitution as a disciplinary field. For cultural studies, it has frequently been noted, is about a great many things: "the struggle to form a more 'organic' kind of intellectual" (Hall, 1980: 46); "the world's new textuality" (Jameson, 1993: 19); "the subjective side of social relations" (Johnson: 43); "illuminating the ways in which power relations are experienced in everyday life" (Kraniauskas: 9); "a central system of practices, meanings and values, which we can properly call dominant and effective" (Williams, 1980: 38) are just some of the proposals for what cultural studies is "about," either programmatically or in its more incisive versions. (It should be noted that not all the providers of these characterizations necessarily endorse the large claims that sometimes accompany attempts at defining "cultural studies.") This diversity of definition notwithstanding, it is useful, despite the caveats that have to be entered about the inevitably whiggish tenor of such narratives, to see the complex institutionalization of cultural studies as consisting of three primary phases, each with its attendant intellectual agendas and political concerns.

In its first phase, which lasted roughly from the late 1950s to the late 1970s and was associated primarily with the exemplary work of Raymond Williams, Richard Hoggart, and E. P. Thompson, and the founding of the influential Birmingham Centre for Contemporary Cultural Studies, cultural studies emerged through an engagement, in some instances with an adversarial edge, with the more conservative understanding of "culture" underwritten by the *Scrutiny* group that coalesced around F. R. Leavis and the critiques of ideology and "false consciousness" associated with Lukacs and the Frankfurt School, though Althusser's account of "interpellation" by "ideological state apparatuses" became much more central for the Birmingham Centre in the early 1970s. The overall objective of this critical enterprise in this early phase of its development was very much the retrieval of what were perceived to be lost or marginalized intellectual and social traditions, enervated by the conviction that the resources of a culture were the possession of all its members and not just a privileged few. Thus, in *The Uses of Literacy* (1957), the prewar working class ethos was used as Hoggart's partly autobiographical context for an analysis of 1950s English popular culture; Thompson's *The Making of the English Working Class* (1963) sought to depict and to revivify for a present-day readership the contradictory *cultural* experiences of a working class that was formed between 1790 and 1832; and Williams' *Culture and Society* (1958) pitted a virtually unacknowledged English Romantic tradition of anticapitalist cultural criticism against its regnant political and economic liberal counterpart. The Birmingham School, primarily in the works of Stuart Hall and Richard Johnson, placed a continued emphasis on popular culture, but wanted at the same time to deepen and extend the principal theoretical categories (*ideology, subjectivity, experience, consciousness*) used in the early writings of its immediate intellectual precursors. Hence the recourse made by the Birmingham School to Althusser and later, and more significantly, Gramsci and his notion of *hegemony.*

In the second phase, which lasted from the late 1970s to the late 1980s, the proponents of British cultural studies continued to focus on the question of the possibility of a left-oriented cultural transformation that had motivated the thinkers in the first phase of its emergence, but complicated their analyses by engaging with feminist theory, race and ethnicity studies, and a little later, queer theory. This development or branching-out also spurred a self-critique of cultural studies' own presuppositions in certain quarters: Cultural studies had purported to be an instrument for the critique of ideology, but its own critiques had up to now been just as oblivious to considerations of gender, race, and sexuality as the ideologies that cultural studies was purporting to critique, and this ideology *in* cultural studies now came in for criticism from some of its own practitioners. The deleterious side to this otherwise welcome enlargement of cultural studies' critical range by its newly directed attention to considerations of race, gender, and sexuality was that cultural studies was now positioned to be a kind of academic identity politics, centered in some cases almost exclusively on the cultural functions of these categories, and concerned almost entirely with "the popular" and a veritable panoply of cultural phenomena reflecting so-called popular taste: hairstyles, Barbie dolls, fast cars, fast food, Elvis impersonators, Michael Jackson and Madonna, domestic animals, snuff videos, tractor pulls and demolition derbies, Disney World and Busch Gardens, dinosaurs, endless numbers of television "soaps," and so on. (This was particularly true of the versions of cultural studies spawned by its American institutionalization, which seemed in most cases to lack the overt political impulses underpinning British cultural studies.) This wholly one-sided emphasis on the demotic and on the "styles" of consumption associated with "the popular" (a kind of "MTV meets Michel de Certeau" in the dismissive formulation of some of the more severe critics) have occasioned critiques (see, for example, the works by Jameson and Morris) of the unremitting "banality" and "parochialism" of many varieties of cultural studies.

In the current phase, from the late 1980s onward, and marked in Britain by the virtual demise of the Birmingham Centre (a victim in part of the Thatcherite *gleichschaltung*), cultural studies has again been affected by forces decisive enough to transform its shape and substance, in particular the revolution in information and telematic sciences and the onset of globalization. These forces, and their associated new modes of production and social forms, affect culture (and thus cultural studies), even as the practitioners of cultural studies continue to reflect on the question that claimed the attention of their colleagues involved in the earlier phases of its development, namely, How is cultural transformation possible? Accompanying this new emphasis on globalization and its repercussions has been the realization that there is now not just *one* cultural studies that does duty for the whole world, so to speak, but a French Cultural Studies, a Spanish Cultural Studies, a German Cultural Studies, an African Cultural Studies, and so forth. The realization that the world today is more than ever a congeries of communities (and that includes nation-states) linked by capitalism has become integral to cultural studies' intellectual agenda in the last decade or so. So just as a decade before cultural studies had enlarged its theoretical armature by incorporating categories from feminist, gender, and queer theories, cultural studies now found itself in a productive engagement with postcolonial theory and subaltern studies, borrowing from the former such notions as *hybridity* to "theorize" the relation between metropolitan and colonial and postcolonial cultures, and from the latter new ways of understanding the asymmetrical relations that obtain between those who possess cultural capital and those who don't (see especially Kraniauskas).

But what has cultural criticism to do in principle with theology and the study of religious traditions? As indicated, theology has always provided, even if only implicitly, the axioms or "grammar" for a cultural criticism. At the same time, a number of ways of undertaking a theologically motivated cultural criticism have shown themselves to be problematic. These include the theologies *of* culture popular in the earlier part of this century, such as Paul Tillich's then-celebrated "method of correlation," which, in essence, involved the use of a theological anthropology (using such concepts as "ultimate concern," "the ground of our Being," etc.) to form a discursive bridge between Christian doctrines (original sin, soteriology) and an analysis of "culture" (employing such notions as "anxiety," "meaninglessness," etc.). Tillich's "method" required the "correlation" of the appropriate Christian doctrine with the requisite description of culture, with the theological anthropology making the relevant transcodings between doctrine and cultural description. Also problematic is a Barthianism that uses a christologically constituted revelation to "overcome" the deliverances of culture. What discredits these approaches is not so much their respective theologies, though there may be problems there as well, but the way in which culture is used in such approaches as a monolithic category, encompassing anything to do with "the human condition" or "immanence," and so forth, so that "culture" becomes, in effect, a general and highly amorphous analogue of "civilization." This "civilization" or "culture" includes the poor and the dispossessed and the powerful and privileged alike, since all are designated as partakers of the same human condition or deemed to belong to the all-encompassing realm of immanence. This flawed politics of theological knowledge has been critiqued by the liberation theologians in particular (though Johann-Baptist Metz pioneered this line of argument in his "critical theology") for its ideological overriding of the plight of those who are victims, and this critique needs to be borne in mind in any theologically sponsored cultural criticism. Most emphatically, there is a chasm between the stable in Bethlehem and the Waldorf Astoria that all theological knowledge must acknowledge! Any definition of "culture" that ends up characterizing it as a seamless totality, thereby occluding more or less significant asymmetries of power and position between human beings, is simply inadequate.

An effective cultural criticism for theology will be one that accords with Christianity's affirmations about the means to attain salvation, the states that coincide with its attainment, and the figures or forms instrumental to this attainment. This criticism, in other words, will be a part of soteriology: A Christian cultural criticism will provide a solution to the "problem" of the world; it will provide its adherents with a way of resolving the problem of a basic recalcitrance of the world.

This soteriologically constituted cultural criticism will have to grant that, in a world constrained by a fundamental recalcitrance that will have to be overcome in the name of redemption, it is always possible that the bringers of redemption will be forced out of sight by a history that cannot have any place for them. Such redemptive and utopian propensities will be hidden and marked by untimeliness as well as being discontinuous with the course of history. As Walter Benjamin pointed out in his "Theses on the Philosophy of History," an effective cultural criticism will provide resources for transcoding these hidden redemptive propensities. If historical conditions stand in the way of the pursuit of liberation, then a theologically framed cultural criticism has to go beyond the boundary framed by these historical conditions. Thought may be defeated by the absence of historical conditions that conduce to liberation, but this cultural criticism has to confront that which defeats thought. Redemption will thus be a never-predictable event, urgent but unanticipatable, "the new." A theologically adequate cultural criticism will make this realization its most basic principle.

deconstruction

David W. Odell-Scott

Deconstruction is associated with a contemporary intellectual movement in philosophy, literary theory, and criticism. The French philosopher Jacques Derrida says that he selected the term *deconstruction* to translate Heidegger's term *destruktion* (*Being and Time*) because the French phonetic equivalent (*destruction*) implied annihilation, which Derrida judged to be more like Nietzschean "demolition" than Heidegger's genealogical study of metaphysics. The French *deconstruction* was customarily associated with a mechanical sense of dis-arranging or dis-assembling, like the disassembling of a whole into parts, as in to de-construct a machine in order to transport it elsewhere for re-construction, or the breaking of a sentence (grammar) into its words, or the de-composing of something in the sense that its own construction fails and it falls apart into its own parts. Thus, de-construct is an un-structuring, or better, un-con-structuring, un-doing, de-composing, un-settling, de-stabilizing. Components and their relations are put into a play that is not an obliteration.

For Heidegger in *Being and Time, destruktion* is the process of tracing an idea (concept, term, or the like) back to its *appearance* when it came to be differentiated with its opposite. Heidegger's studies of the history of thought, and particularly the history of Western metaphysics, is a *destruktion,* an unsettling of the sediment of metaphysics in search of the founding moments or e-vents, when beings came forth as beings, when beings emerged as beings in dynamic differentiation, in opposition to Being. On Derrida's reading, Heidegger's early foundational ontology sought to disclose the "beginning" of metaphysics, when "Being" receded and beings were disclosed. One of Derrida's points of critique is that Heidegger's differentiation of Being and beings at the "beginning" of the history of metaphysics (ontological difference) attempts to establish an "origin" of metaphysics in opposition to what is "derived" or "copied" from the "original." The presupposition that there is an "original" that is superior to its opposite—a "derivative" or "copy"—also deconstructs. Thus, Derrida is suspicious when, on his reading, Heidegger suggests that the *destruktion* of the history of metaphysics can return the thinker to some "original." Derrida questions whether it is possible to have an authentic relation to language as the poetic "saying" of the Being of beings, on which the *construction* of metaphysics is subsequently founded. For Derrida, deconstruction is not the means by which to unearth the origins from which thinking begins or to which thinking could return. Instead, Derrida judges that deconstruction is an event provisionally described as reading, writing, and thinking that undoes, decomposes, unsettles the established hierarchies of Western thought. It is beyond the limits of this short entry to trace out the continued discussion between Derrida and interpreters of Heidegger on this point.

While deconstruction is often associated with *postmodernism,* it differs from much that claims to be postmodern in that deconstruction is primarily a complex, close exegesis of texts—often the very texts identified and evaluated as the primary texts of Western thought. A close reading serves to disclose the *aporia,* the unresolved tensions, conflicts, and contradictions within the text that are often ignored by non-deconstructive exegetes. De Man maintained that the purpose of deconstructive reading is to so respect the text, to read the text so closely, that those places where the text does not make sense to the reader become the very sites in need of elucidation, not in order to master the text, but in order to respect the self-de-composing of the text evident in such aporetic deadlocks, the very places where the text appears to contest or subvert its own stated intent or thesis. The deconstructive reader does not gloss the text, but admits when the reader is helpless in understanding the text. Thus, one of the ways that deconstruction is critical is that the deconstructive reader makes evident the alterity of the text to the contending interpretations, including one's own, and maybe even the interpretation of the author, so as to designate impasses when they occur.

Of interest to the student of religion are the complex ways in which signs or symbols are understood. Augustine in *de Doctrina Christiana* asserted that "a sign is a thing which, over and above the impressions it makes on the senses, *causes something else* to come into the mind as a consequence of itself." This classical definition *(aliquid stat pro aliquo,* Latin), that "a sign stands for something else," is taken to mean that a sign represents something that is not a sign. A sign is "always a sign *of* " and so is dependent upon what it represents in order to be a sign. What is *re-presented* by the sign is assumed to be a presence—defined as that which exists on its own independently of the sign. Thus, what the sign refers to is assumed simply to be, to be present, without need of representation.

A network of differentiations is woven into such ways of thinking:

Sign–signified
sign–presence
re-presentation–presentation
re-presentation–real
dependent–independent

Each of the terms in any dyadic set are not equivalent. One term enjoys privileges over its other. A deconstructive critique proceeds by noting that the bifurcation of sign and signified assumes that there are terms in the discussion that are assumed to be "present" that are themselves *not signs.*

Critical studies of signification begin with the assumption that signs are human inventions and then proceed to study the social, political, psychological, and economic context of sign generation, influence, and use. Let's take an example from contemporary biblical scholarship. One might ask about the adequacies or inadequacies of the presentation of "Jesus" in the canonical gospels. Interpretations that assume a literal correlation between the sign (the name of "Jesus" in the texts) and the signified (the *real* Jesus) are assumed to be un-critical, while those interpretative strategies that explore the complexities of the relation of the sign and the signified, with attention to the influences of the society, politics, economics, and language as well as individual and communal convictions upon the processes of signification are judged to be critical. Much of the difference between contending methods in critical biblical scholarship is over what is identified as the source of a text and the referent of its "signs." To what does the sign refer, and what is the source of the text? While modern critical scholars assume that the source of a particular text is first and foremost its author, they differ over the extent to which the social, linguistic, and political come to influence the author. When all is said and done, they conclude that the author is best able to say what the text means or signifies, that the author's intention enjoys privilege over all subsequent interpretations.

Historical Jesus scholarship has been much concerned with identifying the "sayings" of Jesus, which, scholars argue, were "recorded," "copied," and subsequently "distributed" in the first century. These "sayings" verbally delivered by Jesus and copied in a "text" (yet to be discovered) are assumed to be the (textual) source for much of the material Jesus is "quoted" as having said in the Gospels. So the *written* "sayings" *of* Jesus refer to the *actually spoken* "sayings" *by* Jesus. And because speech is presumed to be more intimate, more immediate and expressive of the speaker than the speaker's own writings, much less another's written report about what the speaker said, then it is further assessed that the *spoken* sayings are the original that the *written* sayings copy. The spoken word of Jesus is the original, the "presence," which the written sayings of Jesus copy and re-present. The Gospels are developed stories that incorporate these written sayings into their story lines. The origin of the written sayings are the oral sayings of Jesus, while the story lines of any particular Gospel are, to a great extent, the work of its author, influenced by social, linguistic, political, and economic factors.

A deconstructive critique of this project would proceed by noting the dyadic structures:

Speaker–Listener
Original–Repeated
Speaker–Reporter
Spoken sayings–Written sayings
Written sayings–Gospel story
Author–Editor

The speaker and the words spoken enjoy privilege over all subsequent listening, reporting, writing, editing, and reading. It is assumed in this line of scholarship that the term *speaker* makes reference to an original, something that is first because it is a source, a real presence that stands as the terminus to all re-presentation. A deconstructive critique would be quick to point out that scholars in the contemporary study of the "historical Jesus" are working with texts and producing texts in a complex inter-textual network of activity, and that nothing is present that is not presented in texts. The presumption in "historical Jesus" scholarship is that at least a few terms have extra-textual reference and so provide a critically determined basis for their inquiry. The "historic" is something outside the text to which the text refers or fails to refer for those writing historical Jesus texts. Some signs refer to things or events that historically (really) existed or happened. A deconstructive critique would point out that even the terms that are judged to refer and that are said to provide a basis for historic Jesus study are meaningful within the context of historic texts and texts about the historic Jesus and that the chain of signification does not "present" a self-evident referent that provides epistemic foundation. So they read and write texts about the "historical Jesus" *as if* the phrase "historical Jesus" were itself *not a sign* among other signs in the texts produced by scholars but a presentation of that which is not a sign, not a text, not an interpretation.

If it is assessed that a set of sayings recorded in a Gospel were actually said by Jesus, the deconstructive critic would proceed by asking, To what does the term *Jesus* refer? The historic Jesus, might be the reply. Then to what does the phrase *historic Jesus* refer? The real, flesh and blood individual. However, the deconstructive critic might retort that the terms *historical, flesh, blood,* and *individual* are themselves signifiers. The deconstructive critique maintains that the claim that a sign signifies something is itself an act of signification, and that the referent of a sign is itself, in turn, a sign that signifies another, which in turn is a sign, and so on.

If we proceed to elucidate what these signifiers signify, then we continue to generate signs that refer to other signs. But, and this is a crucial point, we will not arrive at that which is not a sign. If the scholar intent on asserting that some sayings of Jesus were "actual" sayings of Jesus, then the scholar will employ more and more terms to explicate and elucidate what is meant by the claim, in hopes of satisfying the critic and concluding the discussion. But for the deconstructive critic it does not matter which term, concept, idea, identity, or the like stands as the source, the original, or the unmediated presence. The critical point is that it is commonly assumed in non-deconstructive readings that there is a signifed that is not a sign of another, a source that is not caused by another, which brings the search for signification and causation to a conclusion, a finale, an original. A critique of this process is that even the stated source occurs as a sign in a text, and that such a term does not present a source, an original, an unmediated "presence," but seeks to silence the critic. Even if we were to point at something and say, "I mean this!" such gesturing and speaking de-*sign*-ate something that is then interpreted in terms of the gesturing and speaking. "Oh, are you pointing at 'this'? Is this what you mean?"

For the critic, presence, the unmediated and independent referent, is alluding. It may be promised but never satisfied in the process of signification. Presence is deferred.

Because the signified in turn also signifies something else, "there is nothing outside the text." And those who seek to arrest the play of interpretation, to limit what signs will be used and to state what a particular sign stands for, or that a particular term is not a sign but the presence, the signified, are judged by deconstructionists (a) to be presumptuous in their knowledge of what is beyond signs and (b) to be politically tyrannical. Because texts are clusters of signs that readers and writers continually interpret, texts are open-ended. The possibility of fixing, once and for all, the meaning of any sign, of closing interpretative possibility, is a tyrannical desire. There is always more to say, more to write. And so a deconstructive reading of a text does not hope for the final word as to what a text means, as to what the signs refer to, but rather seeks to open texts that were assumed closed, fixed, settled to interpretative possibilities so that more can be said and written. Thus, reading, writing, and thinking participate in the dynamic and sustaining generation of signs. Interpretation yields interpretation.

A deconstructive critique of the sign-signified bifurcation and the privilege of the signified over the sign is not a simple assertion that everything is a sign. Rather, the points are that the identification of something as a sign in opposition to the signified, and the privileging of the signified over the sign are unfounded, because while what is signified is a referent relative to a sign (and so is identified as a referent because it is referred to by a sign), the referent may in turn serve as a sign for another.

The privilege of speech over writing is a topic of concern in deconstructive critique that deserves at least this brief mention. In much of Western thought the distinction commonly goes like this: A spoken word immediately embodies a thought, whereas a written word is a sign for the spoken word. The intimacy of speech and speaker is evident in that speech ends when the speaker is silent. However, the written word continues to communicate even when the writer is no longer writing, even when the writer is distant to the written text. The spoken word is expressive of the speaker, whereas the written word may be remote to the writer. We read texts written by authors who have been dead for centuries and/or from cultures and languages not our own. Thus, contends Derrida, "logocentricism" or "phonocentricism" (the contention that speech is more expressive of the presence of the speaker than writing is of the writer) is assessed to enjoy identity with the speaker, whereas the written word is "other" in relation to the writer. Derrida critiques the hierarchy, not in service to the superiority of the written word to speech, but as a means to deconstruct the exclusionary and hierarchical structure of the speech/writing bifurcation.

Deconstructive critics assume that a term, concept, idea, and the like are defined in terms of their opposites, in an odd Heraclitean logic in which opposites are what they are by virtue of being in opposition to one another.

However, opposites are not valued as equivalent. In the dyadic network of concepts in any field, one term is in-vested with privilege at the di-vestment of its opposite. This economy sustains an asymmetrical hierarchy in which one notion enjoys privilege over another at the expense of the one divested. The critiques are that there are no isolated entities, for even the contention that something is privileged over another is to declare its relation to others in an intimate network or complex web of relations. Deconstruction seeks to put the oppositional network into critical play. The privileging assessments of an oppositional set are called into question by demonstrating the dependence of the concept invested with privilege on its divested opposite.

A deconstructive reading engages what Derrida calls the pervasive "logic of supplementarity," whereby the divested term in each dyadic set turns out to be *always, already presupposed in any definition of the privileged term*. Take, for instance, the common theological set God and World. It is assumed that the term *God* stands for that which is most original and self-sufficient, while the term *world* refers to God's creation, which is utterly dependent on God in order to be the world. God is independent. The world is dependent. And yet, in order to even begin to speak of God, we already, always presuppose the world. For God to be God, God is already, always, *"God" of the "World."* So, and this is the critical move, which is unsettling, in order for God to be God, for God to be the creator of the world, God is *dependent* on the world to be God. The "world" is a condition necessary for the possibility of God. To be a superior necessitates an inferior, and so the superior is dependent on the inferior to be the superior. Opposites are co-originating and co-dependent.

Let's take, for example, the common dyadic set Man and Woman. In the classical Christian gloss of the creation stories, privilege is given to the second story, in which Woman is created after Man. Woman is Man's second. Adam was created first by God directly from the earth; Woman was created second by God from Adam. The identities in this oppositional pair are elaborated by their associations with other oppositional pairs, in which identifications are made with other concepts, which are also defined in dyadic sets:

Man–Woman
First–Second
God–World
Sacred–Profane
Soul–Body

Because Adam was created first by God from earth, and Woman was created later by God from Adam, Man is causally independent of and superior to Woman, while Woman is assessed to be causally dependent on and inferior to Man. Note the economy by which the terms are invested/divested of value in opposition to each other. Other oppositional sets come into play. Man is said to be closer to God because God created Adam directly out of the earth, whereas Eve was created *from* Adam/*for* Adam. Because Man is identified with God, Woman is identified with God's opposite, the world. Because Man is closer to God, Man is sacred. The opposite of sacred is profane, and so Man's opposite, Woman, is likewise profane. Because Soul is associated with the other first terms, Man is identified with Soul, and Man's opposite, Woman, is identified with Body, which is the opposite of Soul. And in this increasingly complex dyadic network, the privilege of Man over Woman is elucidated in a totalistic economy of theo-cosmic proportions in which Woman is associated with divested terms.

A deconstructive critique proceeds by noting how gender differentiation and identification is produced, how it is that the very notion of Man as first, original, and independent is *already, always dependent* on the notion of Woman as second, copy, and dependent. Man is defined in opposition to Woman, and Woman is defined in opposition to Man. Neither term is privileged in this Heraclitean logic. Each is defined and refined in opposition to the other. The economy of privilege, the investment of one term at the divestment of the other, is dis-established by a deconstructive critique. In order for something to be valued as first, there *already, always* is a second that is necessary if one is to generate the difference, in order for the first to be the first of something. Thus, all attempts to identify an original, a first, a beginning, are self-contradictory by definition, because a first is first to a second, an original is an original to a copy, a beginning is a beginning of that which follows. The privilege of the "original" occurs at the cost of its opposite on which, by definition, the original is dependent as an original. And so a deconstructive critique does not reject one original for another, but calls into question the very project of establishing an original. The ceaseless inversion of the dyadic economy in which opposition remains in play defers attempts for conclusion and so subverts attempts to establish order. Thus, deconstuction affects specific concepts within a dyadic economy and, as well, calls into question the presumed privilege of any network of notions.

deleuze and guattari

George Aichele

Gilles Deleuze (1925–1995) was professor of philosophy at the University of Paris. Félix Guattari (1930–1992) was a psychoanalyst at the LaBorde clinic. Deleuze and Guattari (hereafter D&G) are best known for their books *Anti-Oedipus* and *A Thousand Plateaus,* which form the two-volume work *Capitalism and Schizophrenia.* They propose

> to explore a transcendental unconscious, rather than a metaphysical one; an unconscious that is material rather than ideological; schizophrenic rather than Oedipal; nonfigurative rather than imaginary; real rather than symbolic; machinic rather than structural. (D&G, 1983: 109; see also 1987: 146)

Influenced by both Marxist and Nietzschean thought, D&G re-read Sigmund Freud and neo-Freudian thought in the wake of Jacques Lacan. They are also deeply interested in language, and they draw especially upon the linguistic views of Louis Hjelmslev.

D&G call their investigative procedure "schizoanalysis." They seek, in effect, to psychoanalyze Western civilization itself and, in particular, to analyze the fascination of the Western world with totalitarianism, "to show how, in the subject who desires, desire can be made to desire its own repression" (D&G, 1983: 105). Desire flows freely– "desire is revolutionary in its essence" (1983: 116)–but for that reason, desire is also bound to its own subjection. Therefore, "desire may fix on one of two alternatives. It may affirm itself, or it may choose power as its centre and the establishment of order as its purpose" (Anonymous, 1997).

Like many postmodern thinkers, D&G do not so much offer new information about the world as a new way to *conceive* the world. Schizoanalysis takes the form of an interlinked series of binary oppositions. However, these oppositions do not constitute logical contraries or contradictories, such as good/bad, true/false, or real/unreal. The elements of such logical oppositions cannot both be truly predicated of any one subject. In contrast, for D&G's oppositions, "each [element] takes nourishment from the other, borrows from the other" (1987: 423). The elements in these pairs continually arise out of and inevitably collapse back into each other. Therefore, these elements are paradoxically not elemental, because the identity of each element is itself deconstructed by the potential *within it* of its own "other."

D&G state that there can be no ultimate synthesis, either logical or eschatological, through which the disequilibrium of these oppositions will be overcome. Julia Kristeva describes this "practically infinite...concatenation of deviations" as a "nondisjunction" (1980: 40–41). Therefore, in the following, I call these oppositions *nondisjunctive*. A nondisjunctive opposition is a difference (Derrida's *différance*), which is *prior* to logical or ontological unity and which disrupts the identity of any object that is identified by means of it.

By exploring nondisjunctive oppositions, D&G join the ranks of Kristeva, Roland Barthes, Jacques Derrida, and numerous other poststructural thinkers. D&G's views are especially aligned with those of Michel Foucault (who wrote the preface to *Anti-Oedipus*), and along with Foucault and Michel Serres, among others, D&G suggest (and *A Thousand Plateaus* embodies) a postmodern historical criticism—a criticism that also critiques the foundational concepts and ideological function of "history" itself (D&G, 1987: 23). Following D&G, history can no longer be conceived as an objective, linear, causal sequence lying *behind* texts (or any human relic), or as an external, impartial standard to which the rigorous critic must be responsible. Instead, history will be seen as a "partial object" (1983: 309) that is itself assembled or *produced* here and now by subjective forces of signification and desire.

According to D&G, the "signifying regime" (Foucault's *episteme;* D&G, 1987: 140) that dominates any given era and people appears in the form of specific cultural praxes or "desiring-machines," through which the uncoded material stuff of the "body without organs" is continually "deterritorialized" and then "reterritorialized." The particular desiring-machines vary from one signifying regime to another, but the play of nondisjunctive opposition that they embody remains constant. D&G's schizoanalyses explore in detailed, nonsequential histories some of these desiring-machines, including, among others, the Second Temple of the Jews and the face of Christ.

The phrase "body without organs" is taken from Antonin Artaud (1976: 571) to designate concrete, non-signifying stuff, the "smooth" flow of matter apart from any communicable characteristics. The body without organs is "the *field of immanence* of desire" (D&G 1987: 154; their emphasis). Except as an unavoidable, discarded remainder, the body without organs cannot be known as such. "You never reach the Body without Organs, you can't reach it, you are forever attaining it, it is a limit" (1987: 149–50). "The body without organs is the body without an image" (1983: 8). The body without organs must be presupposed for any thought or utterance whatsoever, but it can only be encountered as an already-coded system (that is, what it is not), a signifying regime through which meaningless bodies are *organ*-ized into meaningful *organ*-isms, such as the self, human society, or the world.

D&G call these meaningful organisms the "full body" (1983: 281). The full body is the world as the product of desire, and desire is always already there, incarnated in the human world. The full body is all that we know, and therefore our world is always a meaningful world.

The earth is the primitive, savage unity of desire and production, the
full body that falls back on the forces of production and appropriates
them for its own as the natural or divine precondition. [I]t is on the
earth that desire becomes bound to its own repression. (1983:
140–41)

The opposition between the body without organs and the full body reflects
the pattern of all of D&G's nondisjunctive oppositions. What is most interesting
to D&G is not the polar extremes, but rather the "plateaus" (following Gregory
Bateson; D&G, 1987: 158) through which the opposed elements shift and
transform into one another. "A plateau is always in the middle, not at the
beginning or the end" (1987: 21). The body without organs is not a pure,
ideal, or absolute state, but it is the point at which opposed elements become
each other: "a pivot…a frontier…a naked full body" (1983: 281).

The sign-system of language is a desiring-machine that transforms the
body without organs into the full body, encoding it into mythical or scientific
objects that we understand and describe. The production of reality occurs
when language carves the body without organs into a signifying regime of
functional units (striated space, material strata, lines of segmentarity or flight).
The signifying regime both produces and is itself produced by struggle over
the sign in which the "faciality" (1987: 115) of the signifier plays an important
role. The face of the signifier refers both to the sign's expression substance,
the meaningless matter from which it is made, and to the fact that as a signifier,
its expression form already signifies. Every signifier signifies at minimum that
it is a signifier. The face of the signifier is the threshold where non-signifying
matter begins to signify—where language appears. The face is the significant
"break" in the "flow" of signifying matter (1983: 36)—in other words, the face
is a desiring-machine, a function that desire produces and in which desire is
produced. "The face is a politics" (1987: 181).

Desiring-machines work by encoding or decoding the endless flow of
meaningless matter on the body without organs. They produce the symbol,
which "is never in a one-to-one relationship with what it means, but always
has a multiplicity of referents" (1983: 181). The symbol is both the product of
desiring-machines and also itself a desiring-machine. In this way, D&G pursue
Umberto Eco's notion (following C. S. Peirce) of unlimited semiosis: There is
no final or ultimate signified (meaning, content) to bring the signifying flow to
a stop. "Desire and its object are one and the same thing: the machine, as a
machine of a machine. Desire is a machine, and the object of desire is another
machine connected to it" (D&G, 1983: 26; see also 1987: 159). Every sign is a
machine, an articulation of signifying desire (another machine) and signified
object (yet another machine), a coupling that is also a break or interruption in
the flow.

The body without organs is never completely encoded. Some portion of
the material flow is always uncoded and uncodable, and it escapes the desiring-
machines (1983: 163, 173). The limitations of the coded flows result in their

failure to signify and even sometimes in the breakdown of the signifying regime itself. These are moments of great interest to schizoanalysis. "[I]t is the displacement of the limit that haunts all societies, the displaced represented that disfigures what all societies dread absolutely as their most profound negative: namely, the decoded flows of desire" (1983: 177).

D&G have no interest in ideology as such, but rather in the nondisjunctive oppositions that make ideology both possible and necessary. One opposition lies between "deterritorialization" and "reterritorialization." Every signifying regime encodes a body that will eventually be deterritorialized (decoded) and then reterritorialized (recoded) into a different regime. For example, "the book assures the deterritorialization of the world, but the world effects a reterritorialization of the book, which in turn deterritorializes itself in the world" (1987: 11). Likewise, writing, or scripture, is the deterritorialization of oral tradition, the verbal sign (1983: 206), which leads eventually to the biblical canon as the reterritorializing of God.

Another nondisjunctive opposition appears between "schizophrenia" and "paranoia," which are the extreme disruption and concentration of identity, respectively. Like culture and history, the human self is an assemblage or *product,* not a given, for D&G. Schizoanalysis refuses the exclusive disjunction of either/or. "Schizophrenia is at once the wall, the breaking through this wall, and the failures of this breakthrough" (1983: 136). In schizophrenia, inclusive or free disjunction (1983: 77) generates unrestrained "desiring-production." The personal self is "dismantled" (1987: 151), and the ego disintegrates into a "little group" (1983: 362). Self-identity is not merely personal, as in classical psychoanalysis, but also communal. "There is no primacy of the individual; there is instead an indissolubility of a singular Abstract and a collective Concrete" (1987: 100). Indeed, schizophrenia reaches its extreme limit in capitalism. Capitalism is the moment when schizophrenia becomes its other, paranoia, which D&G associate with fascism.

This may be clarified by another nondisjunctive opposition, between the "rhizomatic" and the "arborescent." The rhizome is not a single entity, but instead it is a complex network of connections, such as a field of grass or a wolf pack. The rhizome has no fixed center and no clearly defined boundary. In the rhizome, as in schizophrenia, the logical opposition between one and many is undermined. The rhizome deconstructs questions of identity. "A rhizome may be broken, shattered at a given spot, but it will start up again on one of its old lines, or on new lines. Every rhizome contains lines of segmentarity according to which it is stratified, territorialized, organized, signified, attributed, etc., as well as lines of deterritorialization down which it constantly flees" (1987: 9). Deterritorialization produces the rhizome, and thus it is particular, polyvocal, and transitory. However, the "lines of segmentarity" that are essential to defining the rhizome are also the means of its own reterritorialization, its transformation into its other, the arborescent.

Arborescence–centralized, hierarchical organization, such as that of a tree or a large corporation–characterizes the totalizing, paranoid aspect of the signifying regime. In paranoia, the schizophrenic flows are inverted, and the nation, the tribe, and the ego are reterritorialized. The paranoid condition favors that which is sedentary, "biunivocal" (formed into logical oppositions), and universalizing. Paranoia is monotheistic. Paranoia restricts the desiring-machines, which are always potentially schizophrenic. Within the signifying regime, the irresistible flow of signification is countered by the "despotism" of paranoia, which attempts to master the sign and its possible meanings. Paranoia seeks to bring the oscillation of nondisjunctive oppositions to a stop through definitive interpretation of signs that culminates in a full body, a Final Signified. Allegory is arborescent, and midrash is rhizomatic.

Any closed or conclusive exchange of messages belongs to the condition of paranoia. All codes and encodings–all languages, as signifying systems–tend toward paranoia. Any signifying regime is paranoid and despotic, but it also opens up (as *its* inherent other) the possibility of a "postsignifying regime" (1987: 119) that will be subjective and schizophrenic. This echoes Jean-François Lyotard's description of the postmodern as "that which, *in the modern,* puts forward the unpresentable in presentation itself" (1984: 81, his emphasis; see D&G, 1983: 243). The postsignifying regime appears in the signifying regime's failure to signify. For D&G, the postsignifying regime is of most interest, for the postsignifying regime realizes the schizophrenic, rhizomatic flow of desire, and in the emergence of that regime, the totalitarian, paranoid regime is undermined. But not forever.

Another nondisjunctive opposition of interest to biblical scholars is that between the "nomadic war machine" and the "State apparatus." This opposition is more limited in application than those noted above but also more directly relevant to the histories often associated with biblical texts. Once again, that which is centered, sedentary, and "striated"–the State–is opposed to that which is dispersed, mobile, and "smooth"–the nomad (1987: 373–75). The "war machine" is the rhizomatic drive toward "a creative line of flight, a smooth space of displacement" (1987: 423), which only becomes military and totalitarian when it is appropriated and controlled by the State. In the capitalist world, this results in "total war" and culminates in fascism, which is war against the "unspecified enemy."

The body without organs is itself deterritorialized (rhizomatic, schizophrenic, nomadic), and the full body is reterritorialized (arborescent, paranoid, sedentary). These oppositions continually illuminate and augment, but also interfere with, one another. D&G display a preference for the deterritorialized (etc.) side of each pair, as these elements belong to the free flow of desire. Nevertheless, the free flow of desire inevitably leads to its opposite, the suppression of desire, and vice versa.

D&G and the Bible

D&G's writings offer suggestive possibilities for reading the Bible and related texts. D&G admit the possibility of a mixed semiotic, in which various combinations of signifying regimes appear. The "Jewish semiotic" of the Bible is such a mixed semiotic, combining nomadic and State signifying regimes, but also "bearing witness" to a postsignifying regime (1987: 122–23). The prophets give voice to a nomadic machine, and the State apparatus appears in kings and temple institutions (1987: 383). The covenant crisis results from the destruction of the signifying regime centered on the Temple in Jerusalem. The consequent transformations of faith result in profound consequences for understanding of "the book," whether Jewish Tanakh or Christian Bible. As Régis Debray says, in a sentence that could have come from D&G, "The book is what remains of Jerusalem while waiting for Jerusalem: the mobile center of the exile's or nomad's existence" (1996: 149). The one arborescent Temple is replaced by the many rhizomatic scriptures, and controlled signification gives way to unlimited semiosis.

The same pattern appears in the biblical texts themselves. In the story of the Tower of Babel, the desire of nomadic people who migrate to the plain of Shinar is for a State. "Come, let us build ourselves a city, and a tower with its top in the heavens, and let us make a name for ourselves" (Gen. 11:4). The arborescent city and tower (D&G, 1987: 481) that these people build leads inexorably to the rhizomatic dispersion of confused tongues and geographical scattering with which their story concludes. The attempt to encode a name, to reterritorialize, leads to the loss of meaningful language and extreme deterritorialization.

This structure may also be inverted. The story of Pentecost narrates the reterritorialization of the flow of desire. People gather "from every nation under heaven" (Acts 2:5, 9–11) to one centralized place when they hear tongues speaking a single message, "the mighty works of God" (Acts 2:11). The distributed tongues of fire and the schizophrenic speech in many tongues (Acts 2:3–4) are resolved in Peter's speech into the fulfillment and final meaning of the Jewish Scriptures. The decoded glossolalia is recoded into a universal, imperial, and therefore paranoid discourse. Unlike the Babel story, this arborescent consonance does not result in a renewed nomadism. According to the book of Acts, the Gospel does not spread like grass, but grows like a tree.

The postsignifying regime in the Jewish semiotic appears in paradoxical structures of prophecy and election in the Bible. According to D&G, the paradox of the Jewish semiotic unites betrayal and faith: Faith betrays, and betrayal keeps faith. In Hebrew figures such as Cain and Jonah, as in the Greek Oedipus, the postsignifying paradox appears as a deterritorializing "double turning away on a line of flight" (D&G, 1987: 123–24). The paranoid faciality of the signifying regime is transformed through the faith-as-betrayal of biblical characters into a "face-off," a turning away of the signifying face or de-signifying of the signifier, and ultimately a postsignifying "de-facializing" (1987: 190). This postsignifying paradox also appears in the figure of Jesus in the gospels. Jesus is simultaneously nomad-prophet and messiah-king. Jesus signifies a failure to signify of the Jewish semiotic itself, and thus he universalizes the paradox: "He betrays the Jews, he is betrayed by God" (1987: 124; see also 187). Christianity combines the mixed Jewish semiotic with the Roman imperial (State, paranoid) regime, resulting in a new mixture, yet another betrayal and yet another faith.

An extensive bibliography of works by Deleuze and/or Guattari appears in D&G 1987: 579–85.

derrida
Yvonne Sherwood

Jacques Derrida was born in Algeria in 1930, went to France in 1959, and currently divides his time between the *École des Hautes Etudes* in Paris and other institutions in Europe and North America; he is also, like Maurice Blanchot, not dead. Numerous things would interest him about that bland opening sentence, for the conventions of archiving a person for a dictionary ride roughshod over many of the questions he raises. Picking at that sentence (as he picks at other, more interesting sentences), Derrida would be interested in how names survive beyond the death of the person they identify and so "death is structurally implicit in every occurrence or signature of the proper name" (1992b: 19), or how the brutality of scholarship/translation reduces writers and their textual corpora to a few easily wieldable points (reading Yerushalmi reading Freud, he is acutely aware of how "by being dead and by being incapable of responding, Freud can only acquiesce"; 1996b: 41). In fact, you could say that being Derrida gives Derrida rather extreme insight into the absence or deferral of the writing subject, the way in which "one's mortality, infinitude, is inscribed in everything one inscribe[s]" (Bennington and Derrida, 1993: 51), for, as he mused in an interview in one of the many recent conferences "on" him, to be constantly named/quoted/abstracted as "Derrida" is "like being dead without being dead" (1996c: 217).

It's easy to see why someone whose name has been associated with, and held responsible for, Mormon polygamy, Nazism, and the theoretical equivalent of *laissez-faire* capitalism would have a personal as well as a structural interest in the way in which a name functions without the person that it names and marks his/her death. The word *Derrida* has been in circulation long enough for all kinds of clichés to attach themselves to it, many of which are based on misreadings of what could be called "vintage Derrida" (essentially *Of Grammatology* and *Writing and Difference,* collections of Derrida's earliest work from the late 1960s). The pervasive idea of Derrida as a promoter of the "freeplay of the signifier" seems to originate in a misreading of his inaugural essay, "Structure, Sign and Play in the Discourse of the Human Sciences," which is *not* about exiting a nostalgic ("Rousseauistic") origin- and truth-based interpretation for a "Nietzschean" "joyful affirmation of the play of a world of signs," but which *is* about the intrinsic linkages between these two interpretations of interpretation and the impossibility of choosing between them. But somehow the phrase "the joyful affirmation of the play of signs" has been attached to Derrida despite Derrida's own condemnations of the "facile, tedious and naively jubilatory" punning games that have been practiced in the name of deconstruction (Caputo, ed.: 77), despite constant assertions such as "we are not just playing here, turning this little sentence around in order to make it dazzle from every angle" (1992c: 83), and despite the harsh and weary corrections of "stupid and uninformed rumours" that come thick and fast in later works such as *Archive Fever, The Gift of Death, Spectres of Marx,* and *Acts of Literature*. Too easily this misunderstanding mingles with other well-known Derrida-isms—such as "undecideability" and "there is nothing outside the text"—to suggest an interpreter dazzled by the play of undecidables like a deer caught in headlights (Caputo, ed.: 137), caught in a fetishistic relation to words and exulting in the fact that the world is text and only text. Derrida himself is extremely vocal on the error of linguisticism (of seeing everything as language) and, as he engages with topics as far-reaching as Europe, colonialism, and the Internet, it becomes clear that he doesn't mean text/ writing in any conventional sense, and certainly not as some kind of reality-insulated textual playpen.

"Derrida" rightly gets his own space in this dictionary, but he is often subsumed under this thing called "deconstruction" that he is said to have invented (he has often reflected on the attractions of this new sturdy piece of critical machinery—this interpretative crowbar, this method that smacks of "technical rigour" and that gives the critic something to take to and do to texts; see 1992b: 21; 1991b: 273). But Derrida's projects are perhaps better understood in a looser, less disciplined way as "placing in the way of the systematic and the programmatic, reminders of the idiomatic" (1992b: 14), or resisting the institutional structures that harden over and protect our disciplines from restlessness (Caputo, ed.: 62). His work embraces a sense of occasionalism and the haphazard: Rather than working on his magnum opus, his *Phenomenology of Spirit* or his *Being and Time,* he works ad hoc, without an all-embracing heading, often in response to conference invitations. And if one were to try to construct a blunt list of headings for what Derrida has written "on" (if one were trying to put together the idiosyncratic self-set exam paper to which his work was a response), the eclectic topics would include "The Reconfiguration of European Identity after the Fall of the Berlin Wall"; "The Aporetic Obligation Involved in Playing Host to the Other while Respecting His/Her Foreignness"; "Email and the Transformation of the Private and Public Space of Humanity"; "Freud and the Characterisation of Psychology as a 'Jewish Science'"; "The Dangers of Nationalism, Community and Collectivity"; "A Justice Beyond Calculus"; "Nuclear War and the Rhetoric of Deterrance"; and "Marx is 'Dead' (discuss)." Famously, he works within the texts and idioms of others and sets himself diverse texts from anthropology, psychology, philosophy (Marcel Mauss's *The Gift,* Freud's "Note on the Mystic Writing Pad"); only in the area of literature does he show a preference for a certain kind of writing, a writing that resists ideas like "mimesis" and "intention," as he plots his distinctive course through Mallarmé, Ponge, Celan, Joyce, Genet, and Bataille. And in reading these specific texts, he looks for the singularity that threatens generality, for the anomalies that circulate within and open up the system, for the individual case that (in legal terms, and he has a lot to say about the law) is always a falling from, or a declension of, universality. Sometimes he seizes on that aporetic, tongue-tying undecidable "thing" that escapes the binary system (the *pharmakon* and the *Chora* in Plato, the *parergon* in Kant); but always he begins with a few axiomatic presuppositions, or distinctions, to set our thoughts in motion, and then shows how those very presuppositions/distinctions are jeopardized by their rigorous development. Frequently, like Nietzsche, he works by using statements that outrage sense, logic, or morality, such as "a poem is like a hedgehog rolled in a defensive ball on the highway" ("What is Poetry"), or "in the beginning was the telephone" (1992b: 270), or nuclear war is a "fabulous specularisation, a rhetorical figure, a fabulously textual non-event" (1984b: 23). He is, as he confesses, "an incorrigible hyperbolite…prone to exaggerate" (1996d: 48), but such statements about himself should be taken alongside other depictions of himself as, for example, a "conservative person who loves institutions" as a way of, as he puts it, "escaping my own stereotypes" (1992b: 34). (By escaping his own stereotypes, I think he means both the "postmodern" stereotypes of "Derrida" and the stereotypes he is in danger of generating: As he watches over the term *deconstruction* to stop it solidifying into a method, so, in a comic moment in *Monolingualism and the Other,* he expresses anxiety about the term *the Other,* which, he claims, is in danger of degenerating into meaninglessness as an "expression worn enough to give up the ghost"; 1996d: 41.)

As he writes of the "patriarchive" or his "nostalgeria," Derrida clearly surrenders himself to language more than the average philosopher, and he does so because he wants to contest the demotion of rhetoric/metaphor that has governed philosophy since Plato and to problematize the illusion of metaphor and, therefore, risk-free straight-talk. But anyone who goes to Derrida's writing thinking that they will find something literary/poetic *as opposed to* philosophical, any non-philosopher heartened by Richard Rorty's claim that Derrida only uses philosophy as a "comic butt," is likely to be taken aback by what Geoffrey Bennington calls the "rigour of the going through" (Bennington and Derrida, 1993: 62) and the way in which Derrida's work is saturated by its Western philosophical context. Like many twentieth-century thinkers, he takes on the Hegelian axiom that "The Whole is the True" (for him as for Adorno, "The Whole is the False") and he writes explicitly against the hyperjudicialism of Kant's parliament of knowledge in which the philosopher is the absolute source of all legitimation, as the law of law, the justice of justice. Famously, he follows Heidegger in thinking that there is only one metaphysics that shapes all Western thought: He asserts that all thought is governed by the fundamental assumption that something *is* if and only if it is present or presentable (thus objects are present beings, and consciousness is self-presence), though he is emphatic that what he calls Western Metaphysics or Logocentricism is not a single homogeneous system that always presents itself in the same form. If philosophy since Aristotle has rested, as Betrand Russell argues, on three fundamental axioms,

1. the law of identity: "Whatever is, is"
2. the law of contradiction: "Nothing can both be and not be"
3. the law of the excluded middle: "Everything must either be or not be"

then Derrida brings restlessness to philosophy by dwelling on/in the complexities, impurities, and differences that this logic of identity/presence excludes. But at the same time he refuses to characterize himself as a pall-bearer or "one more undertaker in the long history of the deaths of philosophy": It is relatively *easy* to create the illusion of escape, by evoking the fashionable apocalyptic rhetoric of crisis/ends, but the far more difficult task is to show how we must go on working within the reservoir of concepts bequeathed to us by the philosophical tradition because no alternative concepts are available or even conceivable.

How then can we think the relation between Derrida and the Bible, and how can we think his relation to postmodern biblical interpretation? The first point to be made is that Derrida is not that easily conscripted into this thing called postmodernism. On the one hand, he makes statements that can be taken as aphorisms of the postmodern—statements such as "history can never be saturated or closed" (1992c: 7), or the "gathering into itself of the One is not without violence" (1996b: 78–79)—and his essay "The Post Card," like Poe's "The Purloined Letter," has become something of an icon of the postmodern message that subverts classic ideas of communicability and the policing of destinations. But, on the other hand, when he states that "it is never a question of choosing between unity and multiplicity" (Caputo, ed.: 13), or when he speaks of the instruments of traditional criticism as an "indispensable guardrail" that stops "criticism from developing in any direction at all and authorise[s] itself to say almost anything" (1976: 158), Derrida problematizes some of the truisms trotted out in the name of postmodern criticism or presses us to think of them differently (at least if we aim to include *him* in our definitions). Frustratingly for those who would like to define postmodernism by a fundamental set of axioms, he sets up tensions in the postmodern camp, as he reads some of the other texts mentioned in this handbook (Levinas' *Totality and Infinity,* Foucault's *Madness and Civilisation*) with all the attentiveness and disruptiveness that he relates to more typically logocentric texts. For example, in "Cogito and the History of Madness" he takes Foucault to task over his alleged mis-reading of Descartes and questions whether it is really possible to write a vibrant history of madness from the place of madness, or whether it is not actually disingenuous to write as if one were able to loose oneself from a rationalist, *Aufklarisch* repressive.

Derrida's work is orientated by at least a minor obsession with the Bible and is peppered with biblical allusions in overt and covert forms. He is prone to mimic the Bible in its more mystical/aphoristic modes, speaking of "what I heard without hearing, what I understood without understanding" (1996b: 31; cf. Isa. 6:9) or proclaiming like Paul that "I do not want what I want" (Caputo, ed.: 25); he is one of a whole group of contemporary Jewish writers (including Levinas, Jabés, and Bloom) who suggest tangled links between Jewish and postmodern conceptions of Torah/text, and he is prone to take the vocabulary of biblical studies/theology–words like apocalypse, salvation, circumcision, messianicity, Elijah, shibboleth–and to give them back to the biblical scholar/theologian in provocatively distorted forms. More overtly, he proclaims his desire to "read and write in the space or heritage of the Bible," because "everything is in the Bible, everything and the rest" (1992b: 67). In response to a question from John Caputo, he describes the Bible as an "open field" from which he can receive "the most necessary provocations," just as he can from Plato (as he wants to get back to Plato as the horse's mouth, as it were, of philosophy, so perhaps he wants to go back to the Bible as the horse's mouth of Western culture). He has no "stable position" on biblical literature, and indeed sees it as potentially de-stabilizing:

> For me, there is no such thing as "religion." Within what one calls religions–Judaism, Christianity, Islam or other religions–there are again tensions, heterogeneity, disruptive volcanoes, sometimes texts, especially those of the prophets, which cannot be reduced to an institution, to a corpus, to a system. (Caputo, ed.: 21)

It is in this vein that he seizes on the two most iconically disruptive and aporetic biblical texts for his most overtly biblical meditations to date. "The Tower of Babel" reads Genesis 11 as the quintessential narrative of dispersal and confusion, the interruption of the structure by the God who proclaims himself "I am the one I am" and who pronounces confusion in the midst of the imperialist dream of the universal idiom, one people and one lip (Gen. 11:6). *The Gift of Death* reads Genesis 22, through Kierkegaard's *Fear and Trembling,* as opening out into a fundamental split/contradiction between ethics and religion and into the aporia of ethics as "irresponsibilization." In a meditation that takes in (among other texts) Genesis 22, Matthew 6:19-21, and Luke 14:26 (on hating Others for God's sake), Derrida explores the limits of the rational and the responsible that one reaches in granting or accepting death; the demands of the Other in conflict with that of the Great Other, or wholly other (the *tout autre*); and the "absolute dyssymmetry" of human relations with the Divine. He sees Abraham's sacrifice of his son as something monstrous, paradoxical, absolutely singular, *and* as something that happens every day, for though a father taking his son to be sacrificed on the top of a hill at Montmartre would surely be condemned by any civilized society, mechanisms of external debt and other similar inequities mean that this same civilized society puts to death (or allows to die) tens of millions of children *and engages the sacrifice of others to avoid being sacrificed oneself.* Describing deconstruction, provocatively, as "good conscience," he exhorts the biblical religions and civilized society to confront the aporias at their essence by picking at a subversive web of connections between saving and salvation and the economy of "saving oneself." Following Kierkegaard's Christianizing twist at the end of *Fear and Trembling,* but going where even Kierkegaard might hesitate to tread, he ends up musing over the secure celestial coffers in Matthew 6:17–23, and the gaze of the God who rewards what is done in secret, and asking whether it is ever really possible to give a gift/sacrifice that expects nothing in return, or whether there is in "evangelical spiritualism" some kind of "wager on the gaze of God," some kind of "sublime and secret calculation."

The question of how to use or apply "Derrida" in the field of biblical studies remains an open one, and one on which there is still much left to be said. Without being too crassly reductive, I think it is true to say that work to date has divided into two main camps. On one side are the theologians (Hart, Ward, Altizer, Taylor, Caputo) engaging with Derrida's distinctions between a hyper-essentialist negative theology and the anti-essentialism of the "difference" or the "trace," working at the possibility of a deconstructive theology or a "religion without religion," and exploring the apocalyptic and messianic tones of Derrida as a "man of faith." On the other side (and here the numbers are fewer, perhaps because we biblical scholars tend to be more intimidated by philosophy) are the text-orientated critics who have appropriated Derrida by pitting selected biblical texts against themselves and/or against the framing words of commentators (see, for example, Moore on John 4:1–42, Greenstein on Genesis 1–3, and Sherwood on Hosea 1–3). The problems with this distribution magnify the general problems of the theology/biblical studies divide: The theologians who work most closely and brilliantly with Derrida's texts rarely allude to biblical literature and tend to talk globally about "biblical religion" in a way that can seem too abstract and universalizing (and in something of a conflict with Derrida's own emphasis on the particular and on text-immanent critique). John Caputo, for example, powerfully elaborates Derrida's statement on eruptive prophetic texts in terms of ethical monotheism and the singularity of justice that characterizes "biblical religion." But this may smack of idealization to those who work "in" Old Testament/Hebrew Bible, and a biblical scholar familiar with, say, the volcanic, perception-twisting book of Amos might want to take Derrida's comment in a far more text-specific direction.

Much remains to be done with Derrida and the Bible: The rather literal logocentricism of the Johannine prologue seems to be crying out for attention, as are the numerous Hebrew texts that Derrida has said he would like to get closer to if only he "had" more of the language, and because Derrida's work is full of observations from which the biblical scholar can take provocation, there is great potential for going beyond the paradigm of the "deconstructive reading." For example, scattered observations on the way in which the devil exculpates God in dualistic theology (1996b: 13) or observations on the "violence of the hyphen" in the term "Judeo-Christian" may assist in thinking the difference between the "Old" and "New" Testaments and the sublimation or othering of the Jewish that characterizes certain biblical commentaries. As

Derrida meditates on, say, the "homo-hegemony of dominant languages," liberal racisms, and the "indefinitely phantasmatic process of [self]-identification," it becomes clear that this headingless-writer has much to contribute under headings other than "deconstruction" and that his work could equally be "dictionaried" under the headings of "postcolonialism," "autobiography," and "translation." And as he reflects on the aporia of how "certain individuals in certain situations testify to the features of a structure nevertheless universal" (1996d: 20), he offers ways of thinking through that perennial question of postcolonial and gender theory: "How can I be a single instance of 'woman,' or 'the postcolonial subject' and something representative; how can 'I' be at once exceptional and fundamental?"

ethics
Frank M. Yamada

The Postmodern Condition

What is postmodern ethics? At first glance, the two words, *postmodern* and *ethics*, may appear to complicate each other. Jean-François Lyotard, a well-known commentator on the postmodern condition, defines postmodernism as "incredulity toward metanarratives" (Lyotard, 1984: xxiv; 1992). Thus, postmodern thought according to Lyotard seeks to problematize and/or expose modernity's dependence on metadiscourses. In philosophy, the postmodern current is best expressed in the work of Jacques Derrida. Derridian deconstruction seeks to expose the ways in which language attempts to lay hold of transcendence. In a linguistic sense, a signifier is hopelessly traced through with an infinite number of other signifiers, problematizing its relationship to any transcendental signified. Indeed, for Derrida there is no immediate access to extra-textual reality. For him, everything is (in) text. Deconstruction, however, does not lead to an indeterminacy of meaning. On the contrary, Derrida suggests that texts always mean too much:

> I would say that a text is complicated, there are many meanings struggling with one another, there are tensions, there are over-determinations, there are equivocations; but this doesn't mean that there is indeterminacy. On the contrary, there is too much determinacy. That is the problem. (Derrida, 1999: 79)

Deconstruction raises a suspicious eye to any interpretation that would seek to establish itself over another. Thus, it calls into question oppositions that are cherished in the West such as speech over writing, man over woman, and God over humanity, since the privileging of one over another presumes a more immediate access to transcendence or real presence.

Using this brief and oversimplified reduction of deconstruction as a point of entry into postmodernism, and given that ethicists have traditionally viewed their enterprise in terms of universals and foundations (Bauman, 1993: 8–10), one can begin to see the issues at stake in pursuing a postmodern ethics. If Derrida is correct in suggesting that there is no privileged access to transcendence, that is, nothing outside the "text," how is one to think of doing what is right? Does deconstruction, as some of its opponents suggest, promote a kind of moral paralysis–an inherent undecidability–or does ethics

76

after Derrida simply mean that we must think about doing ethics in a different way?

Against Ethics or the Deconstruction of Ethics

John Caputo provides interesting answers to the above questions by proposing something audacious. He confesses, "I am against ethics. Here I stand. I cannot do otherwise" (Caputo, 1993: 1). What Caputo means by "ethics" is that practice of securing foundations upon which one can build a moral society. Ethical discourse attempts, through the application of principles or universals, to aid people in moral living. In this way ethics provides for us the certainty that we are not set adrift in a morally ambiguous universe. Caputo, however, is more compelled by the deconstruction of ethics. Traditionally, ethics has been a sure guide, holding our hands through life's difficult decisions and experiences. The deconstruction of ethics, however, shows that our guide is and has always been just as lost as we are. Such a realization is not the fault of deconstruction or Jacques Derrida, since ethics contains in itself the key to its own undoing. The deconstruction of ethics is "simply passing the word along that one is rather more on one's own than one likes to think, than ethics would have us think" (Caputo, 1993: 4). As the subtitle of *Against Ethics* suggests, Caputo is not simply against ethics or for the deconstruction of ethics. He is also interested in a poetics of obligation. By obligation, Caputo does not mean something metaphysical. Obligation is simply that feeling that compels one to act on behalf of another. It does not come from some higher principle or universal outside the "text," but is relegated to this worldly interaction. Ethics has tried to limit, that is, create a boundary around, obligation. Obligation, however, does not prove to be a willing captor. It is always exceeding what ethics has sought to delimit, to make safe. Obligation, however, is not safe or predictable. For Caputo, "obligation happens." Thus, the deconstruction of ethics "sets obligation loose from its containment or confinement or, better, lets that being-set-loose be seen, even as it exposes the vulnerability, the frailty and fragility of obligation" (Caputo, 1993: 5).

There are certainly some issues that one could raise with Caputo, especially his sometimes awkward privileging of obligation (see Dudiak, 1997). This brief exposition of Caputo's case *Against Ethics,* however, serves as a reminder that ethics as a system of morality or as a foundation for moral order is always open to its own deconstruction, to its own undoing. The deconstruction of ethics, while not necessarily good news (*euanggelion*), will continue to proclaim itself throughout the present discussion. Indeed, it is a specter that haunts all forms of ethical discourse, modern and postmodern.

Deconstruction and Ethics?

Now that we have broached the subject of deconstruction and ethics, we can venture the more intriguing issue of deconstruction's compatibility or incompatibility with ethics. Derrida has addressed the issue of ethics in a recent essay presented for a colloquium titled "Deconstruction and the

Possibility of Justice" (Derrida, 1992a). Derrida admits that deconstruction has been quiet about the problem of justice. He wants to suggest, however, that "what is now called Deconstruction, while seeming not to 'address' the problem of justice, has done nothing but address it, if only *obliquely,* unable to do so directly" (Derrida, 1992a: 10). What Derrida means by this somewhat evasive statement is that one cannot objectify justice–for example, the phrase "justice is x"–without betraying justice, limiting it within the bounds of a particular discourse. Derrida makes a distinction between justice and what he calls "the law" or "the right" (*le droit*). The history of law betrays an attempt to codify justice, to make justice manageable within the bounds of legal concepts. Thus, "the law" or "the right" for Derrida is open to deconstruction. On the other side, however, he states, "Justice in itself, if such a thing exists, outside or beyond law, is not deconstructable...Deconstruction is justice" (Derrida, 1992a: 14–15; Caputo gives extensive commentary on this particular phrase, "justice is not deconstructable," in chapter 4, "In the Name of Justice," of *Against Ethics,* especially 85–92). Derrida does not intend to oppose justice to the law. On the contrary, he suggests that the law proceeds "in the name of justice," though the latter cannot be contained in the law. By attempting to limit justice to a set of legal principles, the law betrays its own intention. Therefore, since justice transcends the law, it opens up the possibility of the law's deconstruction. At the same time, however, just action always requires the law, since it cannot proceed in an unmediated fashion. Even if justice is "outside," or as Caputo suggests, "beneath" the law, it nevertheless requires the process of law. Justice requires action–a decision. Derrida describes the process of making just decisions in terms of undecidability. By undecidability, he does not mean that one is morally paralyzed when confronted with an ethical decision. Such an understanding implies an inherent opposition between undecidability and decision. On the contrary, Derrida suggests,

> Far from opposing undecidability to decision, I would argue that there would be no decision, in the strong sense of the word, in ethics, in politics, no decision, and thus no responsibility, without the experience of some undecidability. If you don't experience some undecidability, then the decision would simply be the application of a programme, the consequence of a premiss or a matrix. So a decision has to go through some impossibility in order for it to be a decision...Ethics and politics, therefore, start with undecidability. (Derrida, 1999: 66)

Thus, Derrida does not understand deconstruction's undecidability as a promotion of moral paralysis. Undecidability is the very possibility of ethical decisions and actions.

Derrida's unpacking of undecidability/decision is helpful in terms of understanding the possible relation between deconstruction and ethics. His discussion, however, does not move the prospects of postmodern ethics forward. Derrida seems to direct his thoughts on justice more toward those who would assume that ethics and deconstruction are incompatible, that is, he questions the question, "What has justice to do with deconstruction?" By showing that justice is the very possibility of deconstruction, and that deconstruction's undecidability is at the very heart of ethical decision making, Derrida has paved the way for postmodern political and ethical action, though he does not take the leap himself. He has marked a space in which we might consider postmodern ethics.

From Derrida to Levinas

The discussion above has focused on deconstruction's inherent undecidability. As we have shown, undecidability in regard to ethics is not moral paralysis. Simon Critchley has gone a step further by proposing that undecidability in deconstruction is actually an ethical move within deconstructive analysis (13–43). Opponents of deconstruction have often characterized the work of Derrida as playing fast and loose with texts. Readers develop this understanding, as shown above, through a misconception of deconstruction's tendency toward undecidability. Critchley, counter to such claims, suggests that Derrida's reading habit, what he calls *clôtural* reading, provides an ethical moment that is crucial to the understanding of deconstruction and to ethics. *Clôtural* reading, according to Critchley, is a strategy that navigates between the double bind of being embedded within a particular discourse while never being limited to that discourse. He identifies two basic moves in a deconstructive reading. The first provides a close-reading or commentary of the text. The second, conditioned by the first, introduces alterity into the text, an "other" that the discourse has attempted to exclude through its own reduction. Thus, the text opens up to deconstruction. Critchley identifies this affirmation of the "other" to be ethically motivated. He says, "The ethical moment that motivates deconstruction is this Yes-saying to the unnameable, a moment of unconditional affirmation that is addressed to an alterity that can neither be excluded from nor included within logocentric conceptuality" (41).

Thus, deconstruction interrupts any discourse that claims immediate access to transcendence by reminding it of the "other" that it attempts to exclude. One can see the ethical implications of such a move. Deconstruction, in its affirmation of alterity, refuses the totalization of any discourse. It reminds us of the minute details that slip the attention of a system—details that may call into question the entire structure of the system's logic. However, Critchley is quick to point out that deconstructing texts and making ethical decisions are two very different tasks. Although he insists that deconstruction is motivated by an ethical drive, Critchley is skeptical of deconstruction's ability to make a difference in ethical decision making, since deconstructive reading requires the suspension of choice or an inherent undecidability. Although Derridian analysis opens up a space in which one can begin to rethink ethics, deconstruction does not move one into the act of deciding. Critchley understands this to be the impasse of deconstruction.

By highlighting Derrida's ethical affirmation of otherness or alterity, Critchley betrays his way through the impasse of deconstruction. Encountering the Other and unconditional ethical imperatives are both major themes in the work of Emmanuel Levinas. Levinas' contribution to the ethical debate is significant. Unlike Heidegger, who conceives of human self-understanding in terms of *Dasein* or Being, Levinas posits that the original and ultimate human experience involves a face-to-face relation with the Other (Levinas, 1985: 77; see also *Totality and Infinity,* in which Levinas articulates his proposal of ethics as the first philosophy). One should not understand this Other in terms of ontology. Levinas understands ontological philosophy as preoccupation with Being. Thus, such a philosophy seeks to subsume all of human experience within categories of existence. Knowledge, therefore, is reflexive. Levinas' primary critique of Heidegger is that he subsumes human relationality to Being. Levinas, however, wants to suggest that it is the encounter with the face of the Other that is primary. Ethics is the first philosophy. Face-to-face with the Other, one is confronted with the fact that something exists outside of oneself. Encountering the Other opens one up to an infinite alterity in that the Other cannot be subsumed into one's own self-understanding. Levinas, therefore, conceives of ethics within a fundamental relationality with the Other. He finds ethics in this original alterity that does not allow the self to exclude otherness or to subsume all otherness into a relation of its own Being.

Levinas confronts a problem, however, when he seeks to elucidate this relationship to the Other. Although he is arguing for the primacy of ethics over ontology, he also is aware that he cannot simply do away with the language of Being. Levinas seeks to question the privileging of ontology while caught within the unavoidable web of ontological language—"the Other is *x.*" He deals with this issue in a later work, *Otherwise than Being.* (Commentators regard this as a response to Derrida's essay "Violence and Metaphysics," which is a deconstructive analysis of Levinasian ethics, on which Critchley provides an excellent commentary, 107–87; for summaries of *Otherwise than Being,* see Critchley: 4–9; and C. Davis: 69–92.) Levinas proposes that philosophy has been preoccupied with what he calls the "Said." This performance of language privileges rationality and the ability to make propositional statements about truth and Being. By focusing primarily on the Said, ontological philosophy has neglected the "Saying." The Saying for Levinas is that moment or event in which one is confronted face-to-face with the presence of the Other. This fundamental experience provides the very condition for the Said, though Saying cannot be comprehended fully within the language of ontology. Critchley articulates Levinas' Saying as "the non-thematizable ethical residue...of language that escapes comprehension, interrupts philosophy, and is the very enactment of the ethical movement from the Same to the Other" (7). Thus, the Saying eludes the particulars of the Said's representation. However, Levinas is not merely pointing to language's inherent imprecision. The Said constantly betrays the Saying since ontological language presupposes the primacy of Being, neglecting the fundamental encounter with the Other.

Levinas' ethics makes the move into the political realm in his discussion of *le tiers* (the third party). Encountering the Other is the primary experience that makes possible the working out of ethical acting and thinking. The realization of a third party, however, disrupts my bi-symmetrical relation to the Other and thus forms the basis for society. *Le tiers* requires me to think about issues that are larger than my own relation to the Other. It creates the necessity for talking about justice for other human beings and the world. It is important to note that Levinas does not envision a universal ethics for all humanity. Obligation to the Other can never be totalized into a system of morals. Levinas seeks, however, for his ethics to be fully rooted in social and political activity. As Davis points out, Levinas dedicates *Otherwise than Being* to the victims of the Holocaust (84). Levinas does not make overt comments about the Holocaust in his book; one can, however, see in his concern for the Other or neighbor a response to the horrible events surrounding World War II. His constant resistance to any universal political program also seem to be motivated by this concern.

The presence of *le tiers* means that ethics must always touch the socio-political ground. Discussion about ethics must move beyond the realm of speculation to the realm of political and social action. As stated above, Critchley takes this move from the ethical to the political as the key to getting beyond the impasse of deconstruction's inherent undecidability. The presence of the third party requires us to think about justice and the application of that justice to promote a moral society. Critchley, following Levinas, argues that it is the task of philosophy to "thematize" such issues, that is, to navigate the space between the Saying and the Said. Philosophical discourse seeks to disrupt any political order that would want to universalize its own position, but philosophy should also attempt to give expression to the Other, to that which the political order attempts to exclude. It is interesting to note that Critchley ends *The Ethics of Deconstruction* with an apology for democracy. He insists that democracy embraces otherness rather than seeking to control it (236–41). Critchley does not want to think of democracy as a static form. In fact, he suggests that "democracy does not exist." We should see democracy as a "task, or a project, to be attempted" (240). Critchley's argument is very dubious at this point; he wants to relate his politics of otherness to a democratic ideal that is not yet realized. Although he wants to avoid comparison with liberal democracy, the comparison is, nevertheless, inevitable. Following his argument against Lacoue-Labarthe and Nancy, who envision the end of politics in favor of analysis of the "political," it is hard not to understand Critchley's conclusion as an apology for a Western politics. Critchley's conclusion is odd in light of his previous argument; one would expect a more critical engagement with a political ideal such as "democracy" or "the democratic." Does not an ethics of otherness imply that one should be more ambitious to expose the ways in which democratic ideals betray the very Other that they are trying to protect? At the same time, Critchley rightly stresses that one should seek to "thematize" the Saying into the Said. Such a project, however, should avoid terms that imply particular political systems (e.g., democracy) in favor of a discourse that would seek to keep systems off balance.

Levinas and Postmodern Ethics

In a recent work, Zygmunt Bauman offers another Levinasian approach to postmodern ethics (1993). He begins by addressing the apparent moral dilemma of postmodernity. He suggests that postmodernism, contrary to popular opinion, does not lead to the erosion of ethics but creates new possibilities in which to think about the ethical task. Bauman contends that modern rationality silenced the human moral spirit by reducing ethics to a series of propositions and universals. Thus, modern ethics repressed the very human element that it was trying to release. Postmodern thought has successfully challenged the presuppositions of modernity, creating a new environment for ethical thinking. It is Bauman's hope that ethical philosophy and political practice will benefit from this new perspective. He is aware, however, that we cannot simply do away with our indebtedness to modernity. Modernist ethics has shaped the ways in which we talk about moral issues such as human rights, justice, and world peace. It is not Bauman's intention to abandon such issues. He suggests, however, that the postmodern condition provides the opportunity for us to think about them in new and novel ways (1993: 3–4).

Bauman starts his study by laying out seven characteristics of postmodern ethics, what he labels as "the marks of moral condition, as they appear once contemplated from the postmodern perspective" (1993: 10). Briefly, they are: (1) Humans are not essentially good or bad, but *morally ambiguous;* (2) morality, contrary to the claims of modernism, is *non-rational;* (3) morality is *aporetic,* that is, there are no unambiguously good choices; (4) morality is not *universalizable;* (5) morality is not only non-rational, but *irrational,* and thus incapable of being systematized; (6) moral responsibility is foundation-less in that ethics begins with a face-to-face encounter with the Other (Levinas), not some ontological starting point of Being; and (7) postmodern ethics does not lead to moral relativism or paralysis but opens up new horizons of possibility for the moral self. Throughout *Postmodern Ethics,* Bauman fleshes out these seven marks within the contexts of modern philosophy, sociology, and political theory. His basic argument is clear: The modernist project, with its emphasis on rationality and universals, has led to the thwarting of the moral conscience. Postmodern thought, according to Bauman, has effectively exposed the modernist project's failings, helping us to see the issues at stake with our eyes wide open. Bauman characterizes postmodernity as *"modernity without illusions"* (1993: 32).

If postmodern thinking is disenchanted with modernity, it is "re-enchanted" with the world in all its complexities, according to Bauman. Human life is fraught with the unpredictable. Modernity's flaw was to see such ambiguity as a problem to be fixed. Postmodernism, with its critique of modern rationality, embraces difficulty rather than shunning it. In terms of ethics, postmodernism would seek to establish the more primary relationship to the Other as the basis of morality rather than the ethical codes and systems produced by modernity. Thus, Bauman's argument re-articulates Levinas' ethics of the Face as a critique of ontological philosophy, the brainchild of modernity. The encounter with the Other cannot be contained within a rational system, and thus ethics is inherently unpredictable. A new kind of wisdom is required to live in a world without universals, what Bauman calls "postmodern wisdom":

> What the postmodern mind is aware of is that there are problems in human and social life with no good solutions, twisted trajectories that cannot be straightened up, ambivalences that are more than linguistic blunders yelling to be corrected, doubts which cannot be legislated out of existence, moral agonies which no reason-dictated recipes can soothe, let alone cure…The postmodern mind is reconciled to the idea that the messiness of the human predicament is here to stay. (1993: 245)

Thus, the postmodern condition produces an ethics that is no longer in denial. Without the systematic constraints of modernity, the moral self is free to pursue what it has always been–an ethical/relational being for the Other.

Bauman has raised some intriguing issues in his work. Some of his most promising and controversial material revolves around how we can or should navigate ourselves ethically in a postmodern world. At points, however, Bauman's suggestions amount to little more than trusting one's own conscience (1993: 245–50). In light of his discussion, however, one would think that more is required. Postmodern realism makes us aware of the fact that we are not alone in the world, that is, we are constantly confronted with others that are affected by our decisions. Part of the obligation of postmodern ethics, therefore, should consist of a raising of the moral conscience. For example, how do local concerns impact the larger human community or the global environment? Such a proposal does not mean that we need to install a system of morality that would provide simple answers to complex problems. Instead, we should seek to reorient the energies of the moral self–the self that is obligated to the Other–toward the problems of the increasingly industrialized world.

Conclusion: Prospects and Trajectories

We began by looking at the postmodern condition and how that condition has impacted ethics. The present discussion is far from comprehensive, though it has attempted to highlight significant trends in the postmodern ethical debate. A few themes begin to emerge. First, postmodern ethics seeks to maintain some form of *alterity* or otherness. Levinas' fundamental relationship with the Other is a significant contribution in this regard. The essence of being human is to be in ethical relationship. We are not solitary beings governed only by our own decisions. We are obligated to something that is beyond us, to another who beckons us. Alterity in ethical discourse also suggests that no system of morality can totally comprehend the encounter with the Other. In fact, postmodern rationality will always seek to question the ways in which ethics betrays itself by trying to limit the Saying to the Said. Second, postmodern ethics is aware of life's complexity. The work of Derrida shows that any attempt to transcend life's web of complex intricacies only leads to inherent contradiction and deconstruction. If Bauman is correct, such a realization is not cause for dismay, but may indeed help us to live more realistically in a life that is characterized by messiness. Last, the postmodern condition need not lead to moral paralysis or indecision. As Derrida has suggested, indecision is the very possibility of ethical decision making. If ethical decisions were not full of ambivalence, contradiction, and irrationality, then human morality would merely be a code that needs application. Postmodern ethics does not provide sure, foolproof answers to the moral issues of modern society. In fact, modernity's attempts to provide such answers may have been its tragic flaw. Postmodern ethicists suggest that life without universals or foundations is not cause for panic but for hope. In the end, ethical decisions are made. The Other beckons us to more authentic ethical relationship. Obligation happens.

fantasy

Tina Pippin

In the last decade, fantasy criticism has taken hold on the margins of postmodern biblical studies. Its present situation bears certain similarities to that of the *Religionsgeschichtlicheshule* in the late 1880s and early 1900s; this school introduced biblical studies to the term *myth*, which Rudolf Bultmann advanced in the twentieth century. At first, *myth* was a shocking term for most biblical scholars, denoting something found in the sacred texts of other religions, but not in the Bible. Gradually *myth* became an accepted term that articulated how ancient, pre-scientific peoples understood their natural world in relation to the supernatural. In examining biblical stories as myths, scholars look at the myths of other ancient cultures of Africa and the Near East. Myth represented their realities and explained the creation and order of their flat earth in a larger universe but also described the action of the divine (for better and for worse) in those worlds.

Then a literary approach to biblical interpretation developed, coincident with the rise of formalism and New Criticism in mid-twentieth-century literary criticism. This perspective argued that the aesthetic value of a literary text warranted close readings of its form and content on its own merit. Thus, biblical texts could be studied as literary "fiction." Fiction, as well as myth, contained truths for the reader, but often these terms raised (and continue to raise) issues of truth and falsity for believers. In academic circles the terms *myth* and *fiction* became acceptable, and literary critics (of both the historical-critical/form-critical and narratological sorts) use these terms as standard.

Like *myth* and *fiction*, *fantasy* raises questions of truth and falsehood. The term *fantasy* has roots in both literature and psychoanalysis. In literature, the works to which it refers (fairy tales and the fantastic, along with the corollaries of science fiction, cyberpunk, and horror) are considered marginal to the "greater works" of fiction. Nor is *fantasy* a respected term in comparative literature circles, and the subgroup of the Modern Language Society, The International Association of the Fantastic in the Arts, which meets yearly at an airport hotel in Ft. Lauderdale, works hard to get their academic disciplines acknowledged as such. And though postmodern biblical criticism is certainly open regarding questions of truth, the term *fantasy* does not hold a vital position in biblical criticism. Biblical scholars have long defended, for example, the book of Job as such against its detractors; to speak of the Bible as fantasy might make it "second rate" literature. Further, it might open it up to charges of lunacy or, at best, childishness.

In the unsaid hierarchy of literary works, fantasy is often considered "lowbrow." Should not all sacred texts be "highbrow" literature? Fantasy also has a connection with the Freudian dreamworld, with meanings that range from harmless childhood story-worlds with happy endings to the deranged hallucinations of a homicidal maniac. Is fantasy, in its literary or psychological forms, creative escape to gain a deeper understanding of reality? Or is fantasy the imaginative vision of the drugged or insane, to be regarded as sometimes of danger to self and others?

The main definitions for fantasy criticism come from Tzvetan Todorov. Todorov applies structuralist analysis to the genre of the fantastic, comparing the genre with the realms of the real and the imaginary. Todorov reflects, "The ambiguity is sustained to the very end of the adventure: reality or dream? truth or illusion?" (1975: 25). Todorov's fantasy criticism is reader-oriented; the reader experiences fear, hope, belief, disbelief, but most of all, hesitation: "'*I nearly reached the point of believing*': that is the formula which sums up the spirit of the fantastic…it is hesitation which sustains its life" (1975: 31). Stories of sea monsters, talking animals (snakes or donkeys), beasts full of horns and eyes, a tower that reaches almost to heaven, a river turning to blood, parting seas, floating ax heads, consultation with mediums and seers, the resurrected dead, a woman impregnated from/with the deity, a tour of a throne room in heaven—all these stories are unbelievable in that they are not part of everyday experience and reality. As the reader enters the world of these stories, she must relate to the "ambiguous vision" of the text by hesitating "between a natural and supernatural explanation of the events described" (1975: 33). It is not so much that one must suspend belief, but one is suspended between belief and disbelief.

In fantasy literature, fantastic events do occur, but such events remain exceptional and not the rule. In the fantastic, the reader follows Cinderella, Alice, Frodo, Moses, or John of Patmos through their adventures, passing through the looking glass and standing in the world the narrator invents. When a reader takes the events of biblical literature "literally," as true historical happenings, she is taking the story out of the world of fantasy into the realm of faith. But the reader who approaches the Bible as fantasy takes the stories "literally" as well; in the immediate experience of reading, a metaphorical, figurative, or scientifically rationalized reading is subsumed under a literal one. For example, Moses parts the sea and the Israelites cross to the other side on dry land. A fantasy critic who reads this story in Exodus will not place questions of the authenticity of the event in history—or of the "reed sea" where Egyptian chariots become bogged down in the swampy mud—on the agenda. Likewise, a reader who emphasizes the Whore of Babylon as a figurative model for the Roman Empire and its imperialism in the colonies misses the true wonder and horror of her presence on the seven-headed beast. Questions of authenticity and figurative equivalence are for scientific investigation, not for experiencing the narrative as fantastic. For Todorov,

The supernatural is born of language, it is both its consequence and its proof: not only do the devil and vampires exist only in words, but language alone enables us to conceive what is always absent: the supernatural. The supernatural thereby becomes a symbol of language, just as the figures of rhetoric do, and the figure is as we have seen, the purest form of literality. (1975: 82)

Fantasy criticism encourages the reader to experience the supernatural events of the text, in some ways by taking the text at "face value," that is, by standing face-to-face with the magical. As D. J. Enright considers, "The supernatural and the natural meet and ignite, illuminating our deepest anxieties and hopes" (1). The scary monsters and flying deities in the clouds all gather around, spinning their fantastic tales.

Todorov further separates the types of fantastic tales into categories. He proposes options that range from the "uncanny" to the "marvelous," with the "fantastic-uncanny" and the "fantastic-marvelous" in between, and often overlapping (1975: 44). The uncanny and fantastic-uncanny (big hints of Freud here) are born mainly out of fear and are the stuff of horror literature (e.g., Edgar Allan Poe). The uncanny is "the supernatural explained"; in other words, the object of horror is not far out of the realm of the rational, and what appears to be supernatural can be accounted for. Stephen King's horror literature works so well because it taps the imagination of supernatural (and for King, sometimes not-so-supernatural) evil and chaos invading the ordered world. Yes, houses can be haunted by ghosts who drive out or kill the inhabitants. And when people die tragically, we may encounter their souls in some not-so-helpful ways. Invisible worlds can intrude into the visible worlds. In the Bible, apocalyptic floods and fires barge into the everyday. Hierarchies of angels and demons are just beyond the visible. Fantasy criticism helps the reader to map the collision of these worlds, tracing the path of fear.

The marvelous and the fantastic-marvelous are at the other end of the spectrum and represent an acceptance of the supernatural (1975: 52). In the fantastic-marvelous the story focuses on supernatural events. According to Todorov, "In the case of the marvelous, supernatural elements provoke no particular reaction either in the characters or in the implicit reader. It is not an attitude toward the events described which characterizes the marvelous, but the nature of these events" (1975: 54). Rosemary Jackson prefers to call the fantastic "a literary *mode* rather than a genre, and to place it between the opposite modes of the marvellous and the mimetic" (32). In other words, fantasy criticism does not dismiss the supernatural, but neither does it accept the supernatural unreservedly. The reader's hesitation is key, and in reading the Bible this hesitation can lead in many paths—toward faith or skepticism, acceptance or cynicism. Fantasy presents so many possibilities for reading; there is room for play and adventure.

Of course, there are "interpretive communities" (to borrow Stanley Fish's term) that want to anchor the supernatural of the Bible in their present spiritual experience. I recently attended a fundamentalist Christian "gold dusting" revival and healing service. In these services the main evangelist and/or certain congregants receive "gold dust" either before or during the service. The dust may come from various sources, all heavenly (according to the narrative of the participants). What is important for the believers is the experience of the fantastic, of an extra-ordinary, supernatural event in the midst of their ordinary (and often painful) lives. In these services, as in apparitions of Mary, the supernatural is bolted (in)to the present. This kind of reading takes the literary framework away from the fantastic; it is like Trekkies who enact the various *Star Trek* roles, dressing in Starfleet uniforms and speaking Klingon. A more biblical example would be Christians who make a pilgrimage to Jerusalem and are seized by a sense of their own messianic identity (the messiah syndrome). These people cross over, take the reading too far by mixing the imaginary with reality. Todorov's theory of the fantastic focuses on the world of the text and the reader entering that world; he posits a clear division that does not always exist in the religious experience of sacred texts (and of course, some count Gene Roddenberry's future vision as sacred, while others connect the dead (?) Elvis with the heavenly court, serving out eternity as a divine intercessor). Todorov gives biblical studies a theoretical sense of the different genres within the genre of the fantastic and an appreciation of the power of these literary forms and their multicultural connections.

But does everyone not dream of flying like Superman or wearing magic, powerful rings or learning to fly high-tech helicopters by plugging for a few seconds into virtual reality? Are not "gold dust" and Trekkie insignias symbols of something that rational folks secretly desire—some proof of the supernatural, of a foretaste of the future in the present, and some experience of the unexplainably miraculous in their ordinary lives? Are readers, especially readers of the Bible, to be satisfied solely with "story"? Fantasy is the mirror, the looking glass, and there is an alternative world on the other side. A character in Kurt Vonnegut's *Breakfast of Champions* calls mirrors *"leaks.* It amused him to pretend that mirrors were holes between two universes...'Don't get too near that leak. You wouldn't want to wind up in the other universe, would you?'" (quoted in Rabkin: 222). Well, some believers want to pass through to the other side, and they create apocalyptic fantasies to live out their desires. Fantasy is certainly the stuff of desire. And even though my religious culture is in a mainstream Protestant denomination, I am drawn to the "wild" stories of the Bible. The difference between the literary fantastic and the acting-out of these fantasies in the gold dusting ceremony is that the participants in the latter experience no hesitation. The dusting *is* supernatural for them; that is the only explanation for the glitter. The biblical text, as mirror, leaks and is a leak of the supernatural. I remain stuck in between, allowing for the gold-dusters' ecstatic spiritual experiences and the event as in itself a fantastic story, while retaining my own staunch skepticism. In other words, the event plays as another fantastic text for me. Meanwhile, I am stuck with a very leaky Bible.

Freud would not let me off the hook so easily. He would say that I have both conscious and unconscious desires to examine. He would certainly question me about my interest in this field. Fantasy criticism also helps me to examine those desires within the spectrum of an ethic of reading. Following Freud, and Lacan, Slavoj Žižek seeks an ethic of fantasy. Žižek points to the particular nature of "fantasy as a 'make-believe' masking a flaw, and inconsistency in the symbolic order" (1991: 156). He notes that "we can acquire a sense of the dignity of another's fantasy only by assuming a kind of distance toward our own, by experiencing the ultimate contingency of fantasy as such, by apprehending it as the way everyone, in a manner proper to each, conceals the impasse of his desire. The dignity of fantasy consists of its very 'illusionary,' fragile, helpless character" (1991: 157). Fantasy is thus a screen for desire; "*through fantasy, we learn 'how to desire'*" (1982: 118; see 1997: 32). What is repressed comes to the surface. Žižek thus speaks of "the paradoxical intermediate role of fantasy: it is a construction enabling us to seek maternal substitutes, but at the same time a screen shielding us from getting too close to the maternal Thing–keeping us at a distance from it" (1989: 119–20). The Bible as fantasy is a place to play out desire for the Divine, screening believers from getting too close to the Mother (or Father) Thing. Eve, the builders of the Tower of Babel, Mary and the other women at the empty tomb, John gazing on the Bride of Christ, all teach their readers desire but also provide a screen, an appropriate distance. The Bible as fantasy allows the reader to gaze on the supernatural from a safe distance, while still being able (if one chooses) to desire heaven, or at least more direct, physical, divine intervention in one's life. "Heaven" is not the end of desire, but its explosion into eternity.

Although this psychoanalytic route provides a base for understanding how fantastic literature operates, a more traditional fantasy criticism takes its lead from the writers of fairy tales and the psychology of identification and desire in this literature. J. R. R. Tolkein, for example, spelled out what the journey into the fantastic is about: Fairy tales have the functions of recovery, escape, and consolation. The reader follows the heroic characters through their adventures and confrontations with good and evil all the way to the happy ending. The lives of readers come into conversation with the lives of the characters, standing before the scary monsters, triumphing over evil. Everyday life is not so mundane after all; the monsters take all sorts of shapes. In his analysis of the political ideologies of fairy tales, Jack Zipes observes, "To have a fairy tale published is like a symbolic public announcement, an intercession on behalf of oneself, of children, of civilization. It is a historic statement" (11). A fairy tale has political value and "to be liberating, it must reflect *a process of struggle* against all types of suppression and authoritarianism and posit various possibilities for the concrete realization of utopia. Otherwise, the words liberating and emancipatory have no aesthetical categorical substance" (178). Jackson relates the idea in this way: "The fantastic traces the unsaid and the unseen culture: that which has been silenced, made invisible, covered over and made 'absent'" (4). Fantastic literature reveals the hidden ideologies of a culture and is always connected with the political. But is the Bible as fantasy a liberating text? It depends on which text (for they are many and particular) and also on the communities of readers. Texts that some readers consider homophobic, racist, or misogynist are liberating for other readers; these texts serve their hegemonic purposes. But even the text itself can oppress; one monarchical dictatorship is substituted for another, ending with the ultimate coup, the armies of God defeating (for a time) the Satan and his followers and establishing an eternal kingdom on earth. Still, Jackson maintains that fantasy is not escape literature, but rather "that fantasies image the possibility of radical cultural transformation through attempting to dissolve or shatter the boundary lines between the imaginary and the symbolic" (178). Religious fantasies aim toward unity (Jackson: 179), an absolute Truth that postmodernism typically rejects. Fantasy criticism can reveal the unseen of culture, and maybe even of the culture of contemporary biblical scholarship.

Fantasy critics and writers are often drawn to the Bible. There are many parallels between the gospels' stories of Jesus and literary works of fantasy, science fiction, and horror, as well as works in other media of the fantastic (film, music, art, the Internet) in popular culture. But few biblical scholars are participating in the conversations with the theory and the theorists, even though interest in cultural studies approaches is growing. George Aichele and I have edited four volumes in which we attempt to bring biblical scholars and fantasy critics into dialogue; volume 60 of the journal *Semeia* (1992) was the first published record of an ongoing investigation. Jack Zipes pronounced in his article for this volume that "the Bible is the seminal work of all fantasy literature" (7). The supernatural is writ large on every page of the Bible. The Bible as fantasy can reinscribe prejudices, heaping the representation of evil on certain people(s) or genders. It has been used as a text reinscribing imperial domination and oppression. But as fantasy literature, the Bible is also subversive and transgressive of the dominant order (Jackson; Aichele and Pippin, 1997b: 14). In some ways the exegetical and hermeneutical process is a journey into fantasy—not in the sense of the psychological state of the interpreter or the biblical authors, however interesting that might be, but as invention of the Real (Lacan's term) into the realm of scholarship. Fantasy criticism asks biblical scholars to stand in a postmodern space that is both in and between the blurry dualities of natural/supernatural and belief/doubt—in a space where the unexpected happens. All sorts of characters meet in this space, even supernatural ones. Fantasy criticism provides another way to encounter these other worlds.

foucault
Mark K. George

The work of French philosopher Michel Foucault (1926–1984) has had a significant impact on twentieth-century thought, and he is generally considered one of the prominent and influential figures in "postmodernism." Foucault's work dealt with topics ranging from philosophy, sociology, medicine, psychology, and psychiatry, to prisons and prison reforms, architecture, geography, and sexuality. His work in these fields challenged established notions and understandings within them, provoking both praise and condemnation from other scholars in those fields. Foucault gained recognition for the originality of his work and rose to prominence in France and then other parts of the world before his untimely death in 1984.

Paul-Michel Foucault was born in Poitiers, France on October 15, 1926. His family was one of some social and economic means, as his father, Paul Foucault, was a surgeon, and his mother, Anne Malapert, was the daughter of a surgeon. Paul-Michel, therefore, grew up with the advantages of a wealthy family. Foucault began his education in Poitiers before moving to Paris in 1945 so he could complete his studies at the prestigious Ecole Normale Supérieure, the training ground for many prominent French intellectuals. When Foucault completed his education, he spent several years teaching and working as a French cultural attaché outside of France (including Sweden, Poland, Germany, and Tunisia), then finally returned to France as a professor of philosophy at the University of Vincennes in 1968. In 1970 Foucault moved to Paris, where he took up a position as professor at the Collège de France, France's premier academic institution. Foucault taught at the Collège de France until his death in Paris on June 25, 1984 (for a fuller discussion of Foucault's life and death, see Eribon, Macey, or Miller).

Foucault's Work

The scope of Foucault's work is testimony to the fact that Foucault did not think of himself simply as a philosopher, at least not in the sense that philosophers study general, universal, or formal structures of human thought or existence. Foucault's chair at the Collège de France was, at his request, in the "History of Systems of Thought," for, as Foucault stated in an interview in 1982, "My field is the history of thought" (Foucault, 1988: 10). Indeed, one might say that Foucault viewed himself as somewhat of an anti-philosopher insofar as he understood his work to be "against the idea of universal necessities in human existence" (1988: 11). Foucault described his work in terms of the history of thought because the question that interested him was revealing the ways by which Western European societies were organized. Foucault sought, among other things, to make people aware of the arbitrariness of institutions, to demonstrate how the institutions and ways of looking at the world that are taken for granted today are the result of certain precise historical changes, and thus to "show which space of freedom we can still enjoy and how many changes can still be made" (1988: 11). Foucault's work, therefore, was always related to political action and social change, not to the simple destruction of society and culture (compare 1988: 14).

Despite his refusal to believe in the idea of universal necessities in human thought, Foucault described his work as concerned with "three traditional problems": (1) knowledge and how that knowledge relates individuals to truth; (2) power (the relationships individuals have with others on the basis of that knowledge); and (3) self, the way in which individuals come to understand and speak about themselves in relation to knowledge and power (1988: 15; I have somewhat modified the way Foucault stated these problems). All three of these ideas–knowledge, power, and self–are present to varying degrees in Foucault's work throughout his career. By focusing his work on these three problems and their development in history (Foucault often begins his books in the seventeenth century and works forward in history; see *Madness and Civilization, Discipline and Punish, The Archaeology of Knowledge*), Foucault was able to write a history of the present, by which he meant that he was able to show how certain ideas or models of humanity developed and came to be accepted as normative, even universal, despite their arising out of particular circumstances and situations (1988: 15). In Foucault's view, only by seeing the arbitrary and constructed nature of the present would it be possible for people to understand how the present, and people's relationships to politics, society, and themselves, might be changed. It is these three problems–power, knowledge, and self–that I will introduce in the remainder of this essay.

Power

Foucault's views on power draw heavily on the work of Friedrich Nietzsche (particularly Nietzsche's *The Will to Power*) and perhaps are more easily described by what Foucault does *not* mean by this idea than by what he *does* mean. When Foucault discusses power, he does not mean by this idea a fixed, quantitative, or physical force, something innately possessed or held by individuals or institutions. He acknowledges that power often is channeled through people or institutions, but this is not due to the inherent "power" of such people or institutions. Rather, Foucault understands power as a force, something present throughout the world and in all people. Power is, therefore, something distinct from authority. Everyone has power, whether they exercise that power individually, in groups, or through institutions (and those institutions can range from small groups of people to governments). The interactions between people, between people and institutions, and among institutions constitute what Foucault calls "force relations."

Power, whether individuals' or institutions', always seeks to become more powerful and influential in society, and thus there is constant interaction, negotiation, and competition among forces. Frequently, forces combine in particular, complex arrangements or configurations in order to achieve more power. These complex power arrangements (or arrangements of forces) can take any number of forms, including social, intellectual, political, religious, economic, medical, juridical, or some other combination. For example, in Foucault's study of juridical practices and penal reforms in *Discipline and Punish,* he shows how public torture in the eighteenth century reflected one arrangement of power, while daily timetables for prisoners in the nineteenth century reflect a different arrangement of power. In the eighteenth century, ideas about the monarchy and theories of law and crime combined in such a way so that public torture of capital criminals was required to restore the idea of the law and the monarch. In the nineteenth century, with the demise of the monarchy and changes in how society was governed and controlled, theories of law and crime combined with new moral and political ideas about the right to punish, the result of which was that torture was considered unnecessary, even abhorrent, and punishment required regimenting criminals' lives through daily schedules and timetables. Theories of governmentality changed; new circumstances brought about changes in how legal power was conceptualized, its aims, and thus how it was enforced.

As a result of the creation of particular, complex arrangements of force relations, power comes to be exercised through certain social institutions and practices, such as banks, the police, medical offices, educational institutions, and professional guilds. What Foucault makes clear is that the power these institutions exercise is not due to some innate quality that they possess, but rather is the result of specific circumstances and historical conditions. Thus, because specific circumstances and conditions made these institutions possible, a change in those circumstances threatens, if not outright negates, the ability of these institutions to continue to exercise their power and to exist in the same way. For example, the rise of historical criticism in the field of biblical studies in seventeenth-century Europe created both certain institutions that could wield power in the interpretation of the biblical text (e.g., universities increased their power and status in society as a result of becoming centers where historical criticism was practiced, a power and status that once was the exclusive claim of churches and synagogues) and experts (those trained in philology, historical critical methodologies, history, and so on) in creating those interpretations. As women and minorities gained greater access to biblical studies in the 1960s and 1970s, new methodologies (such as feminist interpretation and literary criticism) entered the field, and the circumstances in which historical criticism was practiced changed. The complex arrangement of forces that made historical criticism dominant in biblical studies in the past is giving way to a new complex arrangement of forces, in which other people and methods are becoming dominant. Biblical studies exemplifies how Foucault's analyses of institutions and practices are useful for change, because biblical studies is a field in which the ideas and ways of doing things that people take as natural and given in the world arose out of specific circumstances, and therefore, although they are so familiar as to be considered "natural" or "the way things are" (i.e., as universal), they are not, and thus can be changed.

One reason complex arrangements of forces change is due to resistance. Resistance is an integral part of power, because no arrangement of forces can ever include every force or stop the interaction between forces, despite attempts to do so (it is the presence of resisting forces in every form of totalization, be they social institutions or the meaning of literary texts, that J. Derrida and others have pointed out in what has come to be known as deconstruction). Resistance may come in the form of outright opposition to a particular arrangement of forces, or it may be those who, while in basic agreement with a particular arrangement, would have a different focus or emphasis. Yet because resistance is outside the dominant arrangement of forces, this resistance eventually will lead to a new arrangement of forces and a new exercise of power. Social change is, therefore, always possible.

Foucault also recognized that power is not simply coercive. "If power were never anything but repressive, if it never did anything but to say no, do you really think one would be brought to obey it?" (1980: 119). What makes power appealing, and the reason why people accept particular arrangements of forces, is that power is productive. "What makes power hold good, what makes it accepted, is simply the fact that it doesn't only weigh on us as a force that says no, but that it traverses and produces things, it induces pleasure, forms of knowledge, produces discourse" (1980: 119). Power does function in repressive ways in society; Foucault does not deny this aspect of power. But when power is repressive, people and societies are able to acknowledge such repression and reject and resist it. More insidious, in Foucault's view, is the productive aspect of power, because people are less aware of how power affects and controls them. This is because what power produces most clearly is knowledge.

Knowledge

There is an intimate link between power and knowledge. Knowledge is made possible by power, and power is effective because of knowledge. Knowledge of an idea or subject is made possible only because of the particular, complex arrangement of power at work in a particular historical context. Foucault illustrates the relationship between power and knowledge in his study of penal systems in *Discipline and Punish*. In the eighteenth century, under monarchic rule, punishment was exacted on the body of the guilty (as torture) without concern for the soul of the guilty. In the nineteenth century, however, torture was shunned, in part, because there arose a concern for the souls of the guilty and a desire to help them learn from their punishment and be reformed (literally re-formed). The concern for the soul of the guilty arose because new ideas (or knowledge) about humanity and how to shape and transform humanity had arisen.

Examples of power and knowledge also are available in biblical studies. Modern knowledge about the sources in the Hebrew Bible became possible because, among other things, ideas about what constituted scholarly research, what methods were appropriate for that research, how questions should be formulated, what constituted answers, and who was authorized to ask and "produce" such answers changed from earlier periods of biblical study. "Scientific" (or scientifically based) knowledge became valued, and with this change came a change in the type of knowledge that was possible and, therefore, produced. Thus, for example, typological exegesis preceded the "scientific" study of the Bible, but with the rise of "scientific" criticism, such methods, and the knowledge produced by them, became unacceptable (see H. W. Frei, 1974, for a discussion of the changes that took place in the study of the Bible with the introduction of "scientific" methods). In Foucauldian terms, the change in force relations resulted in a new set of questions being made possible, as well as new answers.

Knowledge has both productive and restrictive aspects, as does power. Knowledge gained in medicine and mental health improved the health and well-being of (Western) society, while knowledge gained in the treatment of prisoners made for "more humane" punishments. At the same time, however, this new knowledge was restrictive: New definitions of mental and physical health began to filter throughout society, as did new definitions of behavior and how to treat "inappropriate" behavior. People were required under these new power arrangements to know and control themselves (i.e., to be responsible for themselves) in different ways than before. Yet, because people believed that their self-knowledge benefited themselves (they were healthier, more secure, and able to understand why criminals acted as they did), they willingly participated in supporting, perpetuating, and enforcing these particular power arrangements. Knowledge about medicine, mental health, and legal behavior, in other words, resulted in individuals within society conforming their own behavior to what the legal, medical, and mental health communities defined as "normal," to understand themselves and their subjectivities in terms of these legal, medical, and mental health discourses, and to seek help, for themselves and others, if they came to understand themselves as "abnormal" in some way. Thus, the same knowledge that produces positive effects—a healthier population, the control of disease, the production of medicines for those who are sick—simultaneously serves a repressive function insofar as individuals accept the definitions of "normal" and "health" defined by the legal, medical, and mental health discourses and therefore come to understand themselves in those terms, without realizing there are alternatives. Knowledge provides a subtle, even insidious, way of controlling and regulating people.

Self

The issue of how knowledge and power affect the individual raises the third problem on which Foucault worked: the idea of subjectivity and the creation of a "self." This was the particular focus of Foucault's work near the end of his life. Power and knowledge have their greatest effect on the individual. For Foucault, as for other postmodernists, no individual is a subject prior to the play of force relations on that individual. Foucault is not a Cartesian philosopher, and thus there is no originary, independent consciousness that interacts with the world. Rather, from the very beginning there is power and knowledge (the result of complex arrangements of power), and it is that power and knowledge that inscribe the body (which is simply the site or surface upon which various competing discourses—e.g., ideas about mental and physical health, sexuality, intelligence—impose themselves) and produce in individuals a sense of their own subjectivity and an awareness of their status as "subjects." To the extent that power makes knowledge possible and that knowledge involves humans and human behavior in some way (e.g., health, sexuality, mental processes), this knowledge can be used not only to describe individual human behavior, but to limit and control it. Thus, subjects are simultaneously created and controlled by the knowledge produced about individuals. Furthermore, that knowledge has been created in such a way that individuals participate in that system of control by monitoring themselves and confessing to persons in authoritative positions (e.g., doctors, priests, police) what they know about themselves (and others) and who they are. (This act of confession is a legacy, in Foucault's view, of the Christian tradition.)

The discourses of knowledge by which individuals come to understand themselves as subjects form a "technology of the Self," the means by which individuals are "produced." These technologies also are the means by which individual subjects can be controlled (i.e., governed), for the behavior of individuals can be regulated by the deployment and modification of the knowledges enabled by power and knowledge. Individual subjects thus take up particular relationships with politics and the State because individuals become subjects as a result of discourses that are approved and controlled (or at least influenced) by the State. Individuals know whether or not they are "normal," for example, only insofar as they accept the definitions of "normal" provided by those authorized in a society to establish such definitions (e.g., the American Medical Association, the American Psychological Association) and know themselves well enough to determine whether or not they are in conformity with those definitions. Becoming aware of one's conformity with such definitions requires that one know oneself, and one knows oneself, in Foucault's view, by confessing who and what one is to those in authority, be they dietitians, doctors, priests, psychotherapists, professors, or others.

Foucault and Biblical Studies

Foucault's work in religion largely has been ignored, although recent work is beginning to fill this gap (see Carrette, 2000). Foucault was very aware of the role religion, and particularly the Christian tradition, has played in shaping individuals and society in the West. The impact of Christian tradition was not necessarily through explicit acknowledgment or acceptance of this tradition (although often this was the case), but by shaping the ways in which modern life and society in the West understands and conceptualizes itself.

Foucault's lack of explicit engagement of religion may help to explain why there has been little use of Foucault's thought in biblical studies, although a few biblical scholars have engaged aspects of Foucault's work in interpreting biblical texts. Among New Testament scholars, E. A. Castelli's excellent book *Imitating Paul: A Discourse of Power* was one of the first books published to use Foucault extensively (and persuasively) in reading biblical texts. S. Moore also has employed Foucault in his readings of New Testament texts. In Hebrew Bible studies, I have drawn on Foucault's work in my readings of the stories of Saul and David in 1 Samuel 8–2 Samuel 1, and more indirectly in "Constructing Identity in 1 Samuel 17." I would like to suggest a couple of ways, however, in which I think Foucault offers helpful and interesting tools for biblical studies.

Foucault's studies on the ways in which institutions arise in response to particular circumstances is one way in which his work could be quite helpful in interpreting biblical texts. Castelli's work on the rise of the early church and the role Paul and his correspondence played in establishing what the church was, how it functioned, and how it thought about itself provides an excellent example of the usefulness of Foucault in reading and interpreting such texts. Similar work remains to be done for those portions of the Hebrew Bible that explicitly recount the development of institutions, such as the priestly texts on ritual in the Pentateuch or the texts of Ezra–Nehemiah that describe the organization of the postexilic community. Likewise, whenever questions of identity arise in the Bible, Foucault's work can be helpful in asking what circumstances made possible particular constructions of identity, what knowledge is necessary for identities to be constructed, what is being left out of such constructions, and how those constructions might have been different.

Another way in which Foucault's work can be helpful is for larger, metacritical work in (and on) the field of biblical studies. As a field, biblical studies functions as an institution, a complex arrangement of forces that give the field a particular shape (and even serve to constitute the study of the Bible as a field). The introduction of new methodologies and new persons into the field in the past few decades has challenged the power structures (force relations) that privileged male, European American scholars and has raised questions about the field, such as why some are empowered and authorized to speak while others are not, what methodologies are "appropriate" in biblical studies, how one's location (e.g., social, political, ethnic, racial, gender, sexual orientation) influences one's reading (and should it), and so on. Forces resistant to the dominant configuration of the field have forced it to change, and that process is continuing.

Foucault sought to explain institutions and practices so that people might realize they did not have to accept those institutions and practices as natural or given, but could change them. In like manner, employing Foucault's work in an examination of the field of biblical studies can help those scholars who want to change the field understand how the field came to be, and thus how it might be changed.

gender
Mary Ann Tolbert

Gender from a modernist perspective is generally understood as a set of innate social traits that naturally accompany biological sex. Thus, in modernist thought, gender becomes the universal and essential social correlative of binary biological differentiation. Evidence for this universality has been assumed not only in the study of human society but even in observations of higher primates, where males are observed to be sexually and territorially aggressive, while females are nurturing and sexually passive. Postmodernist thought contests this modernist view of universal binary gender relations in a number of important ways. Rather than describing innate natural traits, gender in the postmodernist perspective is most often asserted to be a socially constructed set of behaviors with deep political roots, and rather than being universal, it is enacted in multiple and different ways in each historical and local setting. Furthermore, the "naturalness" of gender, according to some postmodern theorists, emerges from the pattern of gender identification as a process of performance in which gender-appropriate behaviors are enacted so often that they become "natural." While gender is viewed by most postmodernists as still profoundly implicated in determinations of sex, the binary biological givenness of sex itself is challenged by recognizing it too as a fluctuating social and cultural construction written on the body. The postmodernist perspective on gender is built upon many bases: the insights of the feminist movement, from which most of the concerted theoretical study of gender has come; cognizance of the pervasive influence of ethnocentrism, which has issued increasingly severe criticism of the anthropomorphizing of animal studies; the awareness of the perspectival biases of all scientific theory; and most importantly, an acknowledgment of the great diversity of gender-appropriate performance in many cultures over time, a diversity that earlier studies selectively ignored in their eagerness to prove the universality of bipolar gender relations.

The Gender Debate: Essentialism vs. Constructionism

The relationship of recent feminism and postmodernism is often one of ambivalence and suspicion, and this state of affairs is exemplified nowhere better than in the debate over the nature of gender. To establish solidarity and promote crucial political goals of liberation, U.S. feminists of the 1970s argued that gender was an essential social factor that warranted careful analysis.

Gender was viewed as the universal ascription of unequal social power relations, allowing one gender to dominate and requiring the other to be subordinate, on the foundation of relatively minor biological distinctions. For early feminists, all women were impacted by this unequal ascription to their detriment, while all men were privileged by it. Indeed, the French feminist Monique Wittig asserted that only one gender, the feminine, actually existed, because masculine is synonymous with universal. In addition to pointing out gender inequality, early feminists often transvalued the basic behavioral traits assumed to be innate to each sex, celebrating the ecologically sensitive, embodied, nurturing woman over against the aggressive, death-loving, dominating man.

By the mid 1980s the acceptance of this universal view of gender relations was breaking down within feminist thought through the protests of racially and ethnically marginalized women and lesbians, who argued that the descriptions of this "essential woman" did not include them. A major turning point in this debate came in Elizabeth Spelman's *Inessential Woman: Problems of Exclusion in Feminist Thought.* Spelman began her analysis of gender relations by looking at classical Greek views on gender as articulated by Plato and Aristotle. She argued that Aristotle's discussion of men, women, and slaves in the *Politics* makes it quite clear that gender is as much dependent on *social status* as it is on sex, for while Aristotle says that men are naturally superior to women, he also claims that women are naturally superior to slaves–both female *and* male. Thus, although being male is a necessary condition for superiority, it is not a sufficient condition, for male slaves are superior to no one, not even female slaves. Indeed, Spelman asserted, in Aristotle's view, those who were slaves "by nature" (rather than "by convention," as were those taken in war) had no gender at all, for they were defined completely by their social status. To be a "man" for Aristotle was to be a free citizen, and to be a "woman" was to be the freeborn wife of a "man." Thus, for Aristotle's society, gender and status were inextricably interwoven. Spelman applied this realization concerning the interwoven nature of gender with other social markers to the contemporary situation of racially and ethnically marginalized women in the U.S., arguing that in this case as well the social realities of race or ethnicity were inextricably interwoven with gender to produce qualitatively different experiences of being a "woman." Moreover, Spelman asserted, this interwoven nature of gender made it practically impossible to separate the societal and cultural consequences of gender out from other crucial social factors; in other words, one could not understand what it means to be an African American woman by putting together studies of African American men and white women.

Spelman's work and the work of others, like bell hooks, Adrienne Rich, Audre Lord, and Maria Lugones, broke the theoretical hold of any lingering naive essentialism in feminist thought; there appeared to be no innate, essential traits common to all women *qua* women, and the attempt to assert any always leads to the exclusion of some women as "unwomanly." Rather than being the universal, innate social and psychological complement of bipolar sexual differentiation, gender, in feminist analysis of the late 1980s, revealed itself to be a social construction that could differ significantly between societies and even in sub-groups within the same society. To be a "woman" in modern Western societies was not at all the same reality as being a woman in ancient Greece or Rome, just as to be a white woman in the U.S. was not the same reality as being a Hispanic woman in the U.S.

The assertion that the narrative affirming universal, innate bipolar gender relations is false and that instead gender is constructed, and constructed differently, in diverse local settings, had clear parallels with aspects of postmodern thinking, especially that emerging under the influence of Jean-François Lyotard and Michel Foucault. Some feminists of the late 1980s and early 1990s adopted postmodernism's critique of totalizing metanarratives, like universal bipolar gender relations, as useful understandings for the purposes of feminist theory. However, other feminists warned that the dissolving of the "essential woman" into separate, diverse local genders was disastrous for the political goals of feminism. Even though recognizing that a multitude of "women" with different experiences of gender could still support local and particular responses to discrimination, wide-scale political action opposing the overarching systemic oppression of women could no longer be sustained theoretically because no overarching understanding of "women" existed. Worse still, from their perspective, some poststructualists, who were often included under the wider umbrella of the postmodern movement, like the French Freudian Jacques Lacan, theorized that the phallogocentric basis of civilization was erected precisely on the repression of the feminine, to such an extent that women literally had no language of their own to speak. Edited books like Linda Nicholson's *Feminism/Postmodernism* allowed feminist voices on both sides of the debate to be heard. Was postmodernism the natural partner of feminist theory or yet another male-defined attempt to render women politically powerless and invisible? While some feminists in the 1990s continue to clutch relentlessly on to one side or the other of this debate, many others recognize that both positions are accurate. The advocacy goals of feminist theory and practice can be strengthened by some of the theoretical insights derived from postmodernism, while the potential use of postmodern arguments to undercut decisive social action must be constantly repelled.

Beyond the Essentialism/Constructionism Impasse

Acknowledging the complexity of gender constructions, their inter-dependence with other social factors, and their variability even within a single society pushed feminists to find different grounds for united social action and the assertion of systemic oppression. Because these discussions continue to inform a postmodern understanding of gender, it is worth reviewing some of them briefly. At least three major alternatives to the "essentialist/constructionist" impasse have been proposed. The first follows the lead of Spelman by arguing that the fluidity of gender construction means one must account for many more than two genders, breaking the iron chains of rigid bipolar gender analysis. In U.S. society, lesbians and gay men and every racial and ethnic group potentially produce different realities of gender differentiation. This same multitude of gender relations marks all other cultures, both contemporary and ancient. Hence, ancient freeborn Roman wives and ancient Jewish wives would form two different genders, and Roman female slaves and Jewish female slaves, two others, with different prescribed manners of relating, different dress, different appropriate behaviors, different approved character traits, different experiences of being a "woman," all of which in each case would be assumed to be simply "natural." United action across these different genders is also fluid and sporadic, based on both empathy and common local goals. The building of coalitions, which form and disperse according to need, is the primary political tool of advocacy.

Beginning from the importance of coalitions for feminist politics, the second position, articulated first by Diana Fuss in *Essentially Speaking,* argues for recognizing the gender designation "woman" as a position within a set of power relations rather than the description of attributes. As those social power relations shift, so too does the positionality "woman" (or "man," for that matter). By asserting gender as a relation within a context of social practices, the multiple experiences of gender are acknowledged, as is the shifting nature of gender, for as practices and power relations change, so, too, will the position of gender. To be a woman or a man, then, is adopt the positionality "woman" or "man" within a particular, constantly mutating social, cultural, and historical matrix. For Fuss, moreover, differently positioned females gain unity through political action and discussion, in other words, through coalition-building. In coalition-building, one claims the identity "woman" as a construct in order to change the social and cultural power relations within which one is positioned. As the title of Fuss's book suggests, while gender is a fluid and shifting reality, speaking of an essential identity "woman" is a political necessity, and such a strategy of non-ontological naming is made legitimate, as others as diverse as Gayatri Spivak and Julia Kristeva also argue, both by the conscious identification of women with their gender position and by their commitment to the political process of coalition-building.

The fact that women often experience some empathy or connection with other women, regardless of the relations of power and privilege that differently position them, seems to point to some kinds of commonalities; yet every attempt to name these commonalities, those things essential to a woman, has failed. The third proposal for moving beyond the "essentialist/constructionist" impasse takes this amorphous sense of connection seriously as a starting point for assessing the complexity of gender identification. Iris Marion Young, in *Intersecting Voices: Dilemmas of Gender, Political Philosophy, and Policy,* appropriates Sartre's distinction between two forms of social collectivity, a social series and a social group, to explore both the sense of commonality and the real differences of gender identity. For Sartre, groups are self-conscious social collectives in which members recognize themselves and others to be working for mutually determined, self-conscious purposes. Series, on the other hand, are fluid collectives in which members are passively unified by the material conditions, objects, and actions of themselves and others, which constrain them without their conscious choice or recognition. Sartre illustrates the differences in an example about people waiting for a bus. Those waiting together are a "series," a collective constrained to stand together waiting by the construction of cities, their work or play needs, and the transportation system. They are unlikely to see themselves as connected to the others waiting or to answer the question "Who are you?" with the identity claim "I am a commuter." However, should the bus not arrive, this amorphous series may begin to talk with each other, designate one member to call the transportation office, and actually see themselves as consciously unified toward an action; at this point, for Sartre, the series becomes a group, for all groups develop out of an underlying social series. They become self-conscious about their situation, acknowledge the others around them as similarly situated, and plan definite action. For Young, this distinction has rich possibilities for understanding the experience of gender. Gender is a set of material effects and collectivized habits that fluidly but certainly constrain the range of actions any member of society can perform. In a similar manner, race, ethnicity, sexual orientation, class, and other social factors would form other such constraining social discourses. All people within society are affected by these regulatory sets of social conventions; that is, all people belong to a gender series, a race series, a sexual orientation series, and so forth, and though serialized existence is often felt as limiting, it is so pervasive that it also seems natural. For many within each social series, membership in the series is unconscious or taken for granted. Only when some members from a series bind themselves together to act for certain ends–that is, when certain members of the series become a group–do they become conscious of each other and often claim their membership as an internalized identity. For Young, such a distinction explains why people may sense amorphous and fluid, but real, connections between themselves and other members of their various series without ever necessarily identifying with these others as "women." It also explains why some women or racial or ethnic minorities, for example, can say that being a woman or being black or Hispanic has no effect on their lives. Although it does have an effect in the form of serialized existence, these people have chosen to form their internalized identities around other group agendas. Only those members of a social series who have formed themselves into a social group to affect the conventions of the series are likely to have internalized an identity in terms of being a "woman," "African American," "gay man," and so forth.

Gender as Performance

Analysis of the "naturalness" of gender, which grounded the modern perspective on gender as universal and innate, has led to other important postmodern theories about gender and identity. Judith Butler, in her influential books *Gender Trouble: Feminism and the Subversion of Identity* and *Bodies That*

Matter: On the Discursive Limits of "Sex," argues that the sense of being a gendered subject is actually a production of the repetition of regulated behaviors, so that, rather than subjects constructing gender, gender constructs subjects. Beginning with Nietzsche's insistence that *doing* precedes *being,* Butler contends that the performance of gender-appropriate behaviors precedes, and indeed is constitutive of, the sense of being a gendered subject. Furthermore, using drag as an example, Butler proposes that gender is not an internal, core identity but rather a series of acts and behaviors that are performed on the surface of the body. Unlike drag, however, gender performance is a heavily regulated cultural construct, a ritualized production under continuous forceful constraint. The "naturalness" of these gendered theatricalities arises from their constant, endless forced repetition. Hence, "gender" for Butler is a cultural fiction, produced by a discursive regulatory regime, which through insistence on iterative performance leads to a false sense of gender "identity." Consequently, what appear to be the behavioral results of gender differentiation are, in reality, its source.

In addition, Butler maintains that the pervasive view of society in general, and some feminist critique in particular, that gender, whatever else it might include, always provides a distinction between male and female reveals the underlying cultural regime to be one of enforced heterosexuality. This normative discursive regime unifies gender, anatomical sex, sexual desire, and sexual acts into a simple bipolar system: Men and women are males and females who desire one another and engage in intercourse with each other. While feminists have often denounced the present system as asymmetrical, in that men are constructed as dominant and women as submissive, most feminists, though not all, as Butler points out, have accepted the underlying binary as "natural," neglecting or refusing to notice its heterosexual bias. In fact, among the gay, lesbian, bisexual, and transgendered communities, gender, anatomical sex, sexual desire, and sexual acts are mixed in a variety of disparate ways, demonstrating their basic autonomy and revealing the supposed natural unity of the normative regime to be yet another cultural fiction.

Gender and Sex

In the modern account, and even in some postmodern accounts, the construction of gender is grounded in the presumed givenness of anatomical sex. Not only have feminists like Gale Rubin and queer theorists like Butler contested the assumed connection between gender and sex, but the givenness of anatomical sex itself has also come under intense attack on social, philosophical, and historical grounds. Foucault's influential assessment of sexuality as a historically specific, discursive exercise of power through the constitution of the body recognizes sex itself as a shifting cultural regime of power relations, producing both pleasure and resistance as well as innovation. Sex and sexuality are not eternal products of nature or God's decree, but historically specific, politically informed discursive representations of the material body. The historian Thomas Laqueur, in *Making Sex: Body and Gender from the Greeks to Freud,* demonstrates through the study of medical and anatomical texts from antiquity to the modern period how the very shape of the body has changed with changing power relations between the genders. The ancients believed that only one human body existed with only one set of sexual organs, which in the cooler, imperfect female were held internally while in the hotter, perfect male were present externally. Children generally, though not exclusively, were gestated in the cooler female body because male heat tended to burn up the seed. Laqueur shows that it is only in the anatomical representations and medical and political discourse of the eighteenth and nineteenth centuries that this one sex becomes two opposite sexes, with different physical and social characteristics. Moreover, he demonstrates conclusively that it was not scientific discoveries that brought about the shift in the discursive representation of sex (those came almost a century later), but instead the political necessity to find new grounds for female inferiority and domestication in light of the Enlightenment's toppling of a divinely ordained hierarchical worldview. From a postmodern perspective, sex and gender are both cultural fictions, discursive representations constituting the power relations and practices of bodies in a variety of specific and local configurations. They have no essential meaning or core nature in and of themselves, and one's imagined materiality cannot be used to legitimate constructions of the other.

historiography
Fred W. Burnett

History and the Past

The past and history float free of each other, they are ages and miles apart.

(Jenkins, 1991: 5)

The foundation of all historical writing is that the past once existed and that historians can know and represent it (White, 1989: 19–20). However, since historians have no direct access to any past event, they can only represent the past through writing. What seems to be a banal observation actually is the crucial point in the current debate about what it means to write history. The key question is the epistemological one: Can historians "objectively" know and represent anything about the past, or is the "past" epistemologically irretrievable? Different understandings of whether or not the epistemological "gap" between the present and the past can be bridged provides the terrain on which the so-called history wars are being fought.

The Past Is Known through Language

Postmodern historians generally give a qualified "No" to the epistemological question. They see the past as available to historians only through language and texts. Because few historians today believe that recovering the past "as it was" is possible, or that the attempt should be the main goal of writing history, the issue really is *not* how the historian can know the past "as it was." The ontological fact is that the "past itself" no longer exists; only its textual traces remain, including both written materials and artifacts such as rocks and buildings. For postmodern historians, one's only access to any past event is through reading and interpreting its textual remains and subsequently writing a narrative about it. The crisis and debate about the practice of historical writing stems from the sober admission that the histories historians produce are not—and never will be—the same thing as the past itself (see Berkhofer, Jr., 1988: 435). If histories and the past "are ages and miles apart," then what do historians actually produce, and how?

The Textuality of the Past

> Since textuality is the only bridge to the past, the view of language
> that one holds is crucial for historical practice. Postmodern historians
> emphasize that language does not have a simple referential function
> of providing a "window" into the past; rather than reflecting reality,
> language participates in the creation of (past) reality. Language,
> therefore, has a *constitutive* role in postmodern historical practice: it is
> both the means by which historians create a past, and it is an essential
> part of that creation. The emphasis upon the constitutive role that
> language plays in creating the past is the most important contribution
> of postmodern historians to historiography. (Wilson, 1999: 113–14)

The acknowledgment that language is constitutive for the past is what is
referred to in historical studies as the "linguistic turn." It means that the direct
object of the historian's study is not the "past itself" but that it is any text
about that past *and* the history of interpretation of that text. Previous
interpretations of the sources shape the historian's understanding of their
language and meaning and, consequently, of the past. The language of the
historian's sources has already configured the past in certain ways, and, in
turn, the history of interpretation has framed certain ways for the historian to
understand the sources. Therefore, the textuality of the historian's work is
inevitable. The textual traces of any past event have been doubly framed by
the source documents and by the history of their interpretation. For postmodern
historians, therefore, "history" is defined as an organized re-presentation of
textual traces from the past. "History" is the practice of representing texts that
have themselves already re-presented the past. The *textuality* of the past is the
primary referent of the historian's work, not an object known as the "past
itself."

History as Fictive Narrative

> A historian has to do, not with what actually happened, but only
> with events supposed to have happened…All historians speak
> of things which have never existed except in imagination.
> (Nietzsche, 1971: 307)

If textual sources and histories are not the same as or identical with the
past that they represent, then there is no *necessary* relationship between the
"past" (what happened) and "history" (what is written about what happened).
For example, neither a historian's book about Jesus nor any of the gospels has
necessarily produced any actual events from Jesus' life. Linguistically speaking,
the word *Jesus* exists only as a "sign" (not as the actual historical person), and
what the historian has produced about the sign "Jesus" is yet another text to
be interpreted. What this means is that historians should "consider historical
narratives as what they most manifestly are: verbal fictions, the contents of
which are as much *invented* as *found* and the forms of which have more in

common with their counterparts in literature than they have with those in science" (White, 1978: 82).

Most historians readily acknowledge that the original contexts of past events are lost and that they must construct contexts by which to interpret them. This is different, however, from saying that history is a fictive context that is constructed by the historian and that the fictive context is the real referent and content of the historian's work. Historians usually speak of their heuristic contexts as "the historical milieu," or in biblical studies the "situation-in-life," and then suppose that somehow the past has been made present. "But," as White says, "the presumed concreteness and accessibility of historical milieux, those contexts of the texts that literary scholars study, are themselves products of the fictive capability of the historians who have studied those contexts" (1978: 89). The blurring of the line between history and fiction—for both the production of history and the product—is perhaps the main upshot of the linguistic turn in historical studies.

In summary, for postmodern historians the referent of historical research is not "the past"; it is, rather, the language and constructed contexts of historians. Roland Barthes's conclusion about literary criticism and historical work applies to this point: "The object of criticism is not 'the world' but a discourse, the discourse of someone else: criticism is discourse upon a discourse; it is a second language, or a *metalanguage*...which operates on a first language (or *language object*)" (1972: 258).

History as the Intertextual Product of Discourse

A "discourse" entails both the verbal and non-verbal practices by which a profession conducts itself. To postmodern historians the term *discourse* primarily refers to the way texts and language function so that knowledge is produced within any professional discourse (such as medical, scientific, political, and historical discourses). As Michel Foucault has shown, a discourse defines what its object of study is *and* what counts as knowledge about it (see Burnett, 1990: 65–66; and, forthcoming). In other words, a "discourse" is an institutionalized set of practices that exist at the institutional level as "Truth," and they transcend and control the knowledge that any individual researcher produces.

In biblical studies, historical discourse has involved learning primarily the discourse of historical criticism. Historical-critical discourse has prescribed what sources and methods to use and what conclusions are deemed acceptable as "knowledge" about the past. For example, if a historian is studying the gospel of Matthew, he or she must, of professional necessity, use the concept of the Matthean Community that historical-critical discourse has already constructed as the context by which to read that gospel. However, the "Matthean Community" is a heuristic product of historical-critical discourse, and there is no evidence outside of historical-critical discourse for the existence of a Matthean Community. The general point is that to study "history" is to study a set of texts that historians have linked in certain ways to produce an *intertextual construct*–in this case the Matthean Community–that counts as knowledge about the past (see Kristeva, 1967).

Linguistically speaking, the words *the Matthean Community* are a "sign" or a "signifier" that stand for what is, by definition, absent (namely, the "past itself"). The only linguistic or "historical" referent that can be found for "the Matthean Community" is the intertextual construct that is the upshot of the organization of texts by historians within the discourse of historical criticism. Berkhofer, Jr., summarizes the essential theoretical point:

> The core question that causes all the problems is quite simple: just what is the referent for the word "history?" It cannot be the past as such, because that is absent by definition. If linguistic analysts define words as signs or signifiers that denote objects in their stead, then "history" certainly fits the definition twice over. Normal history exists as a practice because of the very effort needed in the present to imagine (predicate) in the present an absent past actuality presumed to have once existed...Those pasts, however, depend upon still another predication or construction as observed by those interested in the poetics of historical practice. The only referent that can be found for "history"...is the intertexuality that results from the reading of sets of sources combined with...the readings of other historians of these same or other sources as synthesized in the expositions. *"History" refers in actual practice only to other "histories"*...[Postmodern historians] fail to see much...in the distinction drawn by normal historians between fact and fiction, for factual reconstruction is really nothing but construction according to the working of "fictions" of normal history practice, which, in turn, are the premises of both historical realism and realist mimesis. (445, emphasis mine)

It is important to note that the "(inter)textuality of history" does not mean that the Matthean Community never actually existed. It means, rather, that the "actual" community, if there was one, is irretrievably absent and exists now only as an intertextual construct *within scholarship*. All access to the "Matthean Community" is in and through the linguistic practices of the historical discourse that has produced it as a "text." One way to understand the revolutionary inversion of "normal" historiography by postmodern historiography, therefore, is to say that the ontological question (what actually existed and happened) is now secondary to the epistemological issue (what historians claim to know about what might or might not have existed or happened).

Historical Writing as a Literary Act

When Hayden White speaks of the "fictive capability" of historians to produce signs such as the Matthean Community, he is largely concerned about how historians collapse theory into practice. Historians usually assume that the *form* of their histories (their narratives) can be separated from the *content*

(Jesus' actual life). If traditional historians are pressed on the issue, they will acknowledge that their historical accounts are not the same thing as the past event itself ("Yes, surely, my account of Jesus' life is not the same thing as his actual life"). In actual historical practice, though, historians make little epistemological distinction between the past (what actually happened) and "history" (their representations of the past). In this case the historical narrative (the form) about Jesus' life or the Matthean Community subtly becomes part of the assumed and "actual" content of the past. The heuristic Jesus surreptitiously becomes the actual person of history, and the linguistic fiction of the Matthean Community becomes an actual first-century group of Jesus' followers.

In line with traditional historians, biblical scholars also acknowledge that the *form* of their histories is a construction. However, few will agree that the *content* of their constructions is also fictive, that is, that the content (such as the Matthean Community) refers only to their individual imaginations operating within the collective imagination of professional discourses. Instead, biblical scholars generally understand their constructions to be re-constructions that refer and correspond to the past in some measurable way. What postmodern historians are saying is that a historical narrative in both its form and content is not a re-construction of the "past itself" but is a con-struct that refers to the fictive discourse of other historians. In this sense, then, postmodern historians would agree with White's conclusion that the actual practice of historians is indistinguishable from the practice of writing fictional narratives.

Historical Writing as an Ideological Act

When postmodern historians talk about history as fictive, they generally do *not* mean that nothing happened in the past, that what actually happened is irrelevant to writing history and to ethics, or that historians can make up whatever they wish. Postmodern historians are primarily making two points about history as fiction. First, that *as a discourse* "history" imposes meaning on past events. Second, there is no way to prove—except by reference to one's own historical discourse—that these imposed meanings were actually "there" in the past. "History," therefore, has essentially the same epistemological standing as does "fiction." Epistemologically speaking, a historian's meanings and her representation of the past are both imaginary and self-referential: They refer primarily to the historian's own meaning-making discourses. Although White denies that he is a postmodern historian, he summarizes the postmodern point extremely well when he says that historical discourse "is ultimately a second-order fiction, a fiction of a fiction or a fiction of fiction-making" (1989: 27). That is, history is fiction (the imaginative constructions of historians) that refers to fiction (the fiction-making rules of historical discourse or, in biblical studies, the "principles of exegesis").

The crucial distinction to be made is between "facts" and "events": "If there is no such thing as 'raw facts,' but only events under different descriptions, then *factuality becomes a matter of the descriptive protocols used to transform events* *into facts…*We must not confuse 'facts' with 'events.' *Events happen, facts are constituted by linguistic description*" (White, 1989: 35, emphasis mine). In other words, there are no "facts" that exist independently of a discourse. The standard professional stories about Jesus or Matthew's community are not bound to irrefutable evidence in the world; they are stories that historians have agreed to reckon as the truth. In this sense, historical "facts" are not fundamentally different from fiction. Historical "facts" are products of historical discourse, and in that sense they are fictions that enjoy the special status of claiming to be tied to events that really occurred. Postmodern historians, therefore, are not saying that there are no facts, but they are arguing against certain claims about facts, namely, that facts exist as a given prior to the discourse in which they are selected, constructed, and explained.

The postmodern contention is that a historian isolates a set of facts, then constructs a model (or uses an existing model such as the Matthean Community) to account for them, and through the model "naturalizes" the facts into what is already known, namely, the general professional agreements about what count as facts and what explanatory models are appropriate to use. Note carefully: This does not mean that postmodern historians are arguing that "historical accounts have no basis in fact" (Stanford, 1998: 254–55). That is the wrong conclusion to infer, and it collapses the event/fact distinction. It is, rather, that *events* happened, but they are forever lost to historians; what counts as "facts" about those events are selections and products of historical discourse. Postmodern historians believe that the world is real and that events really happened. Their point is not so much the old question of history (reality) versus fiction as it is that the non-fictive and the fictive are never fully separable.

For postmodern historians, therefore, the practice of writing history is ideological production in three minimal ways. First, meanings are imposed on the past by "outsiders" and nonparticipants in the events that are represented. Second, imaginary causal links and explanatory relationships, particularly among past personages, are made by the historian. For example, in the explanatory construct of the Matthean Community, historians must imagine and construct relationships between the followers of Jesus and Jews who are outside that community. These relationships have both ideological and ethical implications, particularly since the historian's realistic discourse presents them as "objective." Finally, the models that historians use are socially inscribed and are, therefore, value-laden. Because there is no necessary relationship between the past and historical narratives, there is no one correct historical account to which all other histories must refer. Furthermore, because of the fact/value (meaning) distinction, *any* historical account could be written otherwise by historians who are inscribed in different power and socio-economic relationships. For historical practice the question has finally become an ethical and political one: Why is any history constructed as it is? Whose interests are served by any historical account? What material effects does this historical account have on people's lives, and what effects does it continue to have?

Historical Writing as an Ethical Act

To reveal the essentially fictive structure of historiography is not to denigrate either such a discipline's use or attained accuracy so much as it is to secure it at its proper ontological status...We do not suggest that historiography is a fiction of the same mode as either mundane fiction, science, or even literary criticism. Historiography...has *its* autonomous value...Only with an awareness of that essentially fictive structure...can the reader or writer of historiography truly take responsibility for it. (S. Delaney, 1978: 85–86)

To enter the current debate about historical practice is to enter at the point of questions about the status of ethical and political issues in writing history (see Schüssler Fiorenza, 1999). Although many excellent suggestions are being made about how to relate ethics and historical practice, no one view prevails (and should not); however, some historians are beginning to ask a common core of questions (such as those listed above) about their work (see Patte). Historians are understanding that to admit that they can never get (and never have gotten) beyond language to the "past itself" is neither to declare the futility of historical work nor to minimize its powerful effects on people's lives (see Adam, 1995a: 45–60). For postmodern historians the constitutive role of *our* language in creating the past is ultimately a call for us to take ethical and political responsibility for what we re-present as "the past" (see Phillips and Fewell, 1997).

identity
Francisco Lozada, Jr.

In the 1990s, contemporary biblical interpretation witnessed a paradigm shift brought about by cultural or liberation hermeneutics and then taken up and supported by postmodern biblical interpreters, namely, the use of identity in the act of biblical interpretation (see Sugirtharajah, 1991; Felder, 1991; Smith-Christopher, 1995). Using identity features such as race, gender, class, sexual orientation, and geography, postmodern biblical interpreters set out to challenge modernism's long-reigning assumption that interpretation is independent of one's identity (see Segovia and Tolbert, 1995a; 1995b; M. West, 1999). In other words, no longer would objectivity—in the Enlightenment's understanding—be the ultimate goal for postmodern biblical interpreters (cf. Bible and Culture Collective, 1995; Adam, 1995a; Appleby et al., 1994; Jencks, 1989). Rather, the goal is to challenge or question those readings or interpretations that claim objectivity and superiority over others. This is done not by inverting superiority on other readings, but by showing how identity or identities, when openly and critically used "in context" with a text at hand, produces different understandings of the text.

In this essay, I will provide a critical review on how identity works within postmodern biblical interpretation by reviewing three studies that are outlined along the lines of three postmodern reading strategies: (1) subversive reading, (2) postcolonial reading, and (3) autobiographical reading. Each reading strategy, working with particular identities, aims to transform the way we understand others and ourselves within an age of postmodernism. In practice, the use of identities in postmodern biblical interpretation involves an analysis of the text, reader, and ideological context. This threefold analysis will be taken into consideration throughout the essay in order to help demonstrate how identity *works* in the act of biblical reading. However, before I proceed, a clearer working postmodern definition of identity and a self-disclosure note are in order.

First, identity is used and understood very broadly among postmodernists (Woodward, 1997; Boyarin, 1994; Segovia, 2000). In the field of postmodern biblical interpretation, *identity* refers primarily to the cultural features, qualities, or temporal and spatial locations of the interpreter in the world before the text, but it can also refer to the identity of a textual character in the world of the text or a historical figure in the world behind the text. Identity is also expressed in a non-essentialist sense. In other words, identity is not understood

113

as immutable, fixed, or primordial, but rather as self-making or constantly reconstructing at different times and different places (Rosaldo, 1989; Hall, 1989: 68–81; Woodward, 1997: 22). For example, postmodern biblical interpreters examine their identities from three settings. It is employed achronically, synchronically, or diachronically. Achronic identity refers to the interpreter's present identity; synchronic identity refers to the interpreter's identity at a particular time; and diachronic identity refers to the identity of the interpreter across different times (Gracia, 2000: 30). Overall, all three kinds of identity are used among postmodern biblical interpreters to illustrate that meaning is never quite fixed or complete.

Second, because I am arguing that what we say is always culturally located by identity, then it is only apropos that I acknowledge an aspect of my identity "in context." I am a Hispanic/Latino American of Puerto Rican descent who has lived all my life in the U.S. and in the shadow of cultural assimilation in the hope of losing my identity(ies). I no longer affirm cultural assimilation or its design to conceal identities. I now apply this conviction against the background of my work in biblical interpretation and teaching (see Lozada, 2000a; 2000b).

Subversive Reading

One way identity is used results in providing another way of reading or interpretation over and against modern interpretations of a particular text and, in the process, shows that knowledge is socially constructed. For postmodern biblical interpreters, all interpretations are inextricably positioned thus; all knowledge is, at the end, contextual. The study that I will focus on uses identity in a subversive way, thus challenging the modernist's claim that meaning and knowledge are something to unearth from the text objectively, independent of one's cultural identity.

This subversive use of identity can best be seen at work in the essay by Randall C. Bailey, "They're Nothing but Incestuous Bastards: The Polemical Use of Sex and Sexuality in Hebrew Canon Narratives" (1995: 121–38). Informed primarily by ideological criticism, Bailey reluctantly draws on source criticism to construct a subversive reading of several narratives. Bailey's reading follows a threefold development centered on the identity of the reader, himself, with regard to three narratives. The first narrative concerns the recurring incident of the patriarch who claims his wife as his sister in order to escape death (Gen. 12, 20, 26); the second is the seduction of Lot (Gen. 19:29–38); and the third narrative, which is the focus of this essay, is the curse of Ham, or Noah's insobriety (Gen. 9:18–28).

Bailey argues that within the narrative of the curse of Ham, those who are characterized as the outsiders (foreigners–Ham and his descendants) are depicted negatively by means of either sexual innuendo or graphic details, thus sanctioning the insiders (Israelites) and even today's readers (Christians) to hate and oppress outsiders (African Americans) through voyeurism. What leads Bailey to such a reading of Genesis 9:18–28 is his experience of being an outsider (a member of the Black African diaspora) whose community is portrayed as having an overt interest in voyeurism, rather than as an insider (a member of the dominant society) in the U.S. with a "normal" (and moral) sexual interest. Bailey's encounter with such an "in-group/out-group" scenario has led him to subvert such an exclusive in/out motif in the Bible and to undercut any appropriation and normalization of this racist insider/outsider motif. As such, Bailey, in keeping with many other postmodern biblical interpreters, is providing another reading; that is, "a reading," not "the only reading" but one reading among many possible readings, to subvert also the notion that the production of knowledge by means of interpretation is univocal and objective. All interpretations are indeed socially and historically conditioned.

For example, in his critical examination of Genesis 9:18–28, an example of sexual innuendo used polemically, Bailey focuses on why all the ambiguities in the text lead the reader to conclude that an act of voyeurism had occurred on the part of Ham by seeing Noah naked, thus leading to a curse of slavery on Ham and his descendants. Informed by source criticism, Bailey argues that the narrative is a conflation of two sources, J and P, with P, immersed within the sexual prohibitions of the Holiness Code in Leviticus 18 and 20, having a heavy and final editing hand on Genesis 9:18–28. As such, Bailey argues that the P school used an old law against Egypt and Canaan (Lev. 18 and 20) as the narrative backdrop behind Genesis 9:18–28, with Ham performing a suspicious sexual act. The purpose of this backdrop, according to Bailey, is not to keep Israel from practicing these sexual taboos, but rather to keep Israel from following the sexual taboos *of the Hamlite line,* whose descendants are Egyptians and Canaanites. In short, the above analysis illustrates how Bailey works with identity in a subversive way. By refusing to conceal or even naturalize his identity universally in his reading of Genesis 9:18–28, Bailey uncovers the myth that knowledge is produced objectively, independent of one's social location. His subversive reading strategy, therefore, does not merely consist of talking about oneself critically; it is also about subverting the insider/outsider opposition in order to challenge any possibility of a universal and objective interpretation grounded on an apartheid type of difference (see Minh Ha, 1990: 371–75). For Bailey, a subversive reading is about producing a different reading, not in order to maintain the insider/outsider opposition, but rather to challenge multiple forms of oppression and dominance.

Postcolonial Reading

Inextricably related to the use of identity in a subversive way is the use of identity from the standpoint of postcolonial theory. The self-disclosure of identity of the flesh-and-blood reader during the reading process, which is considered unconventional among modernist readers, is made known vociferously by many postcolonial readers (see Said, 1978; Kwok, 1995; Sugirtharajah, 1998c; Segovia, 1998). A principal reason behind postcolonial reading, as I see it, is to challenge the colonizing hegemony of the West's normative assumption that to reveal your identity is to fall into an inferior tier of scholarship. However, it is not just about deconstructing conventions of scholarship; using identity in light of postcolonial theory is also about staking a rhetorical and political space among other readings, as evidenced by Bailey's reading above, and, more importantly, decolonizing the reader and the text from colonialism or neo-colonialism.

The essay by Leticia A. Guardiola-Sáenz, "Borderless Women and Borderless Texts: A Cultural Reading of Matthew 15:21–28," is a representative sample of the postcolonial use of identity (1997: 69–81). Guardiola-Sáenz' reading follows a threefold development centered on her reading strategy, identity, and rereading of the plot of the Canaanite woman in Matthew. Informed by postcolonial theory, Guardiola-Sáenz argues in this essay that the ideology of chosenness that is present within the rhetorical strategy of Matthew 15:21–28 subordinates the Canaanite woman in such a way that her identity and voice are erased. The Matthean writer, imbued with an ideology of chosenness, mistreats the Canaanite woman in order to maintain the established, colonial, and ethnic social order of the writer. Reread from the perspective of a postcolonial reader, Guardiola-Sáenz contends that Matthew 15:21–28 has been traditionally read as a story that characterizes the woman as a second-class citizen, rather than as an equal. In other words, the Canaanite woman crosses the "border" not to worship her oppressor (Jesus) but rather to demand restitution; she wants a place at the table as an equal, not as an inferior. Such a rereading of the plot is liberative for Guardiola-Sáenz because it not only recovers the rightful place of the Canaanite woman vis-à-vis the empires of gender, culture, and ethnicity, her rereading also liberates Jesus in that he eventually gives the Canaanite woman her deserved place at the table in the story.

This rereading of the Canaanite woman in Matthew is grounded by and created from the perspective of multiple identities. Similar to Bailey, Guardiola-Sáenz demarcates her social identity along the lines of race/ethnicity–Mexican American–but differently in that her identity as a woman and a dispossessed neighbor are also introduced. Her multiple identities and questions posed to the text locate her as a postcolonial reader. She thus uses this multiple identity to focus her attention in those places in the plot that correlate with her experience of being Mexican American in the U.S., a second-citizen as a woman, and a child of neocolonialism living in the borderlands of the U.S. and Mexico. For instance, she states,

> As a Mexican-American I have read the Canaanite woman's story with the rhetoric of the Other against the rhetoric of Matthew and its readers. I hold that the Canaanite woman is not a humble dog begging for crumbs. She is a dispossessed woman who has awakened from her position as oppressed, and now is coming to confront the empire and demand her right to be treated as human. (79)

As such, she reads the text through multiple identities, going against the plot of the text–the ideology of chosenness–from the perspective of her identities.

In short, what Guardiola-Sáenz's reading demonstrates is that the post-colonial use of identity is inextricably bound with her subversive use of identity. Like Bailey, she is surely working with a hermeneutics of survival, namely, a critique of social and political domination (Bible and Culture Collective: 251–54). This reading strategy is surely growing among biblical scholars, especially among ethnically marginalized women in the U.S. and women from Latin America, Asia, and Africa (see Bird, 1997; Dube, 1998: 118–35). It not only provides a rhetorical and political space among other readings but is also a step forward toward decolonization and liberation for both the reader and text. Rather than totalizing and universalizing through a hermeneutics of positivism, the text is kept unstable and interpretation indeterminable through the use of identity.

Autobiographical Reading

The final area that I will examine in which identity has been used within the field of postmodern biblical interpretation is the approach of autobiographical or personal voice criticism (Anderson and Staley, 1995; Kitzberger, 1999). Autobiographical criticism, as I see it, comes from an interest in exploring how the use of identity works in a much more self-critical way. In so doing, the use of identity in an autobiographical way challenges the long-reigning conventions of biblical interpretation, such as concealing the "I" in order to maintain objectivity as the "proper" way to create scholarly writing. This irruption of the personal pronoun "I"–as I did above–by autobiographical biblical readers not only produces a rhetorical effect by challenging the notion that "legitimate" scholarship can only be written when the public and private spheres are segregated, but, in addition, the emergence of the "I" has a political impact by allowing the "I" to have an even more dominant voice in the interpretive process. It is a political move that does not allow the text to speak for you (Dube, 1998: 119).

An excellent example of the autobiographical use of identity is Jeffrey L. Staley's "Fathers and Sons: Fragment from an Autobiographical Midrash on John's Gospel" (Staley, 1999: 65–85). Informed by an autobiographical approach grounded in cultural studies, Staley provides an interpretation of selected portions of the gospel of John through the genre of personal journal writing. He outlines his reading in fourteen fragments that center on, for example, the nature of fatherhood, his desires as a father, and the relationship between himself and his son, themes also found in the gospel of John. Staley's autobiographical reading of the gospel begins similarly to the gospel, in that he begins with his family roots (fragment one). The reading then moves in the direction of his marriage partner (fragment two), next to fatherhood (fragments three and four), and finally to the "blessings" of children (fragments five through fourteen).

Throughout the fragments, Staley makes himself quite vulnerable, a characteristic that is very real and dangerous for autobiographical critics. By disclosing too much of their personal identities they run the risk of being considered unscholarly. For example, read intertextually in light of the origins of circumcision discussed in John 7:22 and himself, Staley discusses his decision to have his son circumcised (compare Kitzberger: 5). Read intertextually in light of the preempting of the eschatological hour in John 18:11 and himself, Staley comments on his decision to have a vasectomy. Read intertextually in light of the Son's (Jesus') farewell address in John 14:19–20 and himself, Staley narrates his tension at his own young son's kissing him on the lips. These journal entries surely illustrate the vulnerability of disclosing the "I." As Ingrid Rosa Kitzberger confirms in the introduction to the volume in which Staley's essay appears, "exposing oneself the critic makes herself/himself vulnerable, and that is always a risky endeavor" (Kitzberger: 5). Such exposure is a dangerous undertaking because it typecasts the critic as childish, rude, perverted, and, of course, unscholarly, not to mention that it falls into the all-pervasive criticism of opponents who argue that the use of identity leads to the critic's reinscribing herself/himself in the texts that she/he is interpreting (see Moloney: 97–110; Anderson and Staley: 14–15). If the latter is so, the hidden identities, it can be argued, have even more overpowering effects on the texts. However, it can be also be an empowering and liberating experience to "come out," not only for the critic but also for the modern reader. I believe these latter two reasons are why biblical scholars are using autobiographical criticism more frequently, namely, to crush the opposition between the public and private voice in order to show that there is really no difference between eisegesis and exegesis in biblical interpretation. All interpretation is influenced by one's identities.

What Staley's work illustrates with regard to the use of identity in autobiographical interpretation is that identity not only has a subversive motive of challenging modern biblical interpreters with a new form of biblical interpretation (autobiographical) but also has a rhetorical effect that obliterates the distinction between "proper" scholarly writing and "improper" scholarly writing. In other words, Staley's autobiographical approach destabilizes the legitimization of how biblical reading and interpretation are done. The very clash of this distinction is consonant with postmodernism's focus on the indeterminable, and the "unsayable." However, I am not as optimistic as Kitzberger that autobiographical or personal voice criticism will proliferate (Kitzberger: 1–8). Not because I do not believe there is any value in such a reading exercise, but rather because interpreters are always governed by constraints, whether they be institutional constraints (college, university, seminary) or social constraints (family, marriage, or sexual orientation). To resist these constraints is real and dangerous for many critics, both men and women.

Conclusion

All three postmodern reading strategies aim to show that the identities of the interpreters are interconnected with the production of meaning. The subversive strategy uses identity to show that knowledge is socially constructed; the postcolonial strategy employs identity to critique any notion of universality or hegemony, and the autobiographical strategy appropriates identity to challenge the rigidity between the "sayable/unsayable." Overall, all three strategies aim to show that the identities of the interpreters are interconnected with the production of meaning. Furthermore, all three postmodern reading strategies critically employed one or more uses of identity, either achronically (Bailey, Guardiola-Sáenz, and Staley), synchronically (Staley), or diachronically (Bailey, Guardiola-Sáenz, and Staley) to analyze a text in terms of its rhetoric (Bailey), its ideology (Guardiola-Sáenz), or its poetics (Staley). These distinct uses of identity also allow for an investigation of the conditions of racism (Bailey), cultural imperialism (Guardiola-Sáenz), and sexuality (Staley). In so doing, the above critics reconstruct or refashion not only the identity of the texts of ancient Judaism but also the "here and now," in keeping with their social or political aim to contest final and definitive interpretations that reify cultural norms or relations. In other words, taken up as an important factor in postmodern biblical interpretation, identity has made a valuable academic contribution by reminding the academy of the struggles (Bailey and Guardiola-Sáenz) and uncertainties (Staley) of everyday life. In the future, the use of identity and the contestation of identities in biblical interpretation will become more important, especially when the power to represent in the field of biblical interpretation becomes even more diversified nationally and internationally.

ideology
Beverly J. Stratton

"Ideology"–to most biblical interpreters the word has a bad aftertaste. Ideology is what other people have, something responsible scholars seek to eliminate from their work. Church people may have theologies, but they also should avoid letting their ideologies, understood as political positions, govern their interpretation of scripture. Where do these connotations of the term *ideology* come from? What role does ideology play in postmodern biblical interpretation? Do texts have ideologies? Why should scholars and theologians understand and perhaps embrace ideological biblical criticism, and what would this entail?

A Slippery Term

Walter Brueggemann, as editor of the Overtures to Biblical Theology series, observed as recently as 1995 that while the "term ideology reflects an important turn in scholarship...[it is] certainly not yet a word in common or legitimated usage" (in Habel: ix). Two reasons for the lack of scholarly interest in the terms *ideology* and *ideological criticism* may be that these terms are used rather loosely and sometimes have negative connotations.

Modernists and positivists, whether in biblical studies or social sciences, prefer to avoid ideology because they see it as an illegitimate imposition of one's political perspective into scholarship, which should be value-neutral in its aims to discern reality.

Following Marx, materialist and Marxist critics also use the term *ideology* with this negative cast, viewing it as "false consciousness" that allows both dominant and oppressed classes to perpetuate their uneven class relationships. Discerning such false consciousness requires systematic analyses of a society's political, economic, and cultural patterns. Intellectuals with this view of ideology see "ideology critique," the exposing of ideologies, as their moral task.

A third group of scholars views ideology in a more generic and neutral way, as a perspective. For example, in his 1964 essay "Ideology as a Cultural System," Clifford Geertz defines ideologies as "schematic images of social order" (63). Geertz and scholars who see ideology in this neutral way recognize that everyone's interpretation of reality is affected by the ideologies or modes of discourse that shape us. Thus, the lenses through which we see reality and the communities of conversation in which we participate circumscribe our

120

research questions, methods, and results. While positivists presume to avoid ideologies and Marxist critics seek to expose them, scholars in this third group recognize that living within ideologies is unavoidable. It is our human responsibility to select among ideologies to the best of our ability. Chris Weedon observes that "[i]n poststructuralist feminism, we can choose between different accounts of reality on the basis of their social implications" (1987: 29). Some history of the term *ideology* may help to explain this range of positions.

What Is Ideology? Historical Background

When French rationalist philosopher Destutt de Tracy used the term *ideology* in the late 1700s, he intended it to be the science of ideas. Napoleon picked up the term and gave it a derogatory connotation by referring to his opponents as "ideologues." Later, Marx and Engels recognized the role that ideas play in sustaining existing relations of class domination, thus connecting ideology with power and "false consciousness" (for history, see J. Thompson, 1990; Eagleton, 1991; and Kavanagh).

Perhaps the most influential use of ideology in recent Marxist thought is that of French theorist Louis Althusser (1971; reprinted in Žižek, ed., 1994). What Althusser refers to as "state apparatuses" keep the State in power by ensuring that the State will be able to reproduce its relations of production. Repressive state apparatuses (RSAs) are public institutions such as the government, army, legal system, and police power that Althusser claims operate by violence and repression.

While RSAs maintain some order and control, it is ideological state apparatuses (ISAs) that most effectively keep the dominant and lower classes in their place. In contrast to the "repressive state apparatuses" that wield their power through force, ISAs include those aspects of culture and society that most of us willingly embrace, such as schools, religions, families, the media, and other means of inculcating values and shaping worldviews. For Althusser, what ISAs and ideology do is to represent "the imaginary relationship of individuals to their real conditions of existence." (Žižek, ed.: 123) Althusser insists that ideologies exist materially in their practices, yet for him the term *ideology* retains a negative flavor and an association with illusion.

Nevertheless, ideologies function and are sometimes embraced precisely because their worldviews–the ways they represent what is going on in people's lives–largely ring true to their adherents. For example, the green movement is certain that its view of the environment and what is required to preserve a harmonious planetary ecology is the right one–it's not an illusion. African Americans recognize that their lives are affected materially by the ideologies of race and white supremacy. Feminists know that seeing the world as governed by interlocking systems of privilege and oppression, including patriarchy and heterosexism (see Rich, 1980), makes sense out of the experiences of women's lives. Capitalism, consumerism, and a global market seem to be unavoidable realities for modern citizens. According to Althusser, ideologies like these hail us and "interpellate" us as subjects. We come to understand and explain who we are and what our place in the world is by means of the ideologies that we recognize and embrace as well as those we discern and repudiate. Given the range of ideology's history and current usage, the term has a variety of definitions.

Some Definitions

From a positivist social science perspective, Edward Shils defines ideologies as distinct from outlooks, creeds, movements of thought, and programs. Ideologies are explicitly formulated and highly systematized or integrated. They emphasize their distinctiveness, resist innovations, and expect consensus and agreement among their adherents. They are promulgated with authority and affect, and they organize their adherents into communal groups in order to maintain discipline and win others. These communities attempt either to disrupt or transform prevailing institutions and value systems or to withdraw from them (1968: 66, 72).

Alhough Norman Habel (1995) claims to adopt, with Geertz, a more neutral view of ideology, his definitions cohere with Shils's portrait of ideologies belonging to a subset of a society. Habel observes that "a living ideology, as a pattern of beliefs, functions to promote the social and political cause of a particular group in society, to justify its vision, and to promote its interpretation of reality as truth" (12). Similarly, a biblical ideology is a living ideology embodied in a biblical text; it is "a complex and contested set of ideas, values, symbols, and aspirations being promoted with social and political force in a given literary complex to persuade the implied audience within that text of the truth of a given ideology" (11).

Habel draws on Aloysius Pieris' notion of ideology from *An Asian Theology of Liberation* (1988). There, Pieris describes ideology as

> (a) a worldview, (b) essentially programmatic, (c) about a this-worldly future to be realized, not without a struggle, in the socio-political order, (d) with the aid of certain tools of analysis or a method of discernment based on its own (that is, ideological) premises, (e) and requiring by its own intrinsic nature to be transcended by the truth it seeks to articulate. (24)

Operating generally with the notion that ideology is neutral, James Kavanagh explains:

> [I]deology designates a rich "system of representations," worked up in specific material practices, which helps form individuals into social subjects who "freely" internalize an appropriate "picture" of their social world and their place in it. Ideology offers the social subject not a set of narrowly "political" ideas but a fundamental framework of assumptions that defines the parameters of the real and the self... It has the function of producing an obvious "reality" that social subjects can assume and accept, precisely as if it had not been socially produced and did not need to be "known" at all. (310–11)

Ideological Criticism and Biblical Interpretation

Biblical scholars employ ideological criticism in considering the authors, texts, and readers of the Bible. Ideological criticism in relation to the world of the author has interests similar to those of historical and social scientific criticism: discerning and describing the original context, production, and canonization of biblical texts. Ideological critics may seek to uncover the "intentions of the author"—at least insofar as these critics discern and expose the political and social realities of the communities for which a text was originally written and the likely aims and persuasive power it might have had with its first audiences.

Other ideological critics use deconstructive criticism. They identify the dominant interpretation of a text and then show how the wrinkles and gaps in the text undercut this interpretation, revealing blind spots the dominant reading ignores (Phillips, 1994). For example, Carol Newsom (1989) carefully describes how discourse about discourse and ideology in Proverbs 1–9 both supports and undermines the ideology of its speaking father.

Still others read "against the grain" of traditional interpretations of biblical texts simply by reminding scholars that the perspectives and theologies advanced by the narrator are not equivalent to, and therefore should not be equated with, the historical realities and religions of the ancient communities (Clines, 1995).

Ideology in relation to the reader is what traditional interpreters often find most suspect. Feminist scholars read through eyes seeking equality for women. Liberation theologians demand justice for the poor and oppressed. Postcolonial interpreters seek freedom from the chains of colonizers.

The political aims of these interpreters may be worthy, but some in the traditional biblical scholarly community dismiss their work, and the reader-response criticism to which it is related, as marginal. Because such ideological criticism is political, modernists may see it at best as irrelevant to serious scholarship and at worst as foolish or dangerous. Traditional scholars may hold this negative view of reader-influenced criticism because they hold modernist assumptions about the relationship of scholars to the truth and meaning of texts or because those who are church people fear that acknowledging multiple interpretive options will undermine the authority of scripture.

For biblical scholars, "ideological criticism," unfortunately, sounds like the name for a method of biblical interpretation, like text criticism, form criticism, or redaction criticism. While scholars engaged in ideological criticism have specific methodological concerns and are often drawn to particular interpretive methods as described above, the practice itself is less a method and more a hermeneutical stance. That is, ideological critics make particular assumptions about the relationships among author, text, and reader and about the ways that people do and should interpret texts. One of the most debated hermeneutical questions among ideological critics is whether texts have ideologies.

Do Texts Have Ideologies?

Some critics insist that texts have ideologies. This seems obvious, since authors are part of a particular society that shapes their worldviews. Authors likewise intend to shape readers by structuring poetic lines, portraying characters, using narratorial perspective and rhetorical strategies, and delivering arguments in ways that either support or challenge a community's governing ideologies. For example, biblical prophets challenged the opulence and injustice of preexilic Israelite societies, and 1 Timothy argues for women's silence and against their teaching men in the church. Alhough we cannot know the intentions of a biblical text's actual author, it seems reasonable to some critics to say that the text itself has an ideology. Meir Sternberg (1985) may be the most extreme proponent of this position. He finds the Bible's ideology and poetics to be so strong that he claims the Bible has a "foolproof composition" that is impossible to counterread (50), so that the Bible inevitably succeeds in indoctrinating (37). Most biblical ideological critics, however, aim to expose and evaluate what they see as the ideologies of biblical texts (Jobling and Pippin, 1992; Bible and Culture Collective, 1995).

Because of the enormous influence of the Bible on Western culture, groups who feel especially oppressed or liberated by particular texts or ways of reading the Bible often speak about the ideology of a biblical text. For example, some feminists see the Bible's prophetic-liberating tradition as a lens through which to criticize the oppressive patriarchal ideologies of other biblical texts (Ruether, 1983). The Bible, in this view, has texts with multiple ideologies, and readers choose their own texts or principles for selecting a "canon within the canon," possibly deciding that some texts are "irredeemable." Other feminist scholars see the whole Bible as bearing the "patriarchal stamp" of its original cultures and choose to abandon it altogether or to defuse some of its texts or concepts in order to avoid reinscribing its dominating practices (Milne, 1988; Fuchs, 1990).

Feminists are not the only ideological critics who may think of biblical texts as having an ideology that one can choose to embrace or repudiate. South African scholar Itumeleng J. Mosala argues for struggle rather than co-opting or colluding with the Bible's hegemonic texts or its "dominant ideological agendas" (1989: 10). Robert Allan Warrior (1989) reminds liberation theologians that God the liberator is also God the conqueror, authorizing annihilation of Canaanites in already inhabited lands. David Clines (1995), in his metacommentary on the way scholars read Amos, rails against commentators who simply repeat the ideology of the text.

Other critics argue that texts don't have ideologies, people do (Fowl, 1995). Many of these scholars would agree that the "Bible has been used as a weapon of imperialism, sexism, and racism" (Pippin, 1996b: 60), but they would hold its readers accountable for the ways they interpret and use the Bible. Scholars on this side of the debate, like their opposing colleagues, seek to uncover ideologies that shaped biblical authors and their original readers. Rather than saying that a text has a certain ideology, however, they are more likely to refer to a text's representing or promulgating particular value systems held by people. Texts may even reveal multiple ideologies. As 1 Samuel shows, there were both pro-monarchy and anti-monarchy ideologies in ancient Israel. Similarly, Paul's view of the relationship of Gentile Christians to the law differs from that of his presumed early Christian "opponents" in Galatia.

Those ideological critics who hold the view that writers, readers, and interpreters, rather than texts, have ideologies look beyond a text's original composition and communities. Phyllis Trible's 1973 essay "Depatriarchalizing in Biblical Interpretation" broke new ground in scholarship on Genesis 2–3 when she fashioned a new feminist interpretation of that influential text to stand over against traditional readings. Jean Higgins (1976), similarly, highlights the uniformity of readings among traditional views of Eve and seeks to discredit them. Michael Cartwright compares interpretations of the curse of Ham in Genesis 9, noting that while racists used the text to justify slavery, African American Christian preachers reinterpreted it to proclaim their people's royal heritage. He observes "a hermeneutic of 'double-consciousness' " that confronts both the "ideological problems and possibilities of the text of the Bible" (142).

Stephen Fowl argues explicitly that texts don't have ideologies by tracing the interpretation of Abraham narratives over centuries (1995). None of the interpreters of Abraham have correctly identified "the ideology" of the biblical text (nor was that the aim of "precritical" scholars). Instead, each interpreter reads the Abraham narratives in ways that best persuade their communities about particular responses to situations they are facing. In our postmodern context, Fowl argues, to speak about a text's "having" an ideology is as unsophisticated or sloppy as continuing to speak about a text's having a meaning. After the "death of the author" (Barthes, 1977), most theories of interpretation acknowledge that meaning does not reside in texts but rather emerges in the meeting of the worlds of author, text, and reader. Ideologies, like meaning, are not captured in texts to be excavated by diligent scholars. Rather, they shape the ways authors and communities of hearers and readers make meaning of the texts they share.

This position–that texts don't have ideologies, people do–allows scholars to continue to pursue investigations about the ideologies of the authors, editors, redactors, and the communities who have heard the biblical texts as they were told, written, collected, became canonical, and continue to be heard both as sacred scripture and as biblical literature. By insisting on ideologies as belonging to humans rather than texts, we can more easily explain the multiplicity of interpretations of a particular text. We can also hold one another accountable for continuing to read texts, especially such influential texts as the Bible, in ways that oppress some people at the expense of others. This view acknowledges that interpreters have both perspectives and commitments that shape our readings, and it calls us to be responsible readers.

David M. Gunn and Danna Nolan Fewell (1993) illustrate the relationship of ideology to responsible reading by means of one of Aesop's fables. A man claims the superiority of men to lions on the basis of a statue depicting a man defeating a lion. A lion, not persuaded by the man's boast, observes that the statue proves nothing because it was made by a man. The lion in the fable points out that ideologies are part of the way we represent our world to ourselves. Sculptures, paintings, architecture, advertisements, film, and literature—so many aspects of our cultures—both embody and attempt to persuade others of particular ideologies. What viewers and readers find in these art works and artifacts is also shaped by our own identities and the ideologies of the cultures and communities we inhabit. It is not simply a matter of depositing and retrieving particular content, message, or meaning. The "banking model" is no longer an apt metaphor for education, nor is encoding and decoding of messages an adequate model of communication or hermeneutics.

To summarize, biblical ideological critics still argue over whether a text has an ideology. Even so, most adopt a hermeneutical stance with the following assumptions. First, meaning is produced by the interaction among author, text, and reader. Second, texts and their interpretations are shaped through a struggle between competing ideologies. Third, there is no value-neutral interpretation or biblical scholarship. Adopting hermeneutical assumptions like these shows that biblical scholarship may be on the verge of acknowledging postmodern realities that other disciplines have come to terms with in the past century.

Ideology, Postmodernism, and Ethical Biblical Scholarship

A. K. M. Adam has described postmodernism as "antifoundational, antitotalizing, and demystifying" (1995a: 5). Some review of how these aspects of postmodernism have played out in other disciplines during the twentieth century may be helpful in understanding the role played by ideology in arguing for a more modest interpretive epistemology.

Kurt Gödel shocked the world of philosophy and logic in 1931 by demonstrating the rational basis of antifoundationalism. Essentially, he showed that any system as simple and sophisticated as arithmetic is either incomplete or inconsistent; that is, it would include propositions that are true but that cannot be proved true within the system. It is not simply that philosophers have not yet found the right foundation or basis for reason. There is no foundation—no set of assumptions—that could prevent the undesirable consequence of the insufficiency of any proposed system. No foundation can be adequate for what one wants it to do. Like philosophy after Gödel, ideological criticism recognizes that the choice of initial assumptions is somewhat arbitrary, that assumptions shape interpretations, and that no interpretation or set of interpretive assumptions can ever be entirely sufficient.

Physicists have now made peace with paradox. For example, the agreement that light is modeled best by both waves and particles suggests an antitotalizing approach to science. A single totalizing metaphor or schema may be inadequate to the physical reality. Similarly, the creation narratives of

Genesis 1–2 show that ancient Israelites accepted ambiguity and recognized the value of multiple descriptions rather than attempting a totalizing account. Scientists generally, in contrast to some persistent public misconceptions about science that many social scientists and biblical scholars still hold, have abandoned the modernist, positivist view of science, preferring a more realistic recognition that their disciplines operate through models, persuasion, and community protocols. Ideological critics similarly recognize that interpretations must persuade their audiences and that rhetorics function differently within various communities.

Nineteenth-century mathematicians, faced with the realities of non-Euclidean geometries, discovered that truths could be inconsistent yet still "true." For example, a triangle in Euclidean geometry has exactly 180 degrees, but in non-Euclidean geometry (say, on a globe) a triangle might have three right angles, or 270 degrees. Such troubling new knowledge led to a demystifying of the nature of mathematics as a discipline. Its axiomatic basis is now revealed and accepted–even celebrated, as non-Euclidean geometries later proved better suited to the curves of relativity theory's space-time than the prior "truths" of Euclidean geometry. Ideological criticism, likewise, makes claims that are modest, yet still valuable.

Elisabeth Schüssler Fiorenza observes that biblical scholarship as a discipline still clings to scientist assumptions belonging to the "positivist value-neutral stance" that gave birth to its important historical-critical methods (1989: 6). By acknowledging these ideological roots and adopting an ethics of historical reading coupled with an ethics of accountability, she proposes what many scholars who embrace ideological criticism of the Bible hope: that "biblical scholarship can transform its 'ivory tower mentality' in such a way that it can contribute to the public-political articulation of a religious vision for a more humane future of the world" (1989: 6).

By acknowledging the pervasiveness and unavoidability of ideologies, good and bad, biblical interpreters in our rhetorical contexts can choose simply to "play" with texts and market entertaining readings that "sell," or we can assume responsibility to persuade one another and our communities and nations about matters vital to us all through interpretations of biblical texts that have transformed us.

intertextuality
Timothy K. Beal

Intertextuality is a theory that conceives of every text as a set of relations between texts, an intersection of texts that are themselves intersections of other texts, and so on. Every text is a locus of intersections, overlaps, and collisions between other texts. Every text is an *intertext,* that is, a between-text (*inter,* "between"), a paradoxical locus of dislocation, without center and without boundaries.

By *text,* moreover, we are not referring narrowly to written and verbal material. *Text* is used here in its broadest sense as anything that can be read. A poem is a text, but so is a ritual. A Bible is a text, but so is a person. A speech is a text, but so is a face. *Reading,* likewise, must be taken in the very broadest sense, as attending to, looking at, studying. These broad definitions of text and reading are close to anthropologist Clifford Geertz's conception of a text as any cultural form that can be interpreted. Indeed, Geertz's own understanding of culture in terms of *webs* of significance suggests that his definition of text is in many respects intertextual: "As in more familiar exercises in close reading, one can start anywhere in a culture's repertoire of forms and end up anywhere else" (1973: 453). On the other hand, the broader notions of text and reading assumed by the theory of intertextuality need not imply (as does Geertz) that the larger cultural webs in which texts are intertwined, and in which we read them, somehow constitute a complex yet unified cultural whole that carries within it particular meanings to be discovered through interpretation (Masuzawa, 1998: 87–92).

The theory of intertextuality was first developed in relation to Mikhail Bakhtin's notion of dialogism by Julia Kristeva in 1969 as part of a larger critique of modern conceptions of texts as discrete, self-enclosed containers of meaning. Contrary to this conception, intertextuality draws attention to the fact that every text is "constructed as a mosaic of quotations" (1980: 66). Every text is a "field of transpositions of various signifying systems (an inter-textuality)" (1984: 60).

Neither was Kristeva's theory of intertextuality narrowly focused on literary texts. She focused especially on intertextuality as a theory of *intersubjectivity,* that is, on the constitution of any individual subject not as an independent, autonomous agent, but rather as an intersubjectivity, an intersection of multiple, often clashing categories and facets of identity, in which the sum of the parts make up something more and something less than a whole. Just as every text

128

is an intertext, so every subject (every self, every consciousness, every person) is an *intersubject,* a between-space, a centerless field of transpositions of various signifying systems, a more or less unified, more or less stable convergence of personas, roles, voices, images, narratives, and so on.

How might this *theory,* as a way of conceiving of textuality, relate to *method,* as approach or way through (Greek *meta-hodos,* "with way"), in biblical studies? For one, it reveals something important about the process of interpretation itself, namely that one's arrival at a particular interpretation is always a matter of exhaustion and despair. The tracing out of intertextual relations is endless and, quite literally, pointless. Therefore, any interpretive conclusion is a matter of giving up, shutting down, or maybe petering out. The interpreter makes a de-cision, a cut, which cuts off other possible relations, positions roadblocks against other intersections. And where I make my cuts and set up my roadblocks is likely determined not only by accident and oversight but also by the hermeneutical and ideological norms—spoken and unspoken—established within my academic discipline and within my other networks of affiliation and accountability.

Any method in biblical studies is a way through the indeterminacy of intertextuality. Any method opens up interpretive possibilities by cutting others off. The method developed by Michael Fishbane for studying innerbiblical exegesis, for example, focuses on how later Hebrew texts often work from earlier ones within the boundaries of the literary canon of the Hebrew Bible. In so doing it shows how "the Hebrew Bible has an exegetical dimension *in its own right*" (1985: 14). In a somewhat similar vein, Richard Hays's approach (1989; developed from John Hollander, 1981) attends to the literary echoes of specific Hebrew Bible texts in the letters of Paul within the Christian biblical canon. Both of these very fruitful approaches, it is noted, open up interpretation of certain intertextual relations while cutting off others. Both do so, moreover, in a way that takes the closure of a particular canon of scripture for granted, thereby reinforcing those canonical boundaries.

Perhaps the most radical implication that intertextuality carries into biblical studies is an interrogation of the very notions and assumptions of "the biblical" and "the canonical," that is, of the widely presumed possibility of maintaining a secure, closed canon—reduced to particular written texts identified with particular writing subjects originating in particular formative periods for a particular religious tradition. Our commonly held definitions of written texts, writing subjects, origins, and religious traditions are all called into question and potentially dynamited by the theory of intertextuality. Visual, material, and audio culture, whether ancient Near Eastern or contemporary South American, cannot be automatically dismissed or precluded from "the biblical." From the visuality and materiality of writing, ink, pages, scrolls, codices, and books to hypertextual multilingual multibibles; from Donatello's sculpture *David* to Chris Ofili's painting *The Holy Virgin Mary* to Eliseo Subiela's film *Man Facing Southeast;* from Mozart to a sermon on cable television; from a gospel story told in a Guatemalan base community to Laurie Anderson's performance of *Stories from the Nerve Bible:* Where does the biblical stop and the extrabiblical, deuterocanonical, or interpretive begin?

Intertextuality draws attention to the uncontainable and unstable fluidity of "the biblical" as it seeps into and through our various overlapping and clashing constructs of culture and society, past, present, and future; and it demands self-critical honesty, at least, about why and how we cut it off where and when we do.

irigaray
Faith Kirkham Hawkins

> [I]t is necessary to make sexual difference pass from the level of simple naturalness, of instinct, to that of a sexuated subjectivity, respectful of the self and other. This implies a recognition of the other as the representative of a part of nature and spirituality irreducible to the part that I represent…Sexual difference compels us to a radical refounding of dialectic, of ontology, of theology. The negative, the mystery of the unknowable, are unsurpassable in the sexuated relation. (Pluhacek and Bostic: 357)

Among the more recent elements of Luce Irigaray's philosophical interventions has been a "phenomenology of the caress," in which she explores the possibility for "a reciprocal gesture capable of bringing about an awakening to another level of intersubjectivity" (Pluhacek and Bostic: 356). In both method and goal, this project well represents Luce Irigaray's work (she expresses "a horror" of being referred to solely by the patronymic Irigaray; see Hirsh and Olson: 102). Her method has been to examine elements overlooked, ignored, or repressed within the tradition of Western philosophy. Small gestures such as the caress and large questions such as the nature of sexual difference and its implications share the status of the unrecognized within philosophy, and thus both can be found under Luce Irigaray's lens. Her investigations of things repressed within the Western philosophical tradition work toward the goal of challenging the "economy of the Same" that silences the feminine and, indeed, all thought and all entities defined within it as Other. As she herself notes, there is a great deal at stake in this challenge. Were sexual difference taken seriously–that is, were male and female embraced, not as mirror images of one another but within their independent specificity–the world as we conceive it would of necessity be radically reformulated. Yet just such a radical vision guides her philosophical endeavors:

> We still have to await the god, remain ready and open to prepare a way for his coming. And, with him, for ourselves, to prepare, not an implacable decline, but a new birth, a new era in history.

> Beyond the circularity of discourse, of the nothing that is in and of being. When the copula no longer veils the abyssal burial of the other in a gift of language which is neuter only in that it forgets the difference from which it draws its strength and energy. (1993a: 129)

131

The idea that language—and indeed all creation, "from the humblest detail of everyday life to the 'grandest'"—draws its strength and energy from difference is at the very center of Luce Irigaray's work: "This creation would be our opportunity, from the humblest detail of everyday life to the 'grandest,' by means of the opening of a *sensible transcendental* that comes through us, of which *we would be* the mediators and bridges" (1993a: 129; emphasis in the original). She describes three phases within her work, each of which contributes to her larger project of creating discursive space for intersubjective relationships between (and among) women and men. In the first phase, she "showed how a single subject, traditionally the masculine subject, had constructed the world and interpreted the world according to a single perspective" (Hirsh and Olson: 97). *Speculum of the Other Woman* (1974; English Translation 1985), *This Sex Which Is Not One* (1977; ET 1985), and *An Ethics of Sexual Difference* (1984; ET 1993a) most directly represent this portion of her work, though already in *Ethics* she began to move in new directions. In the second phase, she shifted her attention from exposure of "the auto-mono-centrism of the western subject" into explorations of the possibilities for "a second subject." In works such as portions of *Ethics* and *Sexes and Genealogies* (1987; ET 1993b), Luce Irigaray attempted to "define those mediations that could permit the existence of a feminine subjectivity—that is to say, another subject" besides the singular masculine subject allowed within the Western tradition (Hirsh and Olson: 97). Most recently, with works such as *Je, Tu, Nous* (1990; ET 1993c), *I Love to You* (1992; ET 1996), and *Être Deux* (1997), she has explored the relations between (male and female) subjects. However, this schema of the trajectory of her work, even though based on her own description, oversimplifies matters somewhat. Each stage exhibits traces of the processes and goals of the other stages, making it both unwise and difficult to draw sharp lines between the stages as if they were unrelated to one another, or as if they could be understood apart from one another.

For instance, "When Our Lips Speak Together," the final essay of *This Sex,* is both a criticism of the ways in which the Western tradition forbids feminine discourse (the first stage) and an argument for and articulation of that very feminine discourse (the second stage). Moreover, the essay (which is addressed from "I" to "you") already points to the possibilities for and problems facing true intersubjectivity, and thus hints at the third stage of Luce Irigaray's work as well. Just as the earlier works indicate the stages to follow, her latter works both presume and continue to create space for the existence of two true subjects even as they articulate the possibility of "a sexuated subjectivity, respectful of the self and other" (Pluhacek and Bostic: 357). In some ways, her earliest work becomes accessible only in light of her later work, and vice versa, such that Luce Irigaray is best read circularly, in conversation with herself as well as with those to whom she plays interlocutor.

Perhaps because of these complexities, many feminists initially reacted to Luce Irigaray with no small degree of criticism, considering her work essentialist (see Schor, 1994a, for a review of scholarly responses to her early work). Additional factors in this reception of Luce Irigaray's early work in North America include difficulties with and delays in reading her work in translation, the unfamiliarity of her North American readers with the intellectual traditions she engaged, and, perhaps most importantly, the timing of her entrée into the North American consciousness. In the late 1970s and early 1980s, North American feminism was in the throes of "the essentialist debates," such that all feminist scholars were subject to categorization on one or the other side of the divide. Schor's "This Essentialism Which Is Not One: Coming to Grips with Irigaray" marked a turning point both within the essentialist debates in women's studies and within the tide of critical responses to Luce Irigaray's work (Schor, 1994b; originally published in 1989).

In some ways, concern about essentialism is an understandable reaction to texts like *Speculum* and *This Sex,* both of which use the female body as a staging area for theoretical interventions into the economy of the same. In *Speculum,* for instance, Luce Irigaray explores Freudian analyses of female sexual development, and so focuses in great detail on feminine desire, sexuality, and bodies. Through her explication of Freud, she demonstrates that within his work on female sexual development, the male serves as the "norm" against which the female is judged and found to be lacking. A conspicuous example of this is his theory of penis envy, which "drives everything said now and later about female sexuality" (51). Through the critical point of entry offered by feminine sexual development, Luce Irigaray describes not only the phallocentrism (defined by Elizabeth Grosz as "the use of *one* model of subjectivity, the male, by which all others are positively or negatively defined. Others are constructed as variations of this singular type of subject," 1989: 105) of Freud's theories, but also that of the entire "economy of the Same" within which he operates. It is in this sense that the feminine becomes a staging area for her critical inquiries.

Luce Irigaray does not limit herself to the demonstration of the extent to which the phallocentric economy of the Same relies for signification on the repression, denigration, and attempted exclusion of the feminine subject. Rather, she demonstrates the incompleteness of this exclusion of the feminine. The repression or exclusion of the feminine is incomplete because phallocentrism in fact requires the feminine as the negative or mirror that allows the (masculine) subject to exist. Yet the phallocentric economy must attempt to exclude all things feminine: "If woman had desires other than 'penis-envy,' this would call into question the unity, the uniqueness, the simplicity of the mirror charged with sending man's image back to him–albeit inverted. Call into question its flatness" (1985a: 51). As Ellen T. Armour summarizes this element of her argument, "The general grammar of western culture inscribes itself as a cultural imaginary. Matter/world/woman are linked together, rigorously controlled and circumscribed by being relegated to the outside of what really counts even as it/they slip away from circumscription. Though rejected, they also serve as the ground, or raw material, of philosophical speculation" (112).

Luce Irigaray then theorizes all that remains: women's desire, women's sexuality, and women's bodies. Thus, she begins from women's bodies (desire, sexuality), moves from there to critical analysis of the phallocentric economy, and then returns to women's bodies to challenge that economy and further demonstrate its insufficiency as descriptor of human reality. Because of her focus on the feminine, and particularly on feminine desire, sexuality, and bodies, many readers initially took her to be presuming a "feminine essence," presumably universal for all women, and closely related to if not wholly determined by biology. However, it is more accurate–particularly in light of her later works toward an intersubjectivity that respects difference–to see her focus on woman's body, desire, and sexuality as a strategic move. Luce Irigaray undoubtedly has multiple goals within her work, and one of them is assuredly to begin to offer analyses of "the feminine." However, her overarching interest in dismantling the economy of the Same, and her hope of creating space wherein all that is repressed within this economy might speak, suggests that such analyses are not her primary goal, nor are they the center of her work. Thus, to judge her work as if these analyses were at its core is to misunderstand her philosophical project and the manner in which she goes about it.

One clearly strategic element is Luce Irigaray's advocacy and practice of *mimesis.* "One must assume the feminine role deliberately," she contends in *This Sex,* in order to critique and challenge the phallocratic system of Western metaphysics. Mimicry is an indirect approach, in that it "convert[s] a form of subordination into an affirmation, and thus [is] to begin to thwart it." Because the phallocratic economy of the Same recognizes only the masculine Subject, "a direct feminine challenge to this condition means demanding to speak as a 'masculine' subject," which–though possible–"would maintain sexual indifference" (1985b: 76). Moreover, "Speaking (as) woman is not speaking of woman. It is not a matter of producing a discourse of which woman would be the object, or the subject. That said, by *speaking (as) woman,* one may attempt to provide a place for the 'other' as feminine" (1985b: 135).

Herein the strategic and non-essentialist element of Luce Irigaray's mimetic appeal to the feminine becomes clear. The possibility that women could assume the (masculine) subject position and the undesirability of "producing a discourse of which woman would be the object or the subject" indicate that at one level, her argument is not that women are "outside" this system of representation (although they are), but that "the feminine" is. Margaret Whitford offers insight into this conundrum when she notes that, for Luce Irigaray, because women have always and only been defined by and in relation to men, "*woman does not yet exist...*[S]he argues that not only do we still need woman, but that woman has not yet arrived. Essence is not a given, behind us, but a collective creation, ahead of us, a horizon" (1991: 138–39).

Recognition of the strategic role that "the feminine" and the female play within Luce Irigaray's thought is not to suggest that they are primarily metaphorical or strategic. She is, rather, seriously concerned with the nature (identity) of woman, particularly because women have only been the objects of "the masculine gaze," of men's theories. Whitford recognizes that there are essentialist elements within Luce Irigaray's work; she makes no claims that Luce Irigaray is always consistent: "She hovers between a referential and a non-referential discourse, between discursive strategy (the 'two lips') and apparently essentialist ontological strategy (the sexuation of nature…), between mimeticism and prophetic vision" (1991: 135). But Whitford argues that even these have a purpose within the overall and non-essentialist endeavor. Because women are now and always have been omitted from the symbolic order, to avoid any definition of woman (in an attempt to avoid essentialism) is to leave them "homeless." "The problem that Irigaray is dealing with, then, is: how to give women an imaginary and symbolic home, how to introduce women into the symbolic economy, by giving women an identity so that there are two interrelating changing economies, without falling back into identity as sameness" (1991: 136). Whitford's formulation places Luce Irigaray's essentialist gestures into their proper context, notably the goal of "two interrelating changing economies," a goal she expresses herself when she writes of the possibility for a "sexuated relation" or "intersubjectivity."

While it is impossible within the scope of this article to review the full spectrum of the results of her work, one is particularly important to describe here. This is the extent to which her analysis of the economy of the Same and its suppression of the feminine describes the effects of this economy on all of those marked within it as Other. Theorized as the "mirror" of the masculine, the feminine is impossible to see in its independent specificity: "The flat mirror reflects the greater part of women's sexual organs only as a hole" (1985a: 89 n. 92). Such distortion is in fact the fate suffered within this "specular" economy of everything seen only in relation to "the Same." Although she focuses only on sexual difference, it is evident that women and men of color, for instance, are also "reflected" in distorted fashion within the economy of the Same. This distortion is but one effect of being defined as the "Other of the Same"; Luce Irigaray's analysis of the position of women within the economy of the Same suggests several others that are equally (if differently) applicable to diverse groups defined as "other" within the economy of the Same. Because the masculine holds a monopoly on the subject position, the feminine (and by extension, any "other") is limited to an object (and abject) position, unable to act as "subject" in any way. The "Other of the Same" is limited to specific, highly regulated symbolic and practical functions–all of them designed to serve in some way the male subject and the ideology that constructs him. However, just as the feminine position can be adopted mimetically in order to challenge and subvert the economy of the Same, so too can other "outsider" positions offer the potential for such disruption. Although Luce Irigaray considers sexual difference to be the primary difference to which the economy of the Same is indifferent, it is not the only one. Thus, her work offers insight into the conditions of difference within the logic of identity (in her terms, the economy of the Same), insight of considerable force and potential.

Although feminist theologians have begun to practice Irigarayan readings, as well as to examine the role "the divine" plays within her thought, few biblical interpreters have yet mined the possibilities Luce Irigaray offers for new directions in biblical interpretation. These possibilities are far too numerous to outline here, in part because of the complexity and variety within her work. Following her schema of her work, however, it is possible to identify three types of Irigarayan gestures that biblical interpreters and biblical theologians might profitably explore.

One such possibility is to expose, as Irigaray does with Freud, Plato, Kant, and others within the Western philosophical tradition, the ways in which biblical texts operate within and offer support to the phallocentric economy of the Same. This project would follow along the lines of feminist critical engagements with "malestream" theologies, engagements that argued that traditional conceptions of "sin" (for instance, as a form of "pride") and "salvation" resulted from a masculinist perspective masquerading as a universal. Just as Anselm and Luther provide fertile ground for such investigations into and challenges of phallocratic theology, so too do biblical texts ranging from Leviticus to Paul. Thus, this approach would emulate the first stage of Luce Irigaray's work, in which she demonstrated the pervasiveness of the phallocentric perspective within Western philosophical thought. It might also be extended beyond the question of sexual difference, to consider how the economy of the Same shapes biblical constructions of a variety of "others" (such as "the nations" within Hebrew Bible texts, "Jews" within some New Testament texts, etc.).

A second Irigarayan gesture would be to explore the ways in which biblical texts include or provide resources for "the existence of...another subject." From the perspective of biblical theology, of course, the potential for a religious imaginary in which God and humanity are both subjects is one such area to which Irigarayan biblical interpretation might move. Additionally, there is potential for such analysis within the biblical texts as they focus on humans, that is, within their anthropology as well as their theology. For instance, although mimesis within biblical texts has been recognized as an authoritarian gesture (by Elizabeth Castelli, for example), Luce Irigaray's work suggests that we might explore the ways in which marginalized groups within the biblical texts challenge the dominant groups by way of the mimetic play Luce Irigaray enacts. The reliance of female characters on deception, for instance, may be an instance of such *mimesis,* at least to the extent that women rely on the very characteristics attributed to them by the dominant view in order to challenge the power structures upheld by that view. (Feminist interpreters have given significant attention to the deceptive behavior of women characters, particularly within the Hebrew Bible; whether or how this deception enacts Irigarayan *mimesis* remains unexplored.) Moreover, it may not be women alone who practice such mimesis: Men, and also social groups, within the Bible may do so. An additional critical element of this sort of analysis of *mimesis* within the Bible may allow exploration of how potentially "second subjects" (for instance, the early followers of Jesus as a marginalized group within Second Temple Judaism) moved from *mimesis* to dominance, and so enable "history [to] repeat itself, [to] revert to sameness: to phallocratism" (1985b: 33).

A third arena within biblical interpretation to which the work of Luce Irigaray may point is the possibility for "intersubjectivity" within the biblical texts. As Ellen T. Armour expresses it, Luce Irigaray attempts to articulate an alternative economy to the economy of the Same. "This other economy privileges difference rather than sameness and plurality rather than unity. She finds *one* reflection of this economy in a different accounting of women's bodies" (127). There may be other reflections of this economy, which is itself an expression of and the necessary precondition for truly intersubjective relationships, within the Biblical texts. For instance, Luce Irigaray's phenomenology of the caress as the possible expression of such intersubjectivity calls to mind the importance of "touch" within the healing stories of the New Testament. Through Irigarayan analysis of passages such as Luke 8:43–48, biblical interpreters may find wholly new, and potentially intersubjective, answers to the question "Who touched me?"

jameson
Roland Boer

At this moment of rampant transnational capitalism, Fredric Jameson is a welcome figure: a Marxist literary critic of uncommon intellectual and critical ability, increasingly acclaimed as one of the leading critics writing today. Self-consciously working, with others like Terry Eagleton, in creating a Marxist culture in the longue durée of late capitalism, Jameson's relevance for biblical criticism lies in five areas: the crucial questions of Marxist literary criticism; a recovery of its tradition; Marxism and postmodernism; the effort to periodize capitalism; and an untiring focus on utopia, socialism, and capitalism's end.

The Basics

Marxism has generated a terminology that can be forbidding to the neophyte, yet these terms have also pervaded other disciplines—terms such as *class* and *ideology*, denoting the structures of society into various groups according to social, economic, and cultural criteria (class), and the ideas, beliefs, philosophies, religions, and so on that make these classes what they are (ideology). Marxism takes this a step further and notes the inevitable conflict between classes and ideologies, especially between ruling and ruled classes. Another important pair is base (infrastructure) and superstructure: The former designates economics, the production of necessary and luxury items for human survival. It is related to the superstructure—the arena of culture, ideology, politics, the judiciary, and the state—by means of social class (also called the relations of production). For Jameson the final reference point is the base, or economic infrastructure, although he wishes to avoid a crude Marxism where economics becomes determinative.

Against a sense that postmodernism denies history, Jameson insists on history, although highly abstract, as the final horizon. The key term is *mode of production*. Commonly understood to designate the base, Jameson takes it in a more inclusive sense, bringing the whole panoply of items of Marxist analysis—ideology, culture, law, philosophy, state, class, superstructure, base—into the vast epochal term mode of production. These epochs are not static, but continually mutate in the process of time, bringing about different modes of production, such as feudalism, capitalism, or tribal organization, in which the nature and interrelation of the various categories change. But the greatest immediate value of the idea of mode of production is that it functions to relativize the era in which we live—capitalism—as an era with an origin, history, and passing away. There is a potential for such a system to break through the regular logjams of the discipline. For instance, in the continuing debate over the role of archaeological material in the search for Israel's origin, it seems that the material archaeological discoveries give themselves less to specific historical events and sequences than to questions of class and social structure, cultural and religious practice, and economics.

Other terms important for Jameson include the nature and function of dialectics; literature and aesthetics in the light of ideology; the nature and role of commodification and reification; the patterns of domination, hegemony, and alienation; and the labor theory of value, use value, and the four types of exchange value. Because all the items mentioned thus far are features of capitalism, they must affect the way biblical studies operates. To begin with, commodification—a basic economic, social, and ideological feature of capitalism—is already part of the fabric of academia. Biblical studies is commodified through and through, without our knowing it, so to speak, or at least pretending that we don't know. And this takes place at the most mundane level of being paid for a job or task, since we sell labor power or intellectual capital to an employer, write books and articles for a capitalist publishing industry, and compete with each other not only for jobs but for grant funds.

Yet a discipline like biblical studies does not merely replicate capitalism; rather, while taking into its capillaries the patterns of reification and commodification, it may also develop an opposition to precisely these items. Thus, an undercurrent of debate continues about the infiltration of market principles into the academic scene. In the U.S. this may be expected, but in places such as Australia, England, or Scotland there seems to be an assumption that one can resist their introduction. I am skeptical that such resistance is, in fact, possible: It is possible that biblical studies, with the wealth of utopian imagery available to it, may be able to foreshadow something entirely different beyond capitalism.

The way of looking at the situation of contemporary biblical studies in the preceding paragraph is based on one of Jameson's favored models, that of situation and response. Rather than seeing culture, or a particular text, as a mere reflection of a social and economic situation, these items function more commonly as responses to the situation. Such responses may be reflective, but they may also be oppositional, sometimes in a regressive and reactionary manner and at other times in a more utopian and progressive manner.

The Tradition

Marxism now has a distinct tradition of writing and scholarship. It is not as long as biblical studies, but its pedigree includes some great minds: Marx and Engels, Lenin, Mao Zedong, Sartre, Barthes, Brecht, Adorno, Benjamin, Bloch, Althusser, Macherey, Lukacs, Fanon, Gramsci, Eagleton, and Jameson himself.

One of the values of Jameson's work, alongside his interest in popular culture, science fiction, film, video, architecture, postmodernism, modernism, and literary criticism, is his recovery of figures from the tradition. After the Sartre book of 1961, Jameson's first published piece, in 1967, was on T. W. Adorno. Many of the essays that followed were gathered in the critical survey *Marxism and Form* (1971), where Adorno, Benjamin, Bloch, Lukacs, Marcuse, Schiller, and Sartre were presented and discussed. Jameson returned to the tradition with the Adorno book *Late Marxism,* in 1990, and then the recent *Brecht and Method* (1998).

What is noticeable about these figures is the way their names attach to a particular question of the tradition with which they deal: Gramsci on hegemony, Althusser on ideology, Sartre on seriality, Lukacs on reification, Brecht on the estrangement effect, and, of course, Jameson on postmodernism. Needless to say, these writers dealt with far more than these issues, and Jameson is at pains to indicate the complexities of their thoughts.

Yet one of the most urgent tasks of biblical criticism is an introduction to and reflection on this tradition of Marxist literary criticism. It seems to me that a significant part of Jameson's influence on biblical studies lies in drawing attention to the key writers in this tradition, but it also requires a more sustained reflection specifically for biblical critics. (I am in fact working on such a project at the moment: a critical study of Adorno, Benjamin, Bloch, Althusser, Gramsci, Lukacs, Eagleton, and Jameson that seeks not only their importance for biblical studies, but also the deeper thesis that they themselves are enabled in their criticism by biblical criticism.)

Such an effort would provide much-needed alternative perspectives, specifically in light of a Marxist understanding of the function of literature, on crucial areas such as the debate over Israel's origins, the ways political entities are produced, the creation and production of such literature as the Bible in the first place, the development of traditions, and the elusive importance of history (in, for example, the search for the historical Jesus).

Marxism and Metacommentary

A problem that Marxism, like religion, faces within postmodernism is its claim to a grand narrative. I am speaking of the idea of modes of production and the narrative that traces such modes through, from hunting and gathering (primitive communism and tribal society) through neolithic agriculture (hierarchical kinship societies), the Asiatic mode of production (oriental despotism), the ancient mode (slave-based production and oligarchical society), feudalism, capitalism, and communism. This narrative is no less audacious than the Christian, Muslim, Jewish, or any other reading of history, but what tends to be forgotten is that it is not so much an inevitable linear progression as a reflection on the historical forms of various economic and social organizations and the potential for future forms.

While Jameson, as I do, finds the abstract (and therefore, according to Georg Lukacs, highly concrete) notion of modes of production very useful in the interpretation of texts, he is also aware of the challenge to master narratives posed by postmodernism. His response is metacommentary, which is a way of recognizing the plethora of narratives, or interpretations of texts, that arise. For the modes of production narrative, this means that there is less a single sequence than a whole series of possibilities, sequences, and overlaps.

For biblical criticism, metacommentary involves commenting on the commentators (something biblical critics may claim as their own inaugural practice) and allows space for the multiple interpretations to exist, but it also asks about the plausibility of these interpretations and seeks to discern the more persuasive from the less. Thus, it is not merely the text itself that becomes an issue but also the nature of the interpretations, the way they construct their arguments, the methods they display, the strategies of persuasion, and so on (for an example that focuses on Martin Noth, see my *Novel Histories*).

A typical Jameson reading (if there is such a thing) often begins with various interpretive possibilities or options before indicating how they fare in light of a Marxist interpretation. While Jameson agrees that Marxism must take its place as one method among others, ready to risk its neck in the contest of interpretations, he also favors Marxist criticism and often works it so that a Marxist reading will come out on top.

In fact, Jameson also has a distinctive method that attempts to provide some order to the variety that exists within Marxist criticism, and it may be regarded as a particular form of metacommentary for Marxism. The method works at three levels. The first concerns the particular text, focusing on questions of form, ideology, contradiction, and the immediate political history within which the text functions as a response. The second, in a Hegelian move, goes wider, situating the text as one player among a range of others in a contested ideological field. With the ideological focus, class conflict becomes important. The third, which operates with the widest notion of modes of production, seeks traces or figures of such modes in the text being interpreted. Significantly, this method connects the relation between base and super-structure (synchrony) with the history of modes of production (diachrony). The use of this method for biblical interpretation requires a more detailed knowledge of Jameson's work as well as a sensitivity to signals a biblical text gives out at the various levels. Under normal circumstances (that of Jameson himself), not all levels of the analysis work at the same time: Often one will be sufficient.

Periodizing Biblical Studies

There are two final dimensions relevant for biblical studies: The first is the effect on biblical studies of Jameson's vast historicizing effort for capitalism. Working with the assumption that socioeconomic phases have their own cultural dimensions, Jameson has argued that there have been three phases of capitalist culture—realism, modernism, and postmodernism.

Characterized in various ways, the clearest difference between them lies in the signifier-signified relation. In realism, the relation is direct: The signifier points directly to the signified, as in the historical novel in which the description is understood to depict accurately the historical period in question. Once realism is regarded as a particular effect, determined by the ways it is represented, we have modernism, where the relation between signifier and signified is much more tenuous and problematic. For example, what really happened may no longer be found in the text, which now becomes one piece of evidence for the reconstruction of that history. It is assumed that the signified can be located, but the task has become much more difficult.

For Jameson, modernism is the cultural period (roughly 1848 to 1945) that expresses the era of monopoly or imperial capitalism, the phase that saw competition between the imperial nations of Europe for control of the globe, whereas realism belongs to the first emergence of capitalism, to the time of the daring individual entrepreneur and of the first flush of the Enlightenment and its legacy. The earliest stage of contemporary biblical criticism lies in this first stage, particularly the search for the original text that animated text critics like Tischendorf and the development of what was once known as "lower" criticism. The contrast with "higher" criticism, or what we have come to call historical criticism, indicates an unconscious awareness of the periods of biblical criticism. Historical criticism, developed in the period that coincides with modernism, was also acutely aware of the distance between the signifier (the biblical text) and the signified (the history of Israel or of the early church) that historical criticism was designed in the end to produce. The scandal of historical criticism was that it assumed that the text did not refer directly to the history about which it purported to speak.

Postmodernism, the third cultural phase of what is now multi- or transnational capitalism, has virtually dissevered the link between signifier and signified, with the result that the surface-depth model of analysis (the depth provides what is real beyond the surface) of modernism is now discarded. The depth becomes another surface, which is all there is: The "truth is out there," everywhere and multiple. This third cultural phase is connected with the most developed form of capitalism—late capitalism—and it finds a distinct presence in biblical criticism with the breakdown of the dominance of historical criticism and the explosion of various methods for interpreting the Bible: reader response, psychoanalysis, deconstruction, poststructuralism, post-colonialism, feminism, queer theory, ideological criticism, and so on. Beyond these approaches, however, lies the underlying logic of postmodernism itself, which understands the variety of interpretations as a range of competitors, each seeking to outdo and be more persuasive than the other in the marketplace of interpretations.

Utopia, Socialism, and the End of Capitalism

Biblical criticism is not doomed to remain within capitalism, given over forever to market dynamics, for a key item on Jameson's agenda has been the construction within the most overdeveloped capitalist nation on earth of a Marxist culture. Marx argued that the most advanced capitalist places will also be the most decayed and ready for revolution, and so it is appropriate for Jameson to work in the U.S.

This relies on Jameson's notion that culture is not merely a reflection of an economic phase but may also function as a harbinger of something radically different. A Marxist culture, however piecemeal and fledgling, will then provide a partial glimpse of a utopian, that is, socialist or communist, world. If Jameson is right–and in this respect he may well, like Marx, be right–then his work may be regarded as literature that strains toward what is new and almost unthinkable at present.

Although it may initially seem difficult to locate biblical studies within this, one need only think of the wealth of utopian imagery in the Bible to realize that religious texts trade on the expectation of a world radically different from this one, that they seek to provide hope in a religious sense by means of such images. In this way they also provide a flash, every now and then, of a world in which people behave and think radically differently than in this one. This may be best expressed through the fundamental notion of a change in human nature: Both Marxism and religion assume that it is possible.

Yet there is another way in which biblical criticism may be involved– through a realization that biblical criticism is but a subset of the much wider discipline, literary (and cultural) criticism. In this wider context, biblical critics may contribute to the construction of an alternative to capitalism in the production and sharing of writing and teaching. In other words, biblical criticism may form part of the Marxist literary culture that seeks to develop its already healthy life.

Conclusion

I have left until last the question that for many winds its way in with any mention of Marxist criticism: Why Marxism, for biblical criticism, at this historical moment, when communism as a political and social experiment everywhere seems to have failed? I have my own reasons, particularly the symbiotic relation between Marxism and religion, but for Jameson there are two major ones. First, Marxism provides the most comprehensive answer to the personal dilemma of anyone who lives under the vast systems of capitalism, and that is the ability to make sense of the place of the individual within the incomprehensibly huge social situations and historical epochs that normally slip outside one's consciousness. Marxism, is, in other words, the only ideology that makes sense of this relation. Second, far from being obsolete, Marxism is the tool par excellence for interpreting capitalism, since it arose in the hands of Marx as an effort to analyze capitalism with a view to envisaging its demise. Thus, the permutations of capitalism merely generate more refined forms of Marxist analysis rather than augur its departure. Might Marxism also foreshadow the ruin of capitalism?

kristeva
Andrew Wilson

Born in 1941 in Bulgaria, Julia Kristeva is one of a number of eminent and groundbreaking scholars to emerge from the fertile intellectual ground of the Parisian Left Bank in the middle part of the twentieth century. (For a thorough contextualizing of Kristeva's work within the French intellectual scene, see Lechte and Oliver, who both provide particularly detailed and insightful introductions to her work.) Today, her areas of interest range from the intellectual rigors of psychoanalysis, linguistics, and philosophy to the more affective realms of literature, art, and poetry. She has also had an enduring interest in the ideological, with work on sociology, especially political and cultural development, and a pervasive fascination with religion. In addition to her scholarly work, she is steadily becoming known for her works of fiction (such as *The Samurai,* 1992). As a practicing psychoanalyst, she continues to inquire into the nature and significance of the analyst/analysand relationship. Characteristic is Kristeva's tendency to throw these differing areas of inquiry together, often with startling results.

Kristeva's initial work in linguistics began in the 1960s and is notable for her explication of Soviet theorist Mikhail Bakhtin and her interest in the logic of poetic language. (A well-known concept to emerge from her work with Bakhtinian theory is that of "intertextuality"; see Kristeva, 1990: 34–61.) In the 1970s, following closely from this early work, she set about combining language theory with Lacanian psychoanalysis. It was in this period that she formulated her groundbreaking theory of the semiotic, which was to form the basis for much of her future work. (The differences between the discipline of Semiotics and Kristeva's semiotic are discussed in Lechte: xi–xiii.) In the 1980s Kristeva continued her focus on the overlap between linguistics and psychoanalysis, carefully weaving into her discourse the experiences of horror, melancholy, and love, a triad of terms that all owe a debt to her earlier work on the semiotic.

Bearing in mind that this introduction can only really sketch the horizon of Kristeva's startlingly original intellectual developments in a published career spanning the 1960s to the 1990s, let us now narrow the focus somewhat. The course plotted here begins in the 1960s and follows the development of the core concept of the semiotic, looking at its theoretical beginnings in psychoanalysis. From there the trek continues through Kristeva's discussion of the abject as the further implications of the semiotic become apparent, and the journey ends in the 1980s with a brief look at the complex and highly nuanced picture of her discourse on love.

As a linguist, Kristeva looked at the psycho-linguistic structures developed by Jacques Lacan with her own question of how childlike psychic remnants remain hidden within the adult subject. In *Revolution in Poetic Language,* her own concepts of the symbolic and the semiotic, so central to this work, are built on the psychoanalytic tradition first developed by Freud and subsequently reread by Jacques Lacan. (For valuable introductions to psychoanalytic theory, see Anthony, 1994; Ellmann, 1994; Grosz, 1990; Vice, 1996; and Wright, 1984.) Take, for example, concepts such as the Oedipus complex, the twin realms of the Symbolic and Imaginary, and the Mirror Stage; Kristeva's work rests firmly on the foundations set by theoretical concepts such as these—foundations she is not afraid to shake when the need arises.

The Oedipus complex, as one such foundation stone, attempts to account for the emergence of personality, of individuality and self-awareness—in short, the emergence of the speaking subject. This psychic process can be roughly divided into two: the period before the emergence of subjectivity and the period following. Kristeva, however, is not so quick to cleave these two realms so neatly down the middle. In fact, she maintains, they are always elaborately and thoroughly intertwined. It is on this point that she builds her understanding of the semiotic and the symbolic. These terms do not rename or replace Lacan's Imaginary and Symbolic so much as provide necessary coloring and inflection, especially to the Lacanian Imaginary.

The Kristevan symbolic roughly corresponds to Lacan's realm of the Symbolic in that it is the mode of reason and of representation. It is the realm of the self aware, of all that is differentiated and fully present—fully conscious subjectivity. The Kristevan semiotic, like the Lacanian Imaginary, initially refers to the time of undifferentiated union of mother and child and is characterized by the specific qualities marking this time. These qualities are pretty much the inverse of those associated with the Symbolic and as such include the chaotic, irrational, and emotional. Traditionally, these qualities have been allocated to the margins, the repressed and unconscious. Further to this, Kristeva seeks to reconnect the psyche to the actual body, especially the body of the mother. More specifically, she identifies the semiotic in the cry of the child, the sounds and gestures of the baby, and the translation of these characteristics into forms of rhythm, word play and many of the more affective qualities of art, poetry, and music (1984: 26–30).

At first glance, it would appear that these two realms can all too easily be allocated a gender identity, with masculinity encompassing all the qualities of the symbolic and femininity the semiotic. This is true insofar as femininity is relegated to the margins of masculinist discourse and also by Kristeva's own alignment of the semiotic with the body of the mother. But Kristeva, harboring a deep suspicion of identity, stops short of claiming that the semiotic is *inherently* feminine. This move has not always endeared Kristeva to other feminists (Kristeva, 1990: 9–12; Moi, 1994: 163–67; Grosz, 1989: 91–99). For Kristeva, these realms are ungendered, and in her readings she often looks to the work of male poets and writers, such as Lautréamont, Mallarmé, and even Shakespeare, as in some way wielders of the semiotic. Even so, she does speak of the maternal function, the collection of drives or *chora* of the semiotic (1984: 25–30). Just as the symbolic order is disrupted by the semiotic, the semiotic is not entirely without some form of control and regulation, even at the pre-oedipal stage. The semiotic phase is filled with a multitude of primitive drives and impulses, not yet fully developed, conscious, or even rational, but that nonetheless orient and urge the child toward separation, language, and the order of signification. Kristeva uses the Platonic term *chora* as a collective term for these chaotic drives.

The chaotic drives of the semiotic realm, concentrated around the anal and oral modes, are figured toward the *material* separation, negation, and rejection of the mother. As such, they continue to affirm and orient the developmental process in such experiences as birth, weaning, and the rituals of bodily cleanliness in toilet training. These uncontrolled and potentially destructive drives are eventually reigned in, but never altogether controlled by the symbolic "law" of the father–the moment of *symbolic* rejection at the heart of the oedipal complex. In the end, the interaction between the semiotic and the symbolic constitutes for Kristeva the signifying process and thereby makes language possible. In other words, to have meaning, there must be a constant and complex interplay between the modes of the semiotic and the symbolic. And so Kristeva essentially displaces, but does not altogether replace, the Lacanian distinction between the Imaginary and the Symbolic with her own distinction of the semiotic and symbolic. The semiotic remains within the Symbolic as a residue or remnant of the pre-oedipal drives and forces. Its disruptive qualities attest to its always alien motivations. The semiotic is in practice most vividly present (although never actually "present" at all) in those moments when language breaks down. Because of the essential and inseparable interplay between the semiotic and symbolic in language, "*two modalities* of what is, for us, the same signifying process," language for Kristeva is fundamentally heterogeneous (1994: 24–25).

The implications for Kristeva's work on the semiotic become apparent through the provision of a theoretical framework that enables one to speak of that which disrupts and goes beyond language. Now it is possible to speak of the unspeakable. Such observations are, of course, most vividly demonstrated within art, music, literature, and religious discourse and are naturally exemplified in poetic language. For example, in *Black Sun* she writes on Holbein's *Dead Christ* and looks to the writings of Dostoyevsky; in *Maladies of the Soul* she meditates on the work of James Joyce; and in *Tales of Love,* Kristeva investigates Shakespeare, Pergolesi's *Stabat Mater,* Baudelaire, Stendhal, and Bataille among others.

One major difference between Kristeva and Lacan can be seen in Kristeva's move back to the body of the mother. This tactic shifts the analysis of language from a location primarily within the Symbolic realm to a prior stage in which the heterogeneity of language is much more apparent. By taking her discourse back to the body of the mother, Kristeva also questions the over-emphasis on oedipal desire in the signifying process, a move that widens the gap between Kristeva and Lacan still further. These two moves–going back to the body, and displacing desire–bring us to a major term in Kristevan thought: the *abject* (1982). Kristeva describes the abject as neither a subject nor an object; it is not a "thing," but rather it indicates a process. She notices that an overemphasis on desire in the signifying process covered over another, very different, psychic experience. She notes that along with desire, there also seems to be a significant experience of repulsion, even horror, at the heart of the signifying process.

As Kristeva develops the concept of abjection, she pursues her interest in the psychoanalytic status of the mother and her influence on the emerging desires of the child. The child desires but also learns to reject the mother. The rituals of cleanliness, for instance, are begun at this early stage, and the body of the child is separated from the feces it produces. Such separation is crucial in the gradual formation of boundaries and the mapping of the body. It serves to reinforce a sense of inside and outside, which will become important in the symbolic differentiation of subject and object, self and other, semiotic mother and symbolic father (1982: 73).

These instances of rejection set up divisions of clean/unclean, inside/outside, and, ultimately, desire/horror. But just as Kristeva shows that the semiotic and symbolic are not cleanly separable, neither are these divisions able to be so neatly made. The abject is what remains of those chaotic drives that make up the semiotic *chora* once the journey into the symbolic order is "complete." The abject is both inside and outside and so threatens boundaries and distinctions precisely by resisting distinctions, ambiguously inhabiting (but simultaneously not inhabiting) the borders, the margins. To the profound horror of the subject, the abject always threatens to break down and subvert the symbolic order. As Kristeva says, abjection is, fundamentally, "what disturbs identity, system, order" (1982: 4). It is this horror that interests Kristeva, who believes that, by not recognizing the horror of abjection, by repressing and denying the abject, one diminishes a fundamental dimension of the individual and consequently also diminishes the capacity of the individual to cope.

Innumerable cultural rituals have sought to banish, or at least control and distance, the abject. Many such rituals are religious in nature, and Kristeva is particularly interested in those of Jewish Law (1984: 94). Significantly, she comments on the role of Christianity, which, in contrast to other religious traditions, internalizes the contaminating danger of the abject, re-establishing the conflict within. In rejoining the conflict, Christianity also proffers some sort of reconciliation with the maternal principle that is specifically figured by the Virgin Mary and is indicative of what Kristeva terms a revenge of paganism (1982: 116; see also "Stabat Mater" and "A Holy Madness: She and He" in 1987a: 234–63, 83–100). In recent years, there have been a number of forays into biblical studies and theology using Kristevan theory (for examples, see: P. Anderson, 1997: 215–22; Bible and Culture Collective, 1995: 187–224).

Powers of Horror, with its analysis of the separation from the mother, provides the background (and half the story) for Kristeva's study of love in *Tales of Love.* The scene of love is set prior to the acquisition of language, where the tools of the (post-oedipal) symbolic, and therefore the infant's identity, are not yet fully formed. The child, forced to endure a painful separation from the mother, is urged toward an idealized, sublime "other" as a comforting replacement. This phase is illustrated by Lacan in the mirror stage, where the child first recognizes its idealized image in the mirror. Its identification with this image marks an important step along the process of separation from the mother and the development of an ego and identity. Identification with the reflected image depends on first being able to identify the self. But because the drives toward separation and idealization are very much prior to the formation of a fixed identity, identification with this image is at best always a mixture of "self" and "other." An idealized "self/other" can only ever be an imperfect replacement for the real desire to be joined once again with the abjected mother. However, our separation from our mother enables us, as Kristeva will later say, to become *narcissists,* that is, to develop and accept a self identity–an ego-ideal (1987a: 103–21).

Later, when the ego is fully formed in and through language, these semiotic patterns remain as a fundamental sense of loss and emptiness buried deep in the heart of the ego. Our own narcissism attempts to cover over this emptiness, but nothing can ever really compensate for our rending separation from the abjected mother. Accordingly, there always remains a certain instability, not only of the ego, but of the symbolic, and thus of language. Because in some art the semiotic patterns are often more conspicuous, it is here that we can be confronted most vividly by the instability of non-meaning, which lies at the heart of our identity. Confronted with the breach at the core of our being, we effectively stare our own death and annihilation in the face. The renewing process of love can get us through this encounter, but this process does not always run smoothly. When love is absent, our response to the emptiness can lead to depression, melancholia, or even suicide. In *Black Sun,* Kristeva meditates on those experiences of love gone wrong. "When love is not possible, we lose part of ourselves; we begin to die and perhaps then realize that love is life. Such would be our distillation of Kristeva's message" (Lechte: 184).

When love goes wrong, there is a refusal to attach to a substitute subject or object, either real or imagined. The results of this refusal are manifested in a state of melancholia, where sadness itself becomes the only object. Sadness comes to replace that to which the subject would normally become attached, and as such this new "object" is nurtured and cherished as though it were an *actual* object. Kristeva demonstrates in *Black Sun* how this process is played out:

> "I love that object," is what the person seems to say about the lost object [the abjected mother], "but even more so I hate it; because I love it, and in order not to lose it, I imbed it in myself; but because I hate it, that other within myself is a bad self, I am bad, I am non-existent, I shall kill myself"...Consequently the analysis of depression involves bringing to the fore the realization that the complaint against oneself is a hatred for the other. (1989: 11)

Kristeva demonstrates in her readings that these more disturbing elements are played out in many examples of poetry, literature, and art. In elucidating the melancholic, she also spends a great deal of time analyzing the presence and relative balance of the intertwined semiotic and symbolic within accounts of affective experience. Once again religion, particularly the Christian tradition, plays a large role in Kristeva's schema. Religion allows all the essential dramas of the psyche to be played out in full. Christianity internalizes these dramas and thereby conjoins the semiotic and the symbolic *within* rather than *without* the individual (1989: 105–38; 1987a: 234–63).

The renewing power of love allows the oscillation between the semiotic and symbolic to remain without needing to resolve this tension one way or the other. Love provides a path through the crisis of meaning–always faced with the challenge of non-meaning–by embracing both the sublime ideal and the abjected other. In other words, love allows identification through a maintenance rather than a resolution of difference. Kristeva says that love is something spoken, and in this lies its importance for human experience. Kristeva's earliest theories of language return again when we reiterate that language is fundamentally heterogeneous, always a combination of symbolic and semiotic elements. Because of Kristeva's combination of linguistics and psychoanalysis, we can say that it is in and through language that we and others are formed. And her discourse on love reveals that it is language that makes love possible. The interconnectedness of all these areas demonstrates that we are able to and need to love each other because love allows us to function and live in the midst of language. Consequently, by accepting the alien alongside the familiar, by loving, the subject grows used to those moments when confronted with the trauma of difference. In fact, for the ego, this growing ease with difference allows for growth and increased complexity as the ego expands to include difference as part of the self.

In the last part of *Tales of Love,* Kristeva looks to psychoanalysis and to the relationship between the analyst and the analysand in particular as the ideal loving relationship (1987a: 372–83). With a view of Western culture in crisis, caused in part by the breakdown of religious discourse, she sees the ideally balanced psychoanalytic relationship as the new context within which the reclamation of some of the vestiges of story and value can begin (1989: 86).

This impetus continues in *New Maladies of the Soul,* where Kristeva's disillusionment with Western culture becomes more apparent. She argues, using a series of case studies as illustrations, that in the face of this contemporary crisis, psychoanalysis is "one of the few remaining endeavors that will allow change and surprise, that is, that will allow life" (1995: 44). Increasingly, Kristeva turns to religious symbols and stories in an effort to discover anew, within the psychoanalytic relationship, the values so lacking in contemporary culture. It would appear that Kristeva's turn to psychoanalytic practice reveals a desire to usher in a new therapeutic age where psychoanalysis can begin to recreate those positive meanings and values that were once the sole province of religion.

lacan
Ilona Rashkow

Jacques Lacan, the French psychoanalyst whose thought has had such a broad influence on literary theory since the 1960s, considered psychoanalysis as much a part of philosophy as of medicine. Ironically, although Lacan deviated from the mainstream of psychoanalytic thought and was expelled from the International Psychoanalytic Association, he believed himself to be returning *to* Freud rather than departing *from* him.

Despite the fact that Jacques Lacan is not a pro-feminist thinker, feminists have been drawn to his work, since he attempts to "rewrite" Freudianism. Indeed, one of the primary objections to Freudian psychoanalytic theory is his idea of penis envy. (For a number of different perspectives on the current state of the debate between feminists and various kinds of psychoanalysis, see Wright, 1984.) Torok, for example, argues that "penis envy" is not based on biological fact but is a misconception, since a common phallic phase does not characterize the infantile development of both sexes (1964). What Lacan seeks to do is to reinterpret Freud in light of structuralist and post-structuralist theories of discourse. Because Lacan focuses on one's place in society and, above all, one's relationship to language, he shifts the discussion of penis envy from Freud's biological penis to the penis as a philosophical signifier. As a result, many scholars find his writings more relevant to both males and females.

Briefly, where Freud views the mechanisms of the unconscious as generated by libido (sexual energy), Lacan centers the theory of the unconscious on the sense within us of something being *absent.* Lacan describes two "levels" of absence. The less intense awareness of absence can take the form of mere lack (*manque*) or of need (*besoin*). Both of these levels of absence force the psyche to make demands. A deeper feeling of absence takes the higher form of desire (*désir*). Lacan defines *désir* as twofold: First, it is an unconscious feeling toward an object; second, this object can and does desire us in return. Lacan's terms for the universal symbol, or signifier, of *désir* is the *Phallus.* It is important not to confuse the Phallus in this sense with the male sexual organ, the penis. According to Lacanian theory, both sexes experience the absence of and desire for the Phallus–which may be one reason Lacan's restructuring of Freud has appealed to feminists such as Hélène Cixous and Luce Irigaray. Indeed, the sexually critical and liberatory potential of Lacan is that although one sex has an anatomical penis, neither sex can possess the Phallus. As a result, sexuality is incomplete and fractured for *both* sexes.

Moreover, although men and women must line themselves up on one or the other side of the linguistic/sexual divide, they need not align themselves with the side that is anatomically isomorphic.

Lacan's theory of psychosexual development is also a revision of Freud's in that Lacan shifts the description of mental processes from a purely biological model to a semiotic one. For example, Freud discusses the first phase of childhood as the oral phase, in which the child's pleasure comes largely from suckling; the anal phase follows, when the child learns to control and to enjoy controlling the elimination of feces. For Lacan, the analog of the oral phase is the "Mirror-Stage," from six to eighteen months, in which the child's image of his or her bodily self changes from mere formlessness and fragmentation to an identification with a unified shape that the child can see in the mirror. During this development, the child experiences itself as "*le Désir de La Mère,*" the desire of the mother (in both senses–as an object that is itself unconscious and can desire us in return). That is, the baby not only knows that it needs its mother but also feels itself to be what completes and fills the mother's desires (in other words, the child feels *itself* to be "the Phallus"). From this phase Lacan derives the psychic field of the "Imaginary," the state in which a person's sense of reality is grasped purely as images and fantasies of the fulfillment of his or her desires. This stage, begun during the child's second year of life, continues into adulthood.

In Lacanian thought, repression and unconscious occur together with the acquisition of language, at around eighteen months (when Freud's anal stage begins). Lacan derives his ideas of language and the unconscious from the semiotician Ferdinand de Saussure, as he was interpreted by the structuralist anthropologist Claude Lévi-Strauss. Briefly, Lévi-Strauss considered the unconscious as "reducible to a function–the symbolic function," which in turn was merely "the aggregate of the laws" of language (1963: 198). The primary laws of language in structural linguistics are those of the selection and combination of primary basic elements. *Metaphor* is a mode of symbolization in which one thing is signified by another that is like it, that is part of the same paradigmatic class (for example, "a sea of troubles" or "all the world's a stage"). Lacan sees metaphor as equivalent to the Freudian defense of "condensation" (in which one symbol becomes the substitute for a whole series of associations). *Metonymy,* on the other hand, is a mode of symbolization in which one thing is signified by another that is associated with it but not of the same class (for example, the use of "Washington" for "the United States government" or of "the sword" for "military power")–a syntagmatic relationship that Lacan regards as equivalent to Freudian "displacement."

As the child learns the names of things, his or her desires are no longer met automatically; now the child must ask for what he or she wants and cannot request things that do not have names. As the child learns to ask for a signified by pronouncing a signifier, he or she learns that one thing can symbolize another and has entered what Lacan calls the "field of the Symbolic." As Muller and Richardson describe:

From this point on the child's desire, like an endless quest for a lost paradise, must be channeled like an underground river through the subterranean passageways of the symbolic order, which make it possible things be present in their absence in some ways through words. (1982: 23)

At this stage, desires can be repressed, and the child is able to ask for something that metaphorically or metonymically replaces the desired object. Lacan punningly calls this stage of development "*le Nom-du-Père*"– "the Name-of-the-Father"–because language is only the first of the negations and subjections to law that now will begin to affect the child. (In French, the phrase "*le Nom-du-Père*"– "the Name-of-the-Father"–is pronounced exactly the same as "*le Non-du-Père*"– "the no-of-the-Father"–hence its connection to negation and subjection to law.)

Another Lacanian field, less discussed in his writings than the others, is that of the "Real." By this Lacan refers to those incomprehensible aspects of experience that exist beyond images and symbols through which we think and constitute our reality. That is to say, adult humans are always inscribed within language, but language does not constitute the ultimate reality. Because in Lacan's dialectic of desire one object may symbolize another (which is itself a substitute for still another), Lacan says that "the unconscious is structured like a language."

Like Freud, Lacan approaches literature primarily as material that, properly interpreted, illustrates the major concepts of his psychology. His indirect influence on literary theory and criticism has been considerable, primarily because his psychology has affected the philosophy and literary theory of the many French scholars who attended his seminars (and then, by extension, British and American scholars who were influenced by the French). But a strain of direct Lacanian criticism has begun to appear as well in the past several years, in separate essays and in collections such as those edited by Shosana Felman (1981) and Robert Con Davis (1983). Many of these works have taken the form of interpenetrative readings of Lacan and a literary text, by which they inevitably find the basic themes of Lacan's psychology within the text. This seems to be a workable compromise while Lacan's ideas are still relatively unfamiliar. I suspect, however, that as Lacanian criticism becomes more widely accepted, the focus will change. Like Lacanian analysis itself, Lacanian-based readings will be centered more intensely on the Word and the chain of associations that are developed within the text–an approach that may be particularly relevant for biblical scholars.

levinas
Gary A. Phillips

A century which in thirty years has known two world wars, totalitarianisms of the left and right, Hiroshima, the gulags, the genocides of Auschwitz and Cambodia. A century which is drawing to an end with the spectre of the return of all that these barbaric names evoke. Suffering and evil imposed deliberately, but which no reason could limit in the exasperation of reason which has become political and detached from all ethics. (Levinas, 1991: 43; cited in C. Davis: 143).

Totality and Transcendence

War. Genocide. Democide. The ultimate expressions of Totality. The violent excesses of modern social, religious, and political life, evident foremost in the Holocaust, ground Levinas' (and our present) history and give his writings their ethical urgency. After Auschwitz and the Gulag, we are compelled to ask, What, if anything, transcends modernity, transcends reason, transcends the universal and totalizing systems implicated in Western thought and civilization? Is there a vision of the transcendent and of the human that is meaningful today? To rephrase Tolstoy, how then shall we live responsibly? Emmanuel Levinas' (1906–1995) work is an effort to think a way through these issues.

The sociologist Zygmunt Bauman contends that the Gulag anticipates the reality of a severely fragmented postmodern world where the moral life is lived out in a certain austerity, denuded, without the shelter of reason, law, or social contract, "detached from all ethics." Principles-seeking and universality-promoting ethical systems are in shambles (1995: 42). The philosopher Levinas would agree. In the solitude of existence, a solitude made even more solitary by Thought, we desire more than to have our basic physical needs met. Levinas argues that knowledge, philosophy's customary remedy to every concern, is impotent to respond to this desire and to give solace; knowledge fails to give us practical direction out of ourselves and beyond ourselves. Reason only reinforces solitude, assuring the Same old, Same old, because it is wedded to Totality, not Transcendence. What alone gives relief and elevates us is the encounter with the other (for Levinas, either the specific other person, *Autrui*, or that which in general is wholly other than me, *autre*, i.e., alterity), for the other breaks though my solitude from the outside by obligating me. In the obligation to the other, then, I encounter transcendence, the burden of my responsibility, the possibility of justice, my self. In the face of the other, Totality is interrupted in the moment when transcendence, infinity, God, ethics speak.

Described as "the sole moralist of contemporary thought" (Levinas, 1985: viii) and one of the two most important Jewish thinkers of the twentieth century (Gibbs: 4), Levinas labors to find a way beyond Western thought's infatuation with itself and with totalities of every sort–military, philosophical, ideological, even religious. His is an excessive concern to thematize what Plato characterizes as that which exceeds thought, namely the "Good beyond reason." It is a paradoxical but necessary task. The effort to speak about what lies "beyond" thought brings us to the face of the neighbor and to the discovery of a profound burden of responsibility for the other, an "ethics of the other." Interrupting our every attempt to grasp this "outside," the beyond speaks to us concretely in the language of that unsolicited commandment that interrupts every system, every thought, every preoccupation with our selves: "Thou shalt not murder."

In the language of the Hebrew prophets, Levinas' thought is a desire for the first casualty of war–justice, justice for "the widow and the orphan, the stranger and the poor" (Levinas, 1994: 142). The philosopher of the "face," of "exorbitant and infinite responsibility," of "Ethics as First Philosophy," Levinas seeks to describe the radical and uncompromising ethical nature of our relationship to the world, a relationship of obligation prior to any knowledge, belief, or social construction. His provocative writings are both a sharpened phenomenological critique and a prophetic call for responsible philosophical reflection and social action in accord with "another thought of ethics, responsibility, justice, the State" (Derrida, 1996: 335). In the context of a Western philosophical tradition that privileges totalities at the expense of the other, Levinas' expositions on ethics are a "shock wave" undermining the foundation of a modern reasoning habituated to the love of wisdom rather than the wisdom of love, to self and what it knows rather than the other and how I am responsible to her life before all else, even before my own life. Insofar as Levinas attempts to think otherwise than in Greek, he speaks to postmodern concerns.

Jew/Greek or Greek/Jew

Properly speaking, is Levinas a philosopher or religious thinker? A phenomenological thinker or Talmudic exegete? Greek or Jew? He is all these, and more. A contemporary Septuagintist, Levinas writes out of and to the Western classical and Jewish religious traditions. He is at home critically with Tolstoy and Torah, Heidegger and Hayyim of Volozhin. Levinas does not seek "explicity to 'harmonize' or 'conciliate' both traditions" but by their juxtaposition and mutual engagement to disclose those pre-philosophical, originary experiences where meaning–not the meaning of beings that Philosophy admires–begins (Levinas, 1985: 24). Philosophical reflection needs the interruption of the Bible just as each one of us depends on the Other to interrupt our existence. Never static, his language is notoriously thick, poetic, highly repetitive; his thought redundant, likened by Derrida to "the action of waves against the shore" (Derrida, 1965/78: 84 n. 7). His writings struggle to enact formally the impossible task of grasping what lies beyond thought. It is in this way that Levinas erodes–or better, "batters" (Handelman: 180; cited in Davis: 147)–the pillars of Western philosophical systems to expose another foundation, a bedrock far more substantial than Reason or Being: ethics.

Levinas' first major publications, *Totality and Infinity* and *Otherwise than Being or Beyond Essence,* explicate the phenomenological thought of Husserl and Heidegger, two of his teachers, and a wider Western metaphysical tradition that gives pride of place to reflection and self-consciousness. Translator of Husserl's *Cartesian Meditations* (1931), Levinas introduced Husserl and transcendental phenomenology to Sartre and the French intellectual scene. Heidegger's *Being and Time* remained for him a pivotal work– "one of the finest books in the history of philosophy" (1985: 37). But Heidegger's Nazi excesses Levinas never forgave (1990: 25). In *Time and the Other,* Levinas inverts and subverts Heideggerian fundamental ontology by rethinking the nature of time and death. Time is the "very relation of the subject with the Other" (1987: 39); I don't "have time." It is the gift of the other to me that makes time possible.

Levinas has also written extensively on Jewish and religious issues in *Difficult Liberty, Of God Who Comes to Mind, Nine Talmudic Readings, The Time of the Nations,* and *Beyond the Verse,* among other books. An assortment of biblical exegesis, Talmudic commentary, interviews, book reviews, and theological meditations, these writings reflect Levinas' ever-present engagement with Jewish life and thought and his own Jewish experience shaped by the trauma of the Gulag. In seeking "a vision of the human which is still meaningful today" (1994: 155), Levinas draws on philosophical and religious resources. His philosophical concerns with alterity, ethics, transcendence, and responsibility are woven throughout his religious writings, and explicit religious themes ("God"), biblical texts and characters ("Abraham"), and ethical injunctions ("Thou shalt not murder") find a natural home in his philosophical works. It is hardly possible to separate philosophical from religious thought, though commentators will privilege one over against the other. But such a dichotomy misses the point. Each field interrupts, transgresses the other. This disciplinary mixing reflects Levinas' struggle to speak of that which lies outside, indeed ruptures, both philosophical reflection and religious faith, namely, "the idea of the Infinite," or "God" (1998: xiii).

Ethics and More than Being

Western thought is preoccupied with Being and essence. This pre-occupation reveals itself tellingly in the "What is" question. But there is more to "being" than being, Levinas will challenge: "To be or not to be is not the question" (1991a: 5). Levinas interrogates the "What is?" or "being" question that philosophy habitually prefers by countering with a different question, one that asks instead about what is *better* than being. "The most important question of the meaning of being is not: why is there something rather than nothing…but: do I not kill by being?" (1985: 120). Such moral force scandalizes philosophical thinking. Ethics is prior to and has priority over being; ethics is "an-archic," a hyphenated neologism that Levinas uses to give expression to what lies outside of the reach of thought. This and other strange expressions ("dis-inter-ested," "dia-chrony," "to-come," "love-for-the-other," "to-God"[*a-dieu*]) illustrate the way Levinas attempts to think and write outside the categories of thought that are our inheritance from Parmenides to Heidegger. Still, not even Levinas can do without asking the "What is" question. His ethical questioning unmasks a tension and contitutes an interruption in the self-consistent "what is" logic of Western thought's preoccupation with totality (or the "Same") that keeps us in the loop of solitude. Ethics takes us outside ourselves because it alone is attentive to an "exteriority," to a something beyond ourselves. Exteriority is something knowledge can never make room for because knowledge is "always an adequation between thought and what it thinks" (1985: 60). Knowledge is inadequate for gaining purchase on that which lies outside. Reason is never adequate as the response to the needs of my neighbor, only the action of feeding and clothing. Love, however, takes us outside ourselves and our self-interests. This beyond, Levinas claims, at once ruptures and grounds philosophical thought, making ethics "first" philosophy. Ethical questioning thus marks a manner of thinking fractured by linguistic paradox, conceptual contradiction, and, ultimately, an existential unsettledness likened to insomnia.

The Face

How do we escape not only the question of being but the solitude and anonymity of being reinforced by knowledge? It is the face where one approaches the Other and discovers one's humanity…and more. In the face Levinas ties together his conception of language, ethics, and infinity. Strictly speaking, he does not offer a phenomenology of the face, nor is he interested in the construction of a normative ethics. It is not face as such that is the focus of concern, but the relation with the other that is signified when I look into my neighbor's eyes (1985: 86). The relation to the face, Levinas says, is "straightaway ethical" (1985: 86); it refuses reduction to a specific meaning or content. In one sense, one does not "see" the face; the meaning of the face exceeds more than vision can assign to it. Rather, one "hears" the face. "The face speaks" (1985: 87). Levinas employs paradoxical language that recalls Isaiah 2:1 ("The word of the Lord that he saw") in a manner that disrupts the order of knowledge to hear another order—the command "Thou shalt not murder." The face commands me, ordains me, elects me to do everything in my power for the poor to whom we owe all. "Here I am" becomes the appropriate response to the ethical imperative occasioned by the face. Further, this responsibility is a responsibility not just for the specific neighbor but for every other neighbor. Responsibility to the other means nothing less than institutional justice. Citing Rabbi Yohanan: "To leave men without food is a fault no circumstance attenuates: the distinction between the voluntary and the involuntary does not apply here" (1969: 201; cited in I. Stone: 17).

However, withholding food, even murder of another, is possible. One can kill the other. But it is the "face whose *meaning* in saying: 'thou shalt not kill'" (1985: 87) that cannot be killed. The command, the ordination, the election stands even if we fall, because the face signifies far and away beyond ourselves. For this reason, Levinas' thoughts about ethics are neither programmatic nor prescriptive in a traditional sense. His concern is not with constructing ethics but in finding its meaning (1985: 90).

That the face "speaks" means that we are obliged to speak in return; language and responsibility are connected. The concept of face underscores the central importance of language for Levinas. Discourse is the authentic relationship that we have with one another. And it is in discourse that our ethical commitment to one another comes to expression. Language is first and foremost a response to the face; it is the advent of an ethical moment and the moment of ethics. "Here am I" signifies through my speech, announcing my response to the command and my responsibility for other persons. In language, even the quotidian "After you, please," our words give voice to a "Saying" that greets the other and answers to and for him. In every "Said" we encounter a "Saying" that points beyond the actual words themselves to a situation in which I am utterly exposed to my discursive partner. The Said is the domain of ideas, themes, and observations; the Saying is a different domain, the place (it is paradoxically "no-place") where I am exposed to the Other (see Davis: 74–77). The Saying is never coincident with what is Said; it remains elusive, a step ahead of or out of phase with the Said, absent in a certain sense from the words themselves, but present as a trace of the rudimentary condition of exposure to, and thus responsibility for, the other. Philosophical thought has traditionally preoccupied itself with the Said of language, all but ignoring the order of the Saying, which means the ethical and what lies outside the order of Being. But how is it possible for philosophy to remedy this weakness and attend to the Saying if it ever eludes encapsulation in the Said? How is it possible to speak about something as ephemeral as a trace? Is Levinas holding Philosophy up to an impossible standard? Yes. A certain kind of phenomenological description does lead to the discovery that "Saying is to be responsible for others" (1969: 47). But Philosophy needs more. It needs the benefit of the Bible, of Jewish Scriptures. Because of "its impossible chronology, impossible burdens, and its impossible demands which the people of Israel 'do and then hear'" (Stone: 27), the Bible, prophetic speech, and prayers interrupt the Said and foster a recovery of the Saying. Because the biblical text bears interruptive testimony to the originary ethical situation, the philosopher is presented with an opportunity to hear what the Bible has to say about God and humankind.

God and the Bible

Philosophy, no less than Religion, confronts God as a dimension of experience: "The face of the other manifests and is manifest in a moral height which is the dimension of G-d, the revelation of G-d" (Cohen: 193). Philosophy's monumental system-building efforts miss the point terribly that the Infinite is not containable in word, thought, or image. Not a being or in being, God as Infinite is accessible only through relationship with human beings. As such, God as Infinite breaches the system as the command to not kill. God's "presence" is an "absence," a trace left in the face of my sister or brother. The face marks God's passing; the face of the other is where God's glory is manifest. The other (*Autrui*) is wholly other (*autre*). She is also holy. Perhaps it is in the countenance of the Musselman, as described by Primo Levi, whose face is set toward an anonymous, solitary death, that God passes. If so, then in those lifeless eyes, following Levinas, we encounter our excessive and asymmetrical moral responsibility for the other that the system of Auschwitz sought to neutralize. In his face we hear the command to make him first.

The Bible is not alone in marking the trace of God in the human face. The great national literatures also bear witness: "Across all literature the human face speaks–or stammers" (1985: 109). But for Levinas, it is in the "incomparable prophetic excellence" of the Bible's extraordinary characters where the "ethical plenitude and its mysterious possibilities of exegesis…originally signified transcendence" (1985: 23). Levinas frequently returns to Abraham and his words "Here I am" throughout his philosophical writings to signal the erosive power of the biblical witness. The biblical text ruptures being by directing us beyond system and thought to transcendence.

In a post-Holocaust setting, Levinas' writings can be read by theologians and biblical scholars as a reaction to the crisis of modernity and its excessive genuflecting to totalities of every sort. Levinas can also be read as a consolation to a postmodernity deflated by the structural instabilities of the metanarratives of Enlightenment reason and social justice and progress. Levinas' interrogation of the "crisis of being, the otherwise than being" in no way abandons reason or diminishes the importance of working out justice in every facet of social life. To the contrary. Levinas' ethical provocation is a deliberate and emphatic call to question rigorously our way to a severe individual and social responsibility. It is there in the face of the other that I awaken to the call to justice. Such a call to justice should challenge the way biblical scholars read and respond to the biblical text: ethics, not method, as "first exegesis" (see Phillips and Fewell).

If Bauman is correct, the end of the "era of ethics" (i.e., principles-seeking and universality-promoting systems) opens up the possibility of an "era of morality," a vigilant Levinasian morality of the face that does not abandon any other, for every other is wholly–and holy–other. Questions remain: Does such an era to come announce a reenchanted vision of the human that transcends the evil of this tragic past century? Will the Bible continue to interrupt totalities? How will the Bible and those who read it be interrupted by the faces of our neighbors?

lyotard
Gina Hens-Piazza

Among the complex of thinkers who have challenged us to examine the inheritance of the modern era and its critical principles rises the name and contributions of Jean-Francois Lyotard. A French philosopher, Lyotard was born in Versailles in 1924 and was educated in Paris. He went on to teach in various institutions at La Flecke, Sorbonne, Nanterre, Vincennes, and finally, St. Denis until his retirement in 1987. But Lyotard's influence was not confined to France. Founding member of the International College of Philosophy, he was associated with various institutions in Algeria, Germany, and the United States. He taught at the University of California at San Diego, the Johns Hopkins University, Emory, and the University of California at Irvine. Born and educated in the cradle of modernity, Lyotard's early social and political involvements stemmed from the pervasive and formative influence of this post-Enlightenment inheritance.

The modern era infused a mind-set and set forth values developed by Hume, Kant, Descartes, and philosophers of the Enlightenment, as well as their seventeenth-century predecessors, Descartes, Locke, and Newton. Labeled empiricists and rationalists, these shapers of thought promoted a common conception of reason and knowledge. Reason was a fundamental human capacity. It was independent of one's context or cultural constraints. It eclipsed the confines of individualism and of historical conditioning. Surpassing the particularity of thinking and seeing that imprisoned individuals and confined them to a subjectivity, reason served to unveil and guarantee objective facts about the world and about human nature itself. Philosophy even granted it universal status.

The grounds for the advances in science, with which Lyotard later would take issue, are supreme examples of reason at work. They grow out of an assumed intrinsic order in the natural world as well as an inherent organization within society. Science need only employ reason alongside the empirical data, and the objective principles governing both the universe and human nature themselves could be apprehended. It is no surprise that objectivity, science, and reason number among the watch words of modernity.

The impact and promises of reason as universal capacity were not confined to science but were also brought to bear on social theory. Modern social thought assumed that as all humans shared in this common capacity of reason, they all shared a common destiny. Relying on technical and emancipatory reason, people could influence the orientation of history itself, for history too was believed to progress in determinate stages according to reason toward meaning and truth. With the enlistment of reason and the guarantees it carried, people could be responsible for their society. They could navigate world historical progress. They could even achieve happiness.

Such convictions in philosophy and in social theory influenced the development of the political systems during Lyotard's life. Among these were Hitlerism, Stalinism, and colonial domination of what we now understand to be *Western* reason imposed on non-European peoples. The failure of these political and social systems cultivated a growing skepticism of modernity and its promises. Lyotard's early writings not only offer a critical interaction with phenomenology and structuralism, but also serve as a journal of his own intimate wrestling with the tenets of these systems—in particular, with Marxism. In *La Phenomenologie* (1954, trans. 1991), he sets forth critical perspectives on Hegelian dialectics, structuralism, and phenomenology, as well as an enthusiastic exposition of Marxist political theory. It was during the late 1950s to early 1960s that Lyotard had, in fact, affiliated with a leftist Marxist group, *Socialisme on barbarie*, a non-communist organization active in left-wing politics. However, the events of 1968 enkindled a growing pessimism in regard to grand-scale theories of history. In addition, Lyotard's own growing sympathy for student activists during this period coincided with his disenchantment with political theory. They too had abandoned large-scale visions and were motivated by pure opposition to the established order and the fallacies of its claims. A later work, *Discours, Figure* (1971), occasions a more critical analysis of the ideological restrictions of these philosophical systems, with particular attention to Marxist thought and reality. In subsequent years, he mounted an attack on both the "politics of theory" in general and political theory in particular, with Marxism as his target. The affront first echoed in *Economie Libidinale* (1974, trans. 1993) and later culminated in *The Postmodern Condition* (1979, trans. 1984), a report on the state of knowledge. For Lyotard, the promises of rationality had harvested only an abundance of irrationality. Enlightenment values (freedom, progress, truth, and so forth) were bankrupt. Intelligent, purposeful, rational attempts to navigate and comprehend history had only yielded the melancholy lessons of failed political projects and the stubborn facticity of events.

> The "philosophies of history" that inspired the nineteenth and twentieth centuries claim to assure passages over the abyss of heterogeneity or the event. The names which are those of "our history" oppose counterexamples to their claim.—Everything real is rational, everything rational is real: "Auschwitz" refutes speculative doctrine. This crime at least, which is real, is not rational.—Everything proletarian is communist, everything communist is proletarian: "Berlin 1953, Budapest 1956, Czechoslovakia 1968, Poland 1980" (I could mention others) refute the doctrine of historical materialism: the

workers rose up against the Party.–Everything democratic is by and for the people, and vice versa: "May 1968" refutes the doctrine of parliamentary liberalism. The social in its everydayness puts representative institutions in check.–Everything that is the free play of supply and demand is favorable for the general enrichment, and vice versa: the "crisis of 1911 and 1929" refute the doctrine of economic liberalism. And "the crises of 1911 and 1929" refute the post-Keynesian revision of that doctrine. The passages promised by the great doctrinal syntheses end in bloody impasses. Whence the sorrow of the spectators in this bloody end of the twentieth century. (1988: 4)

This passage, a centerpiece of Lyotard's argument, is not intended to land us in a kind of rock-bottom cynicism but to motivate a move beyond the hypnotizing power of Enlightenment projects and their promises. While vestiges of these totalizing programs still persist, such as "the modern tale of the steady conquest of ignorance by knowledge, the unruffled evolution of the Hegelian Idea, the Marxist saga of emancipation from oppression, and the capitalist myth of infinite technological development," postmodernism portends their end (as Terry Eagleton observes in his review of Lyotard's *Just Gaming* and *Le Postmoderne expliqué aux enfants,* 1987: 194). Thus, for Lyotard, the postmodern is characterized first and foremost by "incredulity toward metanarrative" (1984: xxiv), in his now familiar description.

The philosophical, political, and cultural paradigms that define society, systems, and theories constitute the metanarratives. Marxism, empiricism, rationalism, and capitalism number among them. These grand narratives claim to be the stories that disclose the meaning of all other stories. Their status as *meta*narrative stems from the fact that they speak for the many. They have oriented research, fixed results, determined behavior, and defined what is "truth." The incredulity stems from the realization that these "big stories" have deceived us. They have made promises they couldn't keep. They set themselves up as templates that in the end don't orient history or define human destiny. When set against the events of this century, their inherent fallacies are disclosed. Lyotard's observation about Auschwitz, "this crime… which is real, is not rational," hauntingly echoes this deception.

Implied in the events of the past is the evidence of the failure of universal reason as means and guide to reliable facts about the world and human nature. This puts knowledge in a crisis of legitimation. If discourses are no longer able to appeal to grand narratives for legitimation, what is the grounding of knowledge? Lyotard responds by rejecting the unearned status of knowledge and truth as absolute entities. Instead, he redefines them as internal properties of particular "language games." Here, Lyotard takes up the work of Wittgenstein, who first proposed language games as the solution to the problem of establishing the relationship between any statement and the reality to which it referred. These language games and the rules governing them operate only within designated spheres (philosophy, math, football, theology) and therefore have restricted applicability. For example, a move in a philosophical argument would not carry meaning in a basketball game. Hence, something can be true according to one set of rules and false according to another set. No one language game can claim privilege as a "representation of what things are actually like" or even make available "objectively true statements." Science, sports, philosophy, chess, and so forth—each becomes one language game among many. Each is designed for specific purposes and distinguished by specific moves. These plays are self-validating and often afford social identity even to the point of constituting groups or communities.

In biblical studies, ideological criticism has found a home in the postmodern context on such grounds. It recognizes that ideological constraints are operative in the production and in the reception/interpretation of texts. (While there are many different understandings of ideology and how it functions, ideological criticism as practiced in biblical studies seems most indebted to Frederic Jameson, who characterizes ideology as "structural limitation" or a strategy of containment; 1981: 52.) Interpretation of texts implicitly or explicitly engages the particular constraints or games rules of a community or individual (feminist, Marxist, African American, patriarchal). Assuming that language is complex and multivocal, the endless games that can be played produce scores of micro-narratives, or interpretations. In this postmodern playing field, ideological criticism recognizes and invites the heterogeneity of elements of language games over and against the totalizing gestures of grand narratives. These in turn create an affront to any master narrative or macro-interpretation, such as patriarchy.

In addition to his observation of the crisis of legitimation surrounding past notions of knowledge and truth, Lyotard notes that the reign of the grand narratives has also imposed serious constraints on the individual. The teleological confines of these grand schemes have limited individual creativity, controlled the boundaries of what's "thinkable," as well as curtailed the prospects and possibilities of imaginative innovation. In addition, the "big stories" have held a determining power over what's memorable and what counts as history. Moreover, they have gained this status by virtue of their assumed capacity to reveal the single truth behind the many narratives of cultures that make up the world.

In place of these metatruths, Lyotard observes a different world, one that is fashioned by discourse, signs, and symbols. These, in turn, are embedded in cultural systems and the array of language games of groups within these networks. Truth in such a world is not univocal but multiplex. Lyotard's observation, along with the work of various scholars (Raymond Williams, Clifford Geertz, Michel Foucault, etc.), has provided the impetus for the rise of cultural studies in the academy and in biblical studies. In place of seeking out the truth narrated by the grand story of the Bible, cultural studies examines the ways the Bible and culture are mutually influencing each other as well as the claims we make about each of them. Within this arena resides postcolonial studies, with a more focused lens on intercultural reading. For individuals with a past shaped by colonizing powers, the grand narratives of the West have had a particularly catastrophic effect. They have cultivated a passive self, one that is positioned in society but never able to gain a "vantage point" in its activities. For individuals not narrated by the grand accounts, there is no past or story of origin. When postcolonial individuals or groups are featured and free to make their voices heard, they not only disclose the "unrepresentable" in the text but also expose the hegemony of the academy and even of biblical studies and its practices. Hence, when their past begins to be told, the grand narratives appear not so grand or inclusive. The power schemes latent in the grand narratives become clear. It is this disclosure that warrants an alternate course.

Lyotard maps out this new direction as a kind of resistance campaign to these metanarratives. He encourages gradual change brought about by individuals' "skirmishing on the sidelines." In "Lessons in Pragmaticism," he cites as examples individual entrepreneurs in media who help to loosen practices of state monopolies by large broadcasting corporations or individuals in education who employ alternate teaching approaches. These "skirmishes" eventually necessitate that big institutions at least examine their practices and the power issues implicit therein. "You make up little stories, or even segments of little stories, listen to them, transmit them, and act them out when the time is right" (1989: 131). Hence, in his campaign against grand narratives and the power schemes at work in them, Lyotard calls for the promotion and belief in individuals' "little stories."

Why little stories?

Because they are short, because they are not extracts from some great history, and because they are difficult to fit into any great history. Remember the problems the Marxist narrative, to name but one, had with the student episode. How could that be fitted into a web of relations of production and class struggle?...History consists of a swarm of narratives, narratives that are passed on, made up, listened to and acted out; the people does not exist as a subject; it is a mass of thousands of little stories that are at once futile and serious, that are sometimes attracted together to form bigger stories, and which sometimes disintegrate into drifting elements. (1989: 132–33, 134)

Only with the promotion of "the swarm of narratives" can the doom of the grand narratives, their authority and their foundations, be realized. This too provides impetus for cultural and postcolonial studies in the biblical guild. They encourage a multitude of local readings of the biblical tradition as a means to unseat the reigning Western discourse about these stories. Moreover, for the marginalized, this may be the only means of protest and realization of change in the field.

On these terms, Lyotard's project promotes and popularizes a prominent postmodern goal, that is, pluralism. Philosophically, it serves as a basis for politics rooted in heterogeneity and dissension, which honors both "the desire for justice" and "the desire for the unknown" (1984: 67). In his later works he elaborates the program set down in *The Postmodern Condition,* insisting that philosophy, aesthetics, history, and political theory bear witness to heterogeneity and to what has been repressed and forgotten in representations of the past.

Lyotard's proposal is indicative of his post-philosophical position. At the heart of Lyotard's rejection of metanarratives lies his participation in a current philosophical trend, antifoundationalism. Advocates of antifoundationalism include such diverse figures as Derrida, Kuhn, Rorty, Feyerabend, Baudrillard, and Lyotard. Their rejection of the quest for logically consistent, self-evident grounds for philosophical discourse, as well as their alternative promotion of various strategic maneuvers for justification, unite this motley group. For his part, Lyotard courts a skepticism about claims to proof or truth and the foundations that anchor their philosophical argument. Here he echoes the "foundationalist dilemma" summarized by Henry Staten: "There is proof, confirmation, evidence, and then there is what grounds proof, and is in itself capable of being proved" (Henry Staten, *Wittgenstein and Derrida,* 159; cited in Sim).

In place of philosophical foundations and proofs, Lyotard substitutes rhetoric. Because all utterances are bound by rhetoric, it is crucial. Philosophy itself is bound by rhetoric. In place of truth-value certainty, rhetoric takes up residence. It provides the means whereby a philosophy establishes and maintains credibility with an audience. As a means of persuasion, it positions audiences. It evokes emotions, consent, and even dissent. And yes, in the wrong hands it is capable of abuse and excess. Lyotard is acutely aware of the epistemological problems here and the potential tyranny of one susceptible to rhetorical irresponsibility, excess, and abuse of power. Hence, Lyotard's proposal may be subject to the same criticism he levels at foundationalisms and their catalog of abuses. The difference may be in the claims each makes. Foundationalism purports to be in pursuit of truth. According to Lyotard's proposal, antifoundationalism assumes truth to be a fiction. It charges that power constitutes the real goal lurking behind foundationalism's cover. Antifoundationalism strives to unseat the power-wielding of foundations in systems, cultural paradigms, governing bodies. The political dimension embedded in Lyotard's antifoundationalist project becomes clear. But in fact, Lyotard is not hiding behind a philosophical disguise. In *Just Gaming* he candidly claims, "I do not believe myself a philosopher in the proper sense of the term, but a politician" (1985: 10). What motivates this "politician" is a commitment to the individual. He wants to emancipate the individual. This may be the oddness or distinctiveness of Lyotard's postmodernism. He advocates the same goal as modernism, that is, the emancipation of humanity. For him, the postmodern is not a new age, or the dawning of an era on the heels of the apocalyptic demise of the modern. It is not a continuous historical moment, but an event where "little narratives" from individual lives upstage the grand narratives.

What about the Bible in all this? Is the Bible itself a metanarrative and thus to be rejected? In conjunction with the long-standing tradition of the canonical principle, many organized religions claim the Bible as the basis of the unified ethic, worldview, and way of life that they profess. Insofar as the Bible is represented and enlisted as a unified vision prescribing what is good, right, and true for all humanity and its destiny, it would qualify as a "metanarrative." However, recent studies of the biblical writings would assert otherwise. This so-called canon of writings is actually a motley collation of culturally constructed stories. The tales, characters, and lessons that make up the biblical traditions overlap, interweave, contradict, and complement one another. Sometimes they suggest agreement, and sometimes they argue internally about God and the meaning of human existence. Amid this diversity and complexity, no meta-discourse, meta-narrative, or meta-language presides here. They are culturally constrained and generate different responses to the same inquiry. That there are four gospels each representing the Jesus story differently, rather than one proclaiming how it was, is illustrative. Taken together, the biblical texts set forth an elaborate array of "little narratives" inviting the endless supply of readers to spin their interpretive "little stories" in response.

For Lyotard, "the little narrative (which) remains the quintessential form of imaginative invention" also becomes a subversive tactic in the struggle against grand narratives (1984: 67). That is as true in biblical studies as it is in politics. The elevation of the individual requires that the grand narratives, which have restricted or even silenced the personal stories or cultural development of the individual, be abolished. In fact, Lyotard suggests giving "the public free access to the memory and data banks" as one strategy for realizing this goal (1984: 67). And while such a proposal has been judged naive, it demonstrates the gravity of his commitment and concern for the individual over and against systems. "Let us wage war on totalities" so that the individual and not the systems hold power (1984: 82). Only then will individual freedom prevail.

midrash
Daniel Boyarin

Midrash as commentary frequently focuses on the strictly phonetic or sonic aspect of a word; it seems to see meaning in "nothing," in such incidentals as variants of spelling or even the forms of and decorations on letters, and not infrequently finds meanings in words that are the social equivalent of "personal ones." Midrash most frequently (not always) does not proceed by paraphrase, by giving the "meaning" of a passage, but rather by expanding the text via the production of more narrative on the same "ontological" level as the text itself. Extreme (and therefore most revealing) forms of midrash interpret that which, on our theories of language, ought to be "nothing"–parts of words, "meaningless" particles, accidental spelling differences, and even the decorations on letters. It is precisely these features that have produced what might be called "the midrash problem" (Boyarin, 1990). As the great medieval Jewish literary theorist Moses Maimonides remarked of midrashic interpretation, "It cannot be reconciled with the words quoted."

From the posture of Western philosophy (including that of Jews), midrash can only appear as primitive. The signifying practices that characterize midrash as commentary on the canonical and authoritative scripture of Judaism are very similar to linguistic procedures that in other signifying systems (including later Judaism) would belong to practices such as homiletics, poetry, language play, puns, and humor. This is so much the case, indeed, that later forms of Judaism itself interpreted the earlier practice as belonging to the realm of poetry, language play, or homily and *not* commentary.

I cite no less an authority than Maimonides. It would be no exaggeration to say that Maimonides occupies a place in a specific Jewish literary history and theory analogous to that of Aristotle in the discourse of European literature. Maimonides' considerations on the nature of the Bible and the midrash are the *Poetics* of Judaism. Here is Maimonides describing midrash as a signifying practice:

> …Aggadic [midrashic] interpretation, the method of which is well known to those who are acquainted with the style of our Sages. They use the text of the Bible only as a kind of poetical language, *and do not intend thereby to give an interpretation of the text.* As to the value of these midrashic interpretations, we meet with two different opinions. For some think that the midrash contains the real explanation of the text, whilst others, finding that it cannot be reconciled with the words

quoted, reject and ridicule it. The former struggle and fight to prove and to confirm such interpretations according to their opinion, and to keep them as the real meaning of the text; they consider them in the same light as traditional laws. Neither of the two classes understood it, that our Sages employ biblical texts merely as poetical expressions, the meaning of which is clear to every reasonable reader. This style was general in ancient days; all adopted it in the same way as poets do. (Maimonides: 353–54)

Maimonides claims that in order to understand the midrash, we must first have an appropriate conception of what kind of speech it is. After rejecting views that propose that aggada is indeed commentary—either bad or good—Maimonides argues that it is poetry, that is, in his terminology, fiction, in this case, didactic fiction.

In his great modern work on the poetics of midrash, Isaak Heinemann argues against the position of Maimonides:

> However: if the view which Maimonides rejected brought the aggada too close to the plain meaning, his answer [Maimonides'] does not take sufficiently into consideration the difference between the midrash and stories which are purely fictions. It is certainly correct that the *drash* gives greater freedom of movement to the personal character of the interpreter than does the plain sense, and the aggadic drash is "freer" than the halakic, which even Maimonides took seriously... but not infrequently the darshanim cited logical proofs for their midrash and also rejected the interpretations of their colleagues; also the most serious controversies between the Sages of Israel and the sectarians and Christians were carried on with the methods of midrash. (Heinemann: 3)

Heinemann's argument means that midrash is encoded as biblical commentary and not mainly as poetry or homiletic—on its textual surface and in terms of its function within the system of signifying practices of the culture. One does not argue over the referential truth of fictions, nor does one engage in the most fateful controversies of a culture with conceits and quibbles. To take midrash as something else than serious commentary on scripture is analogous to the error of taking ancient historiography as fiction, merely because the "facts" described do not jibe with our reading of documents (see Sternberg: 24–25). Following Heinemann, then, an adequate understanding of midrash would be one in which it is comprehended within the system of signifying practices of which it is a part and not trivialized or reduced by being assimilated to poetry or homiletic.

(This is why it is beside the point to suggest, as some interlocutors have done, that there is nothing unique in midrash; similar practices can be found in other cultures. The question is the place that those practices hold within the signifying systems of those other cultures. On the other hand, I wish it to be absolutely clear that I have nothing at stake in midrash's being unique.

Indeed, to the extent that the explanatory model offered below is at all cogent, the expectation would be to find midrash-like practices in other cultures, given certain sets of cultural conditions and structures. Thus, it would hardly surprise me to find midrash-like commentary in non-Western cultures and even in Greek or Christian ones [earlier or later] that are not dominated by Logos theories of language and signification. Midrash is to be seen in this paper as a token of what commentary might look like in a world without Logos.)

Now, while I would agree that midrash does not intend to give an *interpretation* of the text, interpretation being understood here as a particular kind of commentary, it does certainly function as the most serious kind of reading and commentary on the most authoritative and holy text that Judaism knows. As Simon Goldhill has remarked, any practice of commentary implies a theory of language. The apparent eccentricity of midrash, its frequent-seeming extreme incoherence from the point of view of what counts as commentary in our culture, has to be explained, therefore, via a theory of language. Language itself is embedded in whole systems of signifying practices.

These signifying practices through which rabbinic culture differs all involve a denial of Platonistic splits between the material and the ideal. I wish, however, to avoid strenuously any imputation of some sort of special grace that was visited on "the Jews," or even some subgroup of the Jews, the Rabbis. Contemporary Marxian approaches to historical explanation provide us with modes of thinking about cultural difference that avoid triumphalism and at the same time don't push us in the direction of scientistic, economistic reductionisms.

Marxian classicist George Thomson has proposed a direction for thinking about this issue in remarking on the novelty of the platonic revolution in consciousness (although carefully avoiding, correctly, assigning this revolution to the person of Plato himself):

> As Plato says, the soul is by rights the ruler and master, the body its subject and its slave. This dichotomy of human nature, which through Parmenides and Plato became the basis of idealist philosophy, was something new in Greek thought. To the scientists of Miletos, as to the Achaean chiefs and to the primitive savage, the soul was simply that in virtue of which we breathe and move and live; and although, the laws of motion being imperfectly understood, no clear distinction was drawn between organic and inorganic matter, the basis of this conception is essentially materialist. The worlds of Milesian cosmology are described as gods because they move, but they are no the less material. Nowhere in Milesian philosophy, nor in the Homeric poems, is there anything that corresponds to this Orphic conception of the soul as generically different from the body, the one pure, the other corrupt, the one divine, the other earthly. So fundamental a revolution in human consciousness only becomes intelligible when it is related to a change equally profound in the constitution of human society. (Thomson, 1973: 147; cp. 1955: 239)

It is this revolution in consciousness that enabled, as well, the idea that meaning is abstractable from the matter of text, that the words are bodies and the meanings, souls. The Rabbis, it could be said, maintained against all comers and against all odds a consciousness more similar to that of the "scientists of Miletos [Thales and Anaximander]" than to that of Parmenides, Plato, and most of European thought in their wake (see Boyarin, 1993: 5–6).

I am going to imagine here that midrash came about as the product of a happy accident, the confluence of a highly developed valorization of reading and commentary as the central religious and social practice of a group of people for whom the notions of abstraction and meaning, which we associate so readily with interpretation, had not developed or were being resisted, in part because such notions of meaning were not crystallized at other sites within the cultural system, most notably–dramatically–within the economic and anthropological domains. Moreover, following some of the "best" of recent Marxian theory, the relations between economic signifying practices and others are not simply those of base and superstructure but exist in a much more complex relation of homology (Goux, 1990: 113; Shell, 1978: 4–5). Money is surely one of the most fundamental of symbolic structures within a society and, as such, can be expected to act on other signifying practices and be acted on by them. As Jean-Joseph Goux has written,

> I have gradually reached the conclusion that all processes of exchange and valuation encountered in economic practice set up mechanisms in relation to what I am inclined to term a *symbology,* which is in no way restricted to the economic domain. This symbology entails a system, a mode of symbolizing, which also applies to signifying processes in which are implicated the constitution of the subject, the use of language, the status of objects of desire–the various overlapping systems of the imaginary, the signifying, the real. It is not a matter, then, of ascribing to economic symbology an anterior or causal role. (Goux, 1990: 113)

Marc Shell has also grasped this well: "Whether or not a writer mentioned money or was aware of its potentially subversive role in his thinking, the new forms of metaphorization or exchanges of meaning that accompanied the new forms of economic symbolization and production were changing the meaning of meaning itself" (Shell, 1982: 3–4). The very foundations of philosophy, as a specifically European practice (analogous, of course, but not identical to practices in other human cultures), are grounded in

> bring[ing] together phallos and head...for the ending of the [*Oresteia*] is also concerned with a shift in modes and behavior, as it charts a progression from darkness to light, from obscurity to clarity. Representation of symbolic signs perceived as a form of female activity gives way to the triumph of the male *Logos*. Representation and lyric incantation yield to dialectic and speech, and magic to science. Even more, this "turning away from the mother to the father," as Freud

observed, "signifies a victory of intellectuality over the senses."
(Zeitlin: 111)

Zeitlin proceeds to provide an extensive list of the ontological oppositions grounded in the primary opposition of male as Apollo and female as Erinyes that grow from this "turning" or "victory" (Zeitlin: 112) and that are characteristic of Greek philosophy from some pre-Socratics to Plato and Aristotle. Freud, however, quite mistakenly assigned this "turning" to biblical culture. Neither biblical nor early rabbinic culture, however, made this move toward idealism, toward what Goux has called, quite brilliantly, "paterialism." Both remained as materialistic at least as the Milesian scientists. Biblical and rabbinic cultures resist the abstraction of the male body and the veiling of the penis that produces the phallus, forming, accordingly, a subdominant fiction within the cultural space of the dominant fiction (which subdominant fiction is no less oppressive than the dominant; Boyarin, 1997b: 151–85).

But Isaak Heinemann himself described midrash, long before Derrida, as the "shattering of the Logos" (Heinemann). What is most striking and troubling about midrash is, indeed, its refusal to interpret words as signifiers that are paired with signifieds in any stable fashion. Classical midrash interprets the forms of letters, even decorative flourishes, grammatically required but semantically empty particles, and fragments of words (sometimes taking a part of a Hebrew word and reading it as Greek!). All these phenomena suggest an entirely different sensibility about the meaning of meaning from the logocentric one that drives Western thought (including most Jewish thought from the earliest Middle Ages on).

Interpretation is the dominant mode of commentary in a culture within which value is expressed in terms of an abstract, universal, and in itself substance-free standard: the coin, the Phallus, the father, the Logos. By interpretation I mean virtually all our methods of formal response to texts by which the text is taken to mean something, by which meaning is extractable from a text and presentable, even if incompletely and not exactly, in paraphrase. Even the most extremely antiparaphrastic of Western interpretative methods, for instance the poem-interpretation of the New Critics, still is infinitely more paraphrastic than midrash, which simply refuses to take even the text as verbal icon, preferring almost to read each word, and sometimes each letter, and sometimes the shape of the letter or even its serifs, as a virtual icon in itself. One way to bring this point home would be to insist that, even according to those who would argue that "a poem must not mean but be," the poem remains at least partially translatable. With the modes of linguistic operation that are characteristic of early midrash in place, the text is simply untranslatable (something on the order of the untranslatability of *Finnegan's Wake*). Too many of the features on which midrash founds its meanings are simply artifacts of the materiality of the language in its Hebrew concreteness. Midrash is the dominant mode of commentary in a signifying economy without the "universal equivalent." Famous by now is the moment in talmudic legend when God himself seeks to intervene in midrashic interpretation and is informed that he has no status whatever because the majority of the sages disagree with his interpretation. In commentary, at any rate, for the Rabbis, even the deity is not the measure of all things.

Galit Hasan-Rokem points out in her new book on folk literature in Palestinian midrash, "The discourse of dream interpretation of [the Rabbis] was connected with the dominant interpretative discourse that they employed, the commentary on the Bible and interpretation of written [texts]" (Hasan-Rokem: 109). As Hasan-Rokem has perspicaciously pointed out, rabbinic dream-interpretation practices (as indeed those of the ancient world in general, including such exemplary figures as Artemidorus) seem very similar to modern practices of the interpretation of dream-language, both psychoanalytic and cognitive, such that I would argue that for the Rabbis, the reading of texts was not unlike the interpretation of dreams (Hasan-Rokem: 116). The point is not, as some theorists have claimed, that Freud was somehow influenced by midrash in the development of his interpretation of dreams, but rather that the Rabbis read texts in a dream-interpretation–like fashion (Handelman; Frieden; Hasan-Rokem: 142). As Hasan-Rokem emphasizes, at least one text indicates that the same expertise and spiritual characteristics are requisite for successful dream interpretation and for successful Torah interpretation, or rather that intensive training in the reading of Torah renders one capable of interpreting dream-texts as well (Hasan-Rokem: 118). In other words, I would suggest that language itself was perceived by them in a non-logocentric, or perhaps better stated, not yet fully logocentric modality. For the earliest Rabbis, both the language of dreams and the language of texts work through rebus, through puns, through the concrete forms of letters, through allusions to verses of the Bible, and all the phenomena that Heinemann has referred to as "creative philology," and that we can see are not philology at all but rather a sort of misology.

An elegant example of such misology can be offered from a classical midrash text, a text that has, moreover, important legal consequences, indeed potentially lethal consequences, since it involves the assessment of a verse that deals with capital punishment. It is striking how similar the midrashic understanding adopted in this highly serious context, both in origin (scripture) and in consequence, is to the example of rabbinic dream-interpretation just adduced. In this text, Rabbi Akiva argues, with respect to a verse that includes as the object of capital punishment the plural feminine pronoun *'ethen,* that only one of the two female offenders is, in fact, to be executed. When objected to that the pronoun is plural, Rabbi Akiva's response is that *hen* in Greek means "one!", as far from a logocentric understanding of language as could be imagined. This is in a situation of the most serious religious endeavor imaginable, assessment of the law of Holy Scripture in a capital case.

It is precisely at this site that we mark the difference between midrash and the later logocentricity of Jewish signification practices, as Maimonides gives the absolute difference in meaning of a word that sounds the same in two languages (*'aba* [Hebrew: he wanted] and *'abâ* [Arabic: he refused]; Anidjar) as the basis and cause for a misunderstanding, while for Rabbi Akiva, this is the basis and cause for understanding. As Gil Anidjar has pointed out, language "itself"–assuming such self-identity is still possible–…gets in the way and interferes in the gravest manner, leading one to believe that one *knows* what one has said, or what one has heard. Accurately enough, then, Maimonides remains in the right when he asserts that no knowledge (one may want to say, no meaning, no significiation) is exchanged in the process, since what has been communicated, if at all, is wrong." (Anidjar)

But for Rabbi Akiva, what has been communicated through a *méconnaissance* of Hebrew as Greek is–right. It is exactly in the breakdown between languages that the earlier Rabbi marks the absence of the Logos.

One could claim, however, at this point, that there is not yet any evidence for a different understanding of language per se on the part of the Rabbis, that precisely the comparison between methods of dream-interpretation and Torah-interpretation suggests only a commonality in the understanding of mantic language. It would, accordingly, seemingly be easy to dismiss the thesis of this essay if one could claim that the Rabbis ascribed some special status to Divine language alone and that, with respect to human language, their interpretative methods were identical to those of the "Greeks" and ours. However, this does not seem to be the case. At least some Rabbis used dream-like, midrash-like methods for the application of *contracts* as well (Tosefta Ketobbot 4.9). In other words, I am suggesting that, at least for Rabbi Akiva and his school among the early rabbis, it is precisely the distinction between sacred signifier and language that has not appeared (or has been resisted). Goux describes the platonic revolution in language: "Meaning no longer appears, as the symbolist illusion of sacerdotal writing would have it, to be *adherent* in the signifying material; it exists apart from the sensuous element. A reification of meaning, in the form of a transcendentalized Logos, can then [but has not yet in Rabbi Akiva's midrash] take place" (Goux, 1990: 172). This reification is precisely what is absent in Rabbi Akiva's midrash. Meaning still does appear there to be adherent in the sacerdotal signifying material. As Thomson has pointed out, "[P]uns [are] a universal characteristic of primitive speech, designed to invest it with a magical or mystical significance" (Thomson, 1955: 132); in this respect, midrash has some affinities with some of the most recent practices of literary criticism that take the "matter" of language very seriously indeed. This goes far beyond any facile comparisons of midrash with deconstruction, which are in any case quite questionable (as argued most persuasively by Stern; for the high seriousness of wordplay in a context suprisingly not entirely unlike this one, see Parker: 1–5). Lacan himself, interestingly enough, seems to have had some sense of this difference of rabbinic commentary. Certainly his repeated and famous (some would say notorious) interpretations of "Wo *Es* war, sol *Ich* werden" (Fink: 46) represent a sort of midrash, in the strict sense, on this text, and Lacan himself referred to his commentary on Freud as "talmudic," correctly insisting that he attached more importance to the letter of the text than to its *interpretation* (Lacan: 58)– a sign that the work of midrash continues even in unexpected places.

politics
Eric Thurman

Politically oriented reading is by now a common, if not roundly celebrated, practice in academic biblical studies. Political critics bring to their interpretive interests a concern for the material conditions of people's everyday lives and the complex ways biblical texts may underwrite existing injustices or provide alternative social models and warrants for change. The term *politics*, like its conceptual cousins *ideology* and *ethics,* sometimes lacks crystal-clear definition. The use of these and related terms in biblical scholarship ranges considerably, from a historical focus on the interests driving textual production, to examinations of the roles of biblical texts in various social formations (such as patriarchy), to discussions of ideologies hypostatically encoded in the texts themselves, and to interrogations of the social location of academic biblical studies. Rather than attempt to supply *the* missing signified for *politics,* I aim to exacerbate its elusiveness (without, hopefully, increasing confusion) by highlighting some of the ways postmodern critique at once calls for and complicates our attention to the political aspects of interpretation.

Ideological Criticism

"Ideological criticism," according to *The Postmodern Bible*, "at root has to do with the ethical character of and response to the text and to those lived relations that are represented and reproduced in the act of reading." The authors clarify further, adding that such an interpretive approach "is a deliberate effort to read against the grain—of texts, of disciplinary norms, of traditions, of cultures. It is a disturbing way to read because ideological criticism demands a high level of self-consciousness and makes an explicit, unabashed appeal to justice" (Bible and Culture Collective: 275).

Norman Gottwald's *The Tribes of Yahweh,* published the same year as Jean-François Lyotard's *The Postmodern Condition* (in France), brought to the attention of mainstream biblical studies the lived relations represented in the Exodus and Conquest narratives. Gottwald's innovative approach delineated the social function of Israel's religion using Marxist-informed sociology. His program for political interpretation stated that "only as the full *materiality* of ancient Israel is more securely grasped will we be able to make proper sense of its *spirituality*"(xxv). At the very moment Gottwald brought socioeconomic factors to the foreground in historical biblical research, Lyotard reported the demise of the metanarratives Gottwald named as critical components of historical and constructive theology (Lyotard, 1984: 31–41; Gottwald, 1993a and 1993b). In our postmodern condition, efforts at totalizing analyses such as Gottwald's encounter fierce opposition, especially in the wake of poststructuralism (Bible and Culture Collective, 1995: 272–307). Ideological criticism twenty years after Gottwald's pioneering work (and the work of many others) also devotes considerably more attention to the political nature of biblical interpretation itself.

A roll call of contemporary political biblical scholarship would reveal a virtual congress of critics who self-consciously voice in the name of justice the interests of oppressed and marginalized constituencies (see Adam, 1995a: 45–60; Pippin, 1996b; Bible and Culture Collective: 225–308 for thematic overviews of "ideological criticism"). Joining those critics, postcolonialism (see Moore, in this volume; Sugirtharajah, 1998b) and new historicism (Moore, 1997) have recently found offices in the halls of the biblical academy, while masculinity studies (the theme of the "Bible and Cultural Studies" section of the 1999 SBL annual meeting was "The Man Question;" see also Moore and Anderson, 1998) and queer theory (see Schneider and Stone in this volume; Moore, 1998a) still stand at the door.

As feminist, African American, and postcolonial scholars might remind us, the category "ideological criticism" is of relatively recent vintage, but the *practice* of ideological critique is much older. A postmodern perspective affirms this interpretive legacy's insight that all discourse is politicized. More conventional biblical studies involved in the varieties of historical re-construction or literary criticism are not any less political for failing to investigate or articulate an ideological position. A scholar's "insistence that s/he (or a given text) is 'nonideological' because s/he (or it) disavows any coherent political theory is as silly as would be one's insistence that s/he is 'nonbiological' because s/he has no coherent theory of cell formation" (Kavanagh: 311). In fact, as postmodern theorists maintain, claims to objectivity, disinterestedness, and disciplinary purity all serve to mystify the interpreter's complicity in his or her reading.

Take, for example, the familiar gestures of historical Jesus research. John P. Meier, testifying to widely shared assumptions, suggests that though historians cannot obtain pure objectivity, "pressing towards the goal is what keeps us on track" (Meier, 1991: 5). He admits that "everyone who writes on the historical Jesus writes from some ideological vantage point," but counsels that each scholar ought "to admit honestly one's own standpoint, to try to exclude its influence in making scholarly judgements by adhering to certain commonly held criteria and to invite the correction of other scholars when one's vigilance inevitably slips" (Meier, 1991: 5–6).

Postmodern critics argue, however, that we lack the transcendental reference point by which historians may distinguish between ideological (here meaning "distorted" or "imposed") and "scientifically probable" conclu-sions. In the absence of history in the sense of "what really happened," we have only historiography, the writing of history. We have a discourse, an institutionalized group of practices that arrange intertextual sources into a representation of the "what really happened" (Burnett, in this volume). The historian's linguistic descriptions constitute rather than simply refer to the past. The ability to naturalize and make persuasive a particular recounting depends on fictive devices (like third person narration) and rhetorical tropes that further undermine the historian's putative objectivity (Burnett, 1990; White, 1978; Certeau, 1986b).

Meier's work is a telling example of the inextricably political character of interpretation because his claims to critical self-consciousness make little difference in the conclusions he reaches. Writing a history of Jesus requires an "irreducible theoretical decision" concerning identity and difference—which clues count as evidence and how clues are grouped together or separated (Cousins, 1987: 128). No critic transcends his or her social context in a way that eludes the ideological refractions surrounding these choices. Meier's treatment of Jesus' sayings presents a somewhat obvious case for this point; his lack of engagement with feminist reconstructions of Christian origins offers another. Meier initially brackets the parables to counter the tendency of some scholars to read them as evidence of a Jesus with a wholly "realized eschatology" (Meier, 1994: 290–91); he then produces an eschatological prophet figure not uncomfortable with his own Roman Catholicism (Meier, 1994: 350, 1045). This configuration of what is and what is not relevant to reconstructing Jesus' ministry originates not from the data itself (contra Meier, 1994: 347–48), but from a selective process concerning what, in fact, counts as data. As noted above, this unnatural selection occurs at the level of language and narrative too. All these judgments are unconsciously delimited in advance by the ideologically charged reading formation in which a historian, or any scholar, writes (see Bennett, 1987).

The Ethics of Reading: Whose Ethics? Which Polis?

Recognizing the inescapably political character of biblical interpretation, some scholars call for more sustained efforts toward ethical accountability on the part of readers of the Bible, especially professional critics (for recent examples with important theoretical differences among them, see Adam, 1996; Fowl, 1988; Patte, 1994, 1995; Phillips, 1994; Schüssler Fiorenza, 1999; and Stone, 1997). These critics agree that how we read represents and enacts the kind of politics we (consciously and unconsciously) practice. With Jeffrey Stout, they conclude that "[w]hat begins seeming like a debate over the nature of meaning reveals itself before long as a struggle over what makes literature [in our case, the Bible] worth caring about and what kind of society to strive for" (Stout, 1986: 112).

Recent work by Elisabeth Schüssler Fiorenza and by the tag team of Gary A. Phillips and Danna Nolan Fewell converges on a number of themes highlighted by the ethical turn in biblical studies. Each proposal exhorts interpreters to read "other-wise" (see also Stone, 1997; Heard, 1997; Reinhartz, 1997).

This notion of reading conceives of reading and writing as a perpetual openness to, recognition of, and responsibility to this Other–the otherness of the text itself, the otherness of its writers, the otherness of its readers, and above all the otherness of those individuals who are caught up in the Bible's signifying power as it is deployed both as weapon and tool. (Phillips and Fewell, 1997: 7; compare Schüssler Fiorenza, 1999: 1–14)

Both projects critique hermeneutical foundationalism and putative scientific objectivity (Phillips and Fewell, 1997: 10–14; Schüssler Fiorenza, 1999: 38–46; 58–72). Both also interact with postmodern thought in order to stress the primacy of ethics.

Phillips and Fewell, taking their lead from Emmanuel Levinas, call into question our standard distinction between knowing (epistemology) and doing (ethics). Obligation to the other, on this account, exists prior to any opposition between theory and practice (4–6). Phillips and Fewell ask, "What would happen, for example (and assuming it possible), were we to refuse to distinguish 'ethical reading of Bible' from 'critical reading of Bible?'" (6). Their answer sketches in the voiceless crowds calling to the reader at every level of inquiry (7–10; 16–17). Levinasian deconstruction thrusts the face of the other through the self-confident interpretive facade produced by conventional gestures and assumptions (see also Fewell and Phillips, 1997).

Schüssler Fiorenza articulates a "rhetorical-emancipatory paradigm" for academic biblical studies (1999: 44–55). Drawing from postmodern, postcolonial, and feminist sources, she critiques the regnant value-neutral "scientistic" discourse by highlighting the rhetorical, value-laden nature of language. Her emancipatory focus places marginalized "wo/men" at the center of institutional and interpretive attention. Schüssler Fiorenza aims to reconceptualize biblical scholarship as a public discourse democratically expanding the constituency of the *ekklesia* and promoting "justice and well-being" for all (10–12; 44).

Postmodernism, however, complicates the desire for unambiguously "emancipatory" interpretation or for a form of social justice underwritten by Enlightenment views of subjectivity and equality (Adam, 1995a: 53–54; Bible and Culture Collective: 278, 280, 286, 301–7). Testimony solicited from some of the usual postmodern suspects supports a case against such notions. Habermas (1983), Lyotard (1984), and MacIntyre (1984), for example, each–in very different ways and with conflicting conclusions–point to a crisis of legitimacy in our moral and political vocabularies and institutions. Totalizing theories about justice, the Good, freedom, the proletariat, and so forth are no longer tenable.

Schüssler Fiorenza stresses "over and against some postmodern theories" that "inequalities are not engendered by emancipatory movements and theories of equality, which seek to overcome such unequal otherness" (1999: 159). Rather, the instantiated biases of particular groups "reinforce differences as inequalities" (1999: 159). A postmodern critic might agree and yet reply that the principle of equality *necessarily* "manufacture[s] difference and dissimilarity as inequality" (1999: 159) because "equality" only performs actual political work when employed by partisan groups with local convictions. "Equality," as Luce Irigaray notes, always implies the question, "equal to whom?" (1997a). As an empty concept, "equality" *always* includes *and* excludes when pressed into the service of someone's interests (Fish, 1999). Schüssler Fiorenza papers over this fact when she claims that emancipatory groups define "equality" differently, in a way that "seek[s] to overcome such unequal otherness" (1999: 159). If the interests of the oppressed gained ascendancy, the rules of the language-game of equality would still stand; the players would change sides and a new set of preferences would "reinforce [specific] differences as [principled] inequalities" (1999: 159). The cumulative force of these and other postmodern critiques attenuates the hermeneutical claims made by many liberation biblical critics, suggesting the need for alternative ethical projects (see also Grant, 1999).

The Postmodern Bible obeys the seemingly contradictory imperatives of postmodernism named in this essay's introduction and puts forward a counter-modern ethical proposal. The authors at once announce the political nature of all interpretation and question the basis from which political critique commonly proceeds. For example, they argue that all reading is political, including ideological criticism:

> Even ideological criticism cannot exempt itself from the ideological struggle that takes place in and over texts. The postmodern condition sets the stage for a reading against the grain not only of those historical approaches that would bracket or deny ideology, but also of those literary and cultural critical approaches that would posit a singular, unitary reading of the Bible (ideological or otherwise). (278)

Demonstrating the potential for even liberatory readings to exclude (280–301), the authors consistently point out the dangers of universal, monolithic interpretation. Like the metanarratives of political theory underscored earlier, this hermeneutical strategy secures certainty through the denial of differing voices. Further, the authors assert that "better ideological readings...support and encourage positive social change that affirms difference and inclusion" (302), while maintaining that social change is not "really a goal at all; there is no static teleology in a deconstructive ideological criticism" (306).

This deconstructive practice aims to show just how complicated defining "politics" and offering persuasive critique is from a postmodern stance (see also Fewell and Phillips, 1997; Phillips, 1994; Heard, 1997). However, that stance, at least as defined in *The Postmodern Bible,* also leaves some questions unanswered: What is the basis for their support of difference and plurality? Do all resistant readings run the risk of becoming dominant and thereby oppressive? Is a hypersensitive hermeneutics of suspicion–the constant denaturalizing of readings–the *only* ethical strategy left? How does deconstruction move from ethics to politics? (compare Critchley, 1999: 188–247; Yamada, in this volume).

At this point we may ask how other biblical critics have responded to postmodernism. Two replies stand out. "Anti-postmodernists," as Barry Harvey (in this volume) designates them, reject postmodernism (or at least cardinal aspects of postmodernism) on the grounds that interpretive chaos and vulgar moral relativism inevitably follow when scholars abandon conventional assumptions concerning authorial intent and textual determinacy (see p. 4). Even sophisticated theorists such as Anthony Thiselton and Werner Jeanrond balk at the concept of the social construction of meaning precisely because, on their account, texts lose the power to change the convictions and practices of readers (Thiselton, 1992: 539–50; Jeanrond, 1988: 112). Anti-postmodernists may correctly perceive the political stakes in hermeneutical theory, but those stakes will not be advanced or protected by advocating the necessity of theoretical–as opposed to practical, *political*–controls on interpretation.

Another rejoinder to postmodernism comes from an avowedly theological position. Stephen Fowl's *Engaging Scripture: A Model for Theological Interpretation* articulates an "underdetermined" account of interpretation wherein particular reading formations fashion their readings according to the interests and aims of their community. Fowl accepts (and advances) the postmodern critique of essentialist hermeneutics, but he also questions the ethical resources of deconstruction. The imperative to resist totalizing gestures, Fowl argues, holds only when we encounter the "metaphysics of presence" and its pernicious effects; if, as some suggest, the history of Western thought evinces alternatives to this metaphysics, then other forms of critique may be viable (Fowl, 1998: 48–52). Further, deconstruction equally calls into question readings that support *and* critique morally objectionable practices. "Systematic antideterminacy (as opposed to humility and charity) will paralyze actual attempts to order one's life in accordance with one's interpretation" (Fowl, 1998: 55). Fowl emphasizes the political nature of interpretation by focusing on the concrete communities in which concepts like "justice" and "freedom" take specific and tangible shape through local convictions and practices (Fowl, 1998: 62–97; 1988: 79–80).

Reactions to the politics of postmodern biblical scholarship ultimately fail to separate into neatly identifiable parties. Engagements with postmodern theory continue to be robust and varied. At present, however, it remains the case that "the implications of what it means not to have a telos or a universal ethic or a transcendent truth…have not been sufficiently worked through by biblical critics," perhaps especially critics with overtly political aims (Bible and Culture Collective: 306).

Cultural Criticism and Beyond

Where, then, does this leave us? Right where we've always been: at home with our particular convictions and with those people who commit their lives to what we believe to be true and just (Adam, 1995a: 53–54; Fish, 1999). Nothing follows–no directions for action, no specific political view, no privileged access to new audiences–from the postmodern acknowledgment of unavoidable (though complicated) relationships between politics and academics. As Stanley Fish informs us, "The fact that politics is everywhere has no normative *or* antinormative implications; it provides you with no program, nor does it take any away from you; it points you in no direction but only tells us that, whatever direction you find yourself taking, politics will be there, not as a byway or a danger or an impurity but as the very condition of action" (1999: 126). Local truth claims are all we have and all we need to begin political interpretive work.

Many ideological biblical critics, however, take the "its-politics-all-the-way-down" claim as a prophetic utterance calling interpreters to greater "responsibility" and "accountability." For example, Elisabeth Schüssler Fiorenza expounds an "ethics of accountability that stands responsible...for the ethical consequences of the biblical texts and its meanings" (1999: 15). In a similar vein, *The Postmodern Bible* declares that ideological reading "challenges readers to accept political responsibility for themselves and for the world in which they live," in order to alter "power relationships for the better" (Bible and Culture Collective: 275, 302). Postcolonial critic Roland Boer likewise suggests that biblical studies should contribute to a Marxist "culture that anticipates the end of the capitalist social and economic organization" of imperialism (Boer, 1998: 46).

Each of these summons, and many more like them, indicates a belief that scholars as scholars (a crucial but often unanalyzed qualification) may effect political change. Postmodernism, though, cannot make you a political activist or increase your ethical accountability. Among other things, postmodernism questions the existence of a Public, with a capital "P," to which scholars would be accountable (Fowl, 1988: 78–79). Further, general calls to politicize interpretation appear redundant when made on the heels of acknowledging the unavoidable political character of all discourse. In this light, postmodern critique performs the limited but supremely difficult task of alerting us to *evasions* of politics.

Academic discourse, then, has no necessary or general impact on political discourse. Interpreters who focus on political concerns still abide by the conventions and authorities that constitute the discipline (Fish, 1995: 47–50). Conventions, of course, change; when they do change, "there will be a new understanding of the profession's decorums, but those decorums will still be specific to the profession's practice, which will be internally altered, but not necessarily altered in its relationship to other practices, like the practice of politics, from which it will continue to be distinguished" (Fish, 1995: 44; compare 66–70).

Stephen Fowl represents a species of scholar at home in both academic and political–specifically Christian–habitats. Fowl agrees with Fish that criticism is a professional practice with no general import for extra-academic constituencies (Fowl, 1998: 178–86; Fish, 1995: 19–40, 93–114). Each acknowledges the distinctive goals and procedures of scholastic and political practices (Fowl, 1998: 186–90; Fish, 1995: 41–70). Fowl, however, emphasizes the ad hoc manner in which Christians may engage professional scholarship (179–83); Fish admits such "happy coincidences" between professional and political interests only to downplay their importance (85–87). Where Fish denies the activist academic as a model for professional critics, Fowl exemplifies this breed of scholar by translating academic material into political labor. In Fish's account, it's better to be a big fish in a small academic pond (fish swim in "schools," after all) than a small fish in a sea of partisan barracudas. Fowl's maxim might be "Birds of a feather flock together."

Returning to our local and competing truth claims–claims we never really left behind–also returns us to the historically situated communities and cultures that embody those beliefs. The recent arrival of "biblical/cultural studies" may unearth multiple communities in which critics can work. For example, Abraham Smith calls "African American biblical scholars [to] reach beyond the classroom and the constricting boundaries of particular disciplines to gain nourishment from and provide nourishment for subaltern communities" (1997: 130; compare Fish, 1995: 85–87). By analyzing contingent constellations of biblical texts, audiences, and ideological projects, biblical/cultural studies enrich investigations of the social location of interpretation (Exum and Moore, 1998: 33–35; Glancy, 1998; Sugirtharajah, 1998a). Possibilities for political action only await scholars' imagination and initiative.

Critics committed to effective political work will live and read as citizens of specific constituencies. On this account, political biblical interpretation occurs all the time. In nearly countless ways people employ biblical texts to make sense of their lives and to defend or question specific social formations. When scholars name their allegiances, negotiate their conflicting identities, and engage those reader's lives, they practice ideological biblical criticism.

postcolonialism
Stephen D. Moore

I.

By the 1930s, European colonies and ex-colonies encompassed 84.6 percent of the land surface of the globe (Fieldhouse, 1989: 373; Loomba, 1998: xiii). And although ensuing decades saw the decline of overt colonialism, they also witnessed the escalation of a more insidious phenomenon that would eventually be termed "neo-colonialism," based on the global economic, military, and cultural supremacy of the former colonial powers and newly emergent superpowers (Nkrumah, 1965; Ashcroft, Griffiths, and Tiffin, 1998: 162–63). It is against this imposing backdrop that postcolonial studies has assumed its present contours as an academic enterprise, most notably as a subfield of literary studies (where its impact has been immense), but also as a presence within a broad range of other disciplines, biblical studies included.

Whence the term "post(-)colonial"? It appears to have been coined by historians in the aftermath of World War II and employed in such expressions as "the post-colonial nation-state" (Ashcroft, Griffiths, and Tiffin, 1998: 186). Beginning around the late 1970s, literary critics began to adopt the term, although its usage in literary studies remained sporadic until the early 1990s, when "postcolonial studies" erupted into prominence.

The description "a highly contested field" has become something of a cliché in literary studies, but it perfectly describes postcolonial studies. Even the name of the field has been a hotbed of dispute (Ahmad, 1995; Ashcroft, 1996; McClintock, 1995: 9–15). What is the force of the "post-" in "post(-) colonial," particularly in formulations such as "the post(-)colonial state," "post(-)colonial consciousness" or "post(-)colonial literatures"? Does it imply a clean chronological and ideological break from the colonial "past"? Such a conception of the post(-)colonial is now widely viewed as naive, inadequate, or utopian. It simply cannot account for the complex relations of domination and submission, dependence and independence, desire and revulsion, resistance and collusion that can characterize the exchanges between colonizer and colonized during colonial occupation *and* after official decolonization. Tracing and unraveling these often tortuous relations and affiliations accounts for some of postcolonial theory's most impressive achievements (e.g., Bhabha, 1994). In consequence, the unhyphenated term *postcolonial,* arguably less suggestive of (imagined) chronological or ideological supersession, is now preferred by many critics.

Critical reflection on colonialism presumably began with colonialism itself (taking "colonialism" minimalistically to mean "the implanting of settlements on distant territory" [Said, 1993: 9]). Contemporary histories of postcolonial studies, however, customarily trace its intellectual roots to a disparate group of critics and literary artists, who, operating out of different cultural contexts, engaged in sustained reflection on colonialism and its complex legacies, notably Franz Fanon, C. L. R. James, Albert Memmi, Aimé Césaire, Chinua Achebe, and Ngugi wa Thiong'o. But the work of three further critics constitutes a more immediate resource for contemporary postcolonial studies: Edward Said (his 1978 book *Orientalism,* in particular, is widely seen as having been seminal for the field; see also Said, 1993), Gayatri Chakravorty Spivak (her 1985 manifesto "Can the Subaltern Speak?" has been especially significant; see also Spivak, 1987, 1990, 1998), and Homi Bhabha (his 1994 collection *The Location of Culture* has been a major catalyst in the development of the field). In the work of all three critics, French poststructuralist theory is a central resource for reflecting on colonialism and its effects: Said reads with Foucault, Spivak with Derrida, and Bhabha with Derrida and Lacan. To oversimplify somewhat, much contemporary postcolonial criticism may be broadly classified as "poststructuralist," or, more narrowly, as "deconstructive" (so Ashcroft, Griffiths, and Tiffin, 1998: 192–93), because it entails repeated demonstrations of how texts emanating from colonialist cultures, say–whether standard histories, or travel narratives, or canonical works of literature (Shakespeare's *The Tempest,* Defoe's *Robinson Crusoe,* Conrad's *Heart of Darkness...*)–are enmeshed in ideological formations and networks of contradiction that exceed and elude the consciousness of their authors. The "poststructuralization" of postcolonial studies in the 1980s and 1990s, while accounting for its immense success in a Western literary studies academy that is at once both "politicized" and "poststructuralized," has been a source of concern in certain quarters, however, particularly those in which materialist philosophies, such as Marxism, are seen to supply a more practical basis for social and political action (Ahmad, 1992; Ashcroft, Griffiths, and Tiffin, 1995: Part 4; Gandhi, 1998; San Juan, 1998).

Yet postcolonial criticism is not *a* method of interpretation (any more than is feminist criticism, say) so much as a critical sensibility attuned to a specific range of interrelated textual and historical phenomena. Any example of postcolonial criticism that we might draw on for purposes of illustration is therefore bound to be arbitrary. A convenient (and not unrepresentative) example is nevertheless provided by Edward Said's "Jane Austen and Empire," a much-cited section of his 1993 book *Culture and Imperialism.* Said centers his investigation on Austen's *Mansfield Park.* The modest English estate of the title–the stage for a typical Austenian microdrama of manners and morals–happens in this case to be materially sustained by a second estate, a plantation in Antigua. To this far-off estate Sir Thomas Bertram, the owner of Mansfield Park, makes periodic journeys to manage his business affairs there. Yet, whereas Sir Thomas' arrivals at and departures from Mansfield Park, and his actions and conduct while resident there, are matters of great consequence in the novel, and as such are recounted in detail, as are events at Mansfield Park generally, the Antiguan estate is but the object of a few passing references, and none of the narrative is set there. Antigua, then, is entirely incidental to the action–yet absolutely crucial to it–since Sir Thomas' fortunes and those of his dependents (the cast of characters whom Austen has assembled at Mansfield Park, including the novel's heroine, Fanny Price) hinge on events in Antigua. The occluded relationship between the two estates, unexamined in previous criticism of *Mansfield Park,* is a source of fascination for Said. "How are we to assess Austen's few references to Antigua, and what are we to make of them interpretively?" he muses (89). Sir Thomas' Caribbean estate would have had to be a sugar plantation sustained by slave labor, which was not abolished until the 1830s, Said surmises (*Mansfield Park* was published in 1814). The slave trade, then, was precisely what made the exquisitely refined microcosm of Mansfield Park possible.

> All the evidence says that even the most routine aspects of holding slaves on a West Indian sugar plantation were cruel stuff. And everything we know about Austen and her values is at odds with the cruelty of slavery. Fanny Price reminds her cousin that after asking Sir Thomas about the slave trade, "There was such a dead silence" as to suggest that one world could not be connected with the other because there simply is no common language for both. That is true. But what stimulates the extraordinary discrepancy into life is the rise, decline, and fall of the British empire itself and, in its aftermath, the emergence of a post-colonial consciousness. In order to read more accurately works like *Mansfield Park,* we have to see them in the main as resisting or avoiding that other setting, which their formal inclusiveness, historical honesty, and prophetic suggestiveness cannot completely hide. In time there would no longer be a dead silence when slavery was spoken of, and the subject became central to a new understanding of what Europe was. (Said, 1993: 96)

II.

By the late 1990s, postcolonial studies had begun to make notable inroads in biblical studies. A 1996 issue of the "experimental" biblical studies journal *Semeia* bore the title *Postcolonialism and Scriptural Reading* (see Donaldson, 1996; compare Gallagher, 1994). In 1998 another edited collection appeared, provocatively titled *The Postcolonial Bible* (Sugirtharajah, 1998c); it was the inaugural volume of a projected series itself titled "The Bible and Postcolonialism." That year also saw the appearance of a monograph by Sugirtharajah: *Asian Biblical Hermeneutics and Postcolonialism* (Sugirtharajah, 1998a). In 1999 the *Journal for the Study of the New Testament* put out a thematic issue, *Postcolonial Perspectives on the New Testament and Its Interpretation* (Sugirtharajah, 1999; the next issue of the journal, *JSNT* 74, contained four reviews of *The Postcolonial Bible,* and in *JSNT* 75 *The Postcolonial Bible* answered back in the voice of Fernando F. Segovia). At the time of this writing, the journal *Biblical Interpretation* has also devoted most of an issue to biblical interpretation in postcolonial Hong Kong (Lee, 1999, followed by four response articles, with a reply from Lee) and has approved a proposal for a full issue on postcolonial studies and biblical studies. Also in preparation is an ambitious volume provisionally titled *The Postcolonial Bible Commentary,* loosely modeled on *The Women's Bible Commentary,* and again edited by the ubiquitous Sugirtharajah. The further dissemination of postcolonial studies in biblical studies will also be facilitated by the recent formation of a new program unit within the Society of Biblical Literature titled "New Testament Studies and Postcolonial Studies," due to get underway formally at the 2000 annual meeting of the society. Also worth mentioning is the fact that the program unit was unofficially launched at the 1999 annual meeting, where a special session of the Bible in Africa, Asia, Latin America, and the Caribbean Section was devoted to it–an index of the extent to which the flowering of "indigenous" biblical hermeneutics in the Two-Thirds World, coupled with unprecedented receptivity to such hermeneutics in the West, particularly in North America, guarantees a ready-made audience for postcolonial biblical criticism.

Despite the relatively rapid progress of postcolonial studies within biblical studies, however, an irksome question arises: Is postcolonial studies really relevant to the Bible? Prompting the question is an assumption that tends to permeate the (extrabiblical) literature on colonialism, namely that the latter is a phenomenon whose "real" history begins only with the European colonization of the non-European world in the modern period. This assumption is not without substance. European colonization *was* qualitatively different from pre-capitalist colonial enterprises. European colonizers did more than extract tribute and other forms of wealth from subjugated peoples: They restructured the economies of those peoples, enmeshing them in a symbiotic relationship with their own, and thereby ensuring a constant two-way flow of human and natural resources (slaves, settlers, raw materials, etc.)–and a one-way flow of profits into their coffers (Loomba, 1998: 3–4).

But although colonialism acquired an unprecedented reach and devastating efficiency in the modern period, many earlier empires, not least those of the ancient Near East and the Mediterranean Basin, also engaged in colonization. Postcolonial studies does pose a formidable "translation" problem for students of ancient literature (Gallagher, 1996: 230–33; Jobling, 1999: 117–18)–much the same sort of problem that contemporary literary theory, forged as it is primarily from analysis of modern and postmodern literatures, poses for the biblical "user"–but need not be dismissed on that account. Furthermore, postcolonial studies is by no means narrowly focused on the twin phenomena of colonialism and postcolonialism. A series of other, related phenomena also fall within its orbit: imperialism, Orientalism, universalism, expansionism, exploration, invasion, enslavement, settlement, resistance, revolt, terrorism, nationalism, nativism, negritude, assimilation, creolization, hybridization, colonial mimicry, the subaltern, marginalization, migration, diasporization, decolonization, globalization, and neocolonialism–all intersected by the ubiquitous determinants of language, gender, race, ethnicity, and class. The relevance of many of these concepts to the biblical texts, considered even in their ancient milieux, hardly needs belaboring.

But the agendas for biblical scholarship suggested by postcolonial studies are not limited to ancient texts and contexts. As is well known, the Bible in general, and specific biblical texts in particular, was used in both systematic and ad hoc ways to authorize the conquest and colonization of Africa, Asia, the Americas, and even pockets of Europe itself, ranging from the strategic deployment of the Matthean "Great Commission" in William Carey's immensely influential 1792 pamphlet *An Enquiry into the Obligations of Christians to Use Means for the Conversion of the Heathen* (Sugirtharajah, 1998b: 96–100) to Oliver Cromwell's explicit assumption of the role of the biblical Joshua in the mass slaughter of Irish "Canaanites" in the course of his subjugation in 1649 of the Irish towns of Drogheda and Wexford (Carroll, 1996: 41–42). Such (ab)uses of biblical texts are already a magnet for postcolonial biblical criticism. A third, perhaps less obvious, focus for such criticism is suggested by the fact that the very period when critical biblical scholarship was being invented in Europe–principally the eighteenth and nineteenth centuries–was also the period when European colonization of the globe was in a phase of unprecedented ascent. Needless to say, the former process did not occur in a vacuum, sealed off hermetically, or hermeneutically, from the latter, yet the task of tracing the affiliations and correlations between the two will be a complex one (Segovia, 1998: 58–60).

III.

Let us turn to two exegetical "illustrations" of postcolonial biblical criticism. Richard A. Horsley's "Submerged Biblical Histories and Imperial Biblical Studies" (his contribution to *The Postcolonial Bible*) contains a brief but illuminating reading of Mark. Horsley begins with an eye-opening critique of the history of European and North American Markan scholarship, arguing that the tendency of such scholarship to accept as factual the traditions associating Mark with the imperial metropolis of Rome tacitly assigned this gospel a buttressing role in the grand narrative of Western Christianity; that its tendency to construe Mark as a passion narrative with an extended introduction depoliticized the gospel and emptied its Galilean elements of their significance; that its more recent tendency to read Mark as a narrative of discipleship assimilates the gospel to the individualistic model of Western Christianity, further obscures "the anti-imperial political plot of the Gospel," and reduces Jesus' confrontation with the Roman client rulers to "incidental stage setting" (156). In a reading that continues to bristle with provocative assertions, Horsley goes on to adumbrate an alterative understanding of Mark, one designed to enable its "recovery…as a narrative of imperially subjected peasantries forming a movement of revitalized cooperative social formations based on their own indigenous traditions," and embodying resistance both to exploitative local authorities and alien imperial domination (162; compare 157). The Markan Jesus who emerges from Horsley's essay is hardly a complete stranger; clearly he has much in common with the historical Jesus fleshed out in Horsley's earlier work, as well as with John Dominic Crossan's Jesus and other political Jesus constructs. But Horsley's recent reading in postcolonial theory has apparently enabled him to bring his previous portrait of Jesus in general, and Mark's Jesus in particular, into sharper relief–specifically, elements of it related to colonialism and anti-colonial resistance. (Horsley notes at one point that a postcolonial exegesis of Mark "makes it appear much like the sort of history that recent subaltern studies are striving to construct of the Indian peasantry" [156–57; compare Guha, 1982].) And implicit in Horsley's reading of Mark is the notion that this gospel, properly understood, is consistently anti-imperial in thrust, and hence a sound basis for theological critique of hegemonic ideologies and institutions, including those of today (172).

Another recent postcolonial reading of Mark, however, Tat-siong Benny Liew's "Tyranny, Boundary and Might: Colonial Mimicry in Mark's Gospel," takes issue with interpreters who construe Mark purely or predominantly as a document for liberation. (His targets are Ched Myers, Herman Waetjen, and Robert Hamerton-Kelly; Horsley's essay was not available to him, apparently.) Liew, too, holds that Mark contains elements of an anti-colonial critique. He is not content to stop there, however; he argues that Mark duplicates colonial ideology as much as (or more than?) it resists it. Liew takes up Homi Bhabha's highly influential concept of "colonial mimicry" (Bhabha, 1994: 85–92), but gives it a twist of his own. Bhabha notes how colonial discourses repeatedly enjoin the colonized to internalize and replicate the colonizer's culture–to mimic it, in effect. But this stategy is fraught with risk for the colonizer, argues Bhabha, and replete with opportunity for the colonized, because such mimicry can never be perfect but can all too easily slide over into mockery and thereby menace the colonizer's control. Liew sees Mark, too, as engaged in colonial mimicry–not as active resistance to Roman hegemony, however, but as (unwitting?) reduplication of Roman imperial ideology. Mark's characterization of Jesus is crucial for Liew in this regard. As Liew sees it, Mark is merely intent on replacing one absolutist authority–that of the Roman state–with another–that of Jesus. To demonstate this, Liew analyzes the Markan Jesus' appropriation of the Jewish scriptures, his relations with God, with other Jewish leaders, and with his disciples. Mark's hegemonic characterization of Jesus achieves it climax in the motif of the parousia; then the victorious Christ will annihilate all competing authorities, replicating "the colonial (non)choice of 'serve-or-be-destroyed'" in the process (Liew, 1999: 23; compare Said, 1993: 168), a (non)choice based on the "colonial rationalization" that certain people are simply unworthy of autonomy, or even of life itself (Liew, 1999: 23). The problem for Liew is that by depicting the defeat of power with more power–power in overwhelming measure–Mark is (inadvertently?) mimicking the "might-is-right" ideology that has engendered colonialism and imperialism in the first place (26).

Horsley's and Liew's readings of Mark illustrate the poles between which postcolonial biblical criticism currently oscillates. On the one hand, the biblical text is read more-or-less straightforwardly as an anti-colonial and decolonizing document. On the other hand, the biblical text is read more-or-less straightforwardly as a colonizing document. Less cut-and-dried readings can also be envisioned, needless to say. Simon Samuel, an Indian doctoral student currently completing a full-scale postcolonial reading of Mark at the University of Sheffield, draws more directly than Liew on Bhabha's concept of colonial mimicry, together with the related concepts of hybridity and ambivalence (Bhabha, 1994: 85–92, 112–20, 129–38), to argue that Mark's strategies of colonial reduplication are highly nuanced and contain elements that are genuinely anti-colonial and emancipatory side by side with elements that merely reinscribe colonial ideologies (Samuel, forthcoming).

IV.

Much traditional biblical scholarship reads like postcolonial criticism *avant la lettre*–or else badly done. That hallowed gateway to biblical criticism, for example, the "Old" or "New" Testament introduction (whether the textbook or the course), has derived much of its efficacy and allure from its ability to summon "exotic" empires from the shadows of the biblical texts and parade them before the student: Egypt, Assyria, Babylon, Persia, Greece, Rome. So much biblical scholarship is already a reflection on imperialism, colonialism, and the resistance they inevitably elicit. (With Said [1993: 9], I understand "imperialism" to mean "the practice, the theory, and the attitudes of a dominating metropolitan center ruling a distant territory.") Horsley's edited collection, *Paul and Empire* (Horsley, 1997), is thus able to draw almost exclusively on the resources of mainstream biblical studies to examine its title topic and almost never refers to extra-biblical postcolonial studies. Yet it stands to reason that the latter field would offer significant resources for focusing, sharpening, and enlarging such analyses. And in the process yet another boundary-bursting leaven might ooze its way into biblical studies–and, who knows, might even trickle beyond the borders of biblical studies altogether to effect palpable change in the extra-academic world.

practice
Mary McClintock Fulkerson

The concept of "practice" has a straightforward relevance for interpreters of the Bible: What matters most for a religious faith is living it well. Yet connecting practice with the biblical text is a difficult matter, particularly because of the prominence of the view that textual interpretation is a cognitive act of meaning-discernment, which is to be "applied" later. Given that this modern split of understanding and application has been roundly criticized by philosophers and theologians alike, a next step is to consider work on the category "practice." For thinkers critical of the epistemological subject of modernity, the basis for the problematic cognitive interpreter, practice, or practical understanding, proves an attractive alternative. Attention to practice yields clues for thinking with the Bible in ways more congruent with the complexities of living.

Human understanding is textured and complex. Characterizing the subject as a mind or consciousness whose relation to the world is mediated through representations, the epistemological tradition of this modern subject (inherited from Descartes and Locke; see Taylor, 1989) is strikingly inadequate to its bodied and social character. Ranging from tacit apprehensions to highly reflective discernment, understanding is embodied and social, implicated with power arrangements, and marked by gendered, racialized, and other determinacies, which are rendered invisible by the universal modern subject. To contribute to a postmodern approach to the Bible that appreciates practical understanding as well as the disruptive things such understanding might do to conventional images of biblical interpretation, this essay sketches three contemporary accounts of practice that dissent from the modern subject (and are in that sense "postmodern") and concludes with their implications for a text-related enterprise. Though there are disagreements over characterizing each of the thinkers cited here as "postmodern"–Bourdieu, for example, does not speak of himself with this label, even though some interpreters do–this problem involves the complexities of defining postmodernism. Suffice it to say that, regardless of their additional targets, each is concerned with practice as an alternative to the modern intellectualist subject.

Aristotle's concept of "praxis" was the most developed account of practice among the Greeks, and it continues to have impact today. Praxis, according to the fourth century B.C.E. philosopher, was the doing that achieves the good life for human being (*Nicomachean Ethics:* I, II.4–6, III.6, IV, V, VI.4–13; see

Lobkowicz: 3–57). Agreeing with the ancient Greeks that what is most essentially human is the ethical and political life, Aristotle distinguished praxis from *theoria,* a disciplined life of contemplation. While *theoria* was the highest reach of the good life, *praxis* was its most important dimension, at least for the elite (for a discussion of Aristotelian "elitism," see Okin, 1983, 1989; MacIntyre, 1988). Building on Platonic views, Aristotle advanced appreciation of the polis as the realm for exercise of practical reasoning. His anthropology assumed a universal good for "man" and that it could be measured by the development of virtues or qualities that constituted that good (and subordinate goods), both intellectual and characterological (though there is ambiguity on the degree to which the judgment about this end is really achieved by theoria, which studies the "eternal and unchanging"; Milbank: 347ff.). In what was basically a hierarchy of human activity, Aristotle demoted the doing that produces things, *poesis.* Thus, even as he moved the doing of the good more solidly into the realm of the earthly and the contingent than had his Platonic predecessors, the lesser activities of making were usually distinguished from *praxis.*

This Aristotelian account of practice has been developed by philosopher Alasdair MacIntyre to address what he sees as the fundamentally impoverished state of contemporary moral life. The authority of modern figures of the manager, therapist, and aesthete are the social signs of this impoverishment. As a state of moral incoherence, it results from abandonment of the Aristotelian moral universe and the futility of Enlightenment substitutes. Thus, MacIntyre sees his larger task as a revival of Aristotelian moral thinking. To address particular lacunae in the modern subject, his definition of practice restores notions of the good, virtues, and a (formal) teleological subject, without which he contends there cannot be an intelligible account of moral behavior.

Parsing MacIntyre's definition shows his extension of Aristotle's account of practice through concepts of narrative and tradition to correct for the incoherence of the moral subject. A practice is "any coherent and complex form of socially established cooperative human activity"(1984: 187).What makes a behavior qualify as an action is its intelligibility, for example, reasons may be given for it. However, MacIntyre is not suggesting that good practice is constituted by isolated decisions. What is at stake here is the coherence of a *human life.* MacIntyre develops this Aristotelian concern further with narrative theory: A story unifies the disparate acts that comprise a life by bringing sense to its temporal shape. Extending that coherence to the context in which a life occurs, he shows that a practice is social. A community and its temporally thick set of reasons and arguments—a tradition—grant coherence to lives.

Communities, then, are essential because they make particular contributions: Practice refers to activities "through which goods internal to that form of activity are realized in the course of trying to achieve those standards of excellence which are appropriate to, and partially definitive of, that form of activity" (1984: 187). With the notion that they have internal criteria of excellence, MacIntyre refers to the inherently value-laden character of these activities. When those standards are met, the activity itself is experienced as a good. Internal goods (ends inherent in doing) must be distinguished from external goods (rewards not dependent on doing the activity well). Excellence accrues to the agents' intentional successful activity, rather than being contingently related to a fickle, amoral, or oppressive social context, or to the arbitrary decisions of an uninformed individual choice. A community and its traditions are essential to provide criteria of excellence and wisdom accumulated for knowing how to do something well.

Continuing his definition, a practice has "the result that human powers to achieve excellence, and human conceptions of the ends and goods involved, are systematically extended" (1984: 187). There is a generative character to such activity. MacIntyrean activities are those that in fact develop the best in human life, a judgment only possible when society has teleological language for "the best." While differing from Aristotle on whether activities such as architecture are practices, MacIntyre's is a call for an Aristotle-inspired correction of the modern ateleological subject. Coherent subjects have communal traditions that define inherent goods and ends; ideal practice is distinguishable from institutions and processes of the social formation (institutions are externally related to the goods of practices, on which they seem to impinge only to corrupt; 194ff.). It is a wonderful vision of good practice as inherently creatively expansive.

MacIntyre's account requires the Aristotelian notion of virtues, those human qualities necessary to achieve goods internal to practices (1984: 191–225). These qualities come from a tradition's concept of the ends of life, a theory at odds with the Homeric and utilitarian (or sophist) conceptions of virtue. Only qualities count that constitute the good person in their very exercise, not the qualities that could serve as mere *means* to an end. Thus, skills necessary to make a good product (oddly) and the qualities adherent to a social role are not virtues, nor are qualities deemed necessary to worldly success and disconnected from an account of human telos or teleological (utilitarianism) without a moral order (1984: 121–30, 181–86).

In a discipline shaped by intellectual forces MacIntyre wishes to overturn, sociologist Pierre Bourdieu revives the Greek term *habitus* to make important changes in social science. Although he acknowledges Aristotle's practice–later the Scholastic *habitus*–as background for his work, Bourdieu is not reviving Aristotelian moral theory. His targets are structuralism, with its objectivism, and subjectivism, the isolated Sartrean subject in particular. While Bourdieu's habitus has affinities with MacIntyrean concerns, it provides richer accounts of the range of bodily, tacit, and regularized understanding that is constitutive of agency (1985: 11–24). He also connects habitus with power in more specific ways.

In his fieldwork with traditional Algerian communities and in studies of contemporary French society, Bourdieu develops the concept of habitus as an alternative to the either/or choices of social science: structuralist theories where rules direct behavior, or subjectivist theories where behavior is the result of individual intentionality. Take, for example, a community's sense of honor. An agent does not practice honor because s/he consciously follows a code of communal rules, says Bourdieu; nor does it occur due to an autonomous choosing. Understood as a habitus, this sense of honor "is a permanent disposition, embedded into the agents' very bodies in the form of mental disposition, schemes of perception and thought" (1977a: 1–29, 15; his *Logic of Practice* is a reworking of this material). The sense is formed through an extended communal process both conscious and unconscious. A habitus creates an internalized sense of things–a "feel for the game"–which is the necessary "background" to the highly intentional dimension of practical reasoning. Aristotle's account of practical reasoning is not simply intellectual, given that it assumes a habituated actor, but Bourdieu is better at describing the prereflective character of habituation.

With this account of the relation of agents to the social world, Bourdieu brings together "two dimensions of the social, not two separate sorts of being" (Calhoun: 74). The habituated agent is a "socially informed body." The social world is embedded in an agent as history through the habitus. History thus shapes the present, but not primarily in the highly regulated and codified form that tradition has for MacIntyre. Bourdieu speaks of the "memory of the body"; a culture is borne in the body, which from childhood prereflectively assimilates the knowledge of a community. History is meant in an incarnational way here. As a bodily inheritance, a habitus includes a kinesthetic sense of how to proceed, how to move, how to respond in situations. It divides up and relates to space in particular ways, for practical awareness involves the way a body takes up space in the world; it is an organizing of gestures, posture, bearing, and stance. Necessarily, it is a *gendering* of body, posture, space, and place, and it is ordered by class (1977a: 26, 180–95). Such an account of agency avoids determinism; the habitus is a constantly creative and responsive relation to the world. A habitus carries the past in a regularized dispositional and contextual way. As a pattern in constant negotiation with context, the bodily dispositional response is a "regulated improvisation." When an agent is skilled in a habitus, her practical wisdom enables a continuous decoding of what is going on–reading signs, class, and otherwise; habitus is "self-regulating" as it adjusts to the specifics of a new situation (1977a: 78, 10).

In addition to offering an alternative to objective (structures) versus subjective (individualist) notions of practice, habitus also comes with an analysis of power. Bourdieu thinks that whatever else they are about, agents are always trying to accumulate capital, the symbolic resources of power–the closest he comes to a notion of human nature (he operates with the "innocuous sense" of human nature in contrast to a classic teleological sense; Stout, 1988: 303). The process necessarily takes different forms in traditional homogeneous societies, where intrapersonal relations are the primary context for accumulation, and in contemporary differentiated societies, where self-perpetuating social structures create effects that bypass and complicate the face-to-face setting of habituation (1977a: 159–97; Bourdieu lacks an analysis of capitalism, however–see Calhoun). Consequently, the habitus for Bourdieu is not susceptible to the kind of normative assessment found in the Aristotelian model. Bourdieu deals with cumbersome "units" of power. A practice is a continuum of apprehensions that is not composed of a single intention but includes a range of sensibilities and potential intentions. Its unconscious aspects demand a formulation of the misrecognition of reality. Power analysis for Bourdieu includes the assumption that attempts to protect self-interest (not necessarily conscious) are reproduced by internalized social structures and that relations of class or some form of dominance are constitutive of human situations, and that "learned ignorance" is simply a feature of the overrunning of individual intention by the larger backgrounds of agency. Thus, an assessment based on clearly distinguishable intentions and negligent of the full continuum of the bodily/manual sense–which Aristotelian virtue theory seems to be–would ignore much of what constitutes a habitus (though MacIntyre does not lack a critique of the social formation, the terms of virtue are possible without reference to it).

Bourdieu's work is not lacking in evaluation, however; he employs his own social science tools to challenge the fact-value distinction and other distortions of objectivism. His commitment to the practical context of understanding means that academic knowledge is the residue of a habitus. Academics, like any practice, is embedded in a social world organized around capital-accumulation. Always a critic of theoretical theory, which confuses abstractions for the contingent realities they attempt to map, his work on contemporary French society assesses the social capital and misrecognition in the practices of the academic class (1984). His later work focuses more on a concept of a "field," as well, to better treat the logics of power and capital in differentiated society (arguments that he is postmodern are based on this work on the "discipline"; Lash: 265). While the analysis of an empirical discipline lacks the "normativity" of a philosophical proposal of a moral order and thus (problematically) does not think itself able to propose a teleological account of human nature, Bourdieu's assumption that practical understanding is always a located project is valuational by definition. As an exposé of sorts of the distorting effects of distancing at work in academic pseudo-objectivity, his critique of the habitus of the social scientist operates with an implicitly counterhegemonic eye to reproduction of the interests of dominant classes, as did his critical work on the educational process (1977b; domination prevails even as the elite are nice to the "help," given that the structures maintaining the class divisions are constantly reproduced by the seemingly benign ordinary activities of a habitus of wealth; 1977a: 189–90).

A third account of practice in the work of Michel de Certeau (d. 1986) resonates with postmodern themes of destabilizing and discourse of the Other. While his conversation partners range from historians to literary theorists, anthropologists, and religionists, among others, the work of this Jesuit and historian of sixteenth- and seventeeth-century mysticism eludes disciplinary label or unification. Like Bourdieu, he focused on the particular; Certeau gave extraordinary attention to ordinary practices and their use by the powerless to subvert dominant structures. He described modern society in terms of writing: the replacement of God/church–authorized definitions of the "real" with the authoring of subjects and increasing manipulation by technologies and socioeconomic production. He offered no theory of practice, modernity, or the Other. Instead, Certeau's writing was itself performative– "a new 'style' of practice which resist[ed] the violence of conceptualization by seeking to speak of the Other only through particular others," as one critic says (Bauerschmidt: 5; but consider Certeau's attention to the mode of enunciation, the mode of operation of a speaker, an attention that he carried to all practices, in 1984: 18–24, 154–64). Sharing with MacIntyre and Bourdieu suspicion of modern accounts of knowledge, Certeau exposed the "expert" through ordinary language and displayed the falsification of the abstraction. He highlighted the difference in position of the powerful "observers" and the observed: "The Bororos of Brazil sink slowly into their collective death, and Levi-Strauss takes his seat in the French Academy. Even if this injustice disturbs him, the facts remain unchanged...the intellectuals are still borne on the backs of the common people" (1984: 25). Although theological topics disappeared from his work after the mid-1970s, the Christian faith that he did discuss has a migratory, destabilizing character. He offered many gifts in a postmodern appreciation of the subtle creative possibilities of the small, the moving, and the quotidian, making "a kind of *perruque* (diversionary tactic) of writing itself," as he put it (1984: 28, 2–28; a *perruque* is a diversionary subversive practice, originally practiced by French workers). Certeau wrote of the "shattering" of Christianity (Certeau and Domenach, 1974; Ahearne: 493–503).

Certeau's explicit discussions of practice in *The Practice of Everyday Life* are elaborations of the ways people use what is available to them. In contrast with the Aristotelian practice, Certeau's democratic approach is interested in *poesis* (making) and disrupts the language of capitalist consumption as well. While he shared Foucault's interest in the micro-activities of daily life, Certeau did not concede the overwhelming effect of the disciplinary society and looked for the resistance in ordinary "ways of operating." He thought "making" relevant because it is productive and creative; consuming is active, not simply the passive response of the duped. Certeau was able to see that people deviously find "*ways of using* the products imposed by a dominant economic order" (1984: x–xxiv).

As radically democratic, practices were not tradition-formed communal activity; nor did he follow cultural studies by choosing particular cultural sub-groups–"marginality is not just minority, it is massive and pervasive." Some practices are *strategies,* the practices that take up space and accumulate; they are the maneuvers of institutions. However, his main interest was *tactics*–activities without a base or place. Tactics depend on time and always "manipulate events in order to turn them into 'opportunities.'" They are the tools of the weak, whether it be indigenous peoples' reworking of the colonizing Spanish religion to their advantage, or the walking, talking, reading, and cooking of "everyperson." Activities can be subversive, if, that is, they are considered in their complexity as negotiations with time and space and with logics relative to dominant arrangements (1984: xvii–xxiv, 24–28).

With a powerful sense that Christianity's strategic practices were largely ineffectual in the secular world, Certeau spoke of the Jesus event as the condition for faith, yet in terms of a logic of lack that is part of every event. Certeau meant this as a refusal of universalism. Thus, the incarnation is the inaugural rupture of history, but it cannot be a complete event. It, like the rest of Christian tradition, is necessary as a particular boundary because it forces differentiation. One of the ways he indicates this in terms of Christian relationships is with reference to Jesus, who is "not without the Father." The phrase "not without," borrowed from Heidegger, is a recognition of the relation to the Other; "no one is Christian without the others." Yet there is lack–Jesus' death must happen–for it "permits" and creates "the necessity of being different from these beginnings." Similarly, the New Testament was necessary to contemporary faith, but never as a system or rule-book. The very plurality of gospel accounts of Jesus is the condition of its continued truth. One relates normatively to it when scripture works performatively to create certain relationships, for example, relations like that of Jesus to "the Father" (1971: 341, 338, 335).

We turn to a postmodern "critical practice for texts," as literary critic Catherine Belsey calls it, to help summarize the implications of these accounts of practice for postmodern biblical work. Belsey proposes her account as the postmodern corrective of "expressive realism," which loosely correlates to the hermeneutical subject-text relation characterized as "modern" in this essay. Postmodernism, or more properly, poststructuralism, is the reaction to Saussure. Critical practice comes from a refusal of the modern notion that there is a recoverable "real meaning" to a text. Thus, such a practice aims at "a process of releasing the positions from which the text is intelligible." While our accounts of practice are not primarily text-ordered, they implicitly support such an aim. All three versions assume that language is social, a feature of this critical practice of texts; practical understanding guarantees that. Each also works with a theory of language (such as Wittgenstein's) as fundamentally social. It is this social character that itself helps us to understand the postmodern feature that there can be no single meaning in the text. It also implies that the reader is "a producer of the text." Although they will differ over how, our practice authors' shared interest in communities implicitly multiplies the potential meaning of interpreted objects. As to the productive role of readers, one might say that because each version of practice recognizes the productive character of agents, this carries over naturally to readers, even becoming a

196 Handbook of Postmodern Biblical Interpretation

sort of "specialty" theme for Certeau. Reflecting the complex character of human experience, a final feature of critical practice entails recognition of the impact of the social formation on the reading of a text and, thus, recognition of ideology or misrecognition. On that the authors vary, and we conclude with their distinctive contributions to this outline of critical text practice.

With an account of the tradition-based character of language that entails agreement that texts have multiple meanings constituted by communities, MacIntyre's practice is distinctive for his concern with what would count as the *intelligibility* of a position toward a text. Christian thinkers have been attracted to MacIntyrean practice as a designation for biblical interpretation precisely for this reason. It enhances central commitments of faith and renders "intelligible" alternatives to historical-critical readings of the text. By locating the biblical text in communities with histories, the position authorizes Christian tradition. It relocates issues of truth/falsity and faithfulness/unfaithfulness from the propositional and cognitive to persons' characters. Even with multiple "practices" of scripture thereby made possible, criteria for good reading that come from the ends are provided by the tradition itself. As a rejection of interpretation as an individualistic, autonomous act, MacIntyreans identify this corporate enterprise of scriptural interpretation as one of the core practices of the church (Bass; Fowl and Jones). MacIntyrean practice is most valuable for solving the modern (sometimes) positivist critical disciplines of the academy. The dissolution of the text by historical criticism is addressed by his narrative theory, insofar as the narrative of God's relation to humanity culminating in the Jesus narrative serves to unify the heterogeneity of the Bible and contributes to the unifying telos of the lives shaped by the practice. However, given the absence of the bodily, particularized, and power-related aspects of practical knowledge from MacIntyrean practice, this project has not resulted in accounts of biblical practice where ideological and social location are internal to the analysis. This absence continues in his theological extensions. These authors refer to these realities but lack categories adequate to their exposition (McClendon: 28, 34–46; Fowl and Jones: 111–31. For a gendered use of "practices" see Chopp, 1995).

Bourdieu's account of practice disrupts the location of the text precisely because he does explore the bodied and located character of practical understanding. He would agree with a MacIntyrean that to "practice scripture" is not simply to read it as a book or to exegete it as a canon. The notion that a biblical habitus is a "feel for the game" and regulated improvisation are wonderful ways to think about the characterological effects of good Bible reading in community formation. However, a "habitus of scripture" is located in fields of power relations and requires a look at the "scattering" of scripture as well. In a community habituated by scripture and other specific local as well as dominant political-economic discourses, scripture is "broken apart" by being inscribed in bodies and linked with other cultural phrases; it is gendered, sexualized, and racialized. Just as the hermeneutical relation is not a move from cognitive retrieved meaning to practical application, it is not simply a conscious possession in a mind, nor is it confined to a religious community. In religious life, scripture is first experienced tacitly; it is internalized in bits and pieces and hybridized. It also circulates in spatialized form—in objects, in ritual, in sound bites, in aesthetic experiences, and in North American culture and politics. Bourdieu would have a postmodern theory attend to the spatialized, bodied, and social distribution of the "text," but also to the power relations embedded in that social world. A text disseminated in a poor Appalachian religious space would be habituated differently than one in a wealthy high church space, and the misrecognition that may be ideology will come from analysis of the social nature of this habituation.

The distinctive offering of Certeau to this proliferation of reading communities is not a unified text; nor does he say enough about the "end" of human life so as to relocate evaluation in characterological terms. The New Testament is a "network of text, which is interconnected but not unified." (1971: 339). However, Certeau offers a celebratory display of the productive creativity of reading—but reading by ordinary people. What his view adds to the other two accounts is the invitation to take ordinary Bible practitioners more seriously. Reading can be a subversive tactic. As poachers, ordinary readers can trespass on/with the text, making their own way through its densities and altering it like a renter alters a space occupied temporarily. As with the different realities created by walkers through a city, the readings of such poachers may have little accumulated effects. However, Certeau displays them as rich and artful—serious alternative realities to the distancing abstractions of the experts and mappers. Such a move renders more difficult the definition of a "good" reading; his hints are minimal—in treatments of religious mysticism, he suggests a utopian function for scriptural fables. A miracle story is used to create "a site that is impregnable because it is a nowhere, a utopia" (1984: 17–18, 20; 1982). If anything, his account of practice would lead most clearly to a disruption of the "ownership of the text," as his interest in the use by the powerless moves beyond liberation interests in the marginalized to the ways all "ordinary readers" counter the "experts" with creative use of their codes.

These features of postmodern "critical practice" surely suggest other inquiries and issues. However admirable, practical knowledge is a kind of practical mastery at odds with a highly professionalized society. Yet postmodern biblical practice from Certeau and Bourdieu would offer counter-discourses to the dominant; Bourdieu would have postmodern critical practice ask about the cultural capital accruing to expert theories and control of "right reading" of scripture. Could religious professionals take this seriously? Practical knowledge is embodied. How are bodies corruptly marked by texts in oppressive communities? How are they redeemed? Many are fairly comfortable with the notion that interpretation is communal; the task at hand is exploration of more communities, their inner complexities, misrecognitions, and intersections with the political, cultural, and economic. Surely a postmodern practice of the Bible will release many new relations to the text, if nothing else. More than likely it will continue to burst the boundaries of guilds as we focus on the irreducible mystery of what people do.

process
William A. Beardslee

The Modern World

A quick (and simplified) review of the background can make clearer how process thought can be related to other types of postmodernism. *Postmodernism* is a term for a wide range of responses to the modern world or to "modernism." Here we will term the older stance "the modern," reserving "modernism" for a specific, mostly twentieth-century development. In the older modern culture, which culminated in the nineteenth century, we can note three themes, all of which have provoked postmodern responses.

A first and central mark of the modern was its confidence in reason, more specifically the form of reason that is expressed in the deterministic and mechanistic science that was so widely developed in the nineteenth century. This method was placed in a narrative of human progress that affirmed that many long-standing and seemingly insoluble problems were being solved or would soon be solved by theoretical and applied "scientific reason."

In biblical studies, historical reconstruction of the events that the text reported was a central application of this aspect of modernism. The conviction was that if the student, so to speak, stepped out of the stream of tradition that established the standard interpretation of the Bible, he or she would be able to look at the formative events "from the outside" and see them as they really were. The claim for disinterested objectivity was advanced to counter what were regarded as institutional and traditional controls on interpretation. Rational historical study appeared to be an opening to a larger freedom in religion.

A second, very different trait of the modern was an exploration of inner subjectivity, joined to a belief in the impact of powerful personalities in history and public affairs as well as in literary imagination. This heritage of romanticism was one way of bringing freedom into the deterministic world proclaimed by rational analysis: Events commonly proceeded as determined by their past, but the new insight or the new leadership of a "great man" (as it was then formulated) could inject the new into the flow of public history or culture. This trait of the modern was linked to historical reconstruction in the effort to discover the "great man" Jesus in the various reformulations of the gospel story that were produced in the nineteenth century. It is evident that this motif, like historical reconstruction, is still a lively one.

199

A third mark of the modern that is important for our study was the effort to discern moral laws of universal application. As in so much of modernism, Kant was obviously a central figure here, but the intuition that there is a moral claim that is the same for everyone was a pervasive motif of modernism. The hope for a unification of human society was formulated on the basis of extending the patterns that functioned in (we may fairly say) middle-class Western culture to a universal status. The imperialist implications of this claim were seldom noticed.

Beyond the "Modern" to "Modernism"

These three themes were not articulated in a well-knit intellectual or cultural movement. They were simply presuppositions that were widely shared across much of European and American culture. A challenge to these themes is a trait of most forms of postmodernism. But postmodernism has a different cast when it is viewed as a response to a later and more specific cultural movement, the literary and artistic modernism of the early twentieth century. Modernist writers and artists were reacting against or moving beyond the older modernism by dissecting what they saw as the exhausted visions of the whole, which had given direction to the various modern projects, and reassembling parts of the tradition in new visions of an imagined whole. Joyce, Yeats, and Mann were typical modernists in this sense.

We can clarify the relation of this later stage of the modern to biblical studies by noting the quintessential modernist New Testament scholar–Rudolf Bultmann. His affinity for "the modern" has often been noticed: his mechanistic view of science and his hard-headed historical reconstruction. But his real significance lies in precisely his "modernist" re-imagining of the Christian vision. He worked through a thorough rethinking of the Christian message, which, in effect, took the narrative theme out of it. By reducing the past to "law" and the future to "openness," Bultmann placed all the weight of ultimacy on the moment of decision. The dramatic interplay between memory, expectation, and the present moment as they are known in a story were eliminated. Too often unnoticed is the unquestioning reliance of Bultmann on the Kantian heritage, which set limits on the possibility of knowing what is real and also regarded the will as the distinctive human trait. Process thought, as we shall see, is more radical on both these points.

Conventional Postmodernism

It was as a further development of this twentieth-century modernism that the main varieties of postmodernism emerged. Disillusion with overarching narratives (already in Bultmann) has been a central trait of postmodernism, which has clarified the reasons for such skepticism: An increasing awareness of the role of power claims in the construction of overarching narratives, an exploration of historical location as an ingredient in every cultural and religious expression, and a recognition of the large degree in which coherent cultural products are "linguistically enclosed" are recurring features of the reorientation asked for postmodernism (see Bible and Culture Collective: 2–3 and *passim*).

It is not surprising that a new point of view undertakes to dismantle its predecessors. Postmodern questioning of established cultural norms and practices is more penetrating than that, for this tradition questions not only the structures that it seeks to overcome, but all structures. One could say that the postmodern probing behind the surface assertions of a text (or aesthetic object) can be understood as the transposition of that inward probing into subjectivity, which was so much a mark of one strand of the modern, into the field of forces that constitute a self or a cultural product.

This postmodern dismantling of patterns is directed against the three traits of modernism that we noted above. Most of all, postmodernism rejects the domination of methods of inquiry by the seemingly objective or neutral methodologies that were and are so central to the modern quest to know. Such methods are unmasked and shown to be not neutral but reinforcers of the controlling powers in the society. Postmodernism is equally dismantling of the self, which in Jean François Lyotard's words becomes an assemblage of nodes of communication, with the different nodes responding to different language games.

The third modern trait, the assumption that there is a universal "ought" or moral claim, is equally rejected by uncovering the power claims and interests implied by efforts to establish universal patterns of obligation.

In religion, postmoderism produces two somewhat contrasting patterns. One response is to affirm that if the dominating structures of "liberal," generalized religion have been dismantled, one is free to reaffirm a local tradition, a particular and more traditional form of faith. Naturally, this move is usually taken by postmodernists who are affiliated with a religious tradition that has been contested by the "neutral" and historical methods of the modern (Adam, 1995b).

The other move is to remain in the deconstructive stance toward all structure that would limit and channel religious awareness. From this perspective, the ultimate or transcendent is inherently incapable of being confined to any structure; one may glimpse it when a structure is broken, but a further contact with the transcendent will have to await a further dismantling of some pattern or structure. This move is commonly found in academic circles (it is a leading motif in the Bible and Culture Collective's *Postmodern Bible*), though to some extent it finds expression also in the non-institutional "emerging mysticism" that is so prominent a mark of the contemporary scene (Todd). It is far from as nihilistic as it is often taken to be; rather it is an indirect voice speaking for the marginal and excluded, through critique of the powers.

Process Thought

In its contemporary form, process thought derives from the work of Alfred North Whitehead, work that was done at the height of the "modernist" period. A first way of placing Whitehead and process thought would be to see both as typical, probing, radical modernist re-assemblings of the pieces of thought and culture into a new vision of the whole. This would not be wrong. At the beginning of his great work *Process and Reality: An Essay in Cosmology*, Whitehead

202 Handbook of Postmodern Biblical Interpretation

defines his enterprise, speculative philosophy, as "the endeavor to frame a coherent, logical, necessary system of ideas in which every element of our experience can be interpreted" (3). It should not be forgotten that he also notes the inevitable limitations of language and the impossibility of ever formulating a fully adequate scheme (4).

A very bare outline of the new vision is needed before we address the question of its relevance to postmodernism. In process thought, what is real is what happens; events are real. There is no underlying substance. The event itself is the actuality, an "actual occasion," a droplet of reality. Events, all of them, are also experiences; they have a subjective aspect. "Experience" includes the reception or feeling of immediately preceding occasions that provide the data for the present experience, and also the freedom and self-determination that we know in our everyday experience–though, of course, freedom is trivial in simple occasions. Thus, subject and object are not separate types of reality but alternating aspects of experience. In its moment of coming to be, each occasion or experience is private; then, when it becomes a complete experience, it is an objective reality that offers data to subsequent experiences.

Obviously, we can at best be only marginally and dimly aware of the basic level of experience. Sense experience, which is so often taken to offer basic raw data, is a derived and abstract "presentation" to our conscious awareness. This insight opens the way to the process conviction that though experience is indeed enormously shaped by language and by social setting, it offers a basis for some degree of critical knowledge of reality.

For experience to move into coherent new forms, there must be a universally present limiting and purposive reality that offers direction to each occasion, a direction to which the occasion may or may not respond. Otherwise the ongoing process would simply be a random one. Process thought calls this ordering reality God. God also receives and values each completed experience in God's everlasting nature. Thus, God gives the possibility of direction to the world, but God's power is the power of persuasion. There is no fixed plan; human beings are not "pre-planned," and there will be no unitary, final summing up. It is fundamental to the process vision that there is no sharp line between human reality and other reality.

Charles Hartshorne, the other great contributor to process thought, is close to Whitehead in many ways, but Hartshorne on the one hand is more of a metaphysician, while on the other he has moved further into several postmodern directions: ecological concern and the plurality of religious perspectives, for instance.

The effort to envision reality as a whole, and to do so in public, shared discourse, sets the process project apart from most postmodernism. Yet this effort is tempered in ways that are often not recognized by the process recognition of the relativity of our knowledge.

Exactly like the deconstructive postmodernism we have sketched above, process thought is aimed at dismantling the three traits of the modern that are outlined above. Well before postmodernism emerged from the disillusion of the second half of this century, process thinkers were probing at the same defects in the dominant worldview.

The bare structure of process—the image of reality as the flow of a complex network of successions of occasions or moments of experience—was formulated precisely to overcome the determinism of the older, mechanistic model of reality. Acknowledging the role of deterministic causal connection between events, Whitehead opened up this sequence by showing how we can conceive that freedom, including both chance and purposive action, can also be a fundamental element of reality.

Second, the emphasis on reality as moments of experience, each of which receives from the past and contributes to the future, entails a radically different view of the self from what was (and is) dominant in the modern. Connectedness in a deep sense, so deep that we can say that events are constituted by their relations, or that relations are internal to events, means that the isolated self is a false construct; rather, the self is a connected flow of successive, complexly related occasions.

Perhaps in an even more focused way than in the usual postmoderism, process thought also rejects the image of a neutral, universal law as the basis of ethics. In Whitehead, this comes to expression frequently in his rejection of the image of God as a lawgiver. Process ethics arises from aesthetics and is closer to teleological ethics than to the deontological, duty-based ethics that seemed to so many in the nineteenth century to be the necessary glue for human association as traditional religious sanctions were weakening. (For a fuller yet brief sketch of Whitehead's proposal, see Farmer: 199–253; a useful companion to *Process and Reality* is Sherburne.)

The process perspective has enabled a postmodern interpretation in a wide variety of religious groups. There are evangelical process thinkers (Franklin), as well as Catholic (Bracken) and Jewish (Kaufman). Most of the theology that has been developed from a process perspective has emerged from progressive Protestantism. (For introductory purposes, see Suchocki; see also Cobb and Griffin, Mesle, and for a different perspective, Ogden.)

What has most attracted religious thinkers to process is the possibility of speaking of God in a way that overcomes the gap between a world of faith and a world that manages without God. This means that the immanence of God is the natural starting point for religious inquiry: God is active in every occasion, everywhere, but as a power of persuasion or "proposal." Much in the Christian tradition is congenial to this conviction, far more than commonly appears in older formulations. The process point of view also insists that God is affected by the world—a position that has, in fact, been taken up recently by a wide range of theologians. The correlative is that God is not omnipotent.

Christology has been seen in quite varied ways by process thinkers. In general, process christology has affinities with logos christology—in Christ a power and presence that are everywhere active find their decisive manifestation. The connection between Jesus and Christ is interpreted in process thought with a range of methods; historical study is not excluded, but it is relativized by tradition, by other contemporary methods of study, and especially by a different emphasis in interpretation (see below).

The human being ceases to be the dominator of creation but takes part with God in the continual work of creation. Process theology is Spirit theology in that the constant but changing call of God's spirit is the lure or goad toward change. This note leads to a renewed focus on social responsibility and social ethics among at least some process thinkers (Cobb, 1997, 1999; Daly and Cobb, 1994; Sturm; Gamwell). This note brings process and conventional postmodernism into close affiliation, although process thinkers have tried to form new proposals while much conventional postmoderism has limited itself to critique.

A special contribution of the process perspective is its hermeneutics. Much hermeneutics is oriented toward recovery, whether the recovering of an original meaning or the recovering of an eroded tradition. The aim of process hermeneutics is more forward-looking, to juxtapose the given cultural construct (in this case, the Bible) to the present world of the reader or hearer, in such a way that conflicting claims may be brought into creative tension, so that a new insight may emerge. Both givens are to be taken with equal seriousness, in the conviction that insight may be moved to a new level, to which both clusters of data contribute (Whitehead: 245–47). We can note that here the Bible is basic, but its authority is one of several. (For a thorough treatment of process hermeneutic, see Farmer.)

Of course, interpreters oriented by a process-relational perspective are also attentive to features of the biblical text that are congenial to this point of view, notably the many images of God as persuading or luring God's people and the world (Ford). But the intention is not to make the Bible teach process theology.

Process Postmodernism and Conventional Postmodernism

Process thought comes to its rejection of modernism by a different route than conventional postmodernism. Process thinkers radically deconstruct, but they usually do so in the context of a new proposed pattern. Neither type, however, is foundational in the sense that neither works by first establishing a clear method that can serve as a foundation for the assertions that follow.

One way of understanding their relation is to consider each a finished whole and focus on the contrasts. David R. Griffin has followed this path with rigor and has made his point as the editor of a series of books on "Constructive Postmodern Thought." He summarizes the contrast: "Deconstructive or eliminative postmodernism...eliminates the ingredients necessary for a worldview, such as God, self, purpose, meaning, a real world, and truth as correspondence," while constructive postmodernism "involves a new unity of scientific, ethical, aesthetic, and religious intuitions" and is as much concerned with the new world that must come into being as it is with worldviews (Griffin et al., 1989: xii–xiii). But beyond the clarifying of the contrasts, Griffin's work has been profoundly helpful in pointing to the many transformations, especially of public life, that can be expected if the process perspective is taken seriously. I affirm Griffin's conviction that real, if limited and always somehow perspectival, knowledge of the various dimensions of the world is possible, and I have contributed to his series (Beardslee, 1989). But I also see the need for process thinkers to be attentive to the limits on knowledge that are highlighted by "conventional" postmodernism.

Thus, another approach to the mutual interaction of process post-modernism and what I have called conventional postmodernism is to regard both "movements" as in process and inquire about what is intended by their directions. Deconstruction implies at least a minimal reconstruction; Julia Kristeva speaks of the necessity of shattering a code of behavior before it can be put together again (cited in Bible and Culture Collective: 147). Process thinkers have done radical deconstructing in the process of their recon-structions. There is more in common here than appears at first glance.

A further step is to incorporate insights from both types of discourse into a single inquiry. For example, earlier process thinkers had essayed to sketch a new vision of movement in time that eliminated the (all-too-destructive) apocalyptic symbol of a final end (Farmer: 195–99; Beardslee, 1972), but Catherine Keller has thrown new light on this symbol, which is so deeply embedded in the Western imagination. Using an analysis that is widely drawn from a variety of postmodern thinkers, she helps us to see that we cannot simply choose not to think apocalyptically; the imagery is too deeply built into our whole way of perceiving and existing in the world. To resist the apocalyptic lure we have to neutralize it, to construct "counterapocalyptic" moves that can include but denature elements of this deeply entrenched symbolism (Keller, 1996). I believe that further inquiry of this sort is a major frontier for those who work with the process perspective. The process recognition of the feeling-laden nature of perception can be made more concrete and related to specific social locations by interacting with other forms of postmodernism.

Furthermore, some thoroughgoing deconstructionists are starting to read Whitehead. The important figure here is Gilles Deleuze, who looks at the emerging process rather than the existing world as the key to the mystery of God and creativity (Keller, 1998; Faber). A new form of understanding may emerge, holding these two forms of postmodernism in creative contrast.

We cannot here examine other postmodernisms in relation to process thought, but only notice that feminist postmoderism has drawn, often critically, from both the styles we have examined (Keller, 1986, 1996; Brock). Liberation theology has been a more separate stream, but there have been engagements (Griffin, "Liberation Theology," in Griffin et al.; Pixley).

queer theory
Laurel C. Schneider

Queer theory is not just for or about so-called homosexuals. It is critical theory concerned principally with cultural deployments of power through social constructions of sexuality and gender. The 1978 publication in English of Michel Foucault's first volume of the *History of Sexuality* opened up new ground for thinking critically about the relationship between sexual identity and social power. In the decade following, Foucault's historicized theories of sexuality gave a new language to gay and lesbian—queer—criticisms of heterosexual supremacy. As a result, queer theory emerged as a small but dynamic field of discourse with the appearance of Eve Kosofsky Sedgwick's *Epistemology of the Closet* (1990), David Halperin's *One Hundred Years of Homosexuality* (1990), and Judith Butler's *Gender Trouble* (1990).

In general, queer theory seeks to disrupt modernist notions of fixed sexuality and gender (see Stone and Tolbert in this volume) by appropriating post-structuralist critiques of "natural" identities. Closely tied to analyses of gender, sexuality, and culture, queer theory slants its hermeneutical position decidedly in the direction of historicism and social constructionism. It disrupts sexual identity as a stable signifier by focusing on it as a functional product of historical and social processes. Neither heterosexuality nor homosexuality are givens in the queer frame. Queer theory "queers" taken-for-granted cultural associations concerning all sexual identities (and the social placements that adhere to those identities) by revealing their vulnerability to history and politics, and therefore to change.

Why queer theory employs "queer" in its name is important for understanding the basic presuppositions of the discourse. In theoretical terms, "queer" has come to denote a hermeneutical position similar to other late-twentieth-century theories such as third-wave feminism and postcolonialism, all of which denaturalize or de-essentialize formerly stable identities such as homosexuality, heterosexuality, race, nationality, woman, and man. As a term, queer refers to anything outside the norm. So with heterosexuality as the norm, queer then "naturally" refers to those who are not heterosexual. A difficulty inherent to the task of defining "queer," however, is that the act of definition brings in and domesticates the defined, rendering the queer no longer outside of anything, and so no longer queer—in theory at least. And because queer theory takes on the outsider viewpoint, at least in terms of placements of power based on heteronormative presuppositions, domesticating queerness is a problem for its work.

But historically the term *queer* was a signifier for men who desired sex with other men, introduced in the early twentieth century in some opposition to the pathologizing medical term *homosexual* (coined by a Swiss doctor in 1869). Although a whole lexicon known and deployed only by "queers" has existed at least from the Victorian period onward, terminology that could be picked up and understood by the larger culture and that improved on the usual choice words flung around locker rooms were valued. While in the larger culture queer did become only one of the more polite of a range of derogatory terms for same-sex lovers, it remained in ambiguous tension for so-called queers themselves, making it eventually ripe for theory's plucking.

What paved the way for contemporary queer theory was a transformation in the late 1960s from closet societies to public gay rights organizations and the public discourse on homosexuality that resulted. The most dramatic turning point came in 1969, when patrons of a small Greenwich Village bar in New York called the Stonewall Inn fought back against police harassment. After that the term *gay*—seldom used as a derogatory epithet and so preferred to queer—emerged in the wider culture (to the chagrin of those who thought a perfectly good word was thereby "ruined"). Although it actually was a term taken from late-nineteenth-century slang for "women of dubious morals" (Jagose: 72) and seemed to support assumptions of gay male effeminacy, *gay* basically fit the civil rights ethos of the 1960s and 1970s and by suggesting a more positive self-image and identity.

But civil rights eluded gays. By the mid-1980s, when the AIDS epidemic galvanized a more visible, vocal, and demanding activism, *gay* seemed too tame and parlor-bound for the defiance and desperation of the men who were dying and the lesbians who often were the only ones willing to care and fight for them. *Queer* fit the mood better because it seemed stronger and could be deployed in active opposition to its negative usage. In addition, *gay* had become associated mostly with men, and primarily with a logic of rights that relies for the most part on modernist notions of identity: stable, binary homosexuality in opposition to heterosexuality. As the 1980s closed, the "gay community" had come out of the closet only to discover that it was composed not only of same-sex-loving men and women, but of lesbians who rejected gay identifications, bisexuals, transvestites of all persuasions, and transgendered persons. The word *queer* began to be deployed in order to encompass the emerging diversity of sexual minorities both because it did not seem to be historically attached to any one of them and because it implied defiance of the gay-rights effort to "fit in."

A number of problems arise when queer theory meets biblical studies and theology. One problem revolves around the issue of defining queer vis-à-vis homosexuality (or gay identity); another revolves around the status of homosexuality in history, and yet another concerns the relationship of nondominant sexual identities–however queerly defined–to religious texts, theologies, and traditions. For example, were there *any* homosexuals before the nineteenth century? Some, like classicist Halperin, follow Foucault and say no. Others, such as Mark Jordan, John Winkler, and Bernadette Brooten, qualify this erasure with careful historical attention to language attributed beyond same-sex love to persons ("sodomite," in the case of Jordan's fascinating study of medieval texts, and *tribas,* in the case of Brooten's ground-breaking study of early Christian female homoeroticism). The question is not whether sexual love between same-sex partners has occurred throughout human history (because it surely has) but whether sexual desire, love, and activity alone constitute a sexual identity. This is a vexing problem for scholars who depend on lineages of texts and ideas to formulate interpretation.

In part because of new historical scholarship informed by queer theory, some clear political and methodological differences have emerged between what might be called gay/lesbian liberation writings and queer theory in religious studies. The former concern themselves with problems of exclusion and of justice for gay, lesbian, bisexual, and transgendered people as full persons equal to their heterosexual neighbors in religious communities and textual interpretations. The latter take on the whole paradigmatic system of meaning that produces heterosexuality and homosexuality in the first place, and they view biblical texts and traditions as cultural means of production for that system.

Because queer theory complicates simple associations of homosexuality with persons, queerness is therefore something more transgressive, more productive of difference, and more disruptive of stable, normative sexual identities than what we think of when we use the terms *gay, lesbian,* or *homosexual.* This means that those who argue for gay and lesbian inclusion in biblical studies on the basis of a "natural" (ontological) homosexuality face challenges from two opposing directions. On the one hand, they must defend themselves against the position that sex and sexual desire between men or between women is neither natural nor good. Arguments for homosexuality as a natural variation in human life provide a strong position against these views and account for some of the intense scrutiny of scriptural passages (particularly in the Levitical codes and in Paul) that have long been interpreted as prohibitions.

On the other hand, liberationist strategies of positing a natural homo-sexuality are challenged by queer theory, which rejects essentialist claims about nature and argues instead for radical cultural fabrication in sexual identity and a wider scope to sexual and gender possibilities than the binary constructions of heterosexual and homosexual. A queer theorist engaging the relevant biblical texts on apparent homosexual prohibitions may well accept the prohibitions as such, but will be more interested in their *perceived* necessity and the dynamics of power that they reveal than in any culturally transcendent moral claims that they can possibly make. Indeed, queer theory's radical historicism rejects any claims to deontological authority anywhere except as fabrication and deployment of power.

Scholars who engage queer theory in their work have enlarged and deepened an already wide-ranging debate within biblical studies and theology about the sources and authority of traditions that define social norms and human identities in terms of sin, redemption, good, and evil, particularly as these categories are expressed through gender and race. Queer people are, in one sense, additional "others" to add to the list of those ostracized by social norms originating in the mists of myth and codified in religious doctrines and traditions. But "queer" also represents a convergence of issues and ideas troubling biblical scholarship that only now is beginning to emerge. In her 1992 essay titled "Thinking Sex," Gayle Rubin suggested that "contemporary conflicts over sexual values and erotic conduct have much in common with the religious disputes of earlier centuries. They acquire immense symbolic weight. Disputes over sexual behavior often become the vehicles for displacing social anxieties, and discharging their attendant emotional intensity" (Rubin, 1992: 267). Homosexuality, or perhaps more broadly, queerness, takes shape in contemporary debates in the midst of this anxiety and is certainly fueled by it. Because the status of sexual identity itself is part of the question, the scope of queer studies is necessarily diffuse. Sexual identity and its cultural accoutrements form the content, in other words, of a debate seeking a contested subject when subjects as such are not taken for granted!

This tension leaves visible traces in the literature. *Queer* refers to a particular kind of difference that stands outside and against normative sexual identity and so refers to more than same-sex pairings of men or of women. Queerness qua difference is a difficult target for theory and research, even though theory is its home. For example, where Foucault opened the door for queer theory by critiquing power and identity as cultural productions and by emphasizing a necessary and mutually defining binary relationship between subjugated and dominant identities, his analysis of sexuality did not adequately account for gender. Butler expanded and gave greater depth to Foucault's work by investigating gender as a performance of cultural norms apart from biology and bodies that are produced by and reproduce culture. Sedgwick added a powerful impetus to Foucauldian queer theory by elaborating the necessity of the closet to *hetero*sexual identity production. Along with others, these theorists began to focus on subjugated sexualities as keys to the underside/underpinnings of dominant Western culture, with gender as a primary conceptual tool.

Gender construction and performance in their most radical formulations are closely related to feminist theories of gender and sexual difference (understood as practice, not identity, as Rubin tells Butler in a 1997 interview for the special issue of *differences* titled *Feminism Meets Queer Theory*). But queering feminism and feminist biblical scholarship does raise important critical insights. Everything turns on definitions. As Biddy Martin suggests, if lesbian is defined as a woman who loves women, there is no deep challenge to feminist arguments from nature or to heteronormative conditions for women. But if lesbian is defined in terms of desire and "*difference between women,*" then the category of the lesbian must resist tendencies in some feminist theories to reduce women to a naturalistic norm or, as she calls it, "the fixed ground or maternal swamp of woman-identification" (Martin: 109). Norms cannot abide difference, and perhaps queer lesbianism is actually predicated on difference—not from men, but among women.

Queer theory's adaptation of feminism (the kind of feminism, that is, that argues for the differences gender makes in perspective and meaning) claims that people who do not fit the heterosexual norm do not just live differently (from the norm); they *are* different in the sense that they see differently and constitute a difference that both supports and undermines the givenness of the norm. In other words, the persistent recurrence of homosexuals—literally out of the cradles of heterosexuals—betrays an inessential, arbitrary, produced dimension to sexual identity. At the same time, the persistence of homosexuality supports the normativity of heterosexuality by providing a reminder, always, of what heterosexuality is not.

But difference remains a difficult theoretical target within queer theory. And the differences that gender and race make are particularly problematic still in much of the literature. Michael Warner argues persuasively, for example, that queerness is fundamentally rooted in and always exposes cultural systems of shame about sex (all sex, that is, not just homo-sex). Queers disrupt this shame system and push its buttons precisely because they do not conform to the larger cultural demand that sex be made invisible (and thereby less obviously shameful) through normative, normalizing, and naturalizing practices, assertions, and assumptions. This means that gay and lesbian attempts at normalcy through national organizations that promote the unoffensive and recognizably bourgeois dimensions of gay life elide but can never escape the deeper structure of sexual shame that functions culturally to determine the normal (Warner, 1999).

It is certainly a hallmark of queer theory to think about queerness less in terms of identity and more in terms of socially constructed systems of meaning and practice that implicate everyone. (This, after all, is Kosofsky's point about the closet.) Warner, however, may make too much of a reductionist argument in his claim that queerness exposes and undermines the shame system wrought by heteronormativity. His is an argument that does not deal adequately with the complexities of gendered queerness, and it is unclear how it may apply to the complexities of racialized queerness. The queer reduction in Warner's argument is, at the least, identifiably male. In other words, his is a persuasive argument applied to males because sexual shame for men seems always and forever to be about heteronormativity. Men are shamed who transgress this system, either by evident lack of masculinist behavior or by "bottom" same-sexual practice (regardless of identity, as Warner points out). But women? Sexual *shame* applied to women throughout Western history seems to have little to do with disrupting heteronormativity. Indeed, gender-bending women often come through as reverse heroes rather than victims, even when they are brutally killed (think of Joan of Arc, Pope Joan, or even Brandon Tina). Prostitution and whoredom, on the other hand, are the shaming instruments for women, and neither specifically disrupts heteronormative constraints. Heteronormativity, therefore, cannot be disrupted by queer women based so simply on shame, because sexual shame still functions differently for women and for men. A woman who breaks her gender identification is, sadly, not necessarily transgressing codes of privilege (especially if she succeeds) nearly as radically as a man who breaks his gender identification.

What this discussion reveals is the slippery slope of queer theorizing when it does not take into account other shaping influences, like gender–even when gender may be one of the principal points of queer theorizing. Queer theory cannot, in other words, avoid the difficulties of difference even as it valorizes certain kinds of sexual difference. But queer theory loses its cutting edge if it fails to take seriously the depth of significance and the inseparability of race, class, ethnicity, and gender to queer theorizing. Evelynn Hammonds points out with stunning clarity the importance of racialized sexualities involving complexes of power that configure homophobia–and sexuality–for black lesbians in significantly different ways than for white lesbians (Hammonds, 1997). This is no mere matter of inclusion or exclusion of black experiences in writings on lesbianism. It is a matter of different conclusions based on more thorough investigations of the systems of meaning that structure whole persons and whole worlds in a web of identifications, none of which can be fundamentally isolated for the purposes of study. "Queer" becomes an ever more interesting complex of meanings and processes when the complexity of social meanings and processes are really addressed.

Although queer theory is conceptually fluid enough to encompass a dynamic constellation of interrelated issues, it does not yet resolve them and thus far is not always accountable to other shaping considerations (race in particular). It is still new enough, and contested enough on every level, that beyond Foucauldian critiques of naturalized sexuality queer theory has not, and perhaps should not yet, resolve itself into a "discipline" with an absolute priority of theoretical considerations. Nevertheless, queer theory owes a deep debt to feminism, post-structuralism, civil rights, and AIDS activism, from which its discourse has emerged and against which it often argues and so defines itself.

Years ago, Rosemary Radford Ruether argued that sexism is built on a deep cultural dualism that feminizes evil and therefore requires the persistence of the subjugated female in order to retain the valorization of the masculinized good (see Ruether, 1975, especially part one). Queer theory critically sharpens this broad insight to suggest that normative heterosexuality is a social construction that needs homosexuality in order to retain its norm-defining status. The basic Foucauldian insight that the erasure of the subjugated makes the dominant possible underpins queer readings of the Bible, theology, and history. Queer theory therefore enriches and critiques feminist readings by turning attention to the deep constructions and performances of gender that shape texts and interpretations.

What queer theory principally provides is an intellectual framework for treating sexuality as a meaningful site of difference that could illuminate texts and traditions in helpful if sometimes unsettling ways. This is perhaps the point of greatest tension between queer theory, which destabilizes identities, and lesbian/gay liberationist readings, which seek to legitimate them. Despite queer theory's constant overturning and politicizing of stable identities, however, the intellectual and interpretive tension among queer theory, feminism, and gay/lesbian liberationist activism provides a powerful opportunity for deeper critical thought in religion.

race
Shawn Kelley

When the renowned philosopher G. W. F. Hegel wrote his enormously influential histories of the development of World Consciousness, he made it abundantly clear that Africa had no productive role to play in the elevation of the human spirit (Derrida, 1990: 207–11; Gilroy: 41–71; Gilman, 1982: 93–102; and Walsh: 183–87). This was no mere oversight on his part, no accidental omission of an unfamiliar geographical region. Hegel chose to expel Africa from his narrative of the development of Reason, and he did so because he, like the vast majority of his contemporaries, did not credit Africans with full humanity, with rationality, with civilization, or with history.

"What we properly understand by Africa, is the Unhistorical, Undeveloped Spirit, still involved in the conditions of mere nature, and which had to be presented here only as on the threshold of the World's History" (quoted in Gilman, 1982: 97). Hegel's philosophical analysis of the historical development of *Geist* was breathtakingly original, but his views on Africa were depressingly commonplace. Throughout most of the modern era, white Europeans took their own racial supremacy for granted (see, for example, V. Anderson; Appiah; Baker; Barkan; Cannon; Fredrickson, 1987, 1988; Gates, 1985, 1988; Gilman, 1982, 1991; Gilroy; Goldberg; Gould; Hood; Poliakov; Rose; Said, 1978; West, 1982). This sense of racial entitlement and superiority is one of the few ideas held by the vast majority of intellectuals and religious leaders, political and military leaders, creative artists and literary critics, biological and anthropological scientists. Racial thinking was perceived to be correct, and the racial ranking implicit in the discourse was perceived to be immutable.

The Western sense of immutable racial superiority began to develop in the eighteenth century and was solidified in the nineteenth and early part of the twentieth centuries. (The conventional Christian dread of darkness and blackness is certainly an important component of modern racism, although disagreement does exist on the role that this dread plays; Hood: 26–43 argues that this ancient deprecation is essential to modern racism, while V. Anderson: 51–61, Frederickson, and Gilman place the emphasis on the modern aestheticization and transformation of this traditional apprehension.) It coincided with chattel slavery and with the colonial conquests of Africa, the Middle East, and the Far East, with the Holocaust, and with Hitler's brutal war in the East. It also coincided with the formation of many modern academic disciplines, including the modern versions of theology and biblical scholarship.

213

The Second World War, with its pitiless race war and its racial genocide, represented both the culmination of, and the final moment in, the West's unequivocal sense of racial superiority. A sudden shift occurred in the decades following the Great War–a shift brought about by the postwar devastation of Europe, by the postwar decolonization movements throughout the Third World, by the American civil rights movement, and by the South African anti-apartheid movement. Spurred on by these political events, European and American intellectuals began to confront the most offensive and least intellectually defensible forms of racist thinking (see Baker: 168–212; Barkan: 279–346). No longer would respectable scientists praise magnificent European skulls and hefty European brains (see Gould: 56–145). No longer would respectable artists, poets, and philosophers search for the soul of Aryan culture (see Lang: 61–82). Racism, at least of the most overt and scurrilous sort, was no longer welcome in the house of Being.

This confrontation with the most overt forms of racism hardly solved all the problems caused by the bloody history of imperialist Europe (and America). Subtle and not-so-subtle traces of earlier, virulent racism remain buried in polite language and erudite discourse. Furthermore, it is clear that the hundreds of years of racialized colonization, enslavement, and exploitation continue to influence current social, economic, political, and cultural arrangements. Imperial Europe constructed the intellectual, material, political, and cultural world of modernity, and the descendants of the colonizers tend to reap benefits unavailable to the descendants of the colonized. It is certainly the case that few legitimate intellectuals hold the sort of obnoxious racist prejudices that permeated the thought of most European and American intellectuals throughout most of the modern period. At the same time, the effects of the racialized system that produced these prejudices continue to reverberate throughout the emerging postmodern and postcolonial world.

If we wish to confront the nature and legacy of imperial racism, we need to start by identifying the central strategies of racialized thinking. Racialized thought erases African and indigenous presence from history, silences and marginalizes the voices of nonwhites and non-Europeans, and universalizes the Euro-American point of view. To understand and challenge racism, its effects, and its construction of world history, one must identify and interrogate these ideological strategies of erasure, silencing, marginalization, and universality.

Recovery

Racism functions, in part, by marginalizing and silencing the voices of nonwhites. To put the matter bluntly: Racism has blinded mainstream biblical scholars to the significant presence of dark-skinned Africans in biblical and classical antiquity. The complex process of erasing black Africans from world history was completed in the early part of the nineteenth century. To choose one striking example, for most of Western history Egypt was assumed to be an important cultural and political force in antiquity and was assumed to be at least partly populated by dark-skinned Africans. As Martin Bernal argues, this view of Egypt changed during the first part of the nineteenth century, as intellectual racism was solidified and as Romantic nationalism spread throughout Europe (see Bernal: 189–336). It was at this point that Western scholars began to expunge any traces of African influence from classical antiquity. European intellectuals sought out cultural and racial forefathers in classical antiquity, particularly in ancient Greece. As the progenitor of Europe, classical antiquity must necessarily be free from any Asiatic or African influences. Egypt represented the most serious obstacle to a de-Africanized antiquity, although European intellectuals showed a great deal of ingenuity in responding to the challenge. The de-Africanization of Egypt took many forms (see especially Bernal: 230–46; Felder, 1989: 8–11, 28–36). The philologist Friedrich Schlegel put forth the influential argument that Egypt was able to create a magnificent culture because it had been colonized by Aryans from India (Bernal: 230–33). Hegel, on the other hand, offered a more philosophical explanation for the racial conundrum. Because any historical movement in Africa necessarily "belong(s) to the Asiatic or European World...[Egypt] does not belong to the African Spirit" (Gilman, 1982: 97). Those who accepted the blackness of the Egyptians solved the problem by denying the vitality of Egyptian culture (Bernal: 244). Only one conclusion seemed impossible: that an African culture could be simultaneously civilized and historically influential.

The overt racism that was behind this historiography has long since disappeared, at least in polite company. Anyone today who argued that Africans are, by nature, incapable of civilization would be dismissed as a crank. The racist historiography of the nineteenth century, however, was not the work of cranks. It represented the pinnacle of nineteenth-century learning, and it came to permeate the methods, scholarly consensus, and assured results that continue to influence scholarship today. In Foucault's terminology, much of this racist scholarship has become "normalized" (see Foucault, 1977: 174–94; 1978: 81–91), even as its rather disturbing racial heritage has been forgotten. More recent mainstream scholarship, unaware of conscious effort spent erasing black Africans and other indigenous peoples from world history, has assumed that the conclusions are well grounded. African American scholars, motivated by the desire to discover what has been erased or forcibly marginalized, have established that there was indeed a significant yet often unrecognized black African presence in the biblical text and the biblical world (Bailey, 1991, 1995; Copher: 153–64; Felder, 1989: 8–48; Martin, 1989; Sanders; Waters; and, for further bibliographical references, see Bailey, 1991: 168 n. 14). Africans (designated by the terms Kush, Ethiopia, Nubia, Egypt, and Sheba) appear throughout the Bible both collectively and as individuals (on the question of terminology, see Hood: 24–26; Felder, 1989: 8–11, 32–36; Snowden, 1983: 3). The following praiseworthy and significant biblical characters are almost certainly African: Abraham's maid-wife Hagar (Gen. 16), Moses' wife Zipporah (Num. 12), Jeremiah's benefactor Ebedmelech (Jer. 38:7–13; 39:15–18), Tirhakah the Ethiopian king (Isa. 37:9), the Queen of Sheba (1 Kings 10), Simon of Cyrene (Mt. 27:32), and the Ethiopian eunuch (Acts 8:26–40) (Copher: 153–64; Crowder; Felder, 1989: 8–48; Martin, 1989; Sanders:

57–63). The prophet Zephaniah (see Zeph. 1:1) and Phineas, the grandson of Aaron and progenitor of the Zadokite priesthood (1 Sam. 1:3), are also candidates (Felder, 1989: 12), and Bailey makes an intriguing case for an African Moses in the earliest source material, arguing that the later traditions rework and de-Africanize the earlier traditions (1995: 25–30).

This rich scholarship demonstrates the pervasive presence of African characters in the biblical story. It also demonstrates that there is a considerable difference between the ancient and modern perception of Africans. The modern indifference to Africa, culminating in the tendency to erase Africa and its descendants from the world stage, is nowhere to be found in the Bible, which assumes a sizable African presence in the Greco-Roman world (see also Snowden, 1970: 183–84; 1983: 63–108). The modern animosity to Africans, culminating in chattel slavery and state-enforced segregation and apartheid, is nowhere to be found in the Bible, which stresses African independence, wealth, military power, wisdom, and piety (see Bailey, 1991: 170–83; the classicist Snowden makes a similar claim for Greco-Roman antiquity, especially in 1983: 56, although Hood: 32–43 detects a fair amount of Greco-Roman prejudice against dark-skinned Africans).

Deconstructing Biblical Scholarship

Recovering marginalized or lost voices from history is but one aspect of confronting the legacy of intellectual racism. Important research has been conducted on the pro-slavery and racialized interpretations of the Bible (Bailey, 1996; Felder, 1989: 38–40; Cannon; Copher: 146–50; Gaba; Martin, 1991), on the role that race has played in biblical translations (Bailey and Pippen, 1996; especially the essays by Carroll, Sugirtharajah, and Yilibuw), and on the productive role that the Bible has played in the community and culture of African Americans (Shannon; Smith, 1995; Wimbush). There have also been a number of interesting readings of biblical texts in which nonwhite and/or non-Europeans have brought their own social location to the foreground (Bird et al.; Donaldson; Segovia and Tolbert, 1995a, 1995b; West and Dube). These readings have not only brought a fresh perspective to familiar biblical passages but have also highlighted the degree to which mainstream scholarship is itself a product of its own social location.

Let us dwell, briefly, on the possibility that normative biblical scholarship reflects the ideological and social location of its institutions and practitioners. This implies that there exists a complex relationship between mainstream scholarly methods and racialized Eurocentrism. The scholarly literature cited above often suggests, in rather general terms, that such a relationship exists, although the nature of that relationship has yet to be clearly established (for example, Felder, 1991: 6–7; Meyers: 41–50; Schüssler Fiorenza; Smith, 1997: 117–19). I have been exploring this very question in some detail and for the remainder of the essay would like to sketch my views on how race came to be infused into modern biblical scholarship (Kelley, 1995, 1997, and forthcoming).

Race entered the discipline of biblical scholarship through the back door, as a hidden presupposition buried within the categories that were being appropriated and applied. Modern biblical scholars sought to ground their own work in the most important secular learning of the day. Because these very disciplines were themselves steeped in racial thinking, these same scholars unwittingly projected modern racial ideas back onto antiquity—as we have already seen in the case of Egypt. While erasing Africans from biblical and classical antiquity, scholarship also transformed Jesus and Paul into white, European gentlemen who simultaneously create and reflect the fundamental values of imperial Europe. Two of the secular intellectual movements, Orientalism and racialized Romanticism, proved to be crucial in infusing modern, racist thinking into the very heart of modern biblical scholarship.

First, the nineteenth century, which witnessed the formation of modern scholarship, was a time of unprecedented imperial conquest and of vast social engineering, fueled by the widely held category of race (see Bauman, 1989, 1992 for an analysis of the connection between social engineering, race, and modernity). At the beginning of the nineteenth century, Europe had colonized approximately 35 percent of the non-European world. By the opening of the first World War, however, it had extended its dominance to 85 percent of the planet (Said, 1978: 39–41). This massive imperial conquest directly influenced a number of academic fields, most especially the emerging investigation of the now-conquered Orient. The resulting discipline, Orientalism, reflected the imperial setting out of which it emerged (what follows is indebted to Said's *Orientalism*, one of the most important theoretical books of recent memory). Orientalism became a formidable body of learning that was situated in the elite institutions of higher learning; that was supported by scholarly journals, learned monographs, academic societies, and prestigious university chairs; and that permeated popular culture, elite literature, and a number of academic disciplines (i.e., philosophy, historiography, linguistics).

Orientalists invariably sympathized with the empire they were serving rather than with the colonized subjects whom they were studying. While the discipline they produced was remarkably complex, it did assume a few simple principles: that Orientals possess an immutable racial essence that permeates every aspect of their society and culture; that the principles of externality and backwardness define that racial essence; and that these principles ensure Oriental culture will be necessarily static and moribund while Oriental societies will be necessarily despotic and servile. Because of their moribund culture, Orientals had no contributions to make to modern society. Because of their essentially servile nature, Orientals were fortunate to be ruled by the benign yet iron hand of imperial Europe. This separates Orientals from Africans, who were assumed to have no culture and no political system. According to the logic of modern imperialism, the Oriental world should be colonized, while the African world should be enslaved.

Second, alongside the massive imperial conquest outside of Europe came an equally substantial reorganization within the Continent. Economic, political, cultural, and technological changes swept across the Continent, producing a cultural crisis. This was exacerbated by the Napoleonic imperial conquests, which led to suspicion of the Enlightenment and a decline in the prestige of reason (Beiser, 1992: 1–3, 363–65; Berghahn: 62–72; Schulte-Sasse: 99). Many intellectuals were convinced that the modern world was sinking into pervasive fragmentation, consumerism, and superficiality. The proposed cure, which turned out to be far worse than the disease, was a form of aestheticized, and eventually racialized, nationalism. A healthy society was thought to be grounded in the harmonious, organic, unfragmented relationship between art, culture, language, and society. A healthy society was culturally, linguistically, and racially unified, while an unhealthy society was racially and culturally diverse. This aestheticized ideology nurtured *völkisch* nationalism, blood-and-soil racism, and, eventually, German fascism (see Kelley, 1997: 207–16).

The twin movements of Orientalism and Romantic nationalism created the fundamental racial dynamic that fueled modern scholarship, as the servile and static East inevitably gave way to the liberated and dynamic West. These movements were enormously significant for the modern study of antiquity. We have already seen how the nineteenth century witnessed the radical reevaluation of ancient Egypt. The same would happen with the ancient Orient, with ancient Greece, and with ancient Rome. Before the nineteenth century, the Jews were widely considered to be theological forerunners to Christianity and the Greeks were widely considered to be mildly interesting forerunners to the more important Romans. During the cosmopolitan Enlightenment, the cosmopolitan Romans were favored over the unsophisticated Greeks and the particularistic Jews. This all changed, particularly in Germany, after the upheavals of the early nineteenth century. These upheavals brought about a sudden and dramatic reevaluation of ancient Israel (as external Orientals who bridge the gap between Oriental servility and Western freedom), of ancient Greece (as aesthetically organic, uniquely harmonious, and racial/cultural forerunners to modern Germany and Romantic nationalism), and of ancient Rome (as bloodthirsty, artistically derivative, in the thrall of instrumental reason, and racial/cultural forerunners to modern France and failed cosmopolitanism). The entire trajectory of world history was reconceived along racial lines.

These movements were enormously significant in various phases of the biblical disciplines. Perhaps we can conclude by identifying, for future study, where these movements overlap with biblical scholarship.

(i)   Orientalist linguistics and philology. One of the crucial figures in the formation of the discipline of Orientalism was the biblical scholar Ernest Renan (Said, 1978: 123–48; the standard histories of the discipline of biblical scholarship invariably discuss Renan's expertise in the field of linguistics, yet rarely explore the ideological and racial nature of nineteenth-century Orientalist philology). The influence of Orientalism on modern biblical scholarship, however, can hardly be limited to the modest contributions of Renan, who is primarily significant for solidifying the field and for importing it to biblical scholarship.

(ii) One can see these aestheticized, ideological categories at work in the great histories of Hegel, who in turn greatly influenced the formative biblical scholarship of F. C. Baur and the Tübingen school. Under Tübingen, the Hebrew/Hellene antithesis became the backbone of more than a century's worth of historical criticism. While this antithesis has been stringently challenged by Martin Hengel and Craig Hill on historical and exegetical grounds, insufficient attention has been paid to the way in which it parallels the East/West and colonized/colonizer oppositions and, thereby, to the way in which it inscribes a racialized ideology into its seemingly neutral aesthetic terms.

(iii) One can also see traces of Orientalist and *völkisch* nationalism in Rudolf Bultmann's form criticism. Central to this methodology is the assumption of a direct relationship among the *Volk,* language, and *Kleinliteratur.* Attention could also be paid to the degree to which folklore criticism at the turn of the century had become racialized and the degree to which this scholarship influenced Bultmannian form criticism.

(iv) The philosopher Martin Heidegger, who has exerted enormous influence on biblical scholarship, is particularly interesting here. His History of Being has a complex relationship to Hegel's racialized historiography, and his aesthetics has an equally complex relationship to the racialized aesthetics of Romanticism. Even the seemingly neutral categories of *Being and Time* are thoroughly racialized (see Kelley, 1997). Heidegger himself was radically conservative and was convinced of the intellectual, spiritual, and cultural superiority of the German people. This helps to explain his enthusiastic and vocal support of Adolf Hitler.

(v) Racialized thinking has found its ways into the essential categories of modern thought—history, myth, art, and language. Liberatory movements inevitably incorporate these categories into their critique of racism and Eurocentrism. Perhaps, then, even liberatory critiques are not entirely free from the racialized thinking that they seek to reject. (This is a complex topic that has been discussed with considerable nuance by Appiah, Anderson, and Gilroy. See also Kelley, 1995.) As Appiah has provocatively argued, "Africa" itself may be a colonial rather than an indigenous category. This situation has led Victor Anderson to challenge African American thinkers to move beyond the category of "ontological blackness."

Current scholarship is beginning to recognize the degree to which Orientalism, Romanticism, and aesthetic racism have permeated the classical texts of formative biblical scholarship. This should help future scholars identify traces of these intellectual movements in both mainstream and oppositional scholarship. Only then will the discipline be in a position to truly listen to the voices of those who have been, and who continue to be, marginalized with the help of the category of race.

rhetoric
David S. Cunningham

Rhetoric, a highly contested term, is often used pejoratively, referring either to empty speech ("mere rhetoric") or to outright deception. The standard historical accounts of rhetoric usually take pains to repudiate various negative definitions of the term, including: (1) rhetoric as flowery, excessively ornamental language; (2) rhetoric as "mere" appearance, as opposed to some other, more objective measure of reality; (3) rhetoric as concerned exclusively with style and delivery; and (4) rhetoric as another name for all human communication, regardless of its form. While the fourth definition is troublesome because of its breadth, the other three clearly seek to *restrict* the scope of rhetoric to a range much smaller than it has enjoyed throughout much of its effective-history. In the classical tradition, rhetoric referred broadly to the art of persuasion–primarily in speaking but also in writing.

The Sophists introduced rhetoric as a means of communication that might compete with epic poetry in moving the audience to adopt particular attitudes and to take certain actions. They apparently claimed to practice rhetoric as a political art (*politikê technê:* Plato, *Protag.* 315c), which could teach excellence in the *polis.* They emphasized that, in politics (and in many fields of inquiry), widely varying opinions can justifiably be held; agonistic structures are therefore a standard feature of life. Judgments in such matters are made on the basis not of incontrovertible evidence, but of probability (*eikos*) or opinion (*doxa*). For the Sophists, these terms did not connote unreliability and uncertainty, as we might assume today; they suggested instead that something was apparent, almost obvious. Unencumbered by modernist claims to universally objective certainty, the Sophists believed that probability and verisimilitude were the best one could expect to achieve. Common opinion was considered reliable because of its broad, general appeal among those with whom one is likely to converse.

The later rhetorical tradition judged the Sophists harshly–not so much because of their techniques (as is sometimes thought), but because of their lack of concern for the *moral* assumptions and implications of persuasive discourse. They recognized that communication is facilitated by what binds a community together, but they showed little interest in offering accounts of the proper moral and political *norms* of such communities. Their amoralism generated many of the negative connotations of "sophistic" speech and, by

220

association, lent a pejorative sense to *rhetoric* as well. Writers such as Isocrates attempted to emphasize that the orator must also be a person of good character; but such efforts were drowned by the more general critique of rhetoric, particularly by Plato.

Plato argued that rhetoric is suspect, since it relies on the opinion of the many and is committed to the *particularity* and *fragility* of truth. Rather than relying on "mere" opinion, Plato sought true knowledge or science (*epistêmê*)– a knowledge attainable only through philosophy. Rhetoric, in contrast, was merely a knack or a routine, comparable to cookery (Plato, *Gorg.* 463a). Of course, according to the more general definition of rhetoric as "the art of persuasion," Plato himself was very good at it. Certainly, he succeeded in persuading generations of philosophers, politicians, and educators that his view was the truth; the very success of his argumentative strategies underscores his rhetorical prowess. Moreover, we often read Plato through the objectifying lenses of modernity; perhaps his epistemological commitments are not as foundationalist as they are assumed to be. In the *Phaedrus,* for example, Plato seemed to contemplate a "true philosophical rhetoric" that could lead to truth. Nevertheless, the notion of a rhetoric that could be *true* (in the strong sense that Plato is assumed to be using the word) would be useless for reasoning about the practical affairs with which most people are concerned. Why? Because if the truth could be known for certain and agreed on by all parties, disputation would be unnecessary. Moreover, many writers (e.g., Isocrates) argued that no one could ever achieve the kind of certainty that Plato sought. "In pursuing such knowledge," he believed, "the 'disputers' pursue a phantom and their results are useless to the community" (Ruether, 1969: 3).

The dispute between Plato and the Sophists might be understood another way–namely, that they were pursuing different ends. While Plato was willing to sacrifice "usefulness" for truth, the Sophists were willing to sacrifice "certainty" for progress. This difference can be clarified by Aristotle's division of all inquiry into two categories: analytic and dialectic. Analytic method operates from an agreed-on set of first principles and can claim finality for its results; but because the principles actually "determine" the results (in some sense), its claims cannot be novel. Dialectic method, on the other hand, begins not with first principles but with common opinion (*endoxa*)–that is, with whatever most people consider to be the case. Because common opinion is often wrong and never univocal, dialectic cannot claim absolute finality for its results; nevertheless, its ambiguity makes it able to achieve genuinely new (nontautological) insights.

In the ancient world, these two approaches were not hierarchically ordered; their difference was to be found in their applications. An analytic method is needed when one must be able to demonstrate a clear congruence between a particular outcome and its first principles (as in physics, metaphysics, and logic); but dialectic is more appropriate when first principles are in dispute, or when the goal is to achieve new insight (as in politics, ethics, and poetics).

In these terms, rhetoric is a thoroughly *dialectical* enterprise; it is most useful for those matters that "could be otherwise." Indeed, Aristotle says that "rhetoric is the counterpart [*antistrophê*] of dialectic" (*Rh.* 1354a1). This allusion to the role of the divided chorus in Greek tragedy suggests something of equal importance and purpose but moving in the opposite direction. Like dialectic, rhetoric begins with "common opinion" (*endoxa: Rh.* 1355a14–18; compare *Top.* 100a18–21; *Soph. El.* 183a37–183b1), which is malleable and highly specific to place and time and so cannot be universalized or even generalized. Thus, rhetoric cannot guarantee tautological finality. What would be the use of deliberating about something that could never be otherwise? "Nothing would be gained by it" (*Rh.* 1357a7).

But although similar to dialectic, rhetoric is not identical with it; the two enterprises, like *strophê* and *antistrophê,* move in opposite directions. Dialectic is most appropriate for purely *theoretical* inquiry; but when the discussion turns to *practical* matters—especially in the realms of politics and ethics—the faculty of dialectic is insufficient. Dialectic may move a person's intellect, but it does not necessarily bring about fundamental changes in a person's attitudes and actions. People are induced to such thoroughgoing changes not by dialectical arguments but by rhetorical ones, for only rhetorical arguments are able to attend to the concrete specificity of speaker, audience, and argument.

According to Aristotle, rhetoric is a "faculty" (*dunamis*)—a capacity, an ability, a way of organizing and making sense of the practical exigencies of the world. More specifically, rhetoric is defined as "the faculty of discovering, in the particular case, the available means of persuasion" (*Rh.* 1355b25–6). This involves the discovery and actual construction of arguments that will be appropriate in a given situation. It treats *pathos,* which is concerned with the emotions and tendencies that can be expected of an audience; *êthos,* which is concerned with the character of the speaker; and *logos,* which deals with the arguments themselves. In sum, rhetoric encouraged comparative judgments about the effectiveness of particular arguments in moving audiences to action in contingent matters (matters that "might be otherwise").

Rhetoric had a profound impact in the Hellenistic era and particularly in the Roman era; here, it eventually developed into a more codified and formal system. This is most obvious in Roman rhetoricians; in Quintilian, for example, rhetoric is defined as *bene dicendi scientia*—a specialized knowledge about speaking well (*Inst. Orat.* 2.15.34–38). Roman rhetoric became the standard pedagogical program in the schools, bequeathing to us the five chief categories of rhetoric: the invention and/or discovery of various means of persuasion (*inventio*); the arrangement of these arguments (*dispositio*); the elements of style (*elocutio*); the memorization of the speech (*memoria*); and its appropriate delivery through voice and gesture (*pronunciatio*). This fivefold division tends to place more emphasis on the outward appearance of the speech than on the development of the argument (which is more or less exhausted by the first part, *inventio*).

The Roman rhetoricians provided the basis for most of the distinctively Christian appropriation of rhetoric for some fifteen centuries. Most Christian writers knew Aristotle secondhand, if at all; and even then they often tended to concentrate on his analytical treatises. The Romans were most useful for another reason as well: They had written under a more unified and singular conception of the *polis* than had Aristotle, who was aware of just how greatly matters differed from one Greek city-state to another. The Roman political order, which assumed that there was only one *polis* that really mattered, helped to sustain a similar Christian assumption of that era–even if, for Christians, the true *polis* was the *civitas Dei* rather than the *civitas terrena.*

The New Testament writers clearly manifest rhetorical influences–employing commonplaces and tropes, and attending to the specificity of their audiences ("I have become all things to all people," says Paul, "that I might by all means save some"; 1 Corinthians 9:22). The Fathers knew the art of persuasion, as did their opponents; Origen, in his *Contra Celsum,* demonstrates both. The great fourth-century writers employed tropes and argumentative forms that had been well rehearsed in the schools; obvious examples include the Cappadocians (particularly Gregory of Nazianzus), John Chrysostom, and Augustine, whose *De doctrina Christiana* counsels the appropriation of rhetorical techniques in the service of the gospel.

Christians recognized that their mission ("Go therefore and make disciples of all nations," Matthew 28:19) required them to speak and write persuasively; hence, rhetoric was a natural ally. It helped preachers and theologians to assess audiences, to weigh alternative argumentative forms, and to speak and write with clarity, grace, and wit. Like advocates in the law courts and Roman senators, Christians sought to move their audiences–asking them not just to *think* differently, but to *act* differently (and indeed, to reorder their entire lives). Such appeals are the natural subject-matter of rhetoric, which is thus closely linked with moral philosophy; Aristotle's *Rhetoric* parallels his *Nicomachean Ethics,* while Cicero and Quintilian understood rhetoric as formative for the character of the citizen-orator.

The art of rhetoric thus shaped Christian preaching and polemic from the very beginning, and its influence continued to be felt into the medieval and Reformation eras. Although its significance waned with the rise of other approaches to argument (such as "text and commentary" and scholastic disputation), it significantly shaped the work of writers such as Bonaventure, Luther, and Calvin. Rhetoric flourished in the Renaissance (especially in Italian humanism), but until that time it had undergone little new theoretical development; when Peter Ramus (1515–1572) issued his rationalistic attacks on rhetoric, his primary objects of scorn were still Cicero and Quintilian. Enlightenment rationalism renewed the attacks of Plato, dismissing rhetoric as excessively focused on contingent matters and on the emotions (and thus likely to lead to deception and error).

Critiques of rationalism gave new life to rhetorical theory. John Henry Newman (1801–1890) argued that persuasion takes place not through the intellect alone but also by the movement of the affects and the will–and not through sheer deduction but through the "cumulation of probabilities." Newman's *Essay in Aid of a Grammar of Assent* (1870) is an important post-Enlightenment retrieval of classical rhetorical insights. Friedrich Nietzsche (1844–1900) lectured briefly on classical rhetoric but is better known as a master of its practice, in deconstructing various universalizing pretensions (including those of much Enlightenment theology). In the twentieth century, rhetoric reentered the academy, especially in the United States, in departments of English, speech, and communication studies. Recent influential theorists include Kenneth Burke, Chaïm Perelman, and Brian Vickers, whose magisterial *In Defense of Rhetoric* (1988) is an excellent resource.

The use of rhetoric in biblical studies has fallen into three broad categories. First, biblical texts have been dissected with an eye toward the various elements of language that they have employed in order to persuade. This is similar to the "rhetorical analysis" that has been performed on a wide variety of texts over time. These approaches are usually guided by the classical handbooks, and often offer structural diagrams with the various sections of a text labeled with the traditional parts of a speech (*exordium, probatio,* etc.), or a phrase-by-phrase analysis pointing out the use of tropes and commonplaces.

Secondly, rhetoric has been wedded to certain forms of redaction-criticism (and sometimes, less clearly, to form-criticism) for the purpose of reconstructing hypothetical audiences and attempting to assess the relationship between author and audience. This approach employs a broader appropriation of rhetoric, attending to the whole structure and flow of an argument and to the interrelationship among speaker (writer), audience, and argument. The touchstones are not so much the classical handbooks as the neo-Aristotelian approaches of writers like Burke and Perelman; however, many writers combine both, including George Kennedy, whose *New Testament Interpretation through Rhetorical Criticism* (1984) provided the first book-length statement of this methodology. A survey of its various forms of practice might include the work of Klaus Berger, Vernon Robbins, and Antoinette Wire. This approach has many devotees, but it has also fallen under attack for its necessarily speculative hypotheses (concerning, for example, a text's original audience, or an ancient audience's evaluation of a speaker's character).

Finally, and perhaps most significantly, rhetoric has become a tool for interpreting the biblical texts in ethically significant ways. The focus here is not so much on the relationship between ancient author and ancient audiences, but rather on the relationship between the text and its present-day interpreters and audiences. This approach makes some use of classical rhetorical categories, but its main focus is on describing how the text can be used to persuade in today's contexts. Authors whose work might be included under this rubric are Elizabeth Castelli, Elisabeth Schüssler Fiorenza, and Cynthia Briggs Kittredge. Of course, none of these scholars can be assigned exclusively to any one of these approaches, and still others (such as Neil Elliott and Stephen Fowl) have actively worked to break down any sharp division among the categories.

Also of considerable significance is the study of rhetoric as formative for various Christian thinkers (including their interpretation of the Bible). Tertullian, Gregory of Nazianzus, John Chrysostom, and Augustine have received book-length treatment, as have Calvin, Newman, and Karl Barth. Most recently, rhetoric has been promoted as a methodological framework for Christian theology, based on the claim that theology does not rely on universally recognized first principles (as do, for example, logic and lower-order mathematics). Moreover, many objects of theological study are not empirical and cannot be verified to the satisfaction of all parties. Hence, theology bears fewer similarities to analytical enterprises (such as logic) than it does to such endeavors as politics, law, and even poetry. In some quarters rhetoric has again become a focus in theological education.

Postmodern appropriations of the term *rhetoric* have been, not surprisingly, many and various. For some writers, the descriptions of rhetoric mentioned at the outset of this article and regularly dismissed (rhetoric as flowery, ornamental language, or as "mere appearance") have been taken up in a positive vein and celebrated as an overcoming of the classical paradigm. Celebrations of the ironic play and carnivalesque playfulness of language, in writers from Derrida to Baudrillard, are good examples of this approach. These writers are often charged with some of the same criticisms that met the ancient Sophists; the challenge is always to articulate the moral basis of their claims. In this respect, the work of Levinas and some of the more recent work of Derrida is an important corrective.

Other postmodern interpreters have focused on rhetoric's critical and/or deconstructive potential; Nietzsche is a guiding figure here, and the later work of Michel Foucault is an obvious contemporary representative, examining how particular forms of language (e.g., "madness" or "crime") have been employed to organize, marginalize, and institutionalize. In this genre, one might include studies organized under the general rubric of "the rhetoric of inquiry," which is interested in "how scholars communicate among themselves and with people outside the academy" and "investigat[ing] the interaction of communication with inquiry" (Nelson, Magill, and McCloskey, 1987: ix). Here also one might cite Stanley Fish's observation of the following sign that rhetoric is once again becoming a key category: "In discipline after discipline there is evidence of what has been called the interpretive turn, the realization (at least for those it seizes) that the givens of any field of activity–including the facts it commands, the procedures it trusts in, and the values it expresses and extends–are socially and politically constructed" (Fish, 1989: 485).

Still others argue that a postmodern appropriation of rhetoric will help to move scholars out of their ivory towers and into direct political engagement; here, the work of Terry Eagleton and Frank Lentricchia is particularly powerful. These writers have directly addressed the concern that rhetoric might become an amoral enterprise by putting it in the service of particular political ends. The particular *polis* will differ for different writers; for some, it is the nation-state, but for others, the academy itself (or some other entity) may be understood as a coherent political structure within which specific rhetorical engagement must take place.

Each of these three perspectives is reflected in various theological appropriations of rhetoric in the postmodern era; one can point to advocates of various "rhetorical theologies," whether ironic and playful (Jasper, Taylor), critical (Klemm, Webb), or political (Chopp, Compier). A hybrid of the last two categories is an approach that understands the church as the *polis* (or at least as one of them) within which persuasion should take place (Cunningham, Tracy). Needless to say, most of these writers move among these categories rather freely. Like so much else in the postmodern world, the appropriation of the language of rhetoric is still very much contested.

Rhetoric's adaptability is attested by its use both as a critical tool in deconstructing theological edifices and as a means of setting the traditional claims of the faith in a brighter and more convincing light. As Aristotle and Augustine both emphasized, the art of rhetoric is itself indifferent; its value depends on the ends to which it is employed. Whatever their theological position, Christians throughout history have sought to persuade their audiences, and rhetoric has helped them to do so. Indeed, in describing the goals of theology, Augustine adopted a commonplace from Roman rhetoric: "to teach, to delight, and to move" (*De doct. Chr.* IV.27[74]).

scholarship
Burke O. Long

The word *postmodern* generally denotes cultural transformations in Western Europe and North America as well as altered perceptions of how human beings relate to the intellectual tradition rooted in the European Enlightenment (the *modern*). Postmodern critics construe Enlightenment-based modernity in particular ways and critique widely held convictions that human reason and historically aware empiricism are universal arbiters of truth.

Unruly, variegated, and elusive, postmodernism is not one thing. The term refers to changes in sensibility and outlook as well as to cultural practices often associated with circumstances peculiar to Europe and North America of the late twentieth century. *Postmodern* may describe transformed ways of understanding human beings in relation to modernity; it may also apply to overlapping, interrelated, often conflicting ethical and political responses to contemporary culture and history. Postmodern sensibilities and practices find expression in popular culture as well as in the refined languages of the arts, linguistics, history, law, literature, politics, religion, and the social sciences (Adam, 1995a; Bauman, 1992; Reiss; D. Harvey; Hassan; Natoli and Hutcheon).

One way of thinking about postmodern features of contemporary life is to consider three main trajectories of cultural transformation (Lyotard): (1) the *aesthetic,* where visual, architectural, and literary artists emphasize the ineffable, engage in limitless play of constructed surfaces, and transgress traditional distinctions between elite and mass culture; (2) the *epistemological,* which refers to endemic suspicion toward gestures of mastery such as encompassing theories of understanding, claims to universal knowledge, or meta-narratives that authorize holistic worldviews and national identities. Such efforts toward stabilizing meaning and cultural experiences are countered by a conviction that indeterminacy, fragmentation, incoherence, and ambiguity are inevitable features of knowledge, and that all knowledge is built locally, enmeshed in language, and rooted in particular social, material, and cultural circumstances; (3) the *political* dimension, which associates desire for mastery and knowledge of universal truth, indeed all forms of knowledge, with relationships of political power. In the case of totalizing visions of reality, this means powerful moves to suppress heterogeneity. Postmodernist critiques of modernity thus invite dissenting thought and action aimed at achieving radically democratic, pluralizing, and non-hegemonic ways of constructing both knowledge and the social order.

In all its variety, postmodernism lives in dialectical relation to what it desires to modify. While resisting entrenched ways of Enlightenment modernity, itself a notion constructed out of dissent, a postmodern critic gives no transcendental status to reason, while at the same time taking the Enlightenment's insight into the historicality of human experience to its logical conclusion. Such a critic would expose embedded habits of thought–including the belief that human reason offers a path to universal truth–whose historical contingency has been obscured by long usage, naturalized as universal, or presented as objective and politically neutral. A feminist postmodern reading of a literary text, for example, functions as a political and ethical response to other readings that present themselves as scientifically grounded, as objectively true as rigorous method permits, and as resting on foundations outside the play of gendered (patriarchal) power in personal and institutional relationships. Often carrying an implicit ideology of master knower controlling a world of objects, such objectivizing readings, as Judith Butler writes, make up a "forceful conceptual practice that sublimates, disguises and extends its own power play through recourse to tropes of normative universality." Butler argues that an appeal to normativity, as, for example, resting the truth of a claim on the essential (uncontingent) nature of maleness or femaleness, needs itself to be interrogated to discover what such a "theoretical move that establishes foundations authorizes, and what precisely it excludes and forecloses" (Butler, 1992: 7; Bible and Culture Collective: 1–19).

A postmodern critic tends to locate knowledge, even the powerful presence of scientific rationality itself, in human desire and choice amid changing social and cultural circumstances. Knowledge is presumed to be irremediably partial, ideologically grounded, perspectival, and shaped by vested interest–not, even as a desirable ideal, simply a matter of a unified self "in-here" disinterestedly laying hold of objects "out-there" that are independent of the knower and await deciphering. To a postmodern scholar, knowledge is a culturally bound orderliness imposed on what might be said to be minimally experienced as "reality." Truth about reality, including God, is *socially* constructed. It is rehearsed and legitimated in the practical arenas of language used by individuals who inhabit networks of personal and institutional relationships (Arbib and Hesse). Thus,

> postmodern criticism cannot accept any system of knowledge as absolute or foundational; it cannot accept the premise that some body of knowledge, or subject of knowledge, constitutes a unified totality; and it cannot accept mystifying claims that any intellectual discourse is disinterested or pure…Postmodern knowledge acknowledges that various forces that are ostensibly external to intellectual discourse nonetheless impinge on the entire process of perceiving, thinking,

and of reaching and communicating one's conclusions. (Adam, 1995a: 15)

In most of its higher critical forms, biblical scholarship is a child of the West European Enlightenment tradition and theological interests that pre-date the Enlightenment. On the one hand, premises of scientific rationality and historical empiricism deeply define both methods and products of research, as well as pedagogy, professional credentials, and status. For example, if properly trained and socialized into the guild of modern scholars, and if guided by disciplined use of scientific reasoning, one can, in principle, reach objective understanding of *berit,* or "covenant," and determine its meaning within the ancient biblical world. On the other hand, a metaphysics of transcendence, with its intellectual and social roots sunk deep into antiquity, can identify this biblical idea of covenant with mandates and patterns of timeless reality. Thus, a typical higher critic of the Bible strives for ever more refined and refineable closure on historical as well as transcendental truth, such as God's eternal presence to human beings in covenantal relationship (historically experienced at Mount Sinai) and in "new covenant" Christ-incarnation (historically encountered in Jesus).

A postmodern critic of this method and resulting construal of covenant might ask about its contingent ties to, for example, a narrative of covenant making that excludes women of ancient Israel from its horizon (Ex. 19:14–15); or one might note the cultural specificity–not universality–of this formulation of covenantal theology among Christians, rather than Jews, and its tilt toward a meta-narrative of Christian redemption despite its grounding in scientific historical research. Or again, refusing the modern quest to determine original (and divinely grounded) textual meaning, a scholar might investigate the ethical consequences of holding this idea of monotheistic covenant–one God, one people–to be universally, absolutely, and unalterably true. "This people is to be the exclusive possession of the deity, and none other, and they are to have exclusive desire for this deity, and none other. The Other against whom Israel's identity is forged is abhorred, abject, impure, and in the 'Old Testament,' vast numbers of them are obliterated, while in the 'New Testament,' vast numbers are colonized (converted)" (Schwartz: 18–19).

By adopting postmodern sensibilities and asking such questions of the Bible, indeed by redefining conventional practices and parameters of scholarship, a number of critics have begun to create new bodies of learning about the Bible. Breaking from a modern ideal–a singular Bible held in the keep of specially trained guardians and intensively mined for its original meaning–scholars inclined toward aspects of the postmodern create a culture of dissent. They encourage hermeneutical diversity and free-range, trans-gressive inquiry often carried out in arenas of high-stakes struggle for social change.

Feminist scholarship is a prime example. Whether accepting or rejecting the Bible's religious authority, feminists uncover and resist social and ideological patterns of patriarchy built into the production and reception of the Bible. They examine the consequences of perpetuating those same attitudes in such media as modern scholarship, fictional literature, or the visual arts (Bach; Bal, 1987, 1988, 1992; Exum, 1993, 1996; Ostriker; Pardes; Schüssler Fiorenza, 1985).

Cheryl Exum approaches the Bible as a cultural artifact, not as a text of religious authority. She seeks to undermine its continuing influence on contemporary gender roles and expectations. For example, she opposes the "phallocentric" ideology of Judges 11 (the story of Jepthah and his unnamed daughter) by emphasizing the horror of events when viewed from the vantage point of the daughter. Nameless, and given no voice of resistance to events, Jepthah's daughter dutifully submits to the authority of her father and the austere code of male-centered warrior culture. She is sacrificed to God, to whom Jepthah had earlier vowed that in exchange for military victory he would offer up the first thing he saw upon returning home. "Jepthah carries out the murder, and the deity is implicated. And since this is a literary murder, we shall accuse the narrator of complicity in the crime." In this reading, Exum resists the moral codes embedded within the biblical narrative, gives "voice to biblical women whose experience has been suppressed and distorted by androcentric texts," and exposes the "valorization of submission and glorification of the victim as serving phallocentric interests" (Exum, 1993: 20, 41).

Elisabeth Schüssler Fiorenza similarly struggles with the Bible's anthrocentrism. Nonetheless she honors the Bible's role in formulating Christian theology while rejecting those texts and interpretations that have sustained various kinds of social domination. If the Bible is not to remain a tool for patriarchal oppression of women, then one must look to those biblical "traditions and texts that critically break through patriarchal culture." These are the portions of the Bible, when constituted in a community of women struggling against all forms of oppression, that carry "the theological authority of revelation" (Schüssler Fiorenza, 1985: 33). On this basis, Schüssler Fiorenza undertakes a massive revision of Christian origins–the paradigmatic basis for Christian theology and practice–in ways that will empower women in their struggles for equality in the contemporary church.

Standing on the permeable borders between the modern and the postmodern, Schüssler Fiorenza pursues a historical project well within the canon of Enlightenment-inspired criticism of the Bible while adopting a postmodern suspicion of master narratives that suppress difference and serve the politics of oppression. She uncovers traces of very early church communities in which women exercised apostolic and ministerial leadership. This historical memory, she concludes, was suppressed by post-Pauline and post-Petrine writers, obscured by later church tradition, and ignored by much modern New Testament scholarship. However, the success of the New Testament's "stress on submission and patriarchal subordination...cannot be justified theologically, since it cannot claim the authority of Jesus for its own Christian praxis" (Schüssler Fiorenza, 1985: 334). Even this formulation is rendered problematic in Schüssler Fiorenza's latest work, in which she tries to break the hegemonic hold that conventional ideas about the man Jesus have on Christian theology (Schüssler Fiorenza, 1994).

For biblical scholars concerned with problems of racism, a main question has been, How can the Bible and biblical scholarship, with their roots tangled in racism and sexism as well as in the epistemological assumptions of modernity, provide liberative paradigms for African Americans (D. Williams; Felder)? Delores Williams, for example, offers "womanist theology," and thus creates biblical scholarship that "especially concerns itself with the faith, survival and freedom-struggle of African American women." She resists "black male oppression of black females" as well as "white racism that oppress[es] all African Americans, female and male...But womanist theology also critiques white feminist participation in the perpetuation of white supremacy which continues to dehumanize black women" (Williams: xiv). Biblical Hagar becomes a theological and liberative paradigm, as Williams deconstructs both the biblical text and a tradition of scholarship that has relegated Hagar to a minor role in the master narrative of patriarchal beginnings and Israelite chosenness. Hagar is a slave woman, domestic servant, mother, and a "lone woman/mother (who) struggles to hold the family together in spite of the poverty to which the ruling class economics consign it. Hagar, like many black women, goes into the wide world to make a living for herself and her child, with only God by her side" (Williams: 33).

Postmodern biblical scholarship has also meant investigating how the Bible has been specifically appropriated in various cultural settings, for example, in South African churches or in a theme park or museum exhibition. In these studies, biblical texts emergent in the discourses of their appropriation constitute the foci of scholarly concern rather than, as modern scholarship has usually emphasized, the written canonical text itself. Of interest is

> not just the Bible influencing culture or culture reappropriating the Bible, but a process of unceasing mutual redefinition in which cultural appropriations constantly reinvent the Bible, which in turn constantly impels new appropriations, and biblical scholars find themselves, in their professional capacity, haunting video stores, museums, and other sites of cultural production. (Exum and Moore, 1998: 35)

Feminist scholars give great force to this particular postmodern turn by studying how images of biblical women are reproduced and commodified in visual arts, film, and literature (Bal, 1992; Exum, 1996; Bach, 1997). Taking up a somewhat different cultural question, anthropologist C. Delaney explores the story of Abraham's near sacrifice of Isaac (Genesis 22) in relation to a recent California criminal trial. A father was accused of murdering his daughter but steadily and calmly maintained throughout his trial that God had commanded him, like Abraham, to sacrifice his child. Carol Delaney exposes strangeness in the heart of familiarity. She inquires into the consequences of Jews, Christians, and Muslims continuing to value the biblical paradigm of faithful obedience to God that also involves a problematic notion of paternity (the father owns the son) and a morally questionable ideal of religious devotion (willingness to kill the son). "Why is the willingness to sacrifice the child, rather than the passionate protection of the child, at the foundation of faith? I ask that people imagine how our society would have evolved if protection of the child had been the model of faith" (Delaney, 1998: 253). Other cultural critics chip away at the notion of one God, one people, one Bible–in short, a stable and universally relevant Bible–by highlighting social and ethnic differences among readers (Segovia and Tolbert, 1995a; Mosala, 1996; Wimbush) or by parsing complex relations between Bible translations, interpretations, and colonialist conquests (Bailey and Pippin).

Historiography of biblical scholarship is also undergoing revision. For example, in studying William Foxwell Albright and a few of his influential students during the 1950s, Burke Long traces the efforts and successes of the Albright school in advancing modern study of the Bible. He also explores how members of the school–they referred to themselves as sons and grandsons of Albright–sought to secure political and ideological dominance of mid-twentieth-century American biblical scholarship. In episodes tucked away in private letters, failed projects, and successful publishing programs, Long explores a range of postmodern concerns: power plays to create Albrightean-framed knowledge and social relations that maintain their commanding influence; conceptual and social tensions, tangled with suppressed ideological commitments, that weaken confidence in claims to normativity; fragments of narratives presented in tropes of universality, but encoding local values and programmatic authority for the Albrighteans. Refusing a master narrative, Long offers episodes in the construction of biblical knowledge and "creates a narrative of competing memories (which is) as caught in the web of perspectivity as the actors themselves" (Long: 152).

As is evident, when scholars of postmodern sensibilities do their work, they give up a conviction of being able to occupy a vantage point from which one may know something outside the play of power, interest, and perspective. They engage the politics of cultural and social change in the present, even as, some would argue, other scholars, in their culture of Enlightenment-based scholarship, are complicit with social and institutional forces that resist such changes. The dialectical relationship between modern and postmodern practices supplies the energy of critique and counter-critique. Many scholars continue to develop biblical scholarship under well-established modernist premises, while others assemble their insights out of novel associations, fragmentary narratives, and unusual assemblages of texts and artifacts.

sexuality
Ken Stone

In order to speak meaningfully of "postmodern" perspectives on sexuality, it may first be helpful to identify assumptions about sexuality that can be referred to usefully as "modern" or "modernist." With the increased confidence in science during the eighteenth and nineteenth centuries, it was increasingly argued that the application to sexual matters of methods and paradigms taken from the natural sciences would increase our knowledge of a topic formerly obscured by religious dogmatism and romanticism. It would be incorrect to imply that the resulting tradition of "sexological" research–associated early on with such figures as Krafft-Ebing, Ellis, Hirschfeld, and (to some extent at least) Freud; carried on later by Kinsey and Masters and Johnson; and continuing to the present day in such areas as sociobiology–is or ever was homogenous with respect to presuppositions, methods of research, or political implications (see Robinson, 1976; Bland and Doan, 1998). Nevertheless, it is possible to identify certain recurring features of this tradition of "sexual modernism." These features include a primary focus on the biological and physiological dimensions of sexuality; a corollary understanding of sexuality as a pre-social instinct, the experience and significance of which is thus more or less universal; a tendency, corresponding to the biological focus and qualifying its universalism, to draw sharp, essential distinctions between "male" and "female" sexuality; and a tendency to assume that preferences for certain sexual activities can usefully be classified according to a series of coherent categories corresponding to psychological character type.

It is not certain that sexual modernism has ever had a major direct impact on biblical scholarship. Biblical scholars have probably been influenced more often by the religious moralism that many of the sexologists attacked. But the boundaries between these approaches to sexuality may be less absolute than the sexologists sometimes realized. For example, in spite of the fact that sexology often opposed the moralism of earlier generations, its biologism seldom permitted it to challenge the presupposition that acceptable sexuality was identical to "natural" sexuality, even in those cases where it explicitly set out to expand the boundaries of "natural" sexuality (by, for example, emphasizing that women as well as men were "naturally" characterized by desires for sexual pleasure, or reconceptualizing homosexuality as an inborn disposition toward "inversion"). In any case, a number of the presuppositions of sexual modernism have now been called into question by approaches that

233

stress instead the complexity and instability of that object–"sexuality"–that the sexologists tried to render transparent.

This complexity was already emphasized by Freud in the early years of psychoanalysis (e.g., Freud, 1962). Although Freud's work shares many assumptions with sexology, his theories of sexuality presuppose that psychic life involves specific processes (for example, the workings of the unconscious) that are related to but not identical to the physiological drives emphasized by the sexologists. Moreover, in distinction from many of the sexologists, Freud argues that neither heterosexuality nor homosexuality are inborn dispositions, but rather emerge from an earlier bisexuality by way of a conflict-ridden and precarious journey through processes of desire, identification, and repression. For Freud this journey begins in infancy, where the child's diffuse drive for the pleasurable satisfaction of needs produces psychic representations of previous satisfactions that eventuate in the structures of fantasy. According to Freud, while the drive for satisfaction might be inborn, the psychic restructuring of this drive through fantasy–and hence the constitution of sexuality–is not.

Many of Freud's arguments are difficult to reconcile with the popular view that reproductive heterosexuality is the natural, unproblematic manifestation of a presocial instinct or that other forms of sexuality are problematic deviations from that norm. Rather, all sexuality is for Freud organized at the psychic level through the complex and difficult interaction of somatic, psychic, and social processes. His hypothesis of an early bisexuality and the nervous reactions to this hypothesis from sexologists like Ellis (Weeks, 1989: 152–53) foreshadow contemporary discussions of bisexuality as a phenomenon that destabilizes assumptions about fixed sexual identities (Garber, 1995). Freud's statements about sexuality (as well as those about gender) are often ambiguous and leave room for both conservative and progressive interpretations. Nevertheless, his work continues to attract thinkers conversant with postmodern trends who wish to derive a radical theory of sexuality from a rereading of his work, a theory that can be utilized in the interpretation of a range of texts (e.g., Dollimore, 1991; De Lauretis, 1994, 1998; Bersani, 1986). Although there is, as yet, only a small body of psychoanalytic interpretations of biblical literature (e.g., Bal, 1987: 37–67; Rashkow, 1993), the use of Freudian theories of sexuality to interpret non-biblical texts raises the possibility that biblical scholars will, in the future, also find such approaches fruitful.

In spite of the attraction of Freud for certain postmodern thinkers, alternative approaches sometimes suggest that psychoanalysis shares with sexology a problematic ahistoricism with respect to sexuality. This charge is frequently leveled even against the influential psychoanalytic theorist Lacan, who, in the opinion of some critics (e.g., Segal, 1994; compare Clayton, 1989), rightly refuses to ground sexuality in biology only to universalize the structures of the symbolic order in relation to which sexual desire is thought to be constituted. Thus, in contrast to the sexological emphasis on biology, physiology, and nature, on the one hand, or to the universalizing of such psychoanalytic concepts as the Oedipus complex, on the other hand, there has been a growing emphasis across a number of disciplines on the thoroughly social, cultural, and historical contextualization and constitution of sexuality.

For example, an important but neglected strand of sociological thought argues that all sexual desire and behavior should be understood as the result of complex negotiations between, on the one hand, social scripts and scenarios, with their symbols and role expectations, and, on the other hand, intrapsychic scripting and internal dialogue (Gagnon and Simon, 1973; Simon, 1996). A somewhat more influential anthropological tradition has increasingly demonstrated the cross-cultural variability of both sexual practices and sexual meanings. Although anthropologists such as Malinowski attempted to limit the impact of this cross-cultural variability by, for example, arguing for the biological roots of monogamy, the effect of ethnographic research over time has been to undermine universalizing statements about human sexuality. Thus, where sexology sought to ground its views of sexuality in scientific descriptions of human nature, trends in the social sciences seem to demonstrate the social malleability and production of human nature and the fact that biological and physiological processes associated with sexuality, though unquestionably real, do not contain inherent meanings but rather obtain meaning and impact experience through sociocultural organization and interpretation (Caplan, 1987; Vance, 1989, 1991; Herdt, 1997). If anthropological and sociological analyses question the stability of sexuality across cultures and societies, historical analyses question its stability across time, even within the same culture. Rather than being a single thing, many historians now argue, sexuality assumes different forms in relation to such changing variables as kinship structures; gender relations and ideologies; patterns of residence, mobility, and occupation; economic and class relations; structures of ethnicity and "race"; access to and use of contraception; demarcations of "public" and "private" spheres and a host of other elements of social life (Peiss and Simmons, 1989; Weeks, 1985, 1986, 1989; D'Emilio and Freedman, 1997; Seidman, 1990; Giddens, 1992).

An influential component of this trend toward historicizing sexuality is the work of Foucault, especially the first volume of his *History of Sexuality* (Foucault, 1978). In that volume Foucault contests the notion (presupposed by the sexologists as well as some proponents of the sexual revolution) that the treatment of sexuality in the West during the last three centuries is best understood in terms of a teleological shift from repression to liberation. Foucault emphasizes instead the increasing concern with sexuality in medical, psychiatric, educational, and legal discourses. This "veritable discursive explosion" around sexuality is interpreted by Foucault in terms of an exercise of power that works not so much by repression but rather through such productive mechanisms as observation, specification, classification, diagnosis, and the state management of populations. It is partly as an effect of the power/ knowledge mechanisms of the discourses of sexuality, Foucault argues, that sexuality has come to be understood as that area of life in relation to which the truth of one's self can most reliably be deciphered.

The implications of this analysis of sexuality are both complex and contested. It is clear that, for Foucault, not only the discourses of the sexual sciences but also many of the discourses of sexual liberation need to be reconceptualized, inasmuch as they rely on some notion of an ahistorical "truth of sex" now being uncovered. For some critics, this attempt to question the modern belief that sexuality can "tell us our truth" (Foucault, 1988: 77) threatens to undermine movements for the liberation of sexual minorities. Yet Foucault's interrogation of the process whereby same-sex practices came to be understood in terms of a particular "species" of human being–"the homosexual"–has been crucial for the development of Queer Theory (Halperin, 1995). Moreover, the dual insight that sexuality can profitably be interpreted in terms of power relations, but that these relations are too complex to be understood solely in terms of repression and liberation, has played a key role in many other contemporary discussions of sexuality and potentially raises questions for biblical scholarship as well.

Much recent attention has been given, for example, to the processes of "racialized sexuality" (JanMohamed, 1992) whereby sexuality has been deployed toward the reproduction of "racial" and ethnic inequality through such mechanisms as racial stereotypes (see Carby, 1985; Gilman, 1985; Mercer, 1994). An awareness of such processes raises troubling questions about the tendency of some biblical texts (and some biblical scholars) to associate sexual misconduct with the ethnic "Others" of biblical literature (see Bailey, 1989; Stone, 1997a). A similar sexualization of colonial "Others" by their colonizers has also been examined by scholars associated with postcolonial studies (Stoler, 1991, 1995; McClintock, 1995). Moreover, with the spread of global consumer capitalism it has now become possible to speak of a "global politics of sexuality" (Connell, 1997: 72) whereby race, class, gender, international power relations, and religion all become implicated in such complex phenomena as, for example, international sex tourism (see Davidson, 1998; Brock and Thistlethwaite, 1996). As each of these examples shows, it is the specification of interrelations between sexuality and supposedly nonsexual phenomena, rather than the restriction of sexuality to biological and physiological processes, that has become key to postmodern analyses of sexuality.

Analyses of sexuality in terms of power relations have played an especially important role in feminism, since feminists have long recognized that sexuality is implicated in the oppression of women through such practices as rape, prostitution, pornography, sexual stereotyping, and double standards for male and female sexual behavior. This recognition has even led some feminists to define sexuality almost entirely in terms of gender oppression (e.g., MacKinnon, 1992). Heterosexual intercourse as such is sometimes seen as necessarily suspect under conditions of male domination, inasmuch as the widespread conceptualization of intercourse as the conjunction of male active subject and female passive object is said to involve the "possession," "occupation," and "use" of women by men (Dworkin, 1987). Such discussions may be relevant to the interpretation of biblical representations of sexual contact, for active/passive positions in penetrative intercourse (whether between a man and a woman or between two men) were often understood as isomorphic with dominant/submissive social positions in the ancient world (Winkler, 1990; Halperin, 1990; compare Brooten, 1996; K. Stone, 1996).

At the same time, some feminists caution that this approach to sexuality, while correct in its perception that sexuality is often implicated in the oppression of women, cannot be universalized to cover all instances of sexual contact without falling into another sort of ahistoricism. The assumption that the significance of sexuality can be read more or less directly from "active/ passive" positions in sexual intercourse (an assumption also held by many of the early sexologists as well as some contemporary gay writers [e.g., Bersani, 1987]) tends toward a formal rather than a historical or contextual understanding of sexual meaning. Moreover, this second feminist position argues that, rather than focusing exclusively on the dangers of sexuality for women, analyses of sexuality need to account for women's experiences of pleasure as well. Not only must a totalizing analysis of heterosexual intercourse give way to a recognition of the multiplicity of "heterosexualities" (Segal, 1997: 86; compare Segal, 1994; Katz, 1995; Richardson, 1996), there is also a need to acknowledge the agency that some women in some contexts exercise even through forms of sexuality criticized within feminism. Hence, while pornography, sadomasochism, and lesbian butch/femme roles are often viewed as inherently and necessarily patriarchal, some feminists point out the complexities involved in specifying the meaning of such activities in the lives of individual women and attempt to reclaim the emphasis on freedom of sexual choice that characterized the early second wave of feminism (Vance, 1984; Snitow et al., 1983).

These disputes within feminism are symptomatic of a wider lack of consensus in postmodernity around sexual ethics and values. In the United States in particular, this lack of consensus often centers around a tension between romantic and libertarian approaches to sexuality (Seidman, 1990, 1992). The former approach values sexuality primarily as a means of expressing and strengthening emotional attachments and intimacy. The latter approach, by contrast, understands consensual erotic pleasure in and of itself as a worthwhile goal, even when such pleasure is pursued apart from primary affective bonds, and tends to view norms for sexuality, other than the notion of consent, with suspicion. While both of these approaches arose in the wake of the modern collapse of traditional notions of sexuality as primarily a means toward reproduction, the polarized debate between romanticism and libertarianism has also served as the context for a resurgence of neo-traditionalist attitudes toward sexuality. Whereas libertarian approaches to sexuality tend not to be strongly represented within communities that emphasize biblical interpretation, both romantic and traditionalist attitudes are widespread in such contexts.

As critics point out, all three of these approaches frequently rest on premises that are contested by postmodern thought. Both traditionalism and romanticism tend toward an essentialist view of sexuality in which its significance is thought to be inherent within certain acts or practices, irrespective of context, effects, or the intentions of actors (Seidman, 1992). Traditionalism and romanticism also favor prescriptive approaches to sexuality that fail to come to terms with the diversity of meanings and experiences associated with sexuality (compare Rubin, 1984). Libertarians, on the other hand, place a high value on sexual diversity but often approach sexual ethics in the framework of liberal individualism and frequently avoid qualitative analyses of sexuality. A libertarian ethic tends to emphasize consent as the sole criterion for ethical decision making without considering the difficulties raised for notions of conscious consent by such diverse trends of thought as feminism, psychoanalysis, structuralism, and post-structuralism. Thus, in distinction from traditionalism, romanticism, or libertarianism (though perhaps closer to the latter than either of the former), a postmodern sexual ethics might adopt a pragmatic attitude toward sexuality that appreciates the value of sexual pluralism and diversity while also recognizing the importance of context-specific analyses and evaluations of particular sexual contacts. The need for sexual norms and values is not denied, but such norms and values are acknowledged to be contingent on and relative to the times, places, and populations in relation to which they are elaborated (Seidman, 1992; Weeks, 1997).

If the meanings and experiences associated with sexuality are historical and contextual, as many postmodern trends in the analysis of sexuality imply, then the significance of sexual references in the biblical texts cannot be taken for granted. It is important to remember that such references may presuppose sociocultural frameworks that are very different from our own, frameworks that may themselves be multiple and conflict-ridden. Moreover, if "sexuality" is no one thing but rather a changing effect of the interaction of a range of complex variables, then developments in history and society will no doubt be accompanied by new types of sexual practices, experiences, and meanings unknown to the biblical texts. Recent phenomena such as phone sex and computer sex, for example, continue to produce novel experiences of sexuality that have been, as yet, insufficiently studied. There is little reason to doubt that ongoing social, cultural, and technological changes will require even more, as yet unforeseen, adjustments to our perception of the constellation of practices, pleasures, meanings, risks, and experiences that make up the ever-changing shape of "sexuality."

space
James W. Flanagan

Space has existed since the beginning of time. But human understandings of space and the relationship between space and time have often changed. In recent centuries, Kantian philosophy, Newtonian physics, and Euclidian geometry combined to support confidence in a so-called modernist Cartesian space and time grid. In that perception, three-dimensional space calibrated on x, y, and z axes exists as a static "container" in which events occur throughout time, the fourth dimension.

Twentieth-century discoveries demonstrate the partiality of earlier perceptions. In physics, Einsteinian space-time opened ways to construct and explore worlds that do not rest on Newtonian Enlightenment space and time foundations. The intellectual breakthrough captured in the equation $E = mc^2$ enables developments that will transform life on our planet and in other spaces for the rest of time. As a result, computer technology, moon landings, space travel, and cyberspace communities are reshaping today's spatial consciousness and human aspirations.

Major scientific and technological advances derived from the new understandings run parallel to transformed spatial conceptions in the arts, humanities, and social sciences. There, each has demonstrated again that human perceptions of space are constructed through experiences rooted in economic, political, social, and cultural conditions. History and ethnography from statist and non-statist societies worldwide support this contention. For example, in the medieval period several competing and overlapping spatialities existed until single-point perspective in artistic works contributed to the emergence of centralized territorial sovereignty in nation-states (Edgerton). Among nomadic peoples in Mongolia, chiefly space contrasts with shamanic space (Humphrey). Segmentary tribal societies identify space by peoples rather than by geography (Sack). And Gawan society constructs space by establishing exchange relationships among peoples in the Papua New Guinea region (Munn).

In Western industrialized societies, studies demonstrate that architectural design affects residential social arrangements and other patterns of behavior (Jencks). The economies of Fordist assembly-line production change spatial presuppositions in capitalist societies (D. Harvey). Similarly, it has been argued that because of a common underlying cultural shift, deconstruction in

239

philosophy and literature on one hand and chaos theory in science on the other emerged in the same age (Hayles).

These are but a few of the varied spatialities that can be demonstrated from research across disciplines. The variety and cross-disciplinary associations illustrate two factors. First, the boundaries among realms of daily life as well as the disciplines that examine them are unstable, fluid, and permeable. Second, the changes among life's realms and research disciplines reflect transformations in cultural spatial subtexts, that is, in the worldviews and basic spatial presuppositions that humans act on and use to orient themselves and their surroundings. In light of this, interacting reciprocal influences are easily recognized. Economics is not disconnected from developments in art, sociology goes hand in hand with architecture, and changes in human praxis transform mental perceptions of space. It is relationships such as these and the changes among them that make it possible to contrast postmodern space with spaces of other eras and arenas.

The fundamental importance of space in human thought and action becomes increasingly complex and critical with the advent of globalization and instantaneous electronic communication. These introduce new alternative spatialities that make it impossible to live in or study a single realm of human existence in isolation from all others. The social practices that construct global space operate with different economies, politics, and social and cultural forms. Modes of information displace earlier modes of production (Poster), and spaces of flows replace spaces of places (Castells). By comparison, the technological changes affecting the world today are as momentous as those that gave rise to the Industrial Revolution several centuries ago. We must expect, therefore, that perceptions of space are changing and will continue to change accordingly.

A difference between world spatiality and global spatiality can be noted. The contrast matches that separating a world economy from a global economy (Castells). In the first, former boundaries remain intact and relationships are established that allow agents to transcend the limits of individual space-units. In the latter, boundaries become irrelevant and actions across the globe, nearly instantaneous and universal, are not impeded by them. Individuality and interaction are replaced by integration and complexity.

Postmodern spatiality, as it may be called, is an embedded player in the second milieu. The certainties and spatialities presupposed in the modernist era are now known to be limited to certain domains and experiences, while elsewhere they are either gradually or suddenly being displaced by alternative subtexts. Space itself and spatial understandings, although continuing to operate in a reality-knowledge dialectic, are being expanded and enhanced individually and in tandem. Theoretical bases for these changes are developing in a number of humanities and social science disciplines, especially in spatial fields and studies on critical spatiality.

In the final years of the twentieth century the work of Michel Foucault on heterotopias has influenced many studies on postmodern space (1986: 22). Heterotopias are "spaces of liberty outside of social control" (D. Harvey: 230), or "places of alternate ordering" (Hetherington: 41). Although they may or may not be places of suppression, resistance, and revolt, heterotopias offer alternative spaces that challenge modernist Cartesian three-dimensional space and hegemonic uses of them. The closed-ended object-subject dialectic that controls the modernist perception is forced open by alternative spaces that do not fit easily into earlier molds.

What this means practically is being explored. Here the work of Henri Lefebvre is influential (1991). One who is attempting to extend Foucault's and Lefebvre's insights is geographer Edward W. Soja, who develops the theoretical richness of heterotopias by theorizing "Thirding-as-Othering" and a pair of trialectics that displace the dialectics of modernist spatiality (1996).

Drawing on the experiences and literatures of minorities and oppressed persons, Soja attributes their social occlusion to modernist perspectives and nineteenth- and twentieth-century overemphasis on historicality and sociality. To bring a corrective balance, he calls for openness to alternate spatialities rather than foreclosing on them in favor of modernist material space and mental conceptions of it. Such "Thirding-as-Othering," that is, openness to third or other possibilities, he insists, is a continual need if hegemonies based on modernist space are to be avoided.

Such "Thirding" allows Soja to escape the pretensions of finality implied in the modernist dialectic. He accepts Lefebvre's belief that space is produced in society through a triadic process consisting of "Spatial Practice," "Representations of Space," and "Representational Spaces" (33). For Lefebvre, spatial practice (*espace perçu,* perceived space) produces space by capitalist production and reproduction. It is both medium and outcome of human activity, behavior, and experience. Representations of space (*espace conçu,* conceived space) are the hegemonic, ideological representations associated with this space that obscure its social practices by rendering them invisible. These mental spaces are representations of power, ideology, control, and surveillance. Resistance to these relations must make them visible. Representational spaces or spaces of representations (*espace véçu,* lived space) linked to resistance movements do just that. Associated with the clandestine and underground side of social life, these are spaces as directly lived. They are, therefore, spaces of freedom and change, the heterotopias that Foucault sought to expose.

With Foucault and Lefebvre in the background, Soja proposes ontological and epistemological trialectics. The three "moments" of his ontological trialectic contain each other and cannot be understood in isolation or epistemologically privileged separately. Here, historicality and sociality are joined by a third term, spatiality (1996: 72). Speaking ontologically, each exists and can be known, although, as mentioned above, modern emphases have tended to suppress and ignore spatiality as a necessary ingredient in this trialectic.

The trialectic ontology on its own, however, does not satisfy Soja. It is here that he proposes "Thirding-as-Othering" as a means of escaping the binarisms, dialectics, and opposition that lead to a "closed logic of either/or" that capture physicalist (materialist) and mentalist (idealist) geographers in a hopelessly closed, mutually reinforcing exchange. He wants to avoid the geographer's pitfall, that is, trading the material world and representations of it as if they were object and subject when in fact they are one and the same. Hence, openness to "a third possibility or 'moment' that partakes of the original pairing but is not just a simple combination or an 'in between' position along an all-inclusive continuum" enables one to consider other spatialities (1996: 60).

In order to introduce social spatiality produced through social practice, an epistemology trialectic is proposed. Soja affirms that social space is not a thing but a set of relations produced through praxis. In his trialectic of spatiality, each space has its own epistemology, its own way of being known: Firstspace (perceived space), Secondspace (conceived space), and Thirdspace (lived space). It is important to note, however, that every space is all three.

"Firstspace epistemologies tend to privilege objectivity and materiality, and to aim toward a formal science of space" (1996: 75). Firstspace is the space that geographers have customarily examined. Human occupation, relations between society and nature, architectonics, and "built environments" are examples. This spatiality presents itself as a substantial text to be read, digested, and understood in all it details. As such, Firstspace is conventionally read at two levels, one that concentrates on accurate description of surface appearances, and the other that searches for spatial explanation in exogenous human and biophysical processes.

As understood in modernist geography, Firstspace is positivist, materialist, and becomes increasingly detailed with new technologies such as Global Positioning Systems and satellite imaging. It is the physical world, but it can also be social entities that geographers study. Alone, however, it is fundamentally incomplete and partial (1996: 78).

The boundary separating Firstspace from Secondspace is blurred. Nevertheless, "Secondspace epistemologies are immediately distinguishable by their explanatory concentration on conceived rather than perceived space and their implicit assumption that spatial knowledge is primarily produced through discursively devised representations of space, through the spatial workings of the mind" (1996: 78–79).

Secondspace may be entirely ideational projections into the empirical world from conceived or imagined geographies. Such knowledge of Firstspace is comprehended essentially through thought. Secondspace is the domain of artists and architects who present the world of their imaginations. It encompasses the cognitive maps that, in some cases, become substitutes for "real" maps that plot Firstspace. If Secondspace images are taken seriously as the real world, Firstspace collapses into Secondspace as the latter becomes a substitute for the former.

Soja's description of Thirdspace is not as precise or detailed as the others. Like "Thirding-as-Othering," Thirdspace is a "strategic reopening and rethinking new possibilities" that shift from epistemology to ontology, an "ontological rebalancing act [that] induces a radical skepticism toward all established epistemologies" (1996: 81).

Thirdspaces are the spaces of politics and ideology, where real and imagined are intertwined. For Soja they are filled with capitalism, racism, patriarchy, and other material spatial practices that make the social relations of production, reproduction, exploitation, domination, and subjection concrete. They are the "dominated spaces," the spaces of the peripheries, the margins and the marginalized, the "Third Worlds" that can be found on all scales, in the corpo-reality of the body and mind, in sexuality and subjectivity, in individual and collective identities from the most local to the most global. They are the chosen spaces for struggle, liberation, and emancipation (1996: 68).

Thirdspaces–lived spaces–command Soja's attention. They, he insists, have been lost or suppressed and need to be restored. For critical spatiality, a trialectic that brings lived space into tension with physical space and mental conceptions of it is required, and Soja believes that postmodernism is doing so. To accomplish this, spatiality must be examined critically the same way scholarship has examined history and society critically in order to understand, as far as possible, what happened in the past and is happening in the world today.

Jonathan Boyarin has observed that "'postmodernism' implies not the progressive supersession of the modern, but a critique from within that preserves the freedom of modernism while dismantling its progressivist pretensions to be the last and culminating word" (Boyarin 1994: 438). This description suits postmodern space. It challenges the pretensions of modernist space and opens the possibility of alternatives that have been suppressed. And it seems accurate to observe, as Foucault did as early as 1967, that "the great obsession of the nineteenth century was, as we know, history…The present epoch will perhaps be above all an epoch of space" (Foucault, 1986: 22).

The implications that postmodern spatiality hold for real-life situations and the applications it affords for many disciplines are both varied and serious. Critics cited by Soja, for example, have argued that their lot in life–largely unfavorable and undesired–arises from their spatial exclusion. The Palestinian "problem," the status of African Americans, the so-called Third World, and the proverbial glass ceiling blocking opportunities for women and minorities can all be understood in terms of spatiality. Rationales for the way things are and why they must be that way are cast in historical and social terms while spatial conceptions are omitted. The omission allows a patina of respectability to be introduced whereby the material Firstspace in which the occluded "live" and the Secondspace of the person describing and explaining conditions leaves the hegemonic modernist space intact. The progressivist pretensions are not dismantled.

Categories constructed around postmodern space can also be used for recasting language that at times entraps biblical and religious studies in needless, sometimes endless, debates. In many religious traditions, discussions regarding history versus myth or history versus theology can lead to dissension and devolve into political debates. In some instances, if not most, what is described as myth or theology may be accurately depicted as lived space, Thirdspace. Those on the history side of such debates uncritically assume that religious claims for territorial space, for example, envisage material Firstspace or claimants' Secondspace perceptions of Firstspace. Their objectors may argue or be thought to be arguing that religious longings for territorial space are merely mythological or theological faith-based claims. In fact, the two sides confuse their sources' pretensions for Firstspaces and/or Secondspaces with Thirdspace aspirations. The historicity of exodus, exile, apocalyptic, and similar traditions in any religion are notoriously difficult to evaluate. Understandings of postmodern space suggest that the reason may be that the traditions are voicing unfulfilled but longed-for expectations. In such instances, as with their interpreters, it is their lived space that is ignored, rather than a Firstspace they may or may not have held. In such "readings," critical spatiality is neglected and Thirdspace suppressed. Postmodern space offers avenues to be explored and exploited for ways out of old dilemmas by recovering ontological and epistemological trialectics of spatiality.

theory
Jan Tarlin

Theory is a vexed term in the discourse of mainstream biblical studies. Biblical scholars' difficulties with this term date from well before the advent of the academic prose genre known as "postmodern theory," or simply "theory" for short. Still, as might be expected, the ways in which postmodern theory has been appropriated or rejected within the biblical guild have largely been determined by the previous vicissitudes of the term *theory* within the guild's discourse.

The most generally accepted use of the term *theory* among biblical scholars is as a synonym for *method*. One says, for example, that one wants to apply theories used in the study of secular literature to biblical texts. By deploying the term *theory* in this seemingly commonsense way, one is actually constructing a fairly complex semantic collage, the elements of which include (at least) the following dictionary definitions of *theory* and *method*.

Theory:
- a belief, policy, or procedure proposed or followed as the basis of action
- the body of generalizations and principles developed in association with practice in a field of activity (as medicine, music) and forming its content as an intellectual discipline
- the coherent set of hypothetical, conceptual, and pragmatic principles forming the general frame of reference for a field of inquiry

(Webster's Third: 2371)

Method:
- a procedure or process for attaining an object
- a systematic procedure, technique, or mode of inquiry employed by or proper to a particular science, art, or discipline
- a way, technique, or process of or for doing something

(Webster's Third: 1423)

This definitional collage productively but problematically confuses technique and practice (method) on the one hand with their intellectual/

conceptual basis (theory) on the other in a way that effectively subordinates the latter to the former. That confusion and that subordination have been instrumental in the constitution and development of the discipline of biblical studies practiced in contemporary Western academia. The deflection of theory's bent toward reflection on practice into the methodological/technical trajectory toward "results" has been crucial to the establishment of biblical studies as a modern rigorous, "objective," even "scientific," enterprise fully differentiated from confessional/theological biblical interpretation.

Produced by the German Enlightenment, attached to the *Wissenschaft* tradition, and elaborated in the intellectual environment of Anglo-American positivisms and empiricisms, biblical studies has been mistrustful of sustained reflection on how it knows what it knows. Within the biblical guild, a tacit assumption has prevailed that its beliefs, policies, generalizations, and principles should be seen in the rigor of its arguments and in the validity of its conclusions, but not actually heard as independent voices in its discourse. To emphasize the ways in which "theory" differs from "method" has been regarded as threatening a return to pre-modern "subjective," "unscientific" ways of studying the Bible.

However, this defense of the epochal gains secured by modern Western biblical studies has not been without its price. As Timothy K. Beal and David M. Gunn have argued,

> With the emergence of a positivist historical consciousness in nineteenth-century scholarship...Biblical Studies grew dissociated from the wider intellectual discourse as practitioners pursued ever more single-mindedly the mechanics of their new program. Ironically, with the freedom to read the Bible in a radically fresh way—as a text like any other—came the gradual impositions of new disciplinary limits, as the "historical-critical method" became the measure of legitimate thinking about the text and scholars pressed on toward completing the scientific (*Wissenschaftlich*) understanding of the Bible. (Beal and Gunn, eds.: xi)

During the 1980s some extremely sophisticated attempts were made by biblical scholars to stretch those disciplinary limits without seriously disrupting the discourse of mainstream biblical studies or significantly challenging its values. These attempts involved careful, selective appropriation of concepts and methods from scholarship in fields such as linguistics, philosophy, literary criticism, sociology, and anthropology that could expand the range of biblical scholars' critical reflection without threatening their commitment to "scientific objectivity." To accomplish this task, explicit reflection on the roles of "theory" and "method" in biblical studies became necessary.

Indeed, the first section of Edward L. Greenstein's *Essays on Biblical Method and Translation* is titled "Theory and Method in Biblical Criticism." The relationship between the two titles is instructive. The title of part 1 of Greenstein's book indicates a text that will distinguish between "theory" and "method" and describe their differing functions in the practice of biblical scholarship. However, the prominence of *method* and the absence of *theory* in the title of the book itself promise that its contents will be a contribution to the discourse of mainstream biblical studies: The assimilation and subordination of "theory" to "method" will be maintained.

This promise is explicitly articulated in the portion of the preface where Greenstein orients the reader to the essays that make up part 1 of the book: "[T]heory and method interpenetrate and feed each other as they draw on each other. They are inseparable. One might even propose abandoning the distinction were it not, like 'form' and 'content,' a heuristically useful opposition" (1989a: xii).

For Greenstein, the provisional opposition of *theory* to *method* is heuristically useful because it enables revisionist thinking about what the proper object of systematic, *wissenschaftlich*, biblical scholarship actually is. Theoretical reflection on our methodological practice, Greenstein argues, reveals that biblical scholars have turned our analytical, "objective" lenses in the wrong direction. The goal of an "objectively correct" interpretation of the Bible–or of any other complex text–is an illusion; what can be objectively understood is not the text itself, but rather the conventions and procedures by which interpreters carry out their decidedly subjective work.

The net effect of this argument is to blur the distinction between *theory* and *method,* as what once appeared to be interpretive "methods" are shown to consist of the very beliefs, policies, generalizations, and principles that are the substance of "theory," and these theoretical constructs are found, in turn, to be fit objects for methodical scholarly inquiry. By thus developing an argument in which *theory* and *method* are dialectically transformed one into the other, Greenstein's text reinscribes the problematic relationship between these terms that is so crucial to the discourse of mainstream biblical studies.

To construct his argument that interpretations of texts arise from the subjectivities of interpreters rather than inhering objectively in the texts themselves, Greenstein draws from theoretical reflection by psychologists, philosophers of science, and neo-pragmatist thinkers on the processes of perception and interpretation (1989a: 53–68). From the work of perceptual psychologists including Rudolph Arnheim, Richard L. Gregory, and Julian E. Hochberg, Greenstein takes the insight that there is no such thing as the direct perception of raw sensory input unmediated by thought or memory. "Perception," writes Greenstein, "is itself an interpretive faculty, an active, though largely automatic, implementation of our prior models, presuppositions and analytic strategies" (1989a: 57). What is true of perception itself must hold even more strongly for the highly formalized kinds of perception that go into the observation and experimentation that yield the data from which scientific laws are derived; and, indeed, Greenstein cites theoretical reflections on science by an array of thinkers from Edmund Husserl, through Albert Einstein, to Robert Pirsig, all of whom support the contention that "[t]he root of the [scientific] laws lies in the model in the thinker's imagination" (1989a:

57). And, in turn, what is true of scientific research must certainly be true of investigations in the humanities, where neo-pragmatist thinkers such as Stanley Fish and Richard Rorty have concluded that "we all begin with beliefs or assumptions that guide us in our observations and analyses" (1989a: 60).

Greenstein summarizes his application of this argument to the discipline of biblical studies in a witty response to the scholarly debate occasioned by the publication of John Van Seters' *Abraham in History and Tradition*. This response focuses on the use of the metaphor "pointing evidence" in the discussion of Van Seters' work. Greenstein notes that in contesting Van Seters' maverick view of pentateuchal composition,

> [a]t least four reviewers contended with Van Seters by asserting that the [textual] evidence actually "points" in a different direction. Van Seters has himself used this expression in his reply to criticism. Using language that places truth in the power of the evidence gives the impression that it is not we who rely on our own force of logic or persuasion but that some external "objective" standard articulates the truth for us. "Pointing" evidence, of course, is actually a metaphor, a personification of the data *we* have found, structured, and adduced. We interpret the evidence and we point it. (1989a: 67, Greenstein's emphasis)

If, then, the interpretation of biblical texts is by definition a subjective enterprise, this exercise cannot ground the status of biblical studies as an "objective" academic discipline; there are no absolute criteria by which to evaluate interpretive methods and their results so as to establish which are "correct." No "objective" account can be given of the form and meaning of the biblical text. According to Greenstein, what can be described and discussed, though not evaluated, objectively are precisely the subjective presuppositions that interpreters bring to their reading of texts and the ways in which those presuppositions structure the resulting interpretations:

> When the community (or one of the communities) to which we belong, or choose to belong, accepts a set of assumptions as "facts," we then take them for granted and build our arguments upon them. The various methods in which Biblicists are trained…constitute systems of such facts. One therefore may facilitate discussion and under-standing by laying bare our assumptions and sorting out those of the arguments we criticize. We might discover that our arguments over method are fundamentally differences in assumptions, principles, or beliefs. (1989a: 68)

In other words, what biblical scholars generally call "method" is really "theory" and ought to be the object of a methodical investigation that would form the core of the discipline of biblical studies.

Five years earlier, in his influential book *Reading the Old Testament: Method in Biblical Study* (a work that Greenstein cites approvingly several times), John

Barton had reached a similar conclusion by a different path. Greenstein argues that there exist a myriad of plausible but inherently subjective interpretations of the biblical text based on equally plausible and equally subjective theoretical assumptions. Barton, on the other hand, had argued that biblical interpretation should be pretty much a commonsense enterprise tending to produce the same results wherever and by whomever it is practiced:

> What I should like to imagine is a style of Old Testament studies that would make sense even if all the interpretive decisions had already been made. At the moment each method has to work harder and harder to overturn the conclusions of its predecessors; learned journals are littered with more and more fresh interpretations of particular texts…The truth is that the meaning of very many passages, even of very many whole books, is not very seriously disputed. There is room for exciting new interpretations, but not endless room. In such a situation (and let us imagine it as it may be in fifty, a hundred or two hundred years time), "methods" which yield "results" are of mainly historical interest, for the results have been yielded. Where will be the place of criticism then? (206)

Barton suggests that biblical criticism can place itself in the new landscape that he has mapped once it comes to grips with the fact that

> biblical "methods" are *theories* rather than methods: theories which result from the formalizing of intelligent intuitions about the meaning of biblical texts…[A]t the end of the [reading] process there emerges a distinct impression of what the text means, together with an explanatory theory as to how it comes to mean it. But the theory–which when codified will become source analysis or redaction criticism or whatever–is logically subsequent to the intuition about meaning. It may lead to useful insights into other texts, when they are approached in similar frame of mind…but it can never be a technique which can always be used with the assurance that it will yield correct results. (205, Barton's emphasis)

Once biblicists see that our "methods" are really "theories," Barton argues, we will come to understand that the place of biblical criticism "is not to be always producing new interpretations, but to explain interpretations on which readers can agree" (206). In short, according to Barton, biblical studies should become the methodical, "objective" investigation of the "theories" that it uses as if they were "methods":

> [E]xploring the way we read the Old Testament and asking what our presuppositions are…we might turn again to each of the methods that litter the path of biblical criticism and see in each the key to certain ways we do in fact read the Bible. Instead of asking which method is "right," we might ask what is really going on in the reader

when he [*sic*] is using each of them, what kind of reading they belong to. (206–7)

Both Greenstein's and Barton's arguments contain insights that could have served to generate a sustained critique of, or even significant alternatives to, the way the term *theory* is deployed in the discourse of mainstream biblical studies. Instead, however, both arguments simply produce new and more sophisticated versions of the mainstream discursive maneuvers that confuse *theory* and *method* in ways that subordinate the former to the latter in the interest of establishing that biblical studies is an "objective" discipline. These arguments have proved worth examining at length because they offer such clear examples of the knots into which texts by even the most able mainstream biblical scholars tie themselves when they must come to terms with "theory" and its promptings toward a reflexive self-consciousness that might unsettle the discipline's claims to objectivity.

Given the problematic status of *theory* in the discourse of mainstream biblical studies, it is not surprising that the advent of postmodern theory as a major genre of academic writing in the broad interdisciplinary context of the humanities has not, by and large, been warmly greeted within the biblical guild. Generally, the emergence of theory as an influential scholarly practice has been ignored by biblical scholars; some few have welcomed it, and some quite illustrious ones have cited it as a grave threat to the future integrity of our discipline. All these reactions–denial, excitement, and anxiety–are ways of coping with the realization that, as New Testament critic Stephen D. Moore has noted, "theory is not *confirming* of our conventional exegetical wisdom" (1989: xx, Moore's emphasis).

Postmodern theory undermines the conventional wisdom of the biblical guild in at least three important and related ways. First, the emergence of theory as an academic practice in its own right has highlighted the precariousness of the subordination of theory to method in biblical studies. Second, the trajectory of that practice's development has progressively blurred the boundaries between the human mind and the objects of its investigations. Finally, that blurring has increasingly strengthened the case for arguing that the mind does not discover "the truth" in the objects that it thinks about, but that thought is rather the production of "truth" by the interpenetration of mind and object. These three factors work together to call into question the claims of disciplinary objectivity articulated by the discourse of mainstream biblical studies, whether that discipline is conceived as searching for correct interpretations of texts or for correct understandings of how texts are interpreted.

The three factors outlined above received one of their earliest and most forceful articulations in the work of an author whose texts became one of the most important catalysts for the development of what has emerged as postmodern theory: the German philosopher Martin Heidegger. In the texts collected in *The Question Concerning Technology and Other Essays,* Heidegger argued that the confusion of theory with technique and the further confusion of technique itself with objectivity are constitutive of both modern Western culture and of the science and technology that give that culture its focus. This culture, science, and technology, according to Heidegger, have produced human beings who view themselves either as subjects who discover truth in objects from which they maintain an absolute distance, or, alternatively, as creators who produce truth out of raw materials from which they remain perfectly distinct. Heidegger opposes these views by proposing that human beings are participants in a world from which truth constantly emerges and by which truth is constantly sustained. *Theory,* released from the constraints that Western modernity has imposed on it, would name a way of delineating human participation in the emergence and sustaining of truth.

To release *theory* for this purpose, Heidegger conducts an elaborate etymological investigation of the word's root in classical Greek, *theoria* (focused vision), and of that root's relations with the terms *techne* (art, craft, mode of production) and *aletheia* (truth) (11–14 and 163–67). This investigation, however, is not an exercise in "objective" linguistic history; rather, it is itself a theoretical meditation in which the reader is invited to follow the emergence of new truth from the interpenetration of Heidegger's mind and the ancient Greek language. The truth that emerges from this linguistic meditation is that, at its root, *theory* signifies an act of seeing that participates with the world in the unfolding and sustaining of truth; however, as the Greek root brought forth shoots first in Latin and then in the languages of modern Europe, its original meaning was drastically transformed. In the discourses of modern Western culture, technology, and science, *theory* came to denote an act of visual aggression that forces an objectified world to yield its truth.

According to Heidegger, however, this transformation need not be the final one: "[W]ithin 'theory' understood in the modern way, there yet steals the shadow of the early *theoria.* The former lives out of the latter and indeed not only in the outwardly identifiable sense of historical dependence" (165). Because the viability of the contemporary word *theory* depends on its entire history all the way back to its linguistic root in *theoria,* "theory" has the potential to transform itself by contact with its root. If such a transformation were to take place, theory would become a form of what Heidegger calls "reflection": a kind of thinking that transcends the position of the modern "theorist," who forces truth from an objectified world and thereby produces a present-day form of the ancient Greek practitioner of *theoria:* a careful participant in truth's self revelation (115–82). "Theory" would then become "postmodern theory."

Unfortunately, Heidegger's thought stages a full-scale retreat from the leap into the postmodern that it proposes. Heidegger's goal for the process of reflection is to reach a point where all distinctions between nature, humanity, culture, and language collapse, thereby freeing human communities to simultaneously collaborate in and submit to their destinies by direct participation in "Being itself" (36–41). The reflecting scholar would thus become the voice that articulates the self-revelation of Being as it unfolds in and is unfolded by his or her community (181–82). Thus, via his embrace of a peculiar admixture of mysticism, metaphysics, Romanticism, and nationalism, Heidegger reverts to the modern goal of the objective articulation of empirical truth.

From the early 1950s to the late 1960s a generation of scholars, mostly French, came of age, who took on the challenge from which Heidegger had retreated. These scholars attempted to think past the demarcation of subject and object to participate in the emergence of truth at the point where mind and world interpenetrate, but without appealing to the objective authority of Being to validate their thought. Initially, they situated themselves within discourses—particularly Heidegger's own discourse of phenomenological philosophy, Marxism, Freudian psychoanalysis, and structural linguistics—that had begun, but not completed, important critiques of the basic assumptions of modern Western technology, science, philosophy, and culture. Burrowing from within, these thinkers divested those discourses of their last attachments to the subject/object distinction and the rhetoric of objectivity. Thus divested, those discourses began to articulate their participation in the conjoint enactment by mind and world of truths whose only validation was their lived viability. In this way, an ensemble of discourses that could properly be called "postmodern theory" was generated. To this ensemble belong the structural Marxism of Louis Althusser; the psychoanalytic thought of Jacques Lacan; the aesthetics, ethics, and political philosophy of Jean-François Lyotard; Jacques Derrida's deconstructive philosophy; Paul de Man's deconstructive literary criticism; the psychoanalytic feminisms of Luce Irigaray, Julia Kristeva, Catherine Clement, and Helene Cixous; Michel Foucault's neo-Nietzschean philosophy of power; Jean Baudrillard's Nitetzschean sociology; and the many hybrids they have yielded in succeeding generations of scholars.

What these extremely diverse discourses share in common is a turning of Heidegger's understanding of "theory" on its head; postmodern theory is not so much a way of seeing as it is something to be seen: a performance. To make this point, Stephen D. Moore has neatly inverted Heidegger's etymological argument. "Our word theory," Moore writes, "comes from the Greek *theoria*. Etymologically, therefore, a theory is a sight, a spectacle, a speculation" (1996: 58). Thus, the erosion of the subject/object distinction and the emergence of a truth continually in process from the conjunction of world and mind are not functions of an ongoing revelation of Being, but rather of an ongoing performance by beings. In that performance, generally bumbling, all too often violent, always incomplete, the postmodern theorist seeks to play her or his role.

These scholar-performers have had a major impact on the shaping of academic discourse in the humanities over the last half-century; in biblical studies their influence has barely begun to be felt. Postmodern theory's invitation to abandon the identity of scientist, discoverer, technician, or creator for the equally demanding, but quite different, identity of performer has proved attractive to only a tiny minority in the biblical guild. Whether postmodern theory will have an important influence on the development of biblical studies depends on whether or not a much larger number of biblical scholars find that the internal logic of their work impels them to accept that invitation. What would be the shape of biblical studies if a significant number of its practitioners joined the ranks of those who "know that truth is only an act...[and] never considering their own answers to be satisfying...remain the scandalous authors of the infelicity that never ceases to make history" (Felman, 1983: 150)? We may or may not find out.

translation
Susan Brayford

Once upon a biblical time, there was an outspoken matriarch named Sarah, whose barrenness seemed to present an insurmountable obstacle to the fulfillment of YHWH's promise of innumerable descendants to her husband Abraham. Her inability to conceive a child did not prevent Sarah from conceiving a plan by which her maidservant Hagar would act as a surrogate to provide Abraham a child. However, Hagar's son Ishmael did not meet YHWH's requirements that Sarah herself bear the required heir. When she (over)hears her husband's mysterious visitor predict that she will fulfill her divinely ordained duty within the year, Sarah laughs to herself, wondering if she can still have sexual pleasure, since she is worn out and her husband is old (Gen. 18:12). A few verses later, YHWH criticizes Sarah for her laughter, a remark that most have interpreted as a sign of her lack of faith. However, since Abraham was not criticized for his earlier laughter at the same prediction, I suggest that Sarah's laughter was not primarily one of doubt, but one of delight. She was less concerned about YHWH's divine procreative abilities than about Abraham's human ones. A sampling of several ways in which this verse has been (mis)translated seems to support this possibility.

Translation, the subject of this essay, might seem to have little in common with most of this volume's essays on methods of biblical interpretation. Indeed, postmodern translation theory offers the readers of biblical texts less an actual interpretive method and more an interpretive warning. Let the reader beware. The reason for such caution–that all translation is, at its most basic, interpretation–should come as no surprise to readers of this volume. What might be surprising is where, how, and just how much interpretation occurs before a reader even begins to read the biblical text. Readers not only must acknowledge the multiple biases of the ancient writers and editors, but they also must account for the agendas of ancient, modern, and even postmodern translators. In this essay I will discuss the significance that postmodern translation theory has for biblical interpretation. To show the implications of this theory, I will examine how several different reading communities have translated, and thus interpreted, Sarah's laughing remarks.

In the Beginning...

...there was the Septuagint (hereafter LXX). As the first extant written translation of the Hebrew Scriptures, the LXX also represents the first written interpretation of these scriptures outside the scriptures themselves. The third-century B.C.E. Alexandrian cultural backdrop of this premier Greek translation inevitably influenced, consciously and unconsciously, the lexical decisions of its Hellenistic Jewish translators. Motivated by the desire of diaspora Jews to be able to read their scriptures in the Greek language of their time and place, these learned Alexandrian translators followed no explicit rules for their translation, being guided by "intuition and spontaneity more than conscious deliberation and technique" (Aejmelaeus: 25; see also Barr: 281). The resulting differences between the Greek translation(s) and Hebrew original(s) of different biblical books were explained–or explained away–according to concepts that have dominated biblical translation discourse since antiquity.

Consider, for example, the statement attributed to Ben Sira's grandson, who, in the second century B.C.E., reflected on his translation of his grandfather's book of Sirach:

> You are invited therefore to read it with goodwill and attention, and to be indulgent in cases where, despite our diligent labor in translating, we may seem to have rendered some phrases imperfectly. For what was originally expressed in Hebrew does not have exactly the same sense when translated into another language. Not only this book, but even the Law itself, the Prophecies, and the rest of the books differ not a little when read in the original. (NRSV)

In his own apologetic way, Ben Ben Ben Sira acknowledges the impossibility of translation in much the same way as modern linguistic theorists, who recognize that any rewording, either from one language to another or even within the same language, prohibits complete synonymy (Barnstone: 15–16; compare Steiner: 251). In other words, the source text (ST) cannot equal the target text (TT). From this perspective, the Greek version of Sarah's laughing thoughts are certainly not on target. Instead of pondering the possibility of pleasure, Sarah merely questions whether "it" could happen to her, now that her husband was old (*egelasen de Sarra en heautêi legousa oupô men moi gegonen heôs tou nun ho de kurios mou presbuteros*). In its literary context, "it" could only refer to correcting her inability to have children.

A modern, text-critical explanation of this suppression of Sarah's sexy thoughts points to another aspect of the impossibility of translation, that is, lexical ignorance. Noted LXX scholar John Wevers maintains that the Alexandrian translator probably did not recognize the Hebrew word for pleasure (*'ednah*), because it was a *hapax legomenon* (a word that occurs only one time in the same form in the Hebrew text). As a result, the translator may have read it as two Hebrew words, *d'* and *hnh,* and rendered it as *heôs tou nun,* that is, "until now" (252). I have no quarrel with Wevers' text-critical explanation of *how* the differences may have occurred. However, I maintain that postmodern translation theory can supplement modern explanations by focusing on the social and cultural *significance* of the differences. As I will show below, the ways in which Sarah's thoughts have been translated simultaneously reflect and continue to shape culturally conditioned attitudes about gender and gender roles.

In his disclaimer, Ben Sira's grandson alludes to another ubiquitous topos in translation discourse. Admitting that his translation might not have exactly the same sense as the Hebrew, this early translator hints at the difference between literal (*verbum pro verbo*) translations, later thought to be required for religious and legal texts, and free (*sensus ad sensum*) translations, thought to be more appropriate for literary texts (S. Brock: 69–79). A similar dichotomy characterizes the distinction between formal and dynamic equivalency. While the former assumes that a value-neutral, objective, literal translation process is achievable, the latter acknowledges its impossibility–or unsuitability–and strives for a response in the reader of the TT that is "essentially like" that of the reader of the ST (Nida and Taber: 202). Later expansions of descriptive and prescriptive categories into triadic classifications (e.g., Dryden's metaphrase, paraphrase, and imitation) and even more elaborate schemes to describe the relationship between ST and TT (e.g., Barnstone: 25–29), however, offer little to those interested in interpretation.

These traditional approaches to translation tend not to venture beyond conventional notions about language, equivalence, and meaning. They assume that the source text has an inherent meaning, that this meaning can be translated into another language, and that the success of a translation depends on how closely it corresponds with the meaning of the original. In other words, some degree of equivalence is presumed to be both achievable and desirable. Furthermore, traditional translation theory acknowledges neither the intentional and unintentional biases that translators bring to their work, nor the new creation that results from the act/art of translation. Accordingly, traditional models fail to recognize the "violence" that often accompanies translation.

Beginning Anew

Postmodern theorists, challenging these modern assumptions, ask what if the direction of dependence were reversed so that the meaning of the original text is dependent on the translation (e.g., Gentzler: 144–45)? In Sarah's case, for example, the pleasure that she ponders in the Hebrew original is much more evident when compared with its absence in the Greek translation. In fact, Jacques Derrida prefers the term "transformation" over "translation," because translation modifies the ST to such a degree that it defers and often displaces its meaning (1981: 20). Walter Benjamin goes so far as to characterize translation's transforming quality as a type of afterlife that fulfills the life of the original text (1969a: 70–72). Thus, in her Greek literary afterlife, Sarah is *transformed* from an outspoken Jewish matriarch into a modest Hellenistic matron whose thoughts focus more appropriately on her procreative responsibilities, not on her pleasurable possibilities.

Other postmodern theorists apply reader-response theory to translation and consider translation to be a much broader venture than mere transfer of meaning between languages. Willis Barnstone, for example, associates translation with writing, reading, and interpretation, an act that occurs not on the page, but in the mind. From this perspective,

> the principles of translation from author to translator to reader reveal a series of dependent acts of translation: the author translates the thought by writing a text; the translator reads and interprets the author's text, and then, as the second author, formally translates that interpretation by writing a second text (the translation proper); and the reader translates the second text into her or his own creation. (Barnstone: 22)

The postmodern theory of translation that, in my opinion, offers the most fruitful possibilities for biblical interpretation is that based on cultural studies. This model begins with the modern assumption that meaning and interpretation emerge out of real conditions that can be specifically described. In others' words, "there is always a context in which the translation takes place, always a history from which a text emerges and into which a text is transposed" (Lefevere and Bassnett, 1990: 11). Taking both the texts and their contexts seriously, the cultural studies approach to translation goes beyond the modern sensitivity to the original context and acknowledges institutions of prestige and power within the cultures of both ST and TT (A. Benjamin: 180).

What most clearly distinguishes the cultural studies model of translation theory from more traditional modern methods, however, is its emphasis on translation's bilateral influence. In other words, translation not only *reflects* both its source and receiving culture, but even more importantly, it *shapes* the receiving culture, and often reshapes that of the source. Sherry Simon describes translation as an activity that "destabilizes cultural identities and becomes the basis for new modes of cultural creation" (135). She goes on to characterize translation as a special type of bridge—one that does more than merely connect existing cultural entities. It also "brings into being the realities which it links" (152; see also Overing: 83). She and other scholars who use the cultural studies model of translation theory foreground the translator's role and location(s)—social, political, geographical, economic, and temporal— in the translation process and product, as well as the transformation—both positive and negative— that results from the act of translation.

Some scholars, whose work reflects postcolonial sensitivities, emphasize the often violent nature of translation and question the translators' role in perpetuating the ideological systems associated with the hegemony of the dominant culture. As several contributors to the 1996 *Semeia* volume on translation demonstrate, even the more flexible process of dynamic equivalence often continues "to engender oppression (pun intended!) because of its aim to induce the same oppressive response in the receptor's language as was felt in the source language" (Yilibuw: 31; see also those articles by Pippin, 1996a; A. Smith; Carroll; and Sugirtharajah). Thus, racial, class, and gender oppression are often translated without being transformed. And when transformation does occur, it often results in increased power imbalances between the dominant and marginalized cultures–especially when the biblical text is translated for missionary purposes.

To demonstrate the significance that the cultural studies model of translation theory can have for biblical interpretation, I return to the barren Sarah of Genesis 18:12, as she laughingly ponders the possibility of pleasure for the sake of progeny. Her thoughts of sex allude to the element of female sexual desire that YHWH built into the procreative process (Gen. 3:16). However, both of these explicit references to female sexuality disappear in the LXX translation. Eve will only experience a "turning" (*apostrofē*) toward her husband, and Sarah's musings are limited to the impossibility of bearing children. Their sexuality suppressed, these women are transformed into model Hellenistic ladies who better reflect the more repressive attitudes toward female sexuality described and prescribed in classical Greek literature. Sarah's more circumspect laughter, for example, portrays her as a much better model of Semonides' good wife, that is, one who is "so chaste that she does not even like to listen to other women who talk about sex" (Diehl, frag. 7). The transformed Sarah similarly conforms to Plato's ideal wife, that is, one who engages in sex for procreative purposes only (e.g., *Laws* 8.838–9; *Symposium* 206e).

Even more important for a cultural studies model of translation is its transformative aspect, which "brings into being the realities which it links." In this case, the reality that it brings into being is one in which female sexuality is denied at best and condemned at worst. Consider the patriarch Reuben's misogynist testimony that "women are more easily overcome by the spirit of promiscuity than are men...by decking themselves out they lead men's minds astray, by a look they implant their poison, and finally in the act itself they take them captive" (T. Reu. 5:3–4).

New Testament texts, although not as harsh, nevertheless mirror and perpetuate the LXX's representation of gender roles. The Petrine writer, continuing the domestication of Sarah begun in the LXX, equates Sarah with "the other holy women who used to adorn themselves by accepting the authority of their husbands." Like these women, Sarah "obeyed Abraham and called him lord" (1 Pet. 3:5–6, NRSV). "Peter" conveniently overlooks Abraham's obedience to Sarah (Gen. 16:2), and although Sarah *did* refer to Abraham as "lord," she did so in the context of his possible failure to provide her pleasure (18:12). Sarah's (mis)translated musings that highlight progeny over pleasure would be acceptable to Pastor Timothy's congregation, where childbearing was understood as the only way in which women might be saved from Eve's transgression (1 Tim. 2:14–15). Thus, the domesticated Sarah of the LXX provided a model for early Christian gender roles.

Yet such repressiveness was not universal. Aquila, the second-century C.E. Palestinian translator known for his often awkward literalism, revised the Greek of Genesis 18:12 to read *truferia,* producing a text that can be translated,

"After my being worn out, has there been sexual tenderness to me?" (Wevers: 252). Symmachus' choice of *akmê,* that is, the highest or culminating point of any condition or act, could suggest that Sarah is pondering whether she might reach orgasm. Neither of these Palestinian revisers seemed particularly embarrassed about the physical aspects of Sarah's (a)musing thoughts.

Time travel forward to the twentieth century, when most academic translators and commentators capture the sexual nature of Sarah's *'ednah* by rendering it as "pleasure" or "enjoyment." Although some add apologetic commentary to soften Sarah's sexuality (e.g., Von Rad: 207; Westermann: 273), other commentators more forthrightly acknowledge the sexual overtones in Sarah's laughter. Robert Alter, for example, maintains that the Hebrew *'ednah* "is cognate with Eden and probably suggests sexual pleasure, or perhaps even sexual moistness" (79). Similarly, Nahum Sarna writes that the "Hebrew *ednah* is now known to mean 'abundant moisture' and is an exact antonym of 'withered'" (130). Lexical relationships aside, the physical aspect of "abundant moisture," from a woman's point of view, implies some level of sexual stimulation.

A glance at several English translations of Sarah's thoughts shows that some more accurately reflect the Hebrew original, while others prefer the Greek cover-up. The King James Version (KJV), Revised Standard Version (RSV), and New Revised Standard Version (NRSV) all translate the Hebrew *'ednah* as "pleasure," and The TANAKH (JPS) renders it as "enjoyment." Many, however, highlight Sarah's desire for progeny. The Contemporary English Version (CEV), a self-described "user-friendly" and "mission-driven" translation, "takes into consideration the needs of the hearer, as well as those of the reader, who may not be familiar with the traditional biblical language." Yet it also claims that its text is faithful to the meaning of the original and its accuracy is assured by its direct translation from the BHS. Its "dynamically equivalent" translation– "Now that I am worn out and my husband is old, will I really know such happiness?"–strives for a response from its readers that would be similar to the original readers. Yet in allowing the reader to choose between two meanings for the phrase "know such happiness"–either "the joy of making love" or "the joy of having children"–the CEV essentially admits uncertainty as to what that response should be! The New English Bible (NEB), which purports to express no denominational or doctrinal viewpoint, claims to be a "fresh and authoritative translation." Its translation– "I am past bearing children now that I am out of my time, and my husband is old"– leaves little doubt about what it is (not) authorizing. Like the LXX, the NEB takes away Sarah's "inappropriate" sexual thoughts. Its updated successor, the Revised English Bible (REB), continues the censoring of Sarah's thoughts in its rendering, "At my time of life, I am past bearing children, and my husband is old." These circumspect translations, I maintain, result from ideological, not text-critical, problems with Sarah's thoughts of *'ednah.*

Whether Sarah's laughing thoughts represent her as a sexual Jewish matriarch or a modest Hellenistic matron today, as yesterday, is a matter of culturally conditioned translation. Like the reality brought into being for women as a result of the Greek translation, the reality hoped for among the readership of some modern translations negates the reality of female sexuality and accentuates the more traditional female role of procreation. So, to reiterate, let the reader beware. To carry further Robert Carroll's proposal that Bible translations carry warning labels (52), I suggest that perhaps biblical texts, like films, should display a rating system. Original language texts could carry the "G" label–Go ahead, but be aware of your own biases as you translate these texts. Translations like the RSV and NAB might be rated "PG"–Pretty Good, but be aware that even the more literal translations inevitably are influenced by the multiple locations of their translators. The "R" label would alert readers of translations like the REB that some theological considerations have Regulated the translation. Finally, translations like CEV should carry the "X" rating. The reader should eXpect to read the editors' prepackaged interpretation of the biblical texts.

trauma
Jay Geller

The questions littering the landscapes of German Southwest Africa, Anatolia, Auschwitz, Cambodia, Rwanda, Bosnia, Kosovo…confront the biblical exegete just as they confront all individuals engaged in interpretation: What do they mean? How did they come to be? How do they fit into our master historical narratives? What do they say about humankind? What is the relationship of the exegete's present to these past events? Can one exercise one's hermeneutical vocation without recognizing the possible effects of these events on one's horizon of interpretation? In other words, how does one interpret the Bible at the close of this century of atrocity?

Some, as their meaning-seeking gaze roams from the massacres of the Herero to the dug-up graves of the Kosovars, read apocalyptic signs and biblical prophecy of the End of Days, and others detect the silence (or nonexistence) of Gd. Some find the source of the values and relationships that contribute to, if not engender, these horrors in scripture (C. Delaney, 1998; Schwartz, 1997); conversely, others see scripture as written in response to acts and ideas of that kind. It is to this latter assumption about scripture that studies of the literature of destruction and the experience of survivors (whether victim, perpetrator, survivor, or descendant) may offer some help.

In the wake of these horrors, trauma has become a pivotal notion for such analyses and their concomitant understandings of identities, histories, texts, and discourses (Caruth, 1996; Kirmayer, 1996; Felman and Laub, 1991; LaCapra, 1998; Friedlaender, 1993; Berger, 1999; van Alphen, 1999). Trauma, from the Greek for "wound" and originally referring to an injury to the body (compare a hospital's trauma center), has since the late nineteenth century become increasingly psychologized (Hacking, 1996; A. Young, 1996). While the body may suffer many traumas, contemporary studies of trauma focus on traumatic experiences (terror, disgust, shame, helplessness, depersonalization, dissociation–whether about reality or fantasy) and the effects of such experiences on the mind. Although the experience leaves somato-sensory, iconic, and affective impressions, it cannot be verbalized. Hence, trauma denotes an event that defies one's ability to propositionalize or narrativize experience, that is, one's ability to give it meaning (Herman, 1992; Van der Kolk and Van der Hart, 1995; Krystal, Southwick, and Charney, 1995).

The traumatic experience also has a temporal dimension, which has become a key component of its conceptualization. What often distinguishes a

261

traumatic experience from a horrible one is the former's latency. The delay may occur between the experience and its psychological consequences or symptom formation, or it could be the case that after an initial defensive response to the trauma, the symptoms would appear to have abated, only to return later. Both the trauma and the defensive reaction may leave scars (the provenance of which is no longer recognized) on behavior, body, or social attachment. At some point after the experience, the victim of past trauma relives the event–as if in the present–in nightmare, flashback, or somatic sensation; often the victim acts it out without recognition that he or she is repeating the original situation. Such repetition can manifest itself as phobic avoidance of or compulsive entering into relationships in which a repetition is likely to occur; acting out is also evident when the traumatized individual responds to similar situations in a manner seemingly out of proportion. Such behaviors may also be attempts to work through the trauma and regain control of one's life; working-through often entails a narrative by which the event can be integrated into one's life history or else mastered by transforming the experience into something one controls (Caruth, 1995, 1996; LaCapra, 1998).

For the subject of trauma, the locus of this temporal relationship between the individual's present behavior and thoughts with that past experience is memory: what has been recalled, what has been repressed, and what has been dissociated. While the factuality of this component of trauma is now contested as the proponents of recovered memory oppose those of false memory syndrome (Crews, 1995; Loftus, Feldman, and Dashiell, 1995), what neither contest is how the self-identified victim has narrativized the relationship between the (alleged) recalled experience and her or his present situation. Trauma in both of these competing discourses of recovered versus false memories is characterized as the experience of abuse. The recollected (or repressed, or dissociated) traumatic event (or the belief in its occurrence) explains the sufferers' misery or why they do what they do. That memory, whether recovered or contrived, determines who and what the self is. This experience of trauma also exculpates the individual from responsibility both for the original event and for its consequences on current behavior (Peter's three-time denial of knowing Jesus [Mt. 26:69–75] may be such an example). More, trauma renders the self a victim–the only space today accorded pure innocence. The victim then is free from responsibility for the atrocities that have befallen–or have been committed by–the self or others.

Yet despite the positivistic desire to emphasize the reality of abuse, what is key to the conceptualization of trauma is not that it is an experience that one has had and then forgotten, repressed, or dissociated; rather, it is the recognition that only because that incident was not experienced–that is, not known, not integrated into one's life story, not able to be judged because it exceeds the categories and schema by which we recognize experience–does trauma have its particular effects. The event was not forgotten, for it was never known; only in picking up the traces among the repetitions, affect-laden sensations, phobic reactions, compulsive behaviors, the sense of a dissociated self, can the trauma be reconstructed—known and mastered—the (non)memory recalled. As van der Kolk and van der Hart (1995: 176) write: "Traumatic memories are the unassimilated scraps of overwhelming experiences, which need to be integrated with existing mental schemes, and be transformed into narrative language. It appears that, in order for this to occur successfully, the traumatized person has to return to the memory often in order to complete it." For memory to be effective it must be narrativized.

Trauma has also become collectivized; for example, the Vietnam War has been described as a national trauma, the consequences of which are reflected in U.S. government behavior and Americans' collective memory (Schudson, 1995). Yet it is not just the collective memories disseminated by institutions, monuments, media, textbooks, and family tradition that are social. All retelling is social; the narratives draw on scripts that pervade a culture, and these provide caption and context for somato-sensory perceptions and affects as well as fill in the gaps between these emotion-laden percepts (Wood, 1999; Prager, 1998).

Perhaps no event is more emblematic of this century of genocide and its individual and collective traumas than the Holocaust. The traumas created by the Holocaust afflict not only those victimized in camps, ghettos, asylums, hiding, or forced emigration, but also, as we have come to realize, all those who generate (or fail to generate) discourse about the event. Dealing with trauma is not only manifest in how survivors talk about their experience but also by how historians, writers, and others express themselves (Felman and Laub, 1991; LaCapra, 1998). The conglomeration of events, discourses, behaviors, and structures we call the Holocaust is held to have created a discontinuity, a caesura, an interruption, a question mark in all our categories of understanding and master narratives—it just doesn't fit (Schüssler Fiorenza and Tracy, 1984; Fackenheim, 1990). And this trauma has affected all attempts at historical interpretation of that event: What kind of story can one tell that includes the Holocaust? What kind of history excludes or marginalizes this event? Does, for example, "objective" history of the Holocaust reproduce the values and attitudes that it purports to describe by being as abstract and totalized as the Nazi killing machine and by objectifying the victims, excluding their subjective, affective experience (Friedlaender, 1993)?

The Holocaust has also been traumatic to many Christian scholars of scripture, especially of Christian Scripture: doubly so, as they have not only become aware of and had to confront how much antijudaism lay in the New Testament and in the history of its interpretation, but also how this scripturally based antisemitism contributed to Nazi judeocidal ideology and practice (e.g., Littel, 1975). They have had to reflect on their training as scholars, since a primary resource, the *Theological Dictionary of the New Testament* (*Theologisches Wörterbuch zum Neuen Testament*), was edited by a leading Third Reich theologian, Gerhard Kittel, whose own entries betray antisemitism and whose editorial practices have also come under recent scrutiny (A. Rosen, 1994; Vos, 1984). Less work, however, has been performed on the Hebrew Bible and the history of its interpretation, although some work, for example, on Wellhausen, has been undertaken (Knight, 1983).

While the trauma of the Holocaust has led to new interpretations (and apologetics, a form of denial no less informed by the trauma; indeed, such defenses produce the conditions that contributed to that trauma; LaCapra, 1998), can trauma be employed as a notion internal to the production of biblical texts and narratives? Can the particular characteristics of these writings and stories have been generated in the wake of some earlier (un-worked-through) trauma?

On the eve of the Holocaust, the individual held most responsible for the recognition of the importance of trauma as explanatory principle and as a generator of narratives, Sigmund Freud, addressed its role in the formation of both the Jewish people and their Scripture in *Moses and Monotheism*. Trauma and its consequences had always played a role in the development of Freudian psychoanalysis. Initially, Freud posited that adult seduction of a child was the cause of hysteria when the child grows up. In 1896 the seduction theory assumed a secondary role (but was not not abandoned, as many Freud-bashers allege; Crews, 1998) to infantile sexuality in Freud's understanding of hysteria's genesis; however, trauma remained a key component of Freud's new explanation. Trauma's primary etiological role in individual neurosis underwent a series of ontogenetic (the Oedipus and castration complexes) and voyeuristic (observation of the primal scene) shifts. Further, it was generated more in the realm of fantasy and desire than in actuality—except in Freud's speculations on religious development in which actual parricide is held to have taken place (Freud, 1912–13, 1939). Yet unlike many of his despisers in the recovered memory movement and among oppressed groups (women, postcolonial subjects, etc.), Freud viewed trauma not as an event with inevitable (if variable) consequences, but as a process: "Early trauma–defense–latency–outbreak of neurotic illness–partial return of the repressed" (1939). In *Moses and Monotheism*, Freud proposes an analogy between this process and the development of Judaism as a way of understanding the gap between Moses' original profession of ethical monotheism and its return centuries after its abandonment by the people of Israel. The past event in its actuality is less the precipitating cause than is the relationship of the present—the present of writing, narrating, or redacting—to an event that was never experienced, narrativized, given meaning. That present is the text—whether the Bible or *Moses and Monotheism*.

When Freud, in his London exile, published what proved to be his last completed work, *Moses*, he was met with denunciation and ridicule. Jewish readers in particular were upset by Freud's hypotheses regarding the traumatic events that lay under the TaNaKh. Freud postulated that Moses was an Egyptian noble and follower of Ikhnaten and his monotheistic cult of Aten (following Breasted, 1933). After the death of the pharaoh and the overthrow of his cult, Moses adopted the Hebrews and in turn demanded that they adopt his rigorous ethical monotheism as well as bound them to the Egyptian practice of circumcision. After Moses led the Hebrews out of Egypt, the Hebrews revolted against his stern demands and killed him in the wilderness. Freud continued his story of the Hebrew people as two generations later they joined with the Midianites at Kadesh and adopted their volcano god-demon Yahweh and nonmonotheistic religion. Yahweh was identified with the god of the exodus, and the custom of circumcision was also kept. According to Freud, this "compromise at Kadesh" helped the Hebrews to deal with the trauma of Moses' murder: It aided and abetted the repression of virtually all traces both of the murder and of Moses' Egyptian origins. While the Mosaic tradition was preserved by the Levitical priesthood, it was another six hundred years before monotheism would return with compulsive force (Freud, 1939).

Freud, who took his lead from the suggestive work of Ernst Sellin (1922), argued that Moses' murder was repressed, leaving only bare traces in the text. While the historical motif of Moses the Egyptian has recently been explored by Jan Assmann (1997), Freud has found few defenders for his parricidal speculation. Indeed, concluding his benchmark analysis of Moses, Yerushalmi (1991) engages in a monologue with (the dead) Freud that focuses on his claim that the murder of Moses was repressed. As Yerushalmi argues, the TaNaKh never shies from admonishing the sinful/evil/dreadful deeds of the Israelites; hence, if they had indeed killed Moses, it would have been (masochistically) trumpeted. In his recent work, Richard Bernstein (1998) engages in a monologue with (the living, if absent) Yerushalmi and argues that the TaNaKh does not shy away from how the Israelites bristled under Moses' leadership and how they held homicidal desires toward him that they could not consciously acknowledge. Moreover, if one accepts that the unconscious plays a role in every expression and secretes in distorted form its meanings throughout the text, then indeed the TaNaKh does manifestly represent an effort to deal with a traumatic past, the nature of which can never be known for sure. Textual traces of this hostility would have passed down through the social unconscious—not as meaningful elements but as raw data in need of interpretation, of a midrash. Even Yerushalmi (85) cites the Midrash, which claims that an attempt was indeed made on Moses' life (*Bamidbar Rabbah* 16:13; *Tanhuma,* Shelah 22). The murder need not have taken place; there is no more need for this positivity than for the existence of Gd. Instead, the unsaid of conflicted desires and guilt, of feeling and fantasy, of identity-subverting knowledges that the community fears to recognize shapes what is transmitted. So does the ambivalence of the receivers of the tradition toward those purported forebears who transmitted this material: Absolute fidelity competes with repudiation of those narratives that may no longer make either practical or cognitive sense. (A contemporary, admittedly self-conscious example is the refusal of many congregations to read aloud the last chapter of Esther during Purim services.) Moreover, the receivers may be haunted by postmemories, a notion derived from the experiences of children of Holocaust (and other trauma) survivors: The (parental and community) memories of what predates these children's birth not only affects the lives of the survivors;

their consequent behaviors and (incomplete) narrative accounts of events that their descendants can neither understand nor recreate also dominate the lives and form the identities of those subsequent generations (Hirsch, 1997, 1999). The convergence of these whats, whos, and to whoms, Freud suggests in *Moses and Monotheism,* is the nature of tradition (Freud, 1939; Bernstein, 1998; Robertson, 1988).

Yet it is not for a reconsideration of the factual basis of these hypotheses that Freud's work of biblical interpretation warrants a return; rather, it is for his understanding of the role of trauma, of the role of tradition as the latent transmission of traumatic material awaiting interpretation, in the production of the TaNaKh and of (the return of) the Mosaic religion. More significant perhaps, Freud provides us with ways of understanding scripture's possible traumatic construction and of recognizing–reading–the signs of that construction.

> The text, however, as we possess it today will tell us enough about its own vicissitudes. Two mutually opposed treatments have left their traces on it. On the one hand, it has been subjected to revisions which have falsified it in the sense of their secret aims, have mutilated and amplified and have even changed it into its reverse; on the other hand, a solicitous piety has presided over it and has sought to pre-serve everything as it was, no matter whether it was consistent or contradicted itself. Thus almost everywhere noticeable gaps, disturbing repetitions, and obvious contradictions have come about– indications which reveal things to us which it was not intended to communicate. In its implications the distortion of a text resembles a murder: the difficulty is not in perpetrating the deed, but in getting rid of its traces. (Freud, 1939: 43)

The biblical exegete, then, should attend to those distortions, since "in many instances we may nevertheless count upon finding what has been suppressed and disavowed material hidden away somewhere else, though changed and torn from its context" (Freud, 1939: 43).

The repetitions that we credit to the Deuteronomic source in the TaNaKh, the endless cycle of transgression, punishment, and repentance, may be a case in point. If we consider the traumatic nature of textual construction, such repetitions may be seen not as a trait or trope of oral transmission, nor as moral condemnation of a stiff-necked people, but rather as an acting out of what cannot be integrated into a community's self-understanding (or of a redactor's understanding of his or her community in time; also see Crossan, 1998, on the role of memory in gospel construction). The continuous backsliding of the children of Israel represents a structural repetition of some transgressive action or traumatizing experience that can be neither acknowledged nor restored to some pristine original meaning. These repetitions attempt to give meaning to what "never" had it (i.e., whatever signification may have been given to that event is irretrievable). Alternatively, the text may be the reinterpretation of "traditional" material (often by the adoption of socially sanctioned scripts) to explain present distress. Or rather, some combination of the two: the understanding of traumatic recollection and a hermeneutics that takes the trauma process as its model allow biblical studies to recognize that its text–its historical narrative–is not a description but a distortion that combines an acting-out with an act of mastery together known as interpretation of tradition. Or while Freud speculated about an occluded murder within the TaNaKh to explain what he perceived as textual distortions (among other motivations for his reading), can the New Testament not be read as a series of narratives distorted about the "known" death of the messiah (Smyth, 1999)? Or can the gospel of Matthew be understood as a response to the traumatic split between the Jewish community and the Jesus movement (G. Stanton, 1984)? Finally, if we as scholars endeavor to reconstruct that origin, we too are acting out and interpreting that tradition as well as acting out and interpreting, if not working through, the relationship we, no less than Freud, have with our pasts.

truth
Philip D. Kenneson

Few concepts in the postmodern milieu are as roundly contested as that of truth. Indeed, the debate over the concept of truth (or, more commonly, "truth") within contemporary discourse may exemplify more clearly than any other debate both the abiding influence of certain modern modes of thinking and the difficulties inherent in any attempt to reconceive our most fundamental concepts. Such difficulties stem, in large part, from the interconnectedness of these concepts; more and more people are coming to understand that their conceptions of reality, language, rationality, knowledge, and truth mutually implicate each other. In short, there is no one starting point or fundamental concept that does not already imply or assume a whole host of other commitments. Thus, if postmodern sensibilities about truth are at odds with many earlier understandings of this concept, these differences are the result not simply of an alteration in the notion of truth, but also of shifts taking place across a wide range of basic concepts.

As with most concepts within postmodernism, there is no singular or unitary postmodern understanding or theory of truth, in part, because there are no singular or unitary views of reality, language, rationality, or knowledge. Rather, alongside of the plurality of views regarding each of these notions stand numerous and varied understandings of truth and its diverse functions within present discourse. Given the liminality of our contemporary context and the complexity and contentiousness of the current debates, one can do little more than identify certain points of consensus and critical areas of disagreement. In what follows, therefore, I discuss briefly the consensus that has emerged concerning the epistemological crisis that has given rise to the need for reconceiving the notion of truth. Although many diverse responses to this crisis have been proffered, I briefly sketch three distinguishable ones, each of which identifies the pertinent issues regarding the notion of truth differently. Along the way I will suggest some of the implications of these debates for the practice of biblical interpretation.

During the last quarter of the twentieth century, a consensus emerged across a number of disciplines regarding the bankruptcy of modernist epistemologies, particularly as it relates to their Promethean attempts to secure certainty by establishing indubitable first principles that would ground all subsequent epistemic claims (Rockmore and Singer; Thiel). Indeed, those with postmodern sensibilities usually question the entire modernist fixation on epistemology, a fixation chartered by Descartes' desire to reconstruct the edifice of modern knowledge on foundations more secure than received opinion and authority, both of which were under severe attack at that time (Stout, 1981). This assumption that epistemology must be "first philosophy"– that all responsible philosophy must begin with epistemology and all subsequent philosophical reflection grounded on this foundation–was accepted by nearly all philosophers working out of the two dominant traditions of the West: empiricism and rationalism. Although advocates of these camps disagreed about whether sense experience or the mind's innate ideas provided the necessary epistemological foundations, few philosophers during this period questioned the necessity of securing them. If one doubts the strength and enduring impact of this epistemological legacy, one need only examine the contemporary context, where even the present attempts to leave this legacy behind still bear its imprint. For example, those advocates of a radical skepticism that would deny the very possibility of knowledge seemingly fall prey themselves to the same modernist fixation on epistemology that they would purport to critique and overcome. That is, their claim that no knowledge is possible continues to rely on the same modernist standard for knowledge and certainty that few, if any, forms of human knowledge can attain. But such skepticism is not the only possible response to what many now view as the epistemological dead-end of modernism. For example, others have questioned the narrow way in which knowledge was defined, the way in which radical doubt was widely considered to be the only path to knowledge, and, subsequently, the way in which trust or faith was cordoned off from the knowledge-seeking enterprise (Polanyi; Bernstein, 1983; Hardwig).

Not surprisingly, this spirited interrogation of the modernist epistemological project has had far-reaching impact on certain corollary notions, such as that of truth. Having exposed the inadequacies of simply equating truth with "secure and certain knowledge," critics of modernist epistemologies have created the space for different understandings of the notion of truth. Or said differently, once the historical consciousness that marks modernity turned back on itself to examine the historical character of human standards of knowledge, it was only a matter of time before this project was extended to the notion of truth itself. If all human knowledge is historically and culturally conditioned knowledge, then there is no reason to assume that our understandings of knowledge and truth stand outside this historical and cultural matrix. This is why those working out of a postmodern orientation assume that a society's or culture's notions of truth are inseparable from its historically conditioned understandings of reality, language, rationality, and knowledge.

This leads to the second area of consensus: Most adherents of postmodernism are suspicious of all formal theories, including theories of truth. Such theories, as well as the methodologies premised on them, are to be eschewed, it is argued, because they fail to do the work expected of them, which is to offer universal and ahistorical criteria for discriminating between truth and falsehood. As has often been pointed out, any such criteria would themselves be in need of justification, yet this would require either appealing to the same set of criteria to establish their validity (which would appear to be viciously circular) or appealing to a different set of criteria, a set that would then take the place of the first as being more fundamental, leading to an infinite regress of justificatory claims. As long as a theory of truth remains locked within the modernist epistemological project, this theory will be just as incapable as epistemology is of grounding itself. Thus, while modern philosophy, in privileging epistemology as "first philosophy," sought first to establish a foundationalist epistemology that would serve to both ground and assess all other claims to knowledge, adherents of postmodernism make little or no attempt to ground their discourse in some ostensibly more fundamental discourse (such as a theory of knowledge or a theory of truth) in order to give it more secure footing.

This suspicion about theory has already had an impact on biblical studies, since modernist hermeneutics routinely embody those epistemological assumptions that are now so roundly criticized. As a result, fewer and fewer interpreters of the Bible believe that a theory of interpretation can deliver what it promises: a method for interpreting a text that, if employed, would deliver the truth or meaning of that text. The great hope of hermenuetics was that it would be able to offer, by modeling itself on scientific practice, a means of adjudicating interpretive disputes based solely on appeals to proper method. That is, just as the results of scientific experiments were understood to receive their legitimacy primarily from the method used to secure them, so hermeneutics hoped to offer a theory and method of interpretation that would lend credibility and legitimacy to the interpretations arrived at by means of these methods.

But just as scientists in the last half of the twentieth century have come to acknowledge that their "readings" of the world often say as much about their own interests and assumptions as they do about anything so sublime as "the world as it is in itself," so many practitioners of biblical interpretation have come to acknowledge that human interests and commitments are always implicated in the reading process. No theory if granted, no methodology if followed precisely, can deliver the unadulterated truth or meaning of a text. Indeed, if by truth we mean something like "the way things are apart from anyone's interpretation of them," one is all but forced to admit the seeming vacuity of employing or appealing to the language of "truth" when it comes to interpretive issues. This partly accounts for why the last half-century has witnessed a proliferation of reading strategies whose advocates attempt to acknowledge up front the interests and commitments that inform their readings.

This proliferation of and competition among reading strategies suggests why the debate about postmodernism cannot be neatly separated from the material, historical, social, and political configurations of the contemporary period. As Jameson has argued, this interpretive free-for-all well reflects the conditions imposed by "the cultural logic of late capitalism." Moreover, if knowledge (and therefore truth) is a human production and thereby reflects the interests and extends the aims of those who control the production and reproduction of knowledge, we are then led to attend to a range of concerns different from those that preoccupied earlier thinkers. Writers such as Foucault, for example, have insisted that every discipline operates within a certain "politics of truth" that governs the kinds of discourses that will be regarded as knowledge as well as the epistemic conditions necessary for discriminating between truth and falsehood within that discipline. Thus, those working out of a postmodern orientation are often considerably less interested in demonstrating the truth of certain discourses and more interested in examining the functioning of certain discourses of truth. Moreover, the discourses of truth, as well as the cultural institutions dedicated to the production of truth, are now routinely viewed across the disciplines as inseparable from those cultural narratives that legitimate some forms of knowledge while discrediting others (Lyotard, 1984; Hinchman and Hinchman). Examinations of such issues within the arena of biblical interpretation inevitably lead to questions of interpretive authority and disciplinary power, all of which suggest that questions of "truth" cannot be easily separated from the social and political institutions that exist to authorize and lend legitimacy to certain interpreters and their interpretations. Although some in the academy object that such a view leads to the "politicization" of interpretation and the academy, many with postmodern sensibilities suggest that what is going on is not the politicization of the academy, but the recognition that any academy that exists to credential and therefore authorize some readers as "expert" interpreters was from the beginning already politicized.

To this point we have focused on the general consensus that has emerged regarding why the inherited notion of truth no longer seems intelligible. But the question remains: What, if anything, follows from any of this? How might people proceed once they are convinced that this inherited notion of truth has been discredited? Several responses have been put forward, no one of which has, as yet, claimed widespread acceptance. I offer a brief sketch of three types of responses, all of which accept the critiques of epistemology, but each of which locates these critiques within a different framework of commitments, thereby reconceiving the notion of truth in quite different ways. There are, of course, many other responses possible, not to mention many other ways of mapping them. As an aid in identifying these three types of responses, I have risked naming names, realizing that some of these thinkers fit more comfortably into these pigeonholes than others. Not surprisingly, the positions of many thinkers (such as Derrida) do not fit easily into this scheme, making it possible for advocates of several positions to claim that these writers (when rightly understood!) are advocating something akin to their own positions.

The first type of response, articulated by thinkers such as Rorty, Lyotard, and Fish, proposes what are often referred to as *deflationary* accounts of truth. Such accounts do not necessarily disregard the usefulness of the language of truth, but they do try to undermine its routinely mystifying effects by reconceiving the concept of truth in light of contemporary understandings of the historical and contingent character of human knowing. That is, while modernist accounts of truth presumed that there was something "deep" underlying our uses of the language of truth that philosophy could theorize and regulate, deflationary accounts assume no such depth, but instead, following Wittgenstein, call people to attend to their particular *uses* of the language of truth.

Many who work out of this deflationary model are informed by certain forms of pragmatism as well as by their reflections on the so-called linguistic turn. Here, truth is regarded not so much as "out there" (the objectivist position) or "in here" (the subjectivist position) as it is regarded to be a function of communities of language users. Rather than assuming that truth is another object in the universe to be discovered by looking in a certain way or by employing a particular method that would uncover it, claims to truth are regarded as inseparable from communities of language users who are always part of an ongoing conversation and negotiation not only about what will be regarded as true, but also about how such claims to truth will be adjudicated within this group of people. For this reason, agreements about "the truth of the matter" are always complexly negotiated agreements, even when the texture of those agreements is not plainly visible to those involved. The broader the underlying agreements, the more easily truth claims can be negotiated. This is why Rorty insists that "truth" functions as an honorific, since it points not to the way our words mirror reality but to the agreements people have about how best to talk coherently about the world given the particular projects and interests of their communities. This way of reconceiving truth resonates not only with those working out of pragmatist perspectives but also with many of those working out of social constructionist perspectives (Gergen).

There are several implications of such a view of truth for biblical interpretation, but only two will be mentioned here. First, within such an understanding, the distinction between demonstration and persuasion is blurred. Rather than seeing persuasion as something that one does when demonstration is not possible, persuasion is now commonly regarded as the broader and more inclusive category, with demonstration being a particular subspecies of persuasion made possible by certain shared epistemic conventions. Thus, two biblical scholars with divergent interpretations who nevertheless share the same methodological orientation might consider themselves to be trying to demonstrate to each other the superiority of their own readings. Two scholars with quite different orientations, however, would likely lack the shared agreements to enter into the persuasive process with anything so seemingly determinative as demonstration in mind.

A second important implication for biblical studies concerns the so-called ethics of interpretation (Fowl, 1988). If the activity of reading texts is always implicated in a wider network of interests and purposes, as those working out of this model insist, then one may always ask the following question: What do those who are reading these texts in this way (and encouraging others to do the same) hope to accomplish by so doing? Such questions can no longer be deflected by answers such as "Simply trying to arrive at the meaning or the truth of this text," since such answers continue to presuppose that if one achieved this goal (which those with postmodern sensibilities believe to be illusory), then some desirable and hoped-for change would likely follow. Thus, being asked to attend to the ethics of interpretation urges interpreters to be as mindful (and as honest) as they can about the work they are trying to "do" with texts.

This emphasis on the "political" activity of reading connects to the second type of response, advocated by thinkers as diverse as Habermas, Norris, and Jameson, who believe that many of the postmodernists mentioned above are doomed to political impotence because their position champions a pluralism that undercuts any attempt to challenge the political status quo. As a result, advocates of this second type of response attempt to absorb the critiques of Enlightenment epistemology while still holding on to much of the modernist political agenda (whether that agenda be liberal, Marxist, or some other orientation). Such a position, which is often identified as a kind of "radical modernism" rather than as a form of postmodernism, usually advocates a chastened form of "critical realism," since any attempt to challenge the status quo must be capable of naming and critiquing "the way things are." Moreover, advocates of this position insist that the pragmatists too quickly reduce truth to rational justification, while at the same time failing to observe that all human acts of assertion (MacIntyre, 1994), if not every use of human language (Norris), require a much more substantive notion of truth for their intelligibility. Although the particular projects informed by such a view remain numerous and varied, they all continue to appeal to the notion of truth as a kind of limit construct, insisting that without an ongoing—even if ultimately unsuccessful—attempt to articulate the ways things are, there remains little more than the will to power as a mechanism for change.

A third and quite different tack on these matters, advocated by a group of theologians who espouse what is called "radical orthodoxy," involves questioning the assumed priority given philosophy to adjudicate issues regarding reality, knowledge, and truth. If what grounds our most fundamental beliefs about reality, knowledge, and truth are "foundationless convictions" about the world, humanity, and God rooted in particular narratives, then little is gained by asking a putatively autonomous philosophy to try to establish a more fundamental or secure ground.

Radical orthodoxy asserts that postmodernist epistemologies are suspended between the alternatives of radical skepticism or radical immanentism (the belief that our claims point to nothing beyond ourselves). Radical orthodoxy offers a different alternative: reclaiming certain premodern insights about knowledge and truth that have been chastened by the criticity of modernism. For example, some have argued that premodern epistemologies, unlike their Enlightenment counterparts, did not understand knowledge in primarily representational terms but in terms of participation (Milbank et al., 1999). Indeed, these same authors suggest that the creation of an autonomous discipline of philosophy was itself a contingent event made possible in large part by the sundering of human knowledge from the knowledge of God. The resulting division guaranteed that human knowledge would be incapable of providing grounds for its own claims, a situation that can be rectified, according to this position, only by what one author has called "the liturgical consummation of philosophy" (Pickstock).

This final approach epitomizes well the ways in which postmodern approaches to truth, while certainly not leaving behind the entire modernist epistemological project, have called into question many of the dogmas of modernism, not least of which is the dogma that theological reflection must remain subordinate to putatively more universal modes of philosophical reasoning. If radical orthodoxy is successful in persuading the academy that every position assumes or implies an ontology, and that the choice of an ontology cannot be justified simply on the basis of human reason, then the way is opened to examine different ontologies, including those theological ones that insist that Being is a gift of God. This in turn would create the space to discuss the concept of truth not simply in terms of human reason, but also in terms of participating in the life, knowledge, and worship of God (Marshall; Pickstock). Such a rendering of the notion of truth would have dramatic implications for the practice of biblical interpretation, not least because it would render intelligible again many "pre-critical" forms of interpretation that modernist theories of interpretation had declared illegitimate. Thus, if allegorical and midrashic styles of interpretation—as well as other theological modes of interpretation—are again being taken seriously by many biblical scholars, it is partly because the philosophical assumptions that underwrote their earlier dismissal are no longer considered tenable.

At the end of the day, many people are likely to ask whether a post-modernist conception of truth is really a notion of truth at all. The problem with trying to answer such a question is that it in some ways parallels the situation in which a believer in a geocentric model asks somebody who believes in a heliocentric one whether that person actually believes in a "real" earth. If your concept of "earth" requires that it be the center of the universe for it to count as "earth," then on your account, the person who believes in a heliocentric model does not believe in any earth worth having. But if you are open to having your understanding of what might count as "earth" reshaped, than the answer to this question might be very different. In a similar way, if your concept of "real" truth requires something like "how things really are in themselves, apart from human interests," then you will probably insist that a postmodernist account of truth is not an account of truth at all, or certainly not one worth having. But if you are willing to rethink what you understand by "truth" in order to bring it into line with other conceptions that many contemporary persons have about the character of reality, language, rationality, and knowledge, then it might very well be that a postmodernist reconception of truth might serve some important purposes, not least of which might be to clear the way for at least some interpreters of the Bible to attend to matters that have been considered for too long to be outside the purview of legitimate interpretive practice.

bibliography

Abelove, Henry, Michèle Barale, and David M. Halperin, eds.
1993   *The Lesbian and Gay Studies Reader.* New York: Routledge.
Abrams, M. H.
1971   *Natural Supernaturalism: Tradition and Revolution in Romantic Literature.* New York: W. W. Norton.
Adam, A. K. M.
1995a   *What Is Postmodern Biblical Criticism?* Minneapolis: Fortress Press.
1995b   *Making Sense of New Testament Theology: "Modern" Problems and Prospects.* Macon, Ga.: Mercer University Press.
1996   "Twisting to Destruction: A Memorandum on the Ethics of Interpretation." In *Perspectives on New Testament Ethics.* Ed. Perry V. Kea and A. K. M. Adam. *Perspectives in Religious Studies* 23, no. 1: 215–22.
Aejmelaeus, Anneli
1991   "Translation Technique and the Intention of the Translator." In *VII Congress of the IOSCS. SBLSCS* 31. Ed. Claude E. Cox. Atlanta: Scholars Press, 23–26.
Ahearne, Jeremy
1995   *Michel de Certeau.* Stanford, Calif.: Stanford University Press.
1996   "The Shattering of Christianity and the Articulation of Belief." *New Blackfriars* 77 (November): 493–503.
Ahmad, Aijaz
1992   *In Theory: Classes, Nations, Literatures.* London: Verso.
1995   "Postcolonialism: What's in a Name?" In *Late Imperial Culture.* Ed. Román de la Campa, E. Ann Kaplan, and Michael Sprinker. London: Verso, 11–32.
Aichele, George, and Gary A. Phillips
1995   "Exegesis, Eisegesis, Intergesis." *Semeia* 69/70: 7–18.
Aichele, George, and Gary A. Phillips, eds.
1995   *Intertextuality and the Bible. Semeia* 69/70.
Aichele, George, and Tina Pippin, eds.
1992   *Fantasy and the Bible. Semeia* 60.
1997a   "Special Issue: Fantasy and the Bible." *Journal of the Fantastic in the Arts* 8, no. 2.
1997b   *The Monstrous and the Unspeakable: The Bible as Fantastic Literature.* Sheffield: Sheffield Academic Press.
1998   *Violence, Utopia and the Kingdom of God: Fantasy and Ideology in the Bible.* London/New York: Routledge.
Alcoff, Linda
1991   "The Problem of Speaking for Others." *Cultural Critique* 20: 5–32.
Alter, Robert
1996   *Genesis: Translation and Commentary.* New York: W. W. Norton.
Althusser, Louis
1971   "Ideology and Ideological State Apparatuses." In *Lenin and Philosophy and Other Essays.* Trans. Ben Brewster. London: New Left Books. Rep. in Žižek, ed. *Mapping Ideology,* 100–151 .
Anderson, Janice Capel, and Jeffrey L. Staley, eds.
1995   *Taking It Personally: Autobiographical Criticism. Semeia* 72.
Anderson, Pamela Sue
1997   "Introduction to Kristeva." In *The Postmodern God: A Theological Reader.* Ed. Graham Ward. Cambidge, Mass./Oxford: Blackwell, 215–22.
Anderson, Victor
1995   *Beyond Ontological Blackness: An Essay on African-American Religious and Cultural Criticism.* New York: Continuum.
Anidjar, Gil
1998   *"At Our Place in al-Andalus": Declinations of Context in Jewish Letters.* Ph.D. dissertation, Berkeley, Calif.: University of California.
Anonymous
1997   "Deleuze and Guattari: An Introduction." World Wide Web page at http://130.179.92.25/Arnason_DE/Deleuze.html

Anthony, Elliot
1994   *Psychoanalytic Theory: An Introduction.* Oxford: Blackwell.
Antze, Paul, and Michael Lambek, eds.
1996   *Tense Past. Cultural Essays in Trauma and Memory.* New York: Routledge.
Appiah, Kwame Anthony
1992   *In My Father's House: Africa in the Philosophy of Culture.* New York: Oxford University Press.
Appleby, Joyce, Lynn Hunt, and Margaret Jacob
1994   *Telling the Truth about History.* New York and London: W. W. Norton.
Apter, T. E.
1982   *Fantastic Literature: An Approach to Reality.* London: Macmillian.
Arbib, Michael, and Mary Hesse
1986   *The Construction of Reality.* Cambridge, U.K.: Cambridge University Press.
Armour, Ellen T.
1999   *Deconstruction, Feminist Theology, and the Problem of Difference: Subverting the Race/Gender Divide.* Chicago: University of Chicago Press.
Arnhart, Larry
1981   *Aristotle on Political Reasoning: A Commentary on the Rhetoric.* DeKalb, Ill.: Northern Illinois University Press.
Artaud, Antonin
1976   *Selected Writings.* Trans. Helen Weaver. Ed. Susan Sontag. New York: Farrar, Strauss & Giroux.
Ashcroft, Bill
1996   "On the Hyphen in Post-Colonial." *New Literatures Review* 32: 23–32.
1998   *Key Concepts in Post-Colonial Studies.* London and New York: Routledge.
Ashcroft, Bill, Gareth Griffiths, and Helen Tiffin
1989   *The Empire Writes Back: Theory and Practice in Post-Colonial Literatures.* London and New York: Routledge.
Ashcroft, Bill, Gareth Griffiths, and Helen Tiffin, eds.
1995   *The Post-Colonial Studies Reader.* London and New York: Routledge.
Assmann, Jan
1997   *Moses the Egyptian. The Memory of Egypt in Western Monotheism.* Cambridge, Mass.: Harvard University Press.
Bach, Alice
1997   *Women, Seduction, and Betrayal in Biblical Narrative.* Cambridge, U.K.: Cambridge University Press.
Bailey, Randall
1989   "They're Nothing but Incestuous Bastards: The Polemical Use of Sex and Sexuality in Hebrew Canon Narratives." In F. F. Segovia and M. A. Tolbert, eds., *Reading From This Place.* Vol. 1. *Social Location and Biblical Interpretation in the United States.* Minneapolis: Fortress Press.
1991   "Beyond Identification: The Use of Africans in Old Testament Poetry and Narratives." In Felder 1991, 165–84.
1995   "'Is that Any Name for a Nice Hebrew Boy?' Exodus 2:1–10: The De-Africanization of an Israelite Hero." In Bailey and Grant, 25–36.
1996   "'They Shall Become As White As Snow': When Bad Is Turned into Good." *Semeia* 76, 99–113.
Bailey, Randall, and Jacquelyn Grant, eds.
1995   *The Recovery of Black Presence: An Interdisciplinary Exploration.* Nashville: Abingdon Press.
Bailey, Randall C., and Tina Pippin, eds.
1996   *Race, Class, and the Politics of Biblical Translation. Semeia* 76.
Baker, Lee D.
1998   *From Savage to Negro: Anthropology and the Construction of Race, 1896–1954.* Berkeley: University of California Press.
Bakhtin, M. M.
1968   *Rabelais and His World.* Trans. H. Iswolsky. Cambridge, Mass.: MIT Press.
1981   *The Dialogic Imagination: Four Essays.* Ed. M. Holquist. Trans. C. Emerson and M. Holquist. Austin: University of Texas.
1984   *Problems of Dostoevsky's Poetics.* Ed. and trans. C. Emerson. Minneapolis: University of Minnesota.

1986   *Speech Genres and Other Late Essays.* Ed. C. Emerson and M. Holquist. Trans. V. McGee. Austin: University of Texas.

1990   *Art and Answerability: Early Philosophical Essays.* Ed. M. Holquist and V. Liapunov. Trans. V. Liapunov. Austin. University of Texas.

1993   *Toward a Philosophy of the Act.* Ed. V. Liapunov and M. Holquist. Trans. V. Liapunov. Austin: University of Texas.

Bakhtin, M. M. [*sic*], and Medvedev, P.

1985   *The Formal Method in Literary Scholarship: A Critical Introduction to Sociological Poetics.* Trans. A. Wehrle. Cambridge, Mass.: Harvard University.

Bal, Mieke

1987   *Lethal Love: Feminist Literary Readings of Biblical Love Stories.* Bloomington and Indianapolis: Indiana University Press.

1988   *Murder and Difference. Gender, Genre, and Scholarship on Sisera's Death.* Bloomington, Ind.: Indiana University Press.

1992   *Reading "Rembrandt": Beyond the Word Image Opposition.* Cambridge, U.K.: Cambridge University Press.

Barilli, Renato

1989   *Rhetoric.* Trans. Giuliana Menozzi. Theory and History of Literature. Vol. 63. Minneapolis: University of Minnesota Press.

Barkan, Elazar

1992   *The Retreat of Scientific Racism: Changing Concepts of Race in Britain and the United States Between the World Wars.* Cambridge, U.K.: Cambridge University Press.

Barnstone, Willis

1993   *The Poetics of Translation: History, Theory, Practice.* New Haven: Yale University Press.

Barr, James

1979   "The Typology of Literalism in Ancient Biblical Translations." *MSU* 15. Göttingen: Vandenhoeck & Ruprecht.

Barthes, Roland

1972   *Critical Essays.* Evanston, Ill.: Northwestern University Press.

1977   "The Death of the Author" (French 1968). In *Image Music Text.* Trans. Stephen Heath. New York: Hill and Wang, 142–49.

1986   "The Reality Effect." In *The Rustle of Language.* Trans. Richard Howard. New York: Hill and Wang.

Barton, John

1984   *Reading the Old Testament: Method in Biblical Study.* Philadelphia: Westminster Press.

Bass, Dorothy

1997   *Practicing Our Faith: A Way of Life for a Searching People.* San Francisco: Jossey-Bass.

Bassnett, Susan, and André Lefevere, eds.

1997   *Constructing Cultures.* Topics in Translation. London: Multilingual Matters.

Bataille, Georges

1973a   *Oeuvres complètes.* Paris: Éditions Gallimard.

1973b   *Théorie de la religion.* Paris: Éditions Gallimard.

1985   "The Use-Value of D. A. F. de Sade (An Open Letter to My Current Comrades)." In *Visions of Excess: Selected Writings, 1927–1939.* Ed. Allan Stoekl. Trans. Allan Stoekl with Carl R. Lovitt and Donald M. Leslie, Jr. Minneapolis: University of Minnesota Press, 91–102.

1986a   "Autobiographical Note." *October* 36: 107–10.

1986b   *Erotism: Death and Sensuality.* Trans. Mary Dalwood. San Francisco: City Lights.

1988a   *The Accursed Share, Vol. 1 Consumption.* Trans. Robert Hurley. New York: Zone Books.

1988b   *Guilty.* Trans. Bruce Boone. Venice, Calif.: Lapis Press.

1988c   *Inner Experience.* Trans. Leslie Anne Boldt. New York: State University of New York Press.

1989a   *Theory of Religion.* Trans. Robert Hurley. New York: Zone Books.

1989b   *The Tears of Eros.* Trans. Peter Connor. San Francisco: City Lights.

1991   *The Accursed Share, Vol. 2. The History of Eroticism, Vol. 3. Sovereignty.* Trans. Robert Hurley. New York: Zone Books.

1992   *On Nietzsche.* Trans. Bruce Boone. New York: Paragon House.

1997a   "Love." In *The Bataille Reader.* Ed. Fred Botting and Scott Wilson. Oxford: Blackwell, 94–97.

1997b   "The Psychological Structure of Fascism." In *The Bataille Reader,* 122–46.

Bauerschmidt, Frederick C.
1996   "The Abrahamic Voyage: Michel de Certeau and Theology," *Modern Theology* 12/1:
          1–26.
Bauman, Zygmunt
1989   *Modernity and the Holocaust.* Ithaca: Cornell University.
1992   *Intimations of Postmodernity.* London: Routledge.
1993   *Postmodern Ethics.* Oxford and Cambridge: Blackwell.
1995   *Life in Fragments: Essays in Postmodern Morality.* Oxford and Cambridge: Blackwell.
Beal, Timothy K.
1992   "Glossary." In *Reading Between Texts.* Ed. Danna Nolan Fewell. Louisville, Ky.:
          Westminster/John Knox Press, 21–24.
1992   "Ideology and Intertextuality: Surplus of Meaning and Controlling the Means of
          Production." In *Reading Between Texts,* 27–39.
forthcoming
          "Specters of Moses: Overtures to Biblical Hauntology."
Beal, Timothy K., and David M. Gunn, eds.
1997   *Reading Bibles, Writing Bodies: Identity and the Book.* London: Routledge.
Beardslee, William A.
1972   *A House for Hope: A Study in Process and Biblical Thought.* Philadelphia: Westminster
          Press.
1989   "Christ in the Postmodern Age: Reflections Inspired by Jean François Lyotard." In
          David Ray Griffin, William A. Beardslee, and Joe Holland, *Varieties of Postmodern
          Theology.* Albany: State University of New York Press, 63–80.
Beiser, Frederick
1992   *Enlightenment, Revolution, and Romanticism: The Genesis of Modern German Political Thought,
          1790–1800.* Cambridge, Mass.: Harvard University Press.
Bell, Michael M., and Michael Gardiner, eds.
1998   *Bakhtin and the Human Sciences.* London: Sage Publications.
Belsey, Catherine
1988   *Critical Practice.* London: Methuen, 1980, Routledge.
Benjamin, Andrew
1989   *Translation and the Nature of Philosophy.* London: Routledge.
Benjamin, Walter
1969a   "The Task of the Translator." In *Illuminations: Essays and Reflections.* Ed. Hannah Arendt.
          Trans. Harry Zohn. New York: Schocken, 69–82.
1969b   "Theses on the Philosophy of History." In *Illuminations: Essays and Reflections.* Ed.
          Hannah Arendt. Trans. Harry Zohn. New York: Schocken, 253–64.
Bennett, Tony
1987   "Texts in History: The Determination of Readings and Their Texts." In *Poststructuralism
          and the Question of History.* Ed. Derek Attridge, Geoff Bennington, and Robert Young.
          Cambridge, U.K.: Cambridge University Press, 63–81.
Bennington, Geoffrey, and Jacques Derrida
1993   *Jacques Derrida.* Trans. Geoffrey Bennington. Chicago: University of Chicago Press.
Berger, James
1999   *After the End. Representations of Post-Apocalypse.* Minneapolis: University of Minnesota
          Press.
Berghahn, Klaus
1988   "From Classicist to Classical Literary Criticism, 1730–1806." In Hohendahl 1988,
          13–98.
Berkhofer, Robert F., Jr.
1988   "The Challenge of Poetics to (Normal) Historical Practice." *Poetics Today* 9, no. 2:
          435–52.
Bernal, Martin
1987   *Black Athena: The Afroasiatic Roots of Classical Civilization. Vol. I, The Fabrication of Ancient
          Greece, 1785–1985.* New Brunswick: Rutgers University Press.
Bernstein, Richard J.
1983   *Beyond Objectivism and Relativism: Science, Hermeneutics and Praxis.* Philadelphia: University
          of Pennsylvania Press.
1998   *Freud and the Legacy of Moses.* Cambridge: University of Cambridge Press.
Bersani, Leo
1986   *The Freudian Body: Psychoanalysis and Art.* New York: Columbia University Press.

1987   "Is the Rectum a Grave?" In *AIDS: Cultural Analysis/Cultural Activism*. Ed. D. Crimp. Cambridge, Mass.: MIT Press.

Bhabha, Homi
1992   "Postcolonial Criticism." In *Redrawing the Boundaries*. Ed. Stephen Greenblatt and Giles Gunn. New York: Modern Language Association of America.
1994   *The Location of Culture*. London and New York: Routledge.

Bhabha, Homi, ed.
1990   *Nation and Narration*. London and New York: Routledge.

Bible and Culture Collective
1995   *The Postmodern Bible*. New Haven, Conn.: Yale University Press.

Biguenet, John
1992   *Theories of Translation: An Anthology of Essays from Dryden to Derrida*. Chicago: University of Chicago Press.

Bird, Phyllis, et al., eds.
1997   *Reading the Bible as Women: Perspectives from Africa, Asia, and Latin America*. Semeia 78.

Black, Edwin
1978   *Rhetorical Criticism: A Study in Method*. New York: Macmillan, 1965; reprint, Madison: University of Wisconsin Press.

Blanchot, Maurice
1978   *Death Sentence*. Trans. Lydia Davis. Barrytown, N.Y.: Station Hill Press.
[Fr. 1948]
1982   *The Space of Literature*. Trans. Ann Smock. Lincoln: University of Nebraska Press.
[Fr. 1955]
1986   *The Writing of the Disaster*. Trans. Ann Smock. Lincoln: University of Nebraska Press.
[Fr. 1980]
1988   *The Unavowable Community*. Trans. Pierre Joris. Barrytown, N.Y.: Station Hill Press.
[Fr. 1983]
1988   *Thomas the Obscure*. Trans. Robert Lamberton. Barrytown, N.Y.: Station Hill Press.
[Fr. 1950]
1992   *The Step Not Beyond*. Trans. Lycette Nelson. Albany: State University of New York Press.
[Fr. 1973]
1993   *The Infinite Conversation*. Trans. Susan Hanson. Minneapolis: University of Minnesota
[Fr. 1969] Press.
1995   *The Work of Fire*. Trans. Charlotte Mandell. Stanford, Calif.: Stanford University Press.
[Fr. 1949]
1997   *Awaiting Oblivion*. Trans. John Gregg. Lincoln: University of Nebraska Press.
[Fr. 1962]
1997   *Friendship*. Trans. Elizabeth Rottenberg. Stanford Calif.: Stanford University Press.
[Fr. 1971]
1999   *The Station Hill Blanchot Reader: Fiction and Literary Essays*. Trans. Lydia Davis, Paul Auster, and Robert Lamberton. Ed. George Quasha. Barrytown, N.Y.: Station Hill Press.

Bland, Lucy, and Laura Doan, eds.
1998   *Sexology in Culture: Labelling Bodies and Desires*. Chicago: University of Chicago Press.

Boer, Roland
1996   *Jameson and Jeroboam*. Atlanta: Scholars Press.
1997   *Novel Histories*. Sheffield, U.K.: Sheffield Academic Press.
1998   "Remembering Babylon: Postcolonialism and Australian Biblical Studies." In *The Postcolonial Bible*. The Bible and Postcolonialism 1. Ed. R. S. Sugirtharajah, 24–48.

Borges, Jorge Luis
1984   "Translation." In *Twenty-four Conversations with Borges: 1981–1983*. Trans. Nicomedes Suarez Arauz, Willis Barnstone, and Moemi Escandell. New York: Grove, 49–54.

Boswell, John
1981   *Christianity, Social Tolerance, and Homosexuality: Gay People in Western Europe from the Beginning of the Christian Era to the Fourteenth Century*. Chicago: University of Chicago Press.
1994   *Same-Sex Unions in Premodern Europe*. New York: Vintage Books.

Bottigheimer, Ruth B.
1996   *The Bible for Children: From the Age of Gutenberg to the Present*. New Haven, Conn.: Yale University Press.

Botting, Fred, and Scott Wilson, eds.
1997　　*The Bataille Reader.* Oxford: Blackwell.
Bottum, J.
1994　　"Christians and Postmoderns," *First Things* 40 (February): 28–32.
Bourdieu, Pierre
1977a　*Outline of a Theory of Practice.* Trans. Richard Nice. Cambridge Studies in Social Anthropology. General ed. Jack Goody. Cambridge: Cambridge University Press. (Orig. 1972.)
1977b　*Reproduction in Education, Society and Culture.* With Jean-Claude Passeron. Trans. Richard Nice. Beverly Hills, Calif.: Sage.
1984　　*Homo Academicus.* Trans. Peter Collier. Stanford, Calif.: Stanford University Press.
1990　　*The Logic of Practice.* Oxford: Polity Press. (Orig. French 1980.)
Boyarin, Daniel
1990　　*Intertextuality and the Reading of Midrash.* Bloomington: Indiana University Press.
1993　　*Carnal Israel: Reading Sex in Talmudic Culture.* The New Historicism: Studies in Cultural Poetics 25. Berkeley and Los Angeles: University of California Press.
1994　　*A Radical Jew: Paul and the Politics of Identity.* Berkeley: University of California Press.
1997a　"'An Imaginary and Desirable Converse': *Moses and Monotheism* as Family Romance." In *Reading Bibles, Writing Bodies: Identity and the Book.* Ed. Timothy K. Beal and David M. Gunn. Biblical Limits. London and New York: Routledge, 184–204.
1997b　*Unheroic Conduct: The Rise of Heterosexuality and the Invention of the Jewish Man.* Contraversions: Studies in Jewish Literature, Culture, and Society. Berkeley and Los Angeles: University of California Press.
Boyarin, Jonathan
1994　　"The Other Within and the Other Without." In *The Other in Jewish Thought and History. Constructions of Jewish Culture and Identity.* Ed. Laurence J. Silberstein and Robert L. Cohn. New York: New York University, 424–52.
Bracken, Joseph A.
1991　　*Society and Spirit: A Trinitarian Cosmology.* Selinsgrove, Pa.: Susquehanna University Press.
Breasted, James H.
1933　　*The Dawn of Conscience.* New York: Charles Scribner's Sons.
Brock, Rita Nakashima
1996　　*Journeys by Heart: A Christology of Erotic Power.* New York: Crossroad. (First ed., 1988.)
Brock, Rita Nakashima, and Susan Brooks Thistlethwaite
1996　　*Casting Stones: Prostitution and Liberation in Asia and the United States.* Minneapolis: Fortress Press.
Brock, Sebastian P.
1979　　"Aspects of Translation Technique in Antiquity." *GRBS* 20: 67–87.
Broeck, Raymond Van den
1988　　"Translation Theory after Deconstruction." *Linguistica Antverpiensia* 22: 266–88.
Brooke-Rose, Christine
1981　　*A Rhetoric of the Unreal: Studies in Narrative & Structure, Especially of the Fantastic.* Cambridge, U.K.: Cambridge University Press.
Brooten, Bernadette
1996　　*Love Between Women: Early Christian Responses to Female Homoeroticism.* Chicago: University of Chicago Press.
Brown, Norman O.
1991　　"Dionysus in 1990." In *Apocalypse and/or Metamorphosis.* Berkeley: University of California Press, 179–200.
Bruns, Gerald
1997　　*Maurice Blanchot: The Refusal of Philosophy.* Baltimore: Johns Hopkins University Press.
Buber, Martin, and Franz Rosenzweig
1993　　*Scripture and Translation.* Trans. Lawrence Rosenwald and Everett Fox. Bloomington: Indiana University Press.
Buechner, Frederick
1989　　*The Alphabet of Grace.* San Francisco: Harper & Row.
Burke, Kenneth
1969　　*A Rhetoric of Motives.* New York: Prentice-Hall, 1950; reprint, Berkeley: University of California Press.

1970   *The Rhetoric of Religion: Studies in Logology.* Boston: Beacon Press, 1961; reprint, Berkeley: University of California Press, 1970.

Burnett, Fred W.
1990   "Postmodern Biblical Exegesis: The Eve of Historical Criticism." *Semeia* 51: 51–80.
forthcoming
            Honest to Clio: Postmodern Historical Criticism (tentative title). Sheffield, U.K.: Sheffield Academic Press.

Butler, Judith
1990   *Gender Trouble: Feminism and the Subversion of Identity.* New York: Routledge.
1992   "Contingent Foundations: Feminism and the Question of 'Postmodernism.'" In *Feminists Theorize the Political.* Ed. Judith Butler and Joan W. Scott. New York: Routledge.
1993   *Bodies That Matter: On the Discursive Limits of "Sex."* New York: Routledge.

Calhoun, Craig
1993   "Habitus, Field, and Capital: The Question of Historical Specificity." In *Bourdieu: Critical Perspectives.* Ed. Craig Calhoun, Edward Lipuma, Moishe Postone. Chicago: University of Chicago Press.

Cannon, Katie Geneva
1995   "Slave Ideology and Biblcal Interpretation." In Bailey and Grant 1995, 119–28.

Caplan, Pat, ed.
1987   *The Cultural Construction of Sexuality.* New York and London: Routledge.

Caputo, John D.
1993   *Against Ethics: Contributions to a Poetics of Obligation with Constant Reference to Deconstruction.* Bloomington and Indianapolis: Indiana University Press.
1997   *The Prayers and Tears of Jacques Derrida: Religion Without Religion.* Bloomington: Indiana University Press.

Caputo, John D., ed.
1997   *Deconstruction in a Nutshell: A Conversation with Jacques Derrida.* New York: Fordham University Press.

Carby, Hazel
1985   "On the Threshold of Women's Era: Lynching, Empire and Sexuality in Black Feminist Theory." *Critical Inquiry* 12: 262–77.

Carrette, Jeremy R.
2000   *Foucault and Religion: Spiritual Corporality and Political Spirituality.* London: Routledge.

Carroll, Robert P.
1996   "Cultural Encroachment and Bible Translation: Observations on Elements of Violence, Race and Class in the Production of Bibles in Translation." *Semeia* 76: 39–53.

Cartwright, Michael G.
1993   "Ideology and the Interpretation of the Bible in the African-American Christian Tradition." *Modern Theology* 9, no. 2: 141–58.

Caruth, Cathy
1996   *Unclaimed Experience: Trauma, Narrative, and History.* Baltimore: Johns Hopkins University Press.

Caruth, Cathy, ed.
1995   *Trauma: Explorations in Memory.* Baltimore: Johns Hopkins University Press.

Castelli, Elizabeth A.
1991   *Imitating Paul: A Discourse of Power.* Literary Currents in Biblical Interpretation. Louisville, Ky.: Westminster/John Knox Press.
1994   "Les Belles Infidèles/Fidelity or Feminism? The Meanings of Feminist Biblical Translation." In *Searching the Scriptures.* Vol. 1. *A Feminist Introduction.* Ed. Elisabeth Schüssler Fiorenza. New York: Crossroad: 189–204.

Castells, Manuel
1996   *The Information Age. Economy, Society and Culture.* Vol. 1. *The Rise of the Network Society.* Cambridge, Mass: Blackwell.

Certeau, Michel de
1970   *La possesion de Loudun.* Paris: Gallimard/Julliard.
1971   "How Is Christianity Thinkable Today?" *Theology Digest* 19/4: 334–45.
1974   *Le christianisme éclaté.* With J-M. Domenach. Paris: Seuil.
1982   *The Mystic Fable, Vol. 1, The 16th & 17th Centuries.* Trans. Michael B. Smith. Chicago: University of Chicago Press.
1984   *The Practice of Everyday Life.* Vol. 1. Trans. Steven Randal. Berkeley: University of California Press.

1986a   *Heterologies: Discourse on the Other.* Trans. Brian Massumi. Theory and History of Literature. Vol. 17. Minneapolis: University of Minnesota Press.
1986b   "History: Science and Fiction." In *Heterologies: Discourse on the Other.* Vol. 17.
1987   "La Rupture Instaurice." In *La Faiblesse de Croire.* Ed. Luce Giard. Paris: Éditions de Seuil.
1988   *The Writing of History.* Trans. Tom Conley. New York: Columbia University Press.
1992   *The Mystic Fable, Volume One: The Sixteenth and Seventeenth Centuries.* 2d ed.Trans. Michael Smith. Chicago: University of Chicago Press.
2000   "The Weakness of Believing: From the Body to Writing, a Christian Transit." In *The Certeau Reader.* Ed. Graham Ward. Oxford: Blackwell Publishers, 214–43.

Certeau, Michel de, ed.
1963   Jean-Joseph Surin, *Guide spirituel pour la perfection.* Paris: Descée de Brouwer.
1966   Jean-Joseph Surin, *Correspondance.* Paris: Descée de Brouwer.

Childs, Peter, and Patrick Williams
1997   *An Introduction to Post-Colonial Theory.* London: Prentice Hall.

Chisholm, Dianne
1994   "Irigaray's Hysteria." In *Engaging with Irigaray: Feminist Philosophy and Modern European Thought.* Ed. Carolyn Burke, Naomi Schor, and Margaret Whitford. Gender and Culture. New York: Columbia University Press, 263–83.

Chopp, Rebecca S.
1989   *The Power to Speak: Feminism, Language, God.* New York: Crossroad, 1989.
1995   *Saving Work: Feminist Practices of Theological Education.* Louisville, Ky.: Westminster John Knox Press.

Clark, Katerina, and Michael Holquist
1984   *Mikhail Bakhtin.* Cambridge, Mass.: Harvard University Press.

Clark, Michael J.
1996   *Beyond Our Ghettos: Gay Theology in Ecological Perspective.* Cleveland: Pilgrim Press.
1997   *Defying the Darkness: Gay Theology in the Shadows.* Cleveland: Pilgrim Press.

Clarke, Cheryl
1993   "Living the Texts Out: Lesbians and the Uses of Black Women's Traditions." In *Theorizing Black Feminisms: The Visionary Pragmatism of Black Women.* Ed. Abena Busia and Stanlie James. New York: Routledge.

Clayton, Jay
1989   "Narrative and Theories of Desire." *Critical Inquiry* 16: 33–53.

Clines, David J. A.
1995   *Interested Parties: The Ideology of Writers and Readers of the Hebrew Bible.* JSOTSup 205. Sheffield, U.K.: Sheffield Academic Press.

Cobb, John B., Jr.
1997   *Sustainability: Economics, Ecology, and the Environment.* Maryknoll, N.Y.: Orbis Books.
1999   *The Earthist Challenge to Economism: A Theological Critique of the World Bank.* New York: St. Martin's Press.

Cobb, John B., Jr., and David Ray Griffin
1976   *Process Theology: An Introductory Exposition.* Philadelphia: Westminster Press.

Cohen, Richard A.
1994   *Elevations: The Height of the Good in Rosenzweig and Levinas.* Chicago: University of Chicago Press.

Compier, Don H.
1999   *What Is Rhetorical Theology? Textual Practice and Public Discourse.* Harrisburg, Pa.: Trinity Press International.

Comstock, Gary David
1996   *Unrepentant, Self-Affirming, Practicing: Lesbian/Bisexual/Gay People within Organized Religion.* New York: Continuum.

Comstock, Gary D., and Susan E. Henking, eds.
1996   *Que(e)rying Religion: A Critical Anthology.* New York: Continuum.

Connell, R. W.
1997   "Sexual Revolution." In *New Sexual Agendas.* Ed. L. Segal. New York: New York University Press.

Copher, Charles
1991   "The Black Presence in the Old Testament." In Felder 1991, 146–64.

Cornwell, Neil
1990   *The Literary Fantastic: From Gothic to Postmodernism.* New York: Harvester/Wheatsheaf.
Cousins, Mark
1987   "The Practice of Historical Investigation." In *Poststructuralism and the Question of History.*
        Ed. Derek Attridge, Geoff Bennington, and Robert Young. Cambridge, U.K.:
        Cambridge University Press, 126–38.
Crews, Frederick
1995   *The Memory Wars: Freud's Legacy in Dispute.* New York: New York Review of Books.
Crews, Frederick, ed.
1998   *Unauthorized Freud. Doubters Confront a Legend.* New York: Viking Penguin.
Critchley, Simon
1999   *The Ethics of Deconstruction: Derrida and Levinas.* 2d ed. West Lafayette, Ind.: Purdue
        University Press. (First ed. 1992.)
Crossan, John Dominic
1998   *The Birth of Christianity: Discovering What Happened in the Years Immediately after the
        Execution of Jesus.* San Francisco: Harper San Francisco.
Crowder, Stephanie Buckhanon
1997   "Simon of Cyrene: A Case of Roman Conscription." Unpublished paper presented to
        the "Synoptic Gospels" Section of the Society of Biblical Literature.
Cruikshank, Margaret
1992   *The Gay and Lesbian Liberation Movement.* New York: Routledge.
Cunningham, David S.
1991   *Faithful Persuasion: In Aid of a Rhetoric of Christian Theology.* Notre Dame, Ind.: University
        of Notre Dame Press.
Daly, Herman E., and John B. Cobb, Jr.
1994   *For the Common Good: Redirecting the Economy Toward Community, the Environment, and a
        Sustainable Future.* With Contributions by Clifford W. Cobb. 2d ed., updated and revised.
        Boston: Beacon Press.
Davidson, Julia O'Connell
1998   *Prostitution, Power and Freedom.* Ann Arbor: University of Michigan Press.
Davies, Philip R.
1995   *Whose Bible Is It Anyway?* JSOTSup 204. Sheffield, U.K.: Sheffield Academic Press.
Davis, Colin
1996   *Levinas. An Introduction.* Notre Dame, Ind.: University of Notre Dame Press.
Davis, Robert Con, ed.
1983   *Lacan and Narration: The Psychoanalytic Difference in Narrative Theory.* Baltimore: Johns
        Hopkins University Press.
Debray, Régis
1996   "The Book as Symbolic Object." Trans. Eric Rauth. In *The Future of the Book.* Ed.
        Geoffrey Nunberg. Berkeley: University of California Press, 139–51.
Delaney, Carol
1998   *Abraham on Trial. The Social Legacy of Biblical Myth.* Princeton, N.J.: Princeton University
        Press.
Delaney, Samuel R.
1978   *The American Shore: Meditations on a Tale of Science Fiction by Thomas M. Disch–Angouleme.*
        Elizabethtown, N.Y.: Dragon Press.
De Lauretis, Teresa
1991   "Queer Theory: Lesbian and Gay Sexualities: An Introduction." *Differences: A Journal
        of Feminist Cultural Studies* 3, no. 2: iii–xviii.
1994   *The Practice of Love: Lesbian Sexuality and Perverse Desire.* Bloomington: Indiana University
        Press.
1998   "The Stubborn Drive." *Critical Inquiry* 24: 851–77.
Deleuze, Gilles, and Félix Guattari
1983   *Anti-Oedipus.* Trans. Robert Hurley, Mark Seem, and Helen R. Lane. Minneapolis:
        University of Minnesota Press.
1987   *A Thousand Plateaus.* Trans. Brian Massumi. Minneapolis: University of Minnesota Press.
De Man, Paul
1986   "Conclusions: Walter Benjamin's 'The Task of the Translator.'" In *The Resistance to
        Theory.* Minneapolis: University of Minnesota Press, 73–105.

D'Emilio, John, and Estelle B. Freedman
1997   *Intimate Matters: A History of Sexuality in America.* 2d ed. Chicago: University of Chicago Press.
Derrida, Jacques
1965/1978 "Violence and Metaphysics." In *Writing and Difference.* Trans. Alan Bass. Chicago: University of Chicago Press, 79–153.
1976   *Of Grammatology.* Trans. Gayatri Spivak. Baltimore: Johns Hopkins University Press (1965).
1978   *Writing and Difference.* Trans. Alan Bass. Chicago: University of Chicago Press (1967).
1979   *Spurs: Nietzsche's Styles.* Trans. B. Harlow. Chicago: University of Chicago Press (1976).
1981   *Positions.* Trans. Alan Bass. Chicago: University of Chicago Press.
1984a   "Of an Apocalyptic Tone Recently Adopted in Philosophy." Trans. J. P. Leavey, Jr. *Oxford Literary Review* 6, no. 2: 3–37 (1983).
1984b   "No Apocalypse, Not Now (full speed ahead, seven missiles, seven missives)." *Diacritics* 14 (Summer): 20–31.
1985a   "Des Tours de Babel." In *Difference in Translation.* Ed. J. Graham. Ithaca, N. Y. : Cornell University Press, 165–207.
1985b   *The Ear of the Other: Otobiography, Transference, Translation: Texts and Discussion with Jacques Derrida.* Trans. Peggy Kamuf. New York: Schocken Books (1984).
1987   *The Post Card: From Socrates to Freud and Beyond.* Trans. Alan Bass. Chicago: University of Chicago Press.
1988   *Limited Inc.* Evanston, Ill.: Northwestern University Press.
1989   "How to Avoid Speaking." In *Languages of the Unsayable: The Play of Negativity in Literature and Literary Theory.* Trans. Sanford Budick and Wolfgang Iser. New York: Columbia University Press.
1990   *Glas.* Trans. John P. Leavey, Jr., and Richard Rans. Lincoln: University of Nebraska Press.
1991a   *Given Time. 1. Counterfeit Money.* Trans. P. Kamuf. Chicago: Chicago University Press.
1991b   *A Derrida Reader: Between the Blinds.* Ed. P. Kamuf. New York: Columbia University Press.
1991c   *The Other Heading: Reflections on Today's Europe.* Trans. Pascale-Anne Brault and Michael B. Naas. Bloomington: Indiana University Press.
1992a   "Force of Law: The 'Mystical Foundation of Authority.'" Trans. Mary Quaintance. In *Deconstruction and the Possibility of Justice.* Ed. Drucilla Cornell, Michel Rosenfeld, and David Gray Carlson. New York and London: Routledge, 3–67.
1992b   *Acts of Literature.* Ed. Derek Attridge. London and New York: Routledge.
1992c   *The Gift of Death.* Trans. David Wills. Chicago and London: University of Chicago Press.
1993   *Aporias.* Trans. Thomas Dutoit. Stanford, Calif.: Stanford University Press.
1994   *Spectres of Marx: The State of Debt, the Work of Mourning, and the New International.* Trans. Peggy Kamuf. New York and London: Routledge (1993).
1995a   *The Gift of Death.* Trans. David Wills. Chicago: University of Chicago Press (1992).
1995b   *Points: Interviews, 1974–1994.* Ed. Elisabeth Weber. Trans. Peggy Kamuf et al. Stanford, Calif.: Stanford University Press (1994).
1996a   "Adieu." *Philosophy Today* 40: 334–40.
1996b   *Archive Fever: A Freudian Impression.* Trans. Eric Prenowitz. Chicago: University of Chicago Press (1995).
1996c   "As If I Were Dead: An Interview with Jacques Derrida." In *Applying to Derrida.* Ed. John Brannigan, Ruth Robbins, and Julian Wolfreys. London: Macmillan, 212–26.
1996d   *Monolingualism of the Other, or The Prosthesis of Origin.* Trans. Patrick Mensah. Stanford, Calif.: Stanford University Press.
1999   "Hospitality, Justice and Responsibility: A Dialogue with Jacques Derrida." In *Questioning Ethics: Contemporary Debates in Philosophy.* Ed. Richard Kearney and Mark Dooley. London and New York: Routledge, 65–83.
Detweiler, Robert, ed.
1982   *Derrida and Biblical Studies. Semeia* 23.
Dollimore, Jonathan
1991   *Sexual Dissidence: Augustine to Wilde, Freud to Foucault.* Oxford: Clarendon Press.
Donaldson, Laura, ed.
1996   *Postcolonialism and Scriptural Reading. Semeia* 75.

Dube, Musa
1998   "Savior of the World but Not of This World: A Postcolonial Reading of Spatial
          Construction in John." In *The Postcolonial Bible*. Ed. R. S. Sugirtharajah. Sheffield, U.K.:
          Sheffield Academic Press, 118–35.
Dudiak, Jeffrey M.
1997   "Again Ethics: A Levinasian Reading of Caputo Reading Levinas." In *Knowing Otherwise:
          Philosophy at the Threshold of Spirituality*. Ed. James H. Olthuis. New York: Fordham
          University Press, 172–213.
Dworkin, Andrea
1987   *Intercourse*. New York: Free Press.
Eagleton, Terry
1987   "Awakening from Modernity," *Times Literary Supplement* 4377 (Feb. 20): 194.
1991   *Ideology: An Introduction*. London and New York: Verso.
1996   *The Illusions of Postmodernism*. Cambridge, Mass.: Blackwell.
Edgerton, Samuel Y., Jr.
1975   *The Renaissance Rediscovery of Linear Perspective*. New York: Basic Books.
Eilberg-Schwartz, Howard
1994   *God's Phallus and Other Problems for Men and Monotheism*. Boston: Beacon Press.
Ellmann, Maud, ed.
1994   *Psychoanalytic Literary Criticism*. New York: Longman.
Emerson, Caryl
1997   *The First Hundred Years of Mikhail Bakhtin*. Princeton, N.J.: Princeton University Press.
Enright, D. J., ed.
1995   *The Oxford Book of the Supernatural*. Oxford: Oxford University Press.
Eribon, Didier
1989   *Michel Foucault (1926–1984)*. Paris: Flammarion.
Exum, J. Cheryl
1993   *Fragmented Women. Feminist (Sub)versions of Biblical Narratives*. Valley Forge, Pa.: Trinity
          Press International.
1996   *Plotted, Shot, and Painted. Cultural Representations of Biblical Women*. Sheffield, U.K.:
          Sheffield Academic Press.
Exum, J. Cheryl, and Stephen Moore, eds.
1998   *Biblical Studies/Cultural Studies. The Third Sheffield Colloquium*. JSOTSup. 266. Gender,
          Culture, Theory 7. Sheffield, U.K.: Sheffield Academic Press.
Faber, Roland
1998   "De-Ontologizing God: Levinas, Deleuze, Whitehead." Unpublished paper for the
          25th Anniversary Whitehead Conference.
Fackenheim, Emil
1990   *The Jewish Bible after the Holocaust: A Re-reading*. Bloomington: Indiana University Press.
Farmer, Ronald L.
1997   *Beyond the Impasse: The Promise of a Process Hermeneutic*. Macon, Ga.: Mercer University
          Press.
Felder, Cain Hope
1989   *Troubling Biblical Waters: Race, Class and Family*. New York: Orbis Books.
Felder, Cain Hope, ed.
1991   *Stony the Road We Trod: African American Biblical Interpretation*. Minneapolis: Fortress
          Press.
Felman, Shoshana
1983   *The Literary Speech Act: Don Juan with J. L. Austin or, Seduction in Two Languages*. Trans.
          Catherine Porter. Ithaca, N.Y.: Cornell University Press.
Felman, Shoshana, ed.
1981   *Literature and Psychoanalysis: The Question of Reading: Otherwise*. Baltimore: Johns Hopkins
          University Press.
Felman, Shoshana, and Dori Laub, eds.
1991   *Testimony: Crises of Witnessing in Literature, Psychoanalysis and History*. New York: Routledge.
Fewell, Danna Nolan, ed.
1992   *Reading Between Texts: Intertextuality and the Hebrew Bible*. Literary Currents in Biblical
          Interpretation. Louisville, Ky.: Westminster/John Knox Press.
Fewell, Danna Nolan, and Gary A. Phillips
1997   "Drawn to Excess, or Reading Beyond Betrothal." *Semeia* 77: 23–58.

Fieldhouse, D. K.
1989   *The Colonial Empires.* London: Macmillan.
Fink, Bruce
1995   *The Lacanian Subject: Between Language and Jouissance.* Princeton, N.J.: Princeton
          University Press.
Fish, Stanley
1980   *Is There a Text in This Class? The Authority of Interpretive Communities.* Cambridge, Mass.:
          Harvard University Press.
1989   *Doing What Comes Naturally: Change, Rhetoric, and the Practice of Theory in Literary and
          Legal Studies.* Durham, N.C.: Duke University Press.
1994   *There's No Such Thing as Free Speech (and It's a Good Thing, Too).* Oxford: Oxford University
          Press.
1995   *Professional Correctness: Literary Studies and Political Change.* Oxford: Oxford University
          Press.
1999   *The Trouble with Principle.* Cambridge, Mass.: Harvard University Press.
Fishbane, Michael
1985   *Biblical Interpretation in Ancient Israel.* Oxford: Oxford University Press.
Fisher, Walter R.
1987   *Human Communication as Narration: Toward a Philosophy of Reason, Value, and Action.*
          Columbia, S.C.: University of South Carolina Press.
Flynn, Elizabeth A., and Patrocinio P. Schweickart
1986   *Gender and Reading: Essays on Readers, Texts, and Contexts.* Baltimore: Johns Hopkins
          University Press.
Folkenflik, Robert, ed.
1993   *The Culture of Autobiography: Constructions of Self Representation.* Stanford, Calif.: Stanford
          University Press.
Ford, Lewis S.
1978   *The Lure of God: A Biblical Background for Process Theism.* Philadelphia: Westminster
          Press.
Foucault, Michel
1965   *Madness and Civilization: A History of Insanity in the Age of Reason.* Trans. Richard Howard.
          New York: Random House.
1972   *The Archaeology of Knowledge.* Trans. A. M. Sheridan Smith. New York: Pantheon.
1977   *Discipline and Punish: The Birth of the Prison.* Trans. Alan Sheridan. New York: Pantheon.
1978   *The History of Sexuality. Volume I: An Introduction.* Trans. Robert Hurley. New York:
          Random House.
1979   "What Is an Author?" Trans. Josué Harari. In *Textual Strategies: Perspectives in Post-
          Structuralist Criticism.* Ed. Josué Harari. Ithaca, N.Y.: Cornell University Press, 141–60.
1980   "Truth and Power." In *Power/Knowledge: Selected Interviews and Other Writings, 1972–
          1977.* Ed. Colin Gordon. New York: Pantheon Books, 109–33.
1986   "Of Other Spaces." *Diacritics* 16: 22–27.
1987   "Maurice Blanchot: The Thought from Outside." In *Foucault/Blanchot.* Trans. Jeffrey
          Mehlman and Brian Massumi. Cambridge, Mass.: MIT Press.
1988   "Truth, Power, Self: An Interview with Michel Foucault, October 25, 1982." In
          Technologies of the Self: A Seminar with Michel Foucault. Ed. L. H. Martin, H. Gutman, and
          P. H. Hutton. Amherst: University of Massachusetts Press, 9–15.
Fowl, Stephen E.
1988   "The Ethics of Interpretation, or What's Left Over after the Elimination of Meaning."
          SBL 1988 Seminar Papers. Ed. David J. Lull. Atlanta: Scholars Press.
1995   "Texts Don't Have Ideologies." *Biblical Interpretation* 3, no. 1:1–34.
1998   *Engaging Scripture: A Model for Theological Interpretation.* Oxford: Blackwell.
Fowl, Stephen, and L. Gregory Jones
1997   "Scripture, Exegesis, and Discernment in Christian Ethics." In *Virtues and Practices in
          the Christian Tradition: Christian Ethics after MacIntyre.* Ed. Nancey Murphy, Brad J.
          Kallenberg, and Mark Thiessen Nation. Harrisburg, Pa.: Trinity Press, 111–31.
Franklin, Stephen J.
1990   *Speaking Fundamentally: Alfred North Whitehead's Hermeneutical Metaphysics of Propositions,
          Experience, Language, and Religion.* Grand Rapids, Mich.: Eerdmans.
Fredrickson, George
1987   *The Black Image in the White Mind: The Debate on Afro-American Character and Destiny,
          1817–1914.* 2d ed. Middletown, Conn.: Wesleyan University Press.

1988   "The Social Origins of American Racism." In *The Arrogance of Race: Historical Perspectives on Slavery, Racism and Social Inequality.* Middletown, Conn.: Wesleyan University Press, 189–205.

Freedman, Diane P., Olivia Frey, and Francis Murphy Zauhar, eds.
1993   *The Intimate Critique: Autobiographical Literary Criticism.* Durham, N.C.: Duke University Press.

Freeman, Curtis
1993   "The 'Eclipse' of Spiritual Exegesis: Biblical Interpretation from the Reformation to Modernity." *Southwestern Journal of Theology* 35 (Summer): 21–28.

Frei, Hans W.
1974   *The Eclipse of Biblical Narrative: A Study in Eighteenth and Nineteenth Century Hermeneutics.* New Haven, Conn.: Yale University Press.

Fretheim, Terence E., and Karlfried Froehlich
1998   *The Bible as Word of God: In a Postmodern Age.* Minneapolis: Fortress Press.

Freud, Sigmund
1908   "Creative Writers and Day-Dreaming." In *The Standard Edition of the Complete Psycholog-*
[1907]   *ical Works of Sigmund Freud.* Ed. James Strachey, et al. London: Hogarth Press.
1912–13   "Totem and Taboo." *S.E.* 13
1920   *Three Essays on the Theory of Sexuality.* 4th ed. Trans. and rev. James Strachey. New York:
[1962]   Harper & Row.
1939   "Moses and Monotheism." *S.E.* 23.

Frieden, Ken
1989   *Freud's Dream of Interpretation.* Foreword by Harold Bloom. SUNY Series in Modern Jewish Literature and Culture. Albany: State University of New York Press.

Friedlaender, Saul
1993   *Memory, History, and the Extermination of the Jews of Europe.* Bloomington: Indiana University Press.

Friedman, Jonathan
1985   "Ideology." In *The Social Science Encyclopedia.* Ed. Adam Kuper and Jessica Kuper. London: Routledge, 375–76.

Frow, John
1991   "Michel de Certeau and the Practice of Representation." *Cultural Studies* 5, no. 1: 282–91.

Fuchs, Esther
1990   "Contemporary Biblical Literary Criticism: The Objective Phallacy." In *Mappings of the Biblical Terrain: The Bible as Text.* Ed. Vincent L. Tollers and John Maier. Lewisburg, Pa.: Bucknell University Press, 134–42.

Fuss, Diana
1989   *Essentially Speaking.* New York: Routledge.

Fuss, Diana, ed.
1991   *Inside/out: Lesbian Theories, Gay Theories.* New York: Routledge.

Gaba, Octavius
1995   "Symbols of Revelation: The Darkness of the Hebrew Yahweh and the Light of the Greek Logos." In Bailey and Grant, 143–58.

Gagnon, John, and William Simon
1973   *Sexual Conduct: The Social Sources of Human Sexuality.* Chicago: Aldine Publishing.

Gallagher, Susan VanZanten
1996   "Mapping the Hybrid World: Three Postcolonial Motifs." *Semeia* 75: 229–40.

Gallagher, Susan VanZanten, ed.
1994   *Postcolonial Literature and the Biblical Call for Justice.* Jackson, Miss.: University Press of Mississippi.

Gamwell, Franklin I.
1990   *The Divine Good: Modern Moral Theory and the Necessity of God.* San Francisco: Harper San Francisco.

Gandhi, Leela
1998   *Postcolonial Theory: A Critical Introduction.* New York: Columbia University Press.

Garber, Marjorie
1995   *Vice Versa: Bisexuality and the Eroticism of Everyday Life.* New York: Simon and Schuster.

Gates, Henry Louis, Jr.
1985   "Writing 'Race' and the Difference it Makes." In *"Race," Writing, and Difference.* Ed. Henry Louis Gates, Jr. Chicago: University of Chicago Press, 1–20.

1988   *The Signifying Monkey: A Theory of African-American Literary Criticism.* Oxford: Oxford
            University Press.
Geertz, Clifford
1964   "Ideology as a Cultural System." In *Ideology and Discontent.* Ed. David E. Apter. New
            York: Free Press of Glenco, 47–76.
1973   *The Interpretation of Cultures: Selected Essays.* New York: Basic Books.
Gentzler, Edwin
1990   *Contemporary Translation Theories.* Translation Studies. London: Routledge.
George, Mark K.
1995   *Body Works: Power, the Construction of Identity, and Gender in the Discourse on Kingship.*
            Ph.D. dissertation. Princeton, N.J.: Princeton Theological Seminary.
1999   "Constructing Identity in 1 Samuel 17." *Biblical Interpretation* 7/4 (October): 389–412.
Gergen, Kenneth J.
1994   *Realities and Relationships: Soundings in Social Construction.* Cambridge, Mass.: Harvard
            University Press.
Gibbs, Robert
1991   *Correlations in Rosenzweig and Levinas.* Princeton, N.J.: Princeton University Press.
Giddens, Anthony
1992   *The Transformation of Intimacy: Sexuality. Love and Eroticism in Modern Societies.* Stanford,
            Calif.: Stanford University Press.
Gilman, Sander L.
1982   *Essays on the Image of the Black in Germany.* Boston: G.K. Hall & Co.
1985   *Difference and Pathology: Stereotypes of Sexuality, Race, and Madness.* Ithaca, N.Y.: Cornell
            University Press.
1991   *The Jew's Body.* New York: Routledge.
Gilmore, Leigh
1994   *Autobiographics: A Feminist Theory of Women's Self-Representation.* Ithaca, N.Y.: Cornell
            University Press.
Gilroy, Paul
1993   *The Black Atlantic: Modernity and Double Consciousness.* Cambridge, Mass.: Harvard
            University Press.
Glancy, Jennifer A.
1998   "House Readings and Field Readings: The Discourse of Slavery and Biblical/Cultural
            Studies." In *Biblical Studies/Cultural Studies.* Ed. Cheryl Exum and Stephen Moore.
            460–77.
Glaser, Chris
1996   *Uncommon Calling: A Gay Christian's Struggle to Serve the Church.* Louisville, Ky.:
            Westminster John Knox Press.
Goldberg, David Theo
1993   *Racist Culture: Philosophy and the Politics of Meaning.* Cambridge, Mass.: Blackwell
            Publishers.
Goldhill, Simon
1997   "Wipe Your Glosses." Paper presented at Heidelberg Colloquium.
Gottwald, Norman K.
1979   *The Tribes of Yahweh: A Sociology of the Religion of Liberated Israel, 1250 B.C.–1050 B.C.*
            Maryknoll, N.Y.: Orbis Books.
1993a   *The Bible and Liberation: Political and Social Hermeneutics.* Rev. ed. Ed. Norman Gottwald
            and Richard Horsley. Maryknoll, N.Y.: Orbis Books.
1993b   "Sociological Method in the Study of Ancient Israel." In *The Bible and Liberation: Political
            and Social Hermeneutics.* 142–53.
1993c   "The Theological Task after *The Tribes of Yahweh.*" In *The Bible and Liberation: Political
            and Social Hermeneutics,* 239–49.
Gould, Stephen Jay
1981   *The Mismeasure of Man.* New York: W.W. Norton.
Goux, Jean-Joseph
1990   *Symbolic Economies: After Marx and Freud.* Trans. Jennifer Curtis Cage. Ithaca, N.Y.:
            Cornell University Press.
1992   "The Phallus: Masculine Identity and the 'Exchange of Women.'" Trans. Maria
            Amuchastegui, Caroline Benforado, Amy Hendrix, and Eleanor Kaufman. *Differences*
            4.1: 40–75.

1993   *Oedipus Philosopher.* Trans. Catherine Porter. Meridian: Crossing Aesthetics. Stanford, Calif.: Stanford University Press.

Gracia, Jorge J. E.
2000   *Hispanic/Latino Identity: A Philosophical Perspective.* Malden, Mass. and Oxford: Blackwell.

Graham, Joseph F.
1985   *Difference in Translation.* Ithaca, N.Y.: Cornell University Press.

Grant, George
1995   *Time as History.* Ed. William Christian. Toronto: University of Toronto Press.

Grant, Iain Hamilton
1999   "Postmodernism and Politics." In *The Routledge Critical Dictionary of Postmodern Thought.* Ed. Stuart Sim. New York: Routledge, 28–40.

Grassi, Ernesto
1980   *Rhetoric as Philosophy: The Humanist Tradition.* University Park, Pa.: Pennsylvania State University Press.

Green, Barbara
2000   *Mikhail Bakhtin and Biblical Scholarship: An Introduction.* Atlanta: Society of Biblical Literature.

Greenstein, Edward L.
1989a   *Essays on Biblical Method and Translation.* Atlanta: Scholars Press.
1989b   "Deconstruction and Biblical Narrative." *Prooftexts* 9: 43–71.

Gregg, John
1994   *Maurice Blanchot and the Literature of Transgression.* Princeton, N.J.: Princeton University Press.

Gregg, Richard B.
1984   *Symbolic Inducement and Knowing: A Study in the Foundations of Rhetoric.* Columbia, S.C.: University of South Carolina Press.

Griffin, David Ray, William A. Beardslee, and Joe Holland
1989   *Varieties of Postmodern Theology.* Albany: State University of New York Press.

Grimaldi, William M. A., S.J.
1980   *Aristotle, Rhetoric I: A Commentary.* New York: Fordham University Press.

Grosz, Elizabeth
1989   *Sexual Subversions: Three French Feminists.* Sydney, Australia: Allen & Unwin.
1990   *Jacques Lacan: A Feminist Introduction.* London/New York: Routledge.

Guardiola-Sáenz, Leticia A.
1997   "Borderless Women and Borderless Texts: A Cultural Reading of Matthew 15:21–28." *Semeia* 78: 69–81.

Guha, Ranajit, ed.
1982   *Subaltern Studies, Vol. 1: Writings on South Asian History and Society.* Delhi: Oxford University Press.

Gunn, David M., and Danna Nolan Fewell
1993   *Narrative in the Hebrew Bible.* New York: Oxford University Press.

Habel, Norman C.
1995   *The Land Is Mine: Six Biblical Land Ideologies.* Overtures to Biblical Theology. Minneapolis: Fortress Press.

Habermas, Jürgen
1983   "Modernity–An Incomplete Project." In *The Anti-Aesthetic: Essays on Postmodern Culture.* Ed. Hal Foster. New York: New Press, 3–15.
1984   *The Theory of Communicative Action.* Trans. Thomas McCarthy. Vol. 1. Boston: Beacon Press.
1987   *The Theory of Communicative Action.* Trans. Thomas McCarthy. Vol. 2. Boston: Beacon Press.

Hacking, Ian
1996   "Memory Sciences, Memory Politics." In *Tense Past.* Ed. Paul Antze and Michael Lambek. New York: Routledge.

Halivni, David Weiss
1991   *Peshat and Derash: Plain and Applied Meaning in Rabbinic Exegesis.* New York: Oxford University Press.

Hall, Stuart
1980   "Cultural Studies and the Centre: Some Problematics and Problems." In *Culture, Media, Language: Working Papers in Cultural Studies, 1972–79.* Ed. Stuart Hall et al. London: Hutchinson, 15–47.

1989   "Cultural Identity and Cinematic Representation." *Framework* 36: 68–81.
Halperin, David M.
1990   *One Hundred Years of Homosexuality and Other Essays on Greek Love.* New York: Routledge.
1995   *Saint Foucault: Towards a Gay Hagiography.* Cambridge, Mass.: Harvard University Press.
Halperin, David M., ed.
1996   *Before Sexuality: The Construction of Erotic Experience in the Ancient Greek World.* Princeton, N.J.: Princeton University Press.
Hammonds, Evelynn
1997   "Black (W)holes and the Geometry of Black Female Sexuality." In *Feminism Meets Queer Theory.* Ed. Elizabeth Weed and Naomi Schor. Bloomington: Indiana University Press, 136–56.
Handelman, Susan
1982   *The Slayers of Moses: The Emergence of Rabbinic Interpretation in Modern Literary Theory.* Albany: State University of New York Press.
1991   *Fragments of Redemption: Jewish Thought and Literary Theory in Benjamin, Scholem and Levinas.* Bloomington: Indiana University Press.
Hanson, Ann Ellis
1992   "Conception, Gestation, and the Origin of Female Nature in the *Corpus Hippocraticum.*" *Helios* 19: 31–71.
Hanson, Paul D.
1998   "The World of the Servant of the Lord in Isaiah 40–55." In *Jesus and the Suffering Servant: Isaiah 53 and Christian Origins.* Ed. William H. Bellinger, Jr., and William R. Farmer. Harrisburg, Pa.: Trinity Press International.
Haraway, Donna
1991   *Simians, Cyborgs, and Women: The Reinvention of Nature.* New York: Routledge.
Harding, Sandra
1993   "Reinventing Ourselves as Other: More New Agents of History and Knowledge." In *American Feminist Thought at Century's End: A Reader.* Ed. Linda S. Kaufman. Cambridge, Mass.: Blackwell, 140–64.
Hardwig, John
1991   "The Role of Trust in Knowledge." *Journal of Philosophy* 88 (December): 693–708.
Hart, Kevin
1989   *The Trespass of the Sign: Deconstruction, Theology and Philosophy.* Cambridge, U.K.: Cambridge University Press.
1996   *Losing the Power to Say "I."* Melbourne: Art School Press.
1997   "Derrida." In *The Postmodern God: A Theological Reader.* Ed. G. Ward. Oxford: Blackwell, 159–67.
Hart, Ray L.
1985   *Unfinished Man and the Imagination: Toward an Ontology and a Rhetoric of Revelation.* With an Introduction by Mark C. Taylor. Reprint. Atlanta: Scholars Press. (Orig. 1968.)
Hartshorne, Charles
1948   *The Divine Relativity.* New Haven, Conn.: Yale University Press.
Harvey, Barry A.
1999   *Another City: An Ecclesiological Primer for a Post-Christian World.* Valley Forge, Pa.: Trinity Press International.
Harvey, David
1989   *The Condition of Postmodernity: An Enquiry into the Origins of Cultural Change.* Cambridge, Mass.: Blackwell.
Hasan-Rokem, Galit
1996   *The Web of Life–Folklore in Rabbinic Literature: The Palestinian Aggadic Midrash Eikha Rabba.* In Hebrew. Tel Aviv: Am Oved.
Hassan, Ihab
1987   *The Postmodern Turn: Essays in Postmodern Theory and Culture.* Columbus, Ohio.: Ohio State University.
Hayles, N. Katherine
1991   *Chaos and Order: Complex Dynamics in Literature and Science.* Chicago: University of Chicago.
Hays, Richard
1989   *Echoes of Scripture in the Letters of Paul.* New Haven, Conn.: Yale University Press.

Heard, Chris
1997   "Hearing the Children's Cries: Commentary, Deconstruction, Ethics, and the Book of Habakkuk." *Semeia* 77: 75–89.
Heidegger, Martin
1982   *The Question Concerning Technology and Other Essays.* Trans. William Lovitt. New York: Harper and Row.
Heinemann, Isaak
1970   *Darxei Ha'Agada.* In Hebrew. Jerusalem: Magnes Press.
Hengel, Martin
1974   *Judaism and Hellenism: Studies in their Encounter in Palestine During the Early Hellenistic Period.* Trans. John Bowden. Philadelphia: Fortress Press.
Hennessy, Rosemary
1993   "Queer Theory: A Review of the *differences* Special Issue and Wittig's *The Straight Mind.*" *Signs: Journal of Women in Culture and Society* 18: 964–73.
Herdt, Gilbert
1997   *Same Sex, Different Cultures.* Boulder: Westview Press.
Herman, Judith Lewis
1992   *Trauma and Recovery.* New York: Basic Books.
Hetherington, Kevin
1997   *The Badlands of Modernity.* New York: Routledge.
Higgins, Jean M.
1976   "The Myth of Eve: The Temptress." *Journal of the American Academy of Religion* 44: 639–47.
Hill, Craig C.
1992   *Hellenists and Hebrews: Reappraising Division Within the Earliest Church.* Minneapolis: Fortress Press.
Hill, Leslie
1997   *Blanchot: Extreme Contemporary.* London and New York: Routledge.
Hinchman, Lewis P., and Sandra K. Hinchman
1997   *Memory, Identity, Community: The Idea of Narrative in the Human Sciences.* Albany: State University of New York Press.
Hirsch, Marianne
1997   *Family Frames: Photography, Narrative, and Postmemory.* Cambridge, Mass.: Harvard University Press.
1999   "Projected Memory: Holocaust Photographs in Personal and Public Fantasy." In *Acts of Memory. Cultural Recall in the Present.* Ed. Mieke Bal, Jonathan Crewe, and Leo Spitzer. Hanover, N.H.: University Press of New England.
Hirschkop, Ken
1999   *Mikhail Bakhtin: An Aesthetic for Democracy.* Oxford: Oxford University Press.
Hirsh, Elizabeth, and Gary A. Olson
1995   "'Je–Luce Irigaray': A Meeting with Luce Irigaray." *Hypatia* 10: 93–114.
Hoggart, Richard
1957   *The Uses of Literacy.* London: Chatto & Windus.
Hohendahl, Peter Uwe, ed.
1988   *A History of German Literary Criticism, 1730–1980.* Lincoln: University of Nebraska Press.
Hollander, John
1981   *The Figure of Echo: A Mode of Allusion in Milton and After.* Berkeley: University of California Press.
Hollier, Denis
1989   *Against Architecture: The Writings of Georges Bataille.* Trans. Betsy Wing. London: MIT Press.
Hollier, Denis, ed.
1988   *The College of Sociology.* Trans. Betsy Wing. Minneapolis: University of Minnesota Press.
Holquist, M.
1990   *Dialogism: Bakhtin and His World.* London and New York: Routledge.
Hood, Robert
1994   *Begrimed and Black: Christian Traditions on Blacks and Blackness.* Minneapolis: Fortress Press.

Horsley, Richard A.
1998   "Submerged Biblical Histories and Imperial Biblical Studies." In *The Postcolonial Bible*.
        Ed. R. S. Sugirtharajah. The Bible and Postcolonialism, 1. Sheffield, U.K.: Sheffield
        Academic Press, 152–73.
Horsley, Richard A., ed.
1997   *Paul and Empire: Religion and Power in Roman Imperial Society*. Harrisburg, Pa.: Trinity
        Press International.
Hume, Kathryn
1984   *Fantasy and Mimesis: Responses to Reality in Western Literature*. New York: Methuen.
Humphrey, Caroline
1995   "Chiefly and Shamanist Landscapes in Mongolia." In *The Anthropology of Landscape*.
        Ed. Eric Hirsch and Michael O'Hanlon. Oxford: Clarendon, 135–64.
Irigaray, Luce
1985a   *Speculum of the Other Woman*. Trans. Gillian C. Gill. Ithaca, N.Y.: Cornell University
        Press.
1985b   *This Sex Which Is Not One*. Trans. Catherine Porter with Carolyn Burke. Ithaca, N.Y.:
        Cornell University Press.
1993a   *An Ethics of Sexual Difference*. Trans. Carolyn Burke and Gillian C. Gill. Ithaca, N. Y.:
        Cornell University Press.
1993b   *Sexes and Genealogies*. Trans. Gillian C. Gill. New York: Columbia University Press.
1993c   *Je, Tu, Nous*. Trans. Alison Martin. New York: Routledge.
1996   *I Love to You*. Trans. Alison Martin. New York: Routledge.
1997a   "Equal to Whom?" In *The Postmodern God: A Theological Reader*. Ed. Graham Ward.
        Oxford: Blackwell, 198–213.
1997b   *Être deux*. Paris: B. Grasset.
Irwin, T. H.
1970   "Aristotle's Concept of Signification." In *Language and Logos: Studies in Ancient Greek
        Philosophy Presented to G.E.L. Owen*. Ed. Malcolm Schofield and Martha Craven
        Nussbaum. Cambridge: Cambridge University Press, 241–66.
Irwin, W. R.
1976   *The Game of the Impossible: A Rhetoric of Fantasy*. Urbana, Ill.: University of Illinois Press.
Jackson, David
1990   *Unmasking Masculinity: A Critical Autobiography*. Cambridge, Mass.: Unwin Hyman.
Jackson, Rosemary
1981   *Fantasy: The Literature of Subversion*. London/New York: Methuen.
Jagose, Annamarie
1996   *Queer Theory: An Introduction*. New York: New York University Press.
Jakobson, Roman
1959   "On Linguistic Aspects of Translation." In *On Translation*. Ed. Reuben A. Brower.
        Cambridge, Mass.: Harvard University Press, 232–39.
Jameson, Fredric
1961   *Sartre: The Origins of a Style*. New Haven, Conn.: Yale University Press. Reprint:
        Columbia University Press, 1984.
1971   *Marxism and Form: Twentieth-Century Dialectical Theories of Literature*. Princeton, N.J.:
        Princeton University Press.
1972   *The Prison-House of Language: A Critical Account of Structuralism and Russian Formalism*.
        Princeton, N.J.: Princeton University Press.
1979   *Fables of Aggression: Wyndham Lewis, the Modernist as Fascist*. Berkeley: University of
        California Press.
1981   *The Political Unconscious: Narrative as a Socially Symbolic Act*. Ithaca, N.Y.: Cornell
        University Press.
1988   *The Ideologies of Theory: Essays 1971–1986*. Minneapolis: University of Minnesota Press.
1990a   *Signatures of the Visible*. New York: Routledge.
1990b   *Late Marxism: Adorno, or, the Persistence of the Dialectic*. London: Verso.
1991   *Postmodernism, or, The Cultural Logic of Late Capitalism*. Durham, N.C.: Duke University
        Press.
1992   *The Geopolitical Aesthetic: Cinema and Space in the World System*. Bloomington: Indiana
        University Press.
1993   "On 'Cultural Studies.'" *Social Text* 34: 17–52.
1994   *The Seeds of Time*. New York: Columbia University Press.

1998a   *Brecht and Method.* London: Verso.
1998b   *The Cultural Turn: Selected Writings on the Postmodern, 1983–1998.* London: Verso.
JanMohamed, Abdul
1992   "Sexuality On/Of the Racial Border: Foucault, Wright, and the Articulation of 'Racialized Sexuality.' In *Discourses of Sexuality: From Aristotle to AIDS.* Ed. D. Stanton. Ann Arbor: University of Michigan Press.
Jasper, David
1993   *Rhetoric, Power and Community: An Exercise in Reserve.* London: Macmillan; Louisville, Ky.: Westminster/John Knox Press.
Jeanrond, Werner G.
1988   *Text and Interpretation as Categories of Theological Thinking.* Trans. Thomas J. Wilson. New York: Crossroad.
Jencks, Charles
1989   *What is Post-Modernism?* 3d ed. New York: St. Martin's Press.
1991   *The Language of Post-Modern Architecture.* 6th ed. London: Academy Editions.
Jenkins, Keith
1991   *Re-Thinking History.* London/New York: Routledge.
Jobling, David
1999   Review of R. S. Sugirtharajah, ed., *The Postcolonial Bible. Journal for the Study of the New Testament* 74: 117–19.
Jobling, David, and Tina Pippin, eds.
1992   *Ideological Criticism of Biblical Texts. Semeia* 59.
Johnson, Richard
1986/7   "What is Cultural Studies Anyway?" *Social Text* 16: 38–80.
Jones, Serene
1995   *Calvin and the Rhetoric of Piety.* Columbia Series in Reformed Theology. Louisville, Ky.: Westminster John Knox Press.
Jordan, Mark D.
1997   *The Invention of Sodomy in Christian Theology.* Chicago: University of Chicago Press.
Jost, Walter
1989   *Rhetorical Thought in John Henry Newman.* Columbia, S.C.: University of South Carolina Press.
Jouve, Nicole Ward
1991   *White Woman Speaks with Forked Tongue: Criticism as Autobiography.* New York: Routledge.
Jowett, Benjamin
1861   "On the Interpretation of Scripture." In *Essays and Reviews.* 7th ed. London: Longman, Green, Longman and Roberts. Cited in David C. Steinmetz, "The Superiority of Pre-Critical Exegesis." *Theology Today* 37 (April 1980): 27–38.
Katz, Jonathan Ned
1995   *The Invention of Heterosexuality.* New York: Dutton.
Kaufman, Linda S.
1993   "The Long Goodbye: Against Personal Testimony, or an Infant Grifter Grows Up." In *American Feminist Thought at Century's End: A Reader.* Ed. Linda S. Kaufman. Cambridge, Mass.: Blackwell, 258–77.
Kaufman, William E.
1997   *The Evolving God: Jewish Process Theology.* Lewiston, N.Y.: Edwin Mellen Press.
Kavanagh, James H.
1990   "Ideology." In *Critical Terms for Literary Study.* Ed. Frank Lentricchia and Thomas McLaughlin. Chicago: University of Chicago Press, 306–20.
Keller, Catherine
1986   *From a Broken Web: Separation, Sexism, and Self.* Boston: Beacon Press.
1996   *Apocalypse Now and Then: A Feminist Guide to the End of the World.* Boston: Beacon Press.
1998   "Borders of Chaos: Whiteheadian Cracks in the Postmodern Surface." Unpublished paper for the 25th Anniversary Whitehead Conference.
Kelley, Shawn
1995   "Poststructuralism and/or Afrocentrism." *SBL 1995 Seminar Papers.* Ed. Eugene H. Lovering, Jr. Atlanta: Scholars Press, 226–49.
1997   "Aesthetic Fascism: Heidegger, Antisemitism and the Quest for Christian Origins." In Phillips and Fewell 1997, 195–225.

forthcoming   *The Aryanization of the Bible: Ideology, Methodology, Race, and the Formation of Modern Biblical Scholarship*. Routledge Press.

Kennedy, George A.
1984   *New Testament Interpretation through Rhetorical Criticism*. Chapel Hill: University of North Carolina Press.

Kerr, Heather, and Amanda Nettelbeck
1998   *The Space Between: Australian Women Writing Fictocriticism*. Nedlands, Western Australia: University of Western Australia Press.

Kilcup, Karen L.
1998   "Dialogues of the Self: Toward a Theory of (Re)reading Ai." *Journal of Gender Studies* 7: 5–21.

Kinneavy, James L.
1987   *Greek Rhetorical Origins of Christian Faith*. New York: Oxford University Press.

Kirmayer, Laurence J.
1996   "Landscapes of Memory: Trauma, Narrative, and Dissociation." In *Tense Past*. Ed. Paul Antze and Michael Lambek. New York: Routledge.

Kitzberger, Rosa Ingrid, ed.
1999   *The Personal Voice in Biblical Interpretation*. London: Routledge.

Klemm, David E.
1987   "The Rhetoric of Theological Argument." In *The Rhetoric of the Human Sciences*. Ed. John Nelson, Allan McGill, and Donald McCloskey. Madison: University of Wisconsin Press, 276–97.

Kline, Morris
1953   *Mathematics in Western Culture*. New York: Oxford.

Knight, Douglas A., ed.
1983   *Julius Wellhausen and His* Prolegomenon to the History of Israel. *Semeia* 25.

Kort, Wesley
1996   *Take, Read: Scripture, Textuality, and Cultural Practice*. University Park: Pennsylvania State Press.

Kraniauskas, John
1998   "Globalization is Ordinary: The Transnationalization of Cultural Studies." *Radical Philosophy* 90: 9–19.

Kristeva, Julia
1967   "Word, Dialogue, and Novel." Trans. Alice Jardine, Thomas Gora, and Léon Roudiez. In *The Kristeva Reader*. Ed. Toril Moi. New York: Columbia University Press, 1986.
1980   *Desire in Language: A Semiotic Approach to Literature and Art*. Ed. L. S. Roudiez. Trans. T. Gora, A. Jardine, and L. S. Roudiez. New York: Columbia University Press.
1982   *Powers of Horror: An Essay on Abjection*. New York: Columbia University Press.
1984   *Revolution in Poetic Language*. Trans. M. Waller. New York: Columbia University Press.
1986   "Michel de Certeau." *Libération* 11–12 (Jan.).
1987a   *Tales of Love*. New York: Columbia University Press.
1987b   "Ego Affectus Est. Bernard of Clairvaux: Affect, Desire, Love." In *Tales of Love*. Trans. Leon S. Roudiez. New York: Columbia University Press, 151–69.
1989   *Black Sun*. New York: Columbia University Press.
1990   *The Kristeva Reader*. Ed. Toril Moi. Oxford: Basil Blackwell.
1992   *The Samurai*. New York: Columbia University Press.
1995   *New Maladies of the Soul*. New York: Columbia University Press.

Krystal, John H., Stephen M. Southwick, and Dennis S. Charney
1995   "Post Traumatic Stress Disorder: Psychobiological Mechanisms of Traumatic Remembrance." In *Memory Distortion*. Ed. Daniel Schachter. Cambridge, Mass.: Harvard University Press.

Kwok Pui-lan
1995   *Discovering the Bible in the Non-Biblical World*. New York: Orbis Books.

Lacan, Jacques
1992   *The Ethics of Psychoanalysis*. Ed. Jacques-Alain Miller. Trans. Dennis Porter. New York: Norton.

LaCapra, Dominick
1998   *History and Memory after Auschwitz*. Ithaca, N.Y.: Cornell University Press.

Lang, Berel
1996   *Heidegger's Silence.* Ithaca N.Y.: Cornell University Press.
Laqueur, Thomas
1990   *Making Sex: Body and Gender from the Greeks to Freud.* Cambridge, Mass.: Harvard
          University Press.
Lash, Scott
1990   *Sociology of Postmodernism.* London/New York: Routledge.
Lechte, John
1990   *Julia Kristeva.* London: Routledge.
Lee, Archie C. C.
1999   "Returning to China: Biblical Interpretation in Postcolonial Hong Kong." *Biblical
          Interpretation* 7: 156–73.
Lefebvre, Henri
1991   *The Production of Space.* Trans. Donald Nicholson Smith. Oxford: Blackwell (French,
          1974).
Lefevere, André, ed.
1992   *Translation/History/Culture: A Sourcebook.* Translation Studies. London: Routledge.
Lefevere, André, and Susan Bassnett
1990   "Introduction: Proust's Grandmother and the Thousand and One Nights: The 'Cultural
          Turn' in Translation Studies." In *Translation, History, and Culture.* Ed. André Lefevere
          and Susan Bassnett. London: Pinter, 1–13.
Lentricchia, Frank
1983   *Criticism and Social Change.* Chicago: University of Chicago Press.
Lévi-Strauss, Claude
1963   *Structural Anthropology.* Trans. Claire Jacobson and Brooke Grundfest Schoepf. New
          York: Basic Books.
Levinas, Emmanuel
1969   *Totality and Infinity. An Essay on Exteriority.* Trans. Alphoso Lingis. Pittsburgh, Pa.:
          Duquesne University Press.
1978   *Existence and Existents.* Trans. Alphonso Lingis. The Hague: Martinus Nijhoff.
1985   *Ethics and Infinity. Conversations with Philippe Nemo.* Trans. Richard A. Cohen. Pittsburgh,
          Pa.: Duquesne University Press.
1987   *Time and the Other.* Trans. Richard Cohen. Pittsburgh, Pa.: Duquesne University Press.
1990   *Nine Talmudic Readings.* Trans. Annette Aronowicz. Bloomington: Indiana University
          Press.
1991a   *Otherwise Than Being or Beyond Essence.* Trans. Alphonso Lingis. The Hague: Nijhoff.
1991b   *Entre Nous. Essais sur le penser-à-l'âutre.* Paris: Grasset.
1994   *Beyond the Verse. Talmudic Readings and Lectures.* Trans. Gary D. Mole. Bloomington:
          Indiana University Press.
1998   *Of God Who Comes to Mind.* Trans. Bettin Bergo. Stanford, Calif.: Stanford University
          Press.
Liew, Tat-siong Benny
1999   "Tyranny, Boundary and Might: Colonial Mimicry in Mark's Gospel." *Journal for the
          Study of the New Testament* 73: 7–31.
Linafelt, Tod, and Timothy K. Beal
1992   "Sifting for Cinders: Strange Fires in Leviticus 10:1–5." *Semeia* 69/70: 7–18.
Lionnet, Françoise
1989   *Autobiographical Voices: Race, Gender, Self-Portraiture.* Ithaca, N.Y.: Cornell University
          Press.
Littel, Franklin
1975   *The Crucifixion of the Jews.* New York: Harper & Row.
Lobkowicz, Nicholas
1967   *Theory and Practice: History of a Concept from Aristotle to Marx.* Notre Dame, Ind.: University
          of Notre Dame Press.
Loftus, Elizabeth F., Julie Feldman, and Richard Dashiell
1995   "The Reality of Illusory Memories." In *Memory Distortion.* Ed. Daniel Schachter.
          Cambridge, Mass.: Harvard University Press.
Long, Burke O.
1997   *Planting and Reaping Albright. Politics, Ideology, and Interpreting the Bible.* University Park:
          Pennsylvania State University.

Loomba, Ania
1998   *Colonialism/Postcolonialism.* London and New York: Routledge.
Lovecraft, H. P.
1973   *Supernatural Horror in Literature.* New York: Dover.
Lozada, Francisco, Jr.
2000a   *A Literary Reading of John 5: Text as Construction.* Studies in Biblical Literature. New York: Peter Lang.
2000b   "Ethnic Identity in the Classroom." *Religious Studies News/SBL Edition* 1/1. 1 August 2000. <http://www.sbl-site.org/Newsletter/08_2000/Ethnic Identity1.htm>
Luntley, Michael
1995   *Reason, Truth and Self: The Postmodern Reconditioned.* London: Routledge.
Lyotard, Jean-François
1971   *Discours, Figure.* Paris: Klincksieck.
1984   *The Postmodern Condition.* Trans. Geoff Bennington and Brian Massumi. Theory and History of Literature 10. Minneapolis: University of Minnesota.
1988   *The Differend: Phrases in Dispute.* Trans. Georges van den Abbeele. Minneapolis: University of Minnesota Press.
1989   "Lessons in Pragmaticism." Trans. David Macey. In *The Lyotard Reader.* Ed. Andrew Benjamin, Oxford and Cambridge, Mass.: Basil Blackwell, 122–54.
1991   *Phenomenology.* Trans. Brian Beakley. Albany: State University of New York Press. (French, 1954.)
1992   *The Postmodern Explained.* Minneapolis: University of Minnesota Press.
1993   *Libidinal Economy.* Trans. Iain Hamilton Grant. Bloomington: Indiana University Press. (French, 1974.)
Lyotard, Jean-François, and Jean Loup Thebaud
1985   *Just Gaming.* Trans. Wlad Godzich. Minneapolis: University of Minnesota Press.
Macey, David
1993   *The Lives of Michel Foucault: A Biography.* New York: Pantheon Books.
MacIntyre, Alasdair
1984   *After Virtue: A Study in Moral Theory.* 2d ed. Notre Dame, Ind.: University of Notre Dame Press. (1st ed., 1981.)
1988   *Whose Justice, Which Rationality?* Notre Dame, Ind.: Notre Dame University Press.
1990   *Three Rival Versions of Moral Enquiry: Encyclopaedia, Genealogy, and Tradition.* Notre Dame, Ind.: University of Notre Dame Press.
1994   "Moral Relativism, Truth and Justification." In *The MacIntyre Reader.* Ed. Kelvin Knight. Cambridge, U.K.: Polity Press, 202–20.
MacKinnon, Catharine
1992   "Does Sexuality Have a History?" In *Discourses of Sexuality: From Aristotle to AIDS.* Ed. D. Stanton. Ann Arbor: University of Michigan Press.
Mailloux, Steven
1989   *Rhetorical Power.* Ithaca, N.Y.: Cornell University Press.
Maimonides, Moses
1956   *The Guide for the Perplexed.* Trans. M. Friedländer. New York: Dover.
Manlove, Colin
1992   *Christian Fantasy: From Twelve Hundred to the Present.* South Bend, Ind.: University of Notre Dame Press.
Marcus, Laura
1994   *Auto/biographical Discourses: Theory, Criticism, Practice.* New York: Manchester University Press.
Marshall, Bruce D.
1995   " 'We Shall Bear the Image of the Man of Heaven': Theology and the Concept of Truth." In *Rethinking Metaphysics.* Ed. L. Gregory Jones and Stephen E. Fowl. Oxford: Blackwell, 93–117.
Martin, Biddy
1997   "Extraordinary Homosexuals and the Fear of Being Ordinary." In *Feminism Meets Queer Theory.* Ed. Elizabeth Weed and Naomi Schor. Bloomington: Indiana University Press, 109–35.
Martin, Clarice
1989   "A Chamberlain's Journey." *Semeia* 47, 105–35.

1991   "The *Haustafeln* (Household Codes) in African American Biblical Interpretation: 'Free Slaves' and 'Subordinate Women.'" In Felder 1991, 206–31.

Masuzawa, Tomoko
1998   "Culture." In *Critical Terms for Religious Studies.* Ed. Mark C. Taylor. Chicago: University of Chicago Press, 70–93.

McClendon, J. W.
1994   *Systematic Theology: Doctrine.* Vol. 2. Nashville: Abingdon Press.

McClintock, Anne
1995   *Imperial Leather: Race, Gender and Sexuality in the Colonial Conquest.* New York and London: Routledge.

McDonald, Christie, ed.
1985   *The Ear of the Other: Texts and Discussions with Jacques Derrida.* Trans. Peggy Kamuf. Lincoln: University of Nebraska Press.

McGowan, John
1991   *Postmodernism and Its Critics.* Ithaca, N.Y.: Cornell University Press.

McKnight, Edgar
1988   *Postmodern Use of the Bible. The Emergence of Reader-Oriented Criticism.* Nashville: Abingdon Press.

McNeill, John J.
1993   *The Church and the Homosexual.* Boston: Beacon Press.

Meier, John P.
1991   *A Marginal Jew: Rethinking the Historical Jesus.* Vol. 1.: *The Roots and the Problem and the Person.* New York: Doubleday.
1994   *A Marginal Jew: Rethinking the Historical Jesus.* Vol. 2.: *Mentor, Message, and Miracle.* New York: Doubleday.

Mercer, Kobena
1994   *Welcome to the Jungle: New Positions in Black Cultural Studies.* New York and London: Routledge.

Mesle, C. Robert
1993   *Process Theology: A Basic Introduction.* St. Louis: Chalice Press.

Meyers, William
1991   "The Hermeneutical Dilemma of the African American Biblical Student." In Felder 1991, 40–57.

Milbank, John
1990   *Theology and Social Theory: Beyond Secular Reason.* Oxford: Blackwell.

Milbank, John, Catherine Pickstock, and Graham Ward, eds.
1999   *Radical Orthodoxy: A New Theology.* London: Routledge.

Miles, Richard
1999   "Introduction: Constructing Identities in Late Antiquity." In *Constructing Identities in Late Antiquity.* Ed. Richard Miles. London and New York: Routledge, 1–15.

Miller, James
1993   *The Passion of Michel Foucault.* New York: Simon & Schuster.

Miller, Nancy K.
1991   *Getting Personal: Feminist Occasions and Other Autobiographical Acts.* New York: Routledge.
1997   "Public Statements, Private Lives: Academic Memoirs for the Nineties." *Signs* 22: 981–1015.

Milne, Pamela J.
1988   "Eve and Adam: Is a Feminist Reading Possible?" *Bible Review* 4: 12–21, 39.

Minh-Ha, Trinh T.
1990   "Not You/Like You: Post-Colonial Women and the Interlocking Questions of Identity and Difference." In Gloria Anzaldùa, *Making Face, Making Soul (Haciendo Caras): Creative and Critical Perspectives by Feminists of Color.* San Francisco: Aute Lute Books, 371–75.

Mitchell, W. J. T., ed.
1985   *Against Theory: Literary Studies and the New Pragmatism.* Chicago: University of Chicago Press.

Moi, Toril
1994   *Sexual Textual Politics: Feminist Literary Theory.* London/New York: Routledge.

Moloney, Francis J.
1999   "An Adventure with Nicodemus." In *The Personal Voice in Biblical Interpretation.* Ed. Ingrid Rosa Kitzberger. London: Routledge, 97–110.

Mongia, Padmini, ed.
1996   *Contemporary Postcolonial Theory: A Reader.* London: Arnold.
Moore, Stephen D.
1989   *Literary Criticism and the Gospels: The Theoretical Challenge.* New Haven, Conn.: Yale University Press.
1993   "Are There Impurities in the Living Water that the Johannine Jesus Dispenses? Deconstruction, Feminism and the Samaritan Woman." *Biblical Interpretation* 1: 207–27.
1994   *Poststructuralism and the New Testament: Derrida and Foucault at the Foot of the Cross.* Minneapolis: Fortress Press.
1996   *God's Gym: Divine Male Bodies of the Bible.* New York: Routledge.
1998   "Que(e)rying Paul: Preliminary Questions." In *Auguries: The Jubilee Volume of the Sheffield Department of Biblical Studies.* Ed. David J. A. Clines and Stephen D. Moore. Sheffield, U.K.: Sheffield Academic Press, 250–74.
Moore, Stephen D., ed.
1997   "Biblical Studies and the New Historicism." *Biblical Interpretation* 5, no. 4.
Moore, Stephen D., and Janice Capel Anderson
1998   "Taking It Like a Man: Masculinity in 4 Maccabees." *Journal of Biblical Literature* 117, no. 2: 249–73.
Moore-Gilbert, Bart
1997   *Postcolonial Theory: Contexts, Practices, Politics.* London: Verso.
Moore-Gilbert, Bart, Gareth Stanton, and Willy Maley, eds.
1997   *Postcolonial Criticism.* London: Longman.
Morris, Meaghan
1988   "Banality in Cultural Studies." *Discourse* 10: 3–29.
Morson, G. S., and C. Emerson
1989   *Rethinking Bakhtin: Extensions and Challenges.* Evanston, Ill.: Northwestern University Press.
1990   *Mikhail Bakhtin: Creation of a Prosaics.* Stanford, Calif.: Stanford University Press.
Mosala, Itumeleng J.
1989   *Biblical Hermeneutics and Black Theology in South Africa.* Grand Rapids, Mich.: Eerdmans.
1996   "Race, Class, and Gender as Hermeneutical Factors in the Africana Independent Churches' Appropriation of the Bible." *Semeia* 73: 43–57.
Muller, John P., and William J. Richardson
1982   *Lacan and Language: A Reader's Guide to* Écrits. New York: International Universities Press.
Munn, Nancy D.
1992   "The Cultural Anthropology of Time: A Critical Essay." *Annual Review of Anthropology* 21: 93–123.
Natoli, Joseph, and Linda Hutcheon, eds.
1993   *A Postmodern Reader.* Albany: State University of New York Press.
Nelson, John S., Allan McGill, and Donald N. McCloskey, eds.
1987   *The Rhetoric of the Human Sciences: Language and Argument in Scholarship and Public Affairs.* Madison: University of Wisconsin Press.
Newsom, Carol A.
1989   "Woman and the Discourse of Patriarchal Wisdom: A Study of Proverbs 1–9." In *Gender and Difference in Ancient Israel.* Ed. Peggy L. Day. Minneapolis: Fortress Press, 142–60.
Nicholson, Linda, ed.
1990   *Feminism/Postmodernism.* New York: Routledge.
Nida, Eugene A.
1964   *Toward a Science of Translating: With Special Reference to Principles and Procedures Involved in Bible Translating.* Leiden: E. J. Brill.
Nida, Eugene A., and Charles R. Taber
1982   *The Theory and Practice of Translation.* Leiden: E. J. Brill.
Nietzsche, Friedrich
1971   *The Dawn.* In *The Portable Nietzsche.* Trans. Walter Kaufmann. London: Chatto & Windus.
Nkrumah, Kwame
1965   *Neo-Colonialism: The Last Stage of Imperialism.* London: Nelson.

Noble, Paul R.
1994   "Hermeneutics and Post-Modernism: Can We Have a Radical Reader-Response
        Theory? Part I." *Religious Studies* 30 (December).
Norris, Christopher
1996   *Reclaiming Truth: Contribution to a Critique of Cultural Relativism.* Durham, N.C.: Duke
        University Press.
Nussbaum, Martha C.
1986   *The Fragility of Goodness: Luck and Ethics in Greek Tragedy and Philosophy.* Cambridge,
        U.K.: Cambridge University Press.
Nysse, Richard
1995   "Keeping Company with Nahum: Reading the Oracles against the Nations as Scripture."
        Word & World 15: 412–19.
Nysse, Richard, and Donald Juel
1993   "Interpretation for Christian Ministry." *Word & World* 13: 345–55.
O'Day, Gail R.
1999   "Intertextuality." In *The Dictionary of Biblical Interpretation.* Ed. John H. Hayes. Vol. 1.
        Nashville: Abingdon.
Ogden, Schubert M.
1982   *The Point of Christology.* San Francisco: Harper & Row.
1966   *The Reality of God and Other Essays.* New York: Harper & Row.
1996   *Doing Theology Today.* Valley Forge, Pa.: Trinity Press International.
Okin, Susan Moller
1983   *Women in Western Political Thought.* Princeton, N.J.: Princeton University Press.
1989   *Justice, Gender, and the Family.* New York: Basic Books.
Oliver, Kelly
1993   *Reading Kristeva: Unravelling the Double-Bind.* Bloomington: Indiana University Press.
Olney, James
1980   "Autobiography and the Cultural Moment: A Thematic, Historical, and Bibliographic
        Introduction." In *Autobiography: Essays Theoretical and Critical.* Ed. James Olney.
        Princeton, N.J.: Princeton University Press, 3–27.
Olsen, Lance
1987   *Ellipse of Uncertainty: An Introduction to Postmodern Fantasy.* New York: Greenwood.
Ong, Walter J., S.J.
1982   *Orality and Literacy: The Technologizing of the Word.* New Accents. London: Methuen.
1983   *Ramus, Method, and the Decay of Dialogue.* Rep. Cambridge, Mass.: Harvard University
        Press. (Orig. 1958.)
Ostriker, Alicia Suskin
1994   *The Nakedness of the Fathers: Biblical Visions and Revisions.* New Brunswick, N.J.: Rutgers
        University Press.
Overing, Joanna
1989   "Translation as a Creative Process: The Power of the Name." In *Comparative Anthropology.*
        Ed. Ladislav Holy. London: Basil Blackwell, 70–87.
Pardes, Ilana
1992   *Countertraditions in the Bible: A Feminist Approach.* Cambridge, Mass.: Harvard University
        Press.
Parker, Patricia
1996   *Shakespeare from the Margins: Language, Culture, Context.* Chicago: University of Chicago
        Press.
Paschal, Roy
1960   *Design and Truth in Autobiography.* Cambridge, Mass.: Harvard University Press.
Patte, Daniel
1994   "Acknowledging the Contextual Character of Male, European-American Critical
        Exegeses: An Androcritical Perspective." In *Reading from this Place.* Vol. 1. *Social Location
        and Biblical Interpretation in the United States.* Ed. Fernando F. Segovia and Mary Ann
        Tolbert. Minneapolis: Fortress Press, 35–55.
1995   *Ethics of Biblical Interpretation: A Reevaluation.* Louisville, Ky.: Westminster John Knox
        Press.
Peiss, Kathy, and Christina Simmons, eds.
1989   *Passion and Power: Sexuality in History.* Philadelphia: Temple University Press.

Perelman, Chaïm, and Lucie Olbrechts-Tyteca
1969   *The New Rhetoric: A Treatise on Argumentation.* Trans. John Wilkinson and Purcell Weaver.
           Notre Dame, Ind.: University of Notre Dame Press.
Phillips, Gary A.
1994   "The Ethics of Reading Deconstructively, or Speaking Face-to-Face: The Samaritan
           Woman Meets Derrida at the Well." In *The New Literary Criticism and the New Testament.*
           Ed. Edgar V. McKnight and Elizabeth Struthers Malbon. Valley Forge, Pa.: Trinity
           Press International, 283–325.
Phillips, Gary, and Danna Nolan Fewell
1997   "Ethics, Bible, Reading as if." *Semeia* 77: 1–21.
Phillips, Gary, and Danna Nolan Fewell, eds.
1997   *The Bible and Ethics of Reading. Semeia* 77.
Pickstock, Catherine
1998   *After Writing: On the Liturgical Consummation of Philosophy.* Oxford: Blackwell.
Pieris, Aloysius, S.J.
1988   *An Asian Theology of Liberation.* Faith Meets Faith Series. Maryknoll, N.Y.: Orbis Books.
Pippin, Tina
1996a   "'For Fear of the Jews': Lying and Truth Telling in Translating the Gospel of John."
           Semeia 76: 81–98.
1996b   "Ideology, Ideological Criticism, and the Bible." *Currents in Research: Biblical Studies* 4:
           51–78.
Pixley, George V.
1970   "Whitehead y Marx sobre la dinámica de la historia." *Dialogos* 7: 83–107.
Plate, S. Brent
1997   "Obfuscation: Maurice Blanchot's Religious Recitation of the Limits." *Literature and
           Theology* 11: 239–53.
Plotinus
1987   *Enneads.* Vol. 5. Trans. A. H. Armstrong. Loeb Classical Library. Cambridge, Mass.:
           Harvard University Press.
Pluhacek, Stephen, and Heidi Bostic
1996   "Thinking Life as Relation: An Interview with Luce Irigaray." *Man and World* 29:
           343–60.
Plutarch
1936   *Moralia.* Vol 10. Trans. Harold North Fowler. Loeb Classical Library. Cambridge, Mass.:
           Harvard University Press.
Polanyi, Michael
1962   *Personal Knowledge: Towards a Post-Critical Philosophy.* Chicago: University of Chicago
           Press.
Poliakov, Leon
1974   *The Aryan Myth: A History of Racist and Nationalist Ideas in Europe.* Trans. Edmund Howard.
           New York: Basic Books.
Poster, Mark
1990   *The Mode of Information. Poststructuralism and Social Context.* Chicago: University of
           Chicago Press.
Poteat, William H.
1990   *A Philosophical Daybook: Post-Critical Investigations.* Columbia: University of Missouri
           Press.
Prager, Jeffrey
1998   *Presenting the Past: Psychoanalysis and the Sociology of Misremembering.* Cambridge, Mass.:
           Harvard University Press.
Pucci, Pietro
1992   *Oedipus and the Fabrication of the Father: Oedipus Tyrannus in Modern Criticism and Philosophy.*
           Baltimore: Johns Hopkins University Press.
Rabkin, Eric S.
1976   *The Fantastic in Literature.* Princeton, N.J.: Princeton University Press.
Rad, Gerhard von
1973   *Genesis: A Commentary.* Trans. John H. Marks. Old Testament Library. Philadelphia:
           Westminster Press.
Rashkow, Ilona N.
1993   *The Phallacy of Genesis: A Feminist-Psychoanalytic Approach.* Louisville, Ky.: Westminster/
           John Knox Press.

Reinhartz, Adele
1997   "A Nice Jewish Girl Reads the Gospel of John." *Semeia* 77: 177–93.
Reiss, Timothy
1982   *The Discourse of Modernism.* Ithaca, N.Y.: Cornell University Press.
Rich, Adrienne
1980   "Compulsory Heterosexuality and Lesbian Existence." *Signs: Journal of Women in Culture and Society* 5: 631–60.
Richardson, Diane, ed.
1996   *Theorizing Heterosexuality: Telling It Straight.* Philadelphia: Open University Press.
Robertson, Ritchie
1988   "Freud's Testament: *Moses and Monotheism.*" In *Freud in Exile. Psychoanalysis and Its Vicissitudes.* Ed. Edward Timms and Naomi Segal. New Haven, Conn.: Yale University Press.
Robinson, Paul
1976   *The Modernization of Sex.* New York: Harper & Row.
Rockmore, Tom, and Beth J. Singer
1992   *Antifoundationalism Old and New.* Philadelphia: Temple University Press.
Rorty, Richard
1979   *Philosophy and the Mirror of Nature.* Princeton, N.J.: Princeton University Press.
1989   *Contingency, Irony and Solidarity.* New York: Cambridge University Press.
1991   *Objectivity, Relativism, and Truth.* New York: Cambridge University Press.
Rosaldo, Renato
1989   *Culture and Truth: The Remaking of Social Analysis.* Boston: Beacon Press.
Rose, Paul Lawrence
1992   *Revolutionary Antisemitism from Kant to Wagner.* Princeton, N. J.: Princeton University Press.
Rosen, Alan
1994   "'Familiarly Known as Kittel': The Moral Politics of the *Theological Dictionary of the New Testament.*" In *Tainted Greatness. Antisemitism and Cultural Heroes.* Ed. Nancy Harrowitz. Philadelphia: Temple University Press.
Rosen, Stanley
1987   *Hermeneutics as Politics.* New York: Oxford University Press.
Rubin, Gayle
1992   "Thinking Sex: Notes Toward a Radical Theory of the Politics of Sexuality." In *Pleasure and Danger: Exploring Female Sexuality.* Ed. C. Vance. Rev. ed. London and Boston: Routledge and Kegan Paul, 267–321.
Rubin, Gayle, with Judith Butler
1997   "Sexual Traffic, Interview." In *Feminism Meets Queer Theory.* Ed. Elizabeth Weed and Naomi Schor. Bloomington: Indiana University Press, 68–108.
Ruether, Rosemary Radford
1969   *Gregory of Nazianzus: Rhetor and Philosopher.* Oxford: Clarendon Press.
1975   *New Woman/New Earth: Sexist Ideologies and Human Liberation.* Boston: Beacon Press.
1983   *Sexism and God-Talk: Toward a Feminist Theology.* Boston: Beacon Press.
Sack, Robert D.
1986   *Human Territoriality. Its Theory and History.* Cambridge, U.K.: Cambridge University Press.
Said, Edward
1978   *Orientalism: Western Conceptions of the Orient.* London: Penguin.
1993   *Culture and Imperialism.* New York: Alfred A. Knopf.
Samuel, Simon
forthcoming
          "The Colonial Cross: A Postcolonial Reading of the Gospel According to Mark." Ph.D. dissertation. Sheffield, U.K.: University of Sheffield.
San Juan, Epifanio, Jr.
1998   *Beyond Postcolonial Theory.* New York: St. Martin's Press.
Sanders, Boykin
1995   "In Search of a Face for Simon the Cyrene." In Bailey and Grant 1995, 51–64.
Sarna, Nahum M.
1989   *Genesis: The Traditional Hebrew Text with the New JPS Translation.* JPS Torah Commentary. Philadelphia: JPS.

Schacter, Daniel L., ed.
1995   *Memory Distortion. How Minds, Brains, and Societies Reconstruct the Past.* Cambridge, Mass.: Harvard University Press.

Schneiders, Sandra M.
1989   "Feminist Ideology Criticism and Biblical Hermeneutics." *Biblical Theology Bulletin* 19: 3–10.

Schor, Naomi
1994a   "Previous Engagements: The Receptions of Irigaray." In *Engaging with Irigaray.* New York: Columbia University Press, 3–14.
1994b   "This Essentialism Which Is Not One: Coming to Grips with Irigaray." In *Engaging with Irigaray.* New York: Columbia University Press, 57–78.

Schudson, Michael
1995   "Dynamics of Distortion in Collective Memory." In *Memory Distortion.* Ed. Daniel Schachter. Cambridge, Mass.: Harvard University Press.

Schulte-Sasse, Jochen
1988   "The Concept of Literary Criticism in German Romanticism, 1795–1810." In Hohendahl 1988, 99–177.

Schüssler Fiorenza, Elisabeth
1985   *In Memory of Her. A Feminist Reconstruction of Christian Origins.* New York: Crossroad.
1988   "The Ethics of Biblical Interpretation: Decentering Biblical Scholarship." *Journal of Biblical Literature* 107: 3–17.
1989   "Biblical Interpretation and Critical Commitment." *Studia Theologica* 43: 5–18.
1994   *Jesus. Miriam's Child, Sophia's Prophet: Critical Issues in Feminist Christology.* New York: Continuum.
1999   *Rhetoric and Ethic. The Politics of Biblical Studies.* Minneapolis: Fortress Press.

Schüssler Fiorenza, Elisabeth, and David Tracy, eds.
1984   *The Holocaust as Interruption.* Edinburgh: T. & T. Clark.

Schwartz, Regina
1997   *The Curse of Cain. The Violent Legacy of Monotheism.* Chicago: University of Chicago Press.

Sedgwick, Eve Kosofsky
1989   *Epistemology of the Closet.* Berkeley: University of California Press.

Segal, Lynne
1994   *Straight Sex: The Politics of Pleasure.* London: Virago.
1997   "Feminist Sexual Politics and the Heterosexual Predicament." In *New Sexual Agendas.* Ed. L. Segal. New York: New York University Press.

Segovia, Fernando F.
1998   "Biblical Criticism and Postcolonial Studies: Toward a Postcolonial Optic." In *The Postcolonial Bible.* Ed. R. S. Sugirtharajah. Sheffield, U.K.: Sheffield Academic Press, 49–65.

Segovia, Fernando F., ed.
2000   *Interpreting Beyond Borders.* The Bible and Postcolonialism 3. Sheffield, U.K.: Sheffield Academic Press.

Segovia, Fernando F., and Mary Ann Tolbert, eds.
1995a   *Reading from This Place.* Vol. 1. *Social Location and Biblical Interpretation in the United States.* Minneapolis: Fortress Press.
1995b   *Reading from This Place.* Vol. 2. *Social Location and Biblical Interpretation in Global Perspective.* Minneapolis: Fortress Press.

Seidman, Steven
1990   *Romantic Longings.* New York and London: Routledge.
1992   *Embattled Eros: Sexual Politics and Ethics in Contemporary America.* New York and London: Routledge.

Sellin, Ernst
1922   *Mose und seine Bedeutung für die Israelitisch-jüdische Religionsgeschichte.* Leipzig: A. Deicherlsche Verlagsbuchhandlung.

Sewell, William H., Jr.
1999   "The Concept(s) of Culture." In *Beyond the Cultural Turn.* Ed. Victoria Bonnell and Lynn Hunt. Berkeley: University of California Press, 35–61.

Shannon, David
1995   "'An Ante-bellum Sermon': A Resource of an African American Hermeneutic." In Felder 1995, 98–123.

Shell, Marc
1978   *The Economy of Literature.* Baltimore: Johns Hopkins University Press.
1982   *Money, Language, and Thought: Literary and Philosophical Economies from the Medieval to the Modern Era.* Baltimore: Johns Hopkins University Press.
Shepherdson, Charles
1994   "The Role of Gender and the Imperative of Sex." In *Supposing the Subject(s).* Ed. Joan Copjec. London: Verso, 158–84.
Sherburne, Donald W., ed.
1966   *A Key to Whitehead's* Process and Reality. Bloomington: Indiana University Press.
Sherwood, Yvonne M.
1996   "Derrida Among the Prophets." In *The Prostitute and the Prophet: Hosea's Marriage in Literary-Theoretical Perspective.* Sheffield, U.K.: Sheffield Academic Press, 150–253.
Shils, Edward
1968   "Ideology: The Concept and Function of Ideology." In *International Encyclopedia of the Social Sciences.* New York: Macmillan, 66–76.
Shirato, Tony
1993   "My Space or Yours? De Certeau, Frow and the Meanings of Popular Culture." *Cultural Studies* 7, no. 2: 282–91.
Siebers, Tobin
1984   *The Romantic Fantastic.* Ithaca, N.Y.: Cornell University Press.
Silverman, Kaja
1996   *The Threshold of the Visible World.* London/New York: Routledge.
Sim, Stuart
1986   "Lyotard and the Politics of Antifoundationalism." *Radical Philosophy* (Autumn): 8–13.
Simon, Sherry
1996   *Gender in Translation: Cultural Identity and the Politics of Transmission.* Translation Studies. New York: Routledge.
Simon, William
1996   *Postmodern Sexualities.* New York and London: Routledge.
Smith, Abraham
1995   "Toni Morrison's *Song of Solomon:* The Blues and the Bible." In Bailey and Grant 1995, 107–15.
1996   "The Productive Role of English Bible Translators." *Semeia* 76: 55–68.
1997   "'I Saw the Book Talk': A Cultural Studies Approach to the Ethics of an African American Biblical Hermeneutics." *Semeia* 77: 115–38.
Smith, Sidonie
1987   *A Poetics of Women's Autobiography: Marginality and the Fictions of Self-Representation.* Bloomington: Indiana University Press.
Smith-Christopher, Daniel
1995   *Text & Experience: Towards a Cultural Exegesis of the Bible.* Sheffield, U.K.: Sheffield Academic Press.
Smyth, Damian Barry
1999   *The Trauma of the Cross: How the Followers of Jesus Came to Understand the Crucifixion.* New York: Paulist Press.
Snell-Hornby, Mary
1988   *Translation Studies: An Integrated Approach.* Amsterdam: John Benjamins.
Snitow, Ann, Christine Stansell, and Sharon Thompson, eds.
1983   *Powers of Desire: The Politics of Sexuality.* New York: Monthly Review Press.
Snowden, Frank M., Jr.
1970   *Blacks in Antiquity: Ethiopians in the Greco-Roman Experience.* Cambridge, Mass.: Harvard University Press.
Soja, Edward W.
1996   *Thirdspace: Journeys to Los Angeles and Other Real-and-Imagined Places.* Cambridge, Mass.: Blackwell.
Spelman, Elizabeth
1988   *Inessential Woman: Problems of Exclusion in Feminist Thought.* Boston: Beacon Press.
Spivak, Gayatri Chakravorty
1985   "Can the Subaltern Speak? Speculations on Widow-Sacrifice." *Wedge* (Winter/Spring): 120–30. Excerpted in *The Post-Colonial Studies Reader.* Ed. Bill Ashcroft, Gareth Griffiths, and Helen Tiffin. London and New York: Routledge, 24–28.

1987   *In Other Worlds: Essays in Cultural Politics.* New York: Methuen.
1990   *The Post-Colonial Critic: Interviews, Strategies, Dialogues.* Ed. Sarah Harasym. London and New York: Routledge.
1998   *A Critique of Postcolonial Reason: Toward a History of the Vanishing Present.* Cambridge, Mass.: Harvard University Press.
Staley, Jeffrey L.
1995   *Reading with a Passion: Rhetoric, Autobiography, and the American West in the Gospel of John.* New York: Continuum.
1999   "Fathers and Sons: Fragments from an Autobiographical Midrash on John's Gospel." In *The Personal Voice in Biblical Interpretation.* Ed. Ingrid Rosa Kitzberger. London: Routledge, 65–85.
forthcoming
        "Disseminations: An Autobiographical Midrash on Fatherhood in John's Gospel." *Semeia.*
Stanford, Michael
1998   *An Introduction to the Philosophy of History.* Oxford: Basil Blackwell.
Stanton, Donna, ed.
1992   *Discourses of Sexuality: From Aristotle to AIDS.* Ann Arbor: University of Michigan Press.
Stanton, Graham N.
1984   "The Gospel of Matthew and Judaism." *Bulletin of the John Rylands University Library of Manchester* 66, no. 2: 109–19.
Steiner, George
1975   *After Babel: Aspects of Language and Translation.* New York: Oxford University Press.
Stendahl, Krister
1962   "Biblical Theology, Contemporary." In *The Interpreter's Dictionary of the Bible.* Ed. George Arthur Buttrick. Vol. 1. Nashville: Abingdon Press, 418–32.
Stern, David
1988   "Midrash and Indeterminacy." *Critical Inquiry* 15, no. 1: 132–62.
Sternberg, Meir
1985   *The Poetics of Biblical Narrative: Ideological Literature and the Drama of Reading.* Indiana Studies in Biblical Literature. Bloomington: Indiana University Press.
Stoler, Ann Laura
1991   "Carnal Knowledge and Imperial Power: Gender, Race, and Morality in Colonial Asia." In *Gender at the Crossroads of Knowledge: Feminist Anthropology in the Postmodern Era.* Ed. M. di Leonardo. Berkeley: University of California Press.
1995   *Race and the Education of Desire.* Durham, N.C.: Duke University Press.
Stone, Ira
1996   *Reading Levinas/Reading Talmud.* Philadelphia: Jewish Publication Society.
Stone, Ken
1996   *Sex, Honor and Power in the Deuteronomistic History.* Sheffield, U.K.: Sheffield Academic Press.
1997a   "The Hermeneutics of Abomination: On Gay Men, Canaanites, and Biblical Interpretation." *Biblical Theology Bulletin* 27: 36–41.
1997b   "Biblical Interpretation as a Technology of the Self: Gay Men and the Ethics of Reading." *Semeia* 77: 139–55.
Stout, Jeffrey
1981   *The Flight from Authority: Religion, Morality, and the Quest for Autonomy.* Notre Dame, Ind.: University of Notre Dame Press.
1986   "The Relativity of Interpretation." *The Monist* 69: 103–18.
1988   *Ethics after Babel: The Languages of Morals and Their Discontents.* Boston: Beacon Press.
Stuart, Elizabeth, et al.
1997   *Religion Is a Queer Thing: A Guide to the Christian Faith for Lesbian, Gay, Bisexual and Transgendered People.* Cleveland: Pilgrim Press.
Sturm, Douglas
1998   *Solidarity and Suffering: Toward a Politics of Relationality.* Albany: State University of New York Press.
Suchocki, Marjorie Hewitt
1997   *God, Christ, Church: A Practical Guide to Process Theology.* New rev. ed. New York: Crossroad. (First ed., 1986.)
Sugirtharajah, R. S.
1991   *Voices from the Margin: Interpreting the Bible in the Third World.* New York: Orbis Books.

1996   "Textual Cleansing: A Move from the Colonial to the Postcolonial Version." *Semeia* 76: 7–20.
1998a   *Asian Biblical Hermeneutics and Postcolonialism: Contesting the Interpretations.* Maryknoll, N.Y.: Orbis Books.
1998b   "A Postcolonial Exploration of Collusion and Construction in Biblical Interpretation." In *The Postcolonial Bible.* Ed. R. S. Sugirtharajah. Sheffield, U.K.: Sheffield Academic Press, 91–116.
Sugirtharajah, R. S., ed.
1998c   *The Postcolonial Bible.* The Bible and Postcolonialism, 1. Sheffield, U.K.: Sheffield Academic Press.
1999   *Postcolonial Perspectives on the New Testament and Its Interpretation. Journal for the Study of the New Testament* 73 (thematic issue).
forthcoming
            The Postcolonial Bible Commentary. Sheffield, U.K.: Sheffield Academic Press.
Suleiman, Susan R., and Inge Crosman, eds.
1980   *The Reader in the Text: Essays on Audience and Interpretation.* Princeton, N.J.: Princeton University Press.
Suleri, Sara
1995   "Criticism and Its Alterity." In *Borders, Boundaries, and Frames: Essays in Criticism and Cultural Studies. Essays from the English Institute.* Ed. Mae Henderson. New York: Routledge, 171–82.
Taber, Charles R.
1978   "Translation as Interpretation." *Interpretation* 32: 130–43.
Taylor, Charles
1989   *Sources of the Self: The Making of the Modern Identity.* Cambridge, Mass.: Harvard University Press.
Taylor, Mark C.
1984   *Erring: A Postmodern A/theology.* Chicago: Chicago University Press.
1986   *Deconstruction in Context: Literature and Philosophy.* Chicago: Chicago University Press.
Thiel, John E.
1994   *Nonfoundationalism.* Minneapolis: Fortress Press.
Thiselton, Anthony
1992   *New Horizons in Hermeneutics: The Theory and Practice of Transforming Biblical Reading.* Grand Rapids, Mich.: Zondervan.
Thompson, E. P.
1963   *The Making of the English Working Class.* London: Gollancz.
Thompson, John B.
1990   *Ideology and Modern Culture: Critical Social Theory in the Era of Mass Communication.* Stanford, Calif.: Stanford University Press.
Thomson, George
1955   *Studies in Ancient Greek Society.* Vol. 2. *The First Philosophers.* London: Lawrence and Wishart.
1973   *Aeschylus and Athens: A Study in the Social Origins of Drama.* London: Lawrence and Wishart.
Thomson, J. A. K.
1970   *The Ethics of Aristotle: Nicomachean Ethics.* London: Penguin Books. (Reprint.)
Todd, Douglas
1996   *Brave Souls: Writers and Artists Wrestle with God, Love, Death, and the Things That Matter.* Toronto: Stoddart.
Todorov, Tzvetan
1975   *The Fantastic: A Structural Approach to a Literary Genre.* Ithaca, N.Y.: Cornell University Press.
1984   *Mikhail Bakhtin: The Dialogical Principle.* Trans. W. Godzich. Minneapolis: University of Minnesota Press.
Tolkien, J. R. R.
1965   "On Fairy Stories." In *Twig and Leaf.* Boston: Houghton, 3–48.
Tompkins, Jane P., ed.
1980   *Reader-Response Criticism: From Formalism to Post-Structuralism.* Baltimore: Johns Hopkins University Press.
1988   "Me and My Shadow." *New Literary History* 19: 168–78.

Torok, M.
1964   "L'Envie Du Pénis Sous La Femme." In *La Sexualité Feminine: Nouvelle Recherche Psychanalyse.* Paris: Payon.
Toury, Gideon
1979   *In Search of a Theory of Translation.* Tel Aviv: Porter Institute for Poetics and Semiotics.
Tracy, David
1981   *The Analogical Imagination: Christian Theology and the Culture of Pluralism.* New York: Crossroad.
1991   *Dialogue with the Other: The Inter-Religious Dialogue.* Louvain Theological and Pastoral Monographs. Vol. 1. Leuven: Peeters Uitgeverij; reprint, Grand Rapids, Mich.: Eerdmans. (Orig., 1990.)
Trible, Phyllis
1973   "Depatriarchalizing in Biblical Interpretation." *Journal of the American Academy of Religion* 41: 30–48.
Tull, Patricia K.
1999   "Rhetorical Criticism and Intertextuality." In *To Each Its Own Meaning: An Introduction to Biblical Criticisms and Their Application.* Rev. and exp. ed. Ed. Steven L. McKenzie and Stephen R. Haynes. Louisville, Ky.: Westminster John Knox Press.
Turner, Denys
1995   *Eros and Allegory: Medieval Exegesis of the Song of Songs.* Kalamazoo, Mich.: Cistercian Publications.
Valesio, Paolo
1980   *Novantiqua: Rhetorics as a Contemporary Theory.* Advances in Semiotics. Ed. Thomas A. Sebeok. Bloomington: Indiana University Press.
van Alphen, Ernst
1999   "Symptoms of Discursivity: Experience, Memory, and Trauma." In *Acts of Memory: Cultural Recall in the Present.* Ed. Mieke Bal, Jonathan Crewe, and Leo Spitzer. Hanover, N.H.: University Press of New England.
van Herk, Aritha
1991   *In Visible Ink: Crypto-frictions.* Edmonton, Alberta, Canada: NeWest Publishers.
1992   *A Frozen Tongue.* Sydney: Dangaroo Press.
van der Kolk, Bessel, and Otto van der Hart
1995   "The Intrusive Past: The Flexibility of Memory and the Engraving of Trauma." In *Trauma.* Ed. Cathy Caruth. Baltimore: Johns Hopkins University Press.
Vance, Carole
1989   "Social Construction Theory: Problems in the History of Sexuality." In D. Altman, et al., *Homosexuality, Which Homosexuality?* Amsterdam: Uitgeverij An Dekker/Schorer.
1991   "Anthropology Rediscovers Sexuality: A Theoretical Comment." *Social Science and Medicine* 33, no. 8: 875–84.
Vance, Carole, ed.
1992   *Pleasure and Danger: Exploring Female Sexuality.* Rev. ed. London and Boston: Pandora Press.
Veeser, H. Aram, ed.
1996   *Confessions of the Critics.* New York: Routledge.
Venuti, Lawrence, ed.
1991   *Rethinking Translation: Discourse, Subjectivity, Ideology.* New York: Routledge.
Vice, Sue, ed.
1984   *Psychoanalytic Criticism: Theory and Practice.* London/New York: Methuen.
1996   *Psychoanalytic Criticism: A Reader.* Cambridge, U.K.: Polity Press.
Vickers, Brian
1988   *In Defense of Rhetoric.* New York: Oxford University Press; Oxford: Clarendon Press.
Volosinov, V. I.
1973   *Marxism and the Philosophy of Language.* Trans. L. Matejka and I. Titunik. Cambridge, Mass.: Harvard University Press.
1987   *Freudianism: A Critical Sketch.* Ed. I. Titunik and N. Bruss. Trans. I. Titunik. Bloomington: Indiana University Press.
Vos, J. S.
1984   "Antijudaismus/Antisemitismus im *Theologischen Wörterbuch zum Neuen Testament.*" *Nederlands Theologisch Tijdschrift* 38 (1984): 89–110.

Wall, Thomas Carl
1999   *Radical Passivity: Levinas, Blanchot, Agamben.* Albany: State University of New York Press.
Walsh, W. H.
1971   "Principle and Prejudice in Hegel's Philosophy of History." In *Hegel's Political Philosophy: Problems and Perspectives.* Ed. Z. A. Pelczynski. Cambridge, U.K.: Cambridge University Press, 181–98.
Ward, Graham
1996   "The Voice of the Other." *New Blackfriars* 77: 518–28.
2000   *The Certeau Reader.* Cambridge, Mass.: Blackwell.
Warner, Michael
1999   *The Trouble With Normal: Sex, Politics, and the Ethics of Queer Life.* New York: Free Press.
Warrior, Robert Allan
1989   "Canaanites, Cowboys, and Indians: Deliverance, Conquest, and Liberation Theology Today." *Christianity and Crisis* 49 (September 11): 261–65.
Wasserstrom, Jeffrey N.
1998   "Are You Now or Have You Ever Been Postmodern?" *The Chronicle of Higher Education* 45, no. 3 (September 11).
Waters, John
1991   "Who Was Hagar?" In Felder 1991, 187–205.
Watson, Francis
1995   "A Response to Professor Rowland." *Scottish Journal of Theology* 48: 518–20.
1997   *Text and Truth: Redefining Biblical Theology.* Edinburgh: T. & T. Clark.
Webb, Stephen H.
1991   *Re-Figuring Theology: The Rhetoric of Karl Barth.* SUNY Series in Rhetoric and Theology. Ed. David Tracy and Stephen H. Webb. Albany: State University of New York Press.
1993   *Webster's Third New International Dictionary of the English Language.* Springfield, Mass.: Merriam-Webster.
Weed, Elizabeth, and Naomi Schor, eds.
1997   *Feminism Meets Queer Theory: Books from Differences.* Bloomington: Indiana University Press.
Weedon, Chris
1987   *Feminist Practice & Poststructuralist Theory.* Cambridge, Mass.: Blackwell.
Weeks, Jeffrey
1985   *Sexuality and Its Discontents: Meanings, Myths and Modern Sexualities.* London and Boston: Routledge and Kegan Paul.
1986   *Sexuality.* London and New York: Routledge.
1989   *Sex, Politics and Society: The Regulation of Sexuality Since 1800.* 2d ed. New York and London: Longman.
1997   "Sexual Values Revisited." In *New Sexual Agendas.* Ed. L. Segal. New York: New York University Press.
West, Cornel
1982   *Prophesy Deliverance! An Afro-American Revolutionary Christianity.* Philadelphia: Westminster Press.
1986   "Ethics and Action in Fredric Jameson's Marxist Hermeneutics." In *Postmodernism and Politics.* Ed. Jonathan Arac. Minneapolis: University of Minnesota Press, 123–44.
1989   *The American Evasion of Philosophy: A Genealogy of Pragmatism.* Madison: University of Wisconsin Press.
West, Gerald O.
1995   *Biblical Hermeneutics of Liberation: Modes of Reading the Bible in the South African Context.* 2d ed. Maryknoll, N.Y.: Orbis Books.
West, Gerald, and Musa W. Dube, eds.
1996   *"Reading With": An Exploration of the Interface Between Critical and Ordinary Readings of the Bible. African Overtures. Semeia* 73.
West, Mona
1999   "Reading the Bible as Queer Americans: Social Location and the Hebrew Scriptures." *Theology and Sexuality* 10: 28–42.
Westermann, Claus
1984   *Genesis 12–36: A Commentary.* Trans. John Scullion. Minneapolis: Augsburg.

Wevers, John W.
1992   *Notes on the Greek Text of Genesis.* SBLSCS 35. Atlanta: Scholars Press.
White, Hayden
1973   *Metahistory: The Historical Imagination in Nineteenth-Century Europe.* Baltimore: Johns Hopkins University Press.
1978   *Tropics of Discourse. Essays in Cultural Criticism.* Baltimore: Johns Hopkins University Press.
1989   "'Figuring the Nature of the Times Deceased': Literary Theory and Historical Writing." In *The Future of Literary Theory.* Ed. Ralph Cohen. New York: Routledge, 19–43.
Whitehead, Alfred North
1978   *Process and Reality: An Essay in Cosmology.* Corrected ed. Ed. David Ray Griffin and Donald W. Sherburne. New York: Free Press. (First ed., 1933.)
Whitford, Margaret
1991   *Luce Irigaray: Philosophy in the Feminine.* London: Routledge.
Williams, Delores S.
1993   *Sisters in the Wilderness. The Challenge of Womanist God-Talk.* Maryknoll, N.Y.: Orbis Books.
Williams, Patrick, and Laura Chrisman, eds.
1994   *Colonial Discourse and Post-Colonial Theory: A Reader.* New York: Columbia University Press.
Williams, Raymond
1958   *Culture and Society, 1780–1950.* London: Chatto & Windus.
1980   "Base and Superstructure in Marxist Cultural Theory." In *Problems in Materialism and Culture.* London: Verso.
1983   *Keywords: A Vocabulary of Culture and Society.* Rev. ed. London: Fontana.
Wilson, Norman J.
1999   *History in Crisis? Recent Directions in Historiography.* Upper Saddle River, N.J.: Prentice Hall.
Wimbush, Vincent
1995   "The Bible and African Americans: An Outline of an Interpretive History." In Felder 1995, 81–97.
1998   "Interrupting the Spin: What Would Happen Were African Americans to Become the Starting Point for the Academic Study of the Bible?" *Union Seminary Quarterly Review* 61: 52–76.
Wimsatt, William K., Jr., and Monroe Beardsley
1954   "The Intentional Fallacy." In *The Verbal Icon.* Lexington: University of Kentucky Press, 3–18.
Winkler, John J.
1990   *The Constraints of Desire: The Anthropology of Sex and Gender in Ancient Greece.* New York and London: Routledge.
Wittgenstein, Ludwig
1953   *Philosophical Investigations.* 3d. ed. Trans. G. E. M. Anscombe. New York: Macmillan.
Wittig, Monique
1992   *The Straight Mind.* Boston: Beacon Press.
Wood, Nancy
1999   *Vectors of Memory. Legacies of Trauma in Postwar Europe.* Oxford: Berg.
Woodward, Kathryn, ed.
1997   *Identity and Difference: Culture, Media, and Identities.* London: Sage/Open University.
Wright, Elizabeth
1984   *Psychoanalytic Criticism: Theory in Practice.* London: Methuen.
Yee, Gale A.
1995   "Ideological Criticism: Judges 17–21 and the Dismembered Body." In *Judges and Method: New Approaches in Biblical Studies.* Ed. Gale A. Yee. Minneapolis: Fortress Press, 146–70.
Yerushalmi, Yosef Hayim
1991   *Freud's Moses: Judaism Terminable and Interminable.* New Haven, Conn.: Yale University Press.
Yilibuw, Dolores
1996   "Tampering with Bible Translation in Yap." *Semeia* 76: 21–38.

Young, Alan
1996   "Bodily Memory and Traumatic Memory." In *Tense Past.* Ed. Paul Antze and Michael
            Lambek. New York: Routledge.
Young, Iris Marion
1997   *Intersecting Voices: Dilemmas of Gender, Political Philosophy, and Policy.* Princeton, N.J.:
            Princeton University Press.
Young, Robert J. C.
2000   *Postcolonialism: An Historical Introduction.* Oxford: Blackwell.
Zeitlin, Froma
1996   "The Dynamics of Misogyny: Myth and Mythmaking in Aeschylus's *Oresteia.*" In *Playing
            the Other; Gender and Society in Classical Greek Literature.* Women in Culture and Society.
            Chicago: University of Chicago Press, 87–119.
Zipes, Jack
1988   *Fairy Tales and the Art of Subversion: The Classical Genre for Children and the Process of
            Civilization.* New York: Methuen.
Žižek, Slavoj
1991   *Looking Awry: An Introduction to Jacques Lacan through Popular Culture.* Cambridge, Mass.:
            MIT Press.
1993   *Tarrying with the Negative: Kant, Hegel, and the Critique of Ideology.* Durham, N.C.: Duke
            University Press.
1994   *The Metastases of Enjoyment: Six Essays on Woman and Causality.* London/New York:
            Verso.
1996   "'I Hear You with My Eyes'; or, The Invisible Master." In *Gaze and Voice as Love Objects.*
            Ed. Renata Saleci and Slavoj Žižek. Durham, N.C.: Duke University Press, 90–126.
1997   *The Plague of Fantasies.* London/New York: Verso.
Žižek, Slavoj, ed.
1994   *Mapping Ideology.* London: Verso.

index

Achebe, Chinua, 183
Adam, A. K. M., vii–ix, 8–13, 113, 126, 175, 176, 177, 179–80, 201, 227–29
Adorno, Theodor, 70–72, 139, 140
Aejmelaeus, Anneli, 254–55
Ahearne, Jeremy, 42–43, 194
Ahmad, Aijaz, 182
Aichele, George, 62–68, 90
Akiva, R., 172–73
Albright, William Foxwell, 232
Alcoff, Linda, 18
allegory, allegorical interpretation, 9, 66, 274
Alter, Robert, 259
Althusser, Louis, 51–52, 121–22, 139, 140, 252
Altizer, Thomas, 74
Anderson, Janice Capel, 17–18, 117, 175
Anderson, Pamela Sue, 147–48
Anderson, Victor, 213, 219
Anidjar, Gil, 172–73
Anthony, Elliot, 145
anti-postmodernism, 1–7
Appiah, Kwame Anthony, 213–19
Appleby, Joyce, 113
Aquila, 258–59
Aquinas, Thomas, 49–50
Arbib, Michael, 228
Aristotle, 70–72, 100, 189–94, 221–23, 226
Armour, Ellen T., 133, 137
Arnheim, Rudoph, 247–48
Arnold, Matthew, 49–50
Artaud, Antonin, 63
Ashcroft, Bill, 182, 183
Assmann, Jan, 265–66
Augustine, 14–15, 50–51, 56, 223, 225, 226
author, 8–13, 24–25, 39–40, 56–57, 123, 124–26

autobiography, 14–19, 36, 113, 117–19

Bach, Alice, 229
Bailey, Randall C., 114–17, 119, 215–16, 231–32, 236
Baker, Lee D., 213
Bakhtin, M. M., 20–27, 128, 144
Bal, Mieke, 5, 229, 231–32, 234
Barkan, Elazar, 213–14
Barnestone, Willis, 255–57
Barr, James, 254–55
Barth, Karl, 53–54, 218
Barthes, Roland, 8–11, 47–48, 63, 108, 125, 139
Barton, John, 249–50
Bass, Dorothy, 196
Bassnett, 257
Bataille, Georges, 28–34, 37, 71, 146
Bateson, Gregory, 64
Baudelaire, Charles, 146
Baudrillard, Jean, 28, 165, 225, 252
Bauerschmidt, Frederick C., 42, 194
Bauman, Zygmunt, 5, 76, 82–83, 154–55, 159, 217, 227
Baur, F. C., 219
Beal, Timothy K., 28–34, 128–30, 246
Beardslee, Monroe, 8
Beardslee, William A., 199–205
being/Being, 30–31, 36–37, 55–56, 80–81, 82–83, 103–4, 155–59, 219, 251–52, 274
Beiser, Frederick, 218
Bell, M., 27
Belsey, Catherine, 195–96
Benjamin, A., 257
Benjamin, Walter, 54, 139, 140, 256

race, 49, 52, 74–75, 100, 103, 113, 116–17, 124, 185, 206, 200–211, 213–19, 230–31, 235–36, 243
Rad, Gerhard von, 259
Ramus, Peter, 223
Rashkow, Ilona N., 151–59, 234
Reinhartz, Adele, 176
Reiss, Timothy, 227
Renan, Ernest, 218
rhetoric, 18–19, 27, 70, 71, 72, 87, 165, 175–76, 177, 220–26, 252
Rich, Adrienne, 100–101, 121–22
Richardson, Diane, 152–53, 237
Rilke, Ranier Marie, 39
Robbins, Vernon, 224
Robertson, Ritchie, 265–66
Robinson, Paul, 233
Rockmore, Tom, 268–69
Rorty, Richard, 5, 70–72, 165, 247–48, 272
Rosaldo, Renato, 113–14
Rose, Paul Lawrence, 213
Rosen, Alan, 263–64
Rosen, Stanley, 6
Rousseau, Jean-Jacques, 15
Rubin, Gayle, 104–5, 208–10, 238
Ruether, Rosemary Radford, 124, 211, 221
Russell, Bertrand, 70–72

Sack, Robert D., 239
Said, Edward, 115–16, 183–84, 187, 188, 213, 217–19
Samuel, Simon, 187–88
San Juan, Epifanio, Jr., 183
Sanders, Boykin, 215
Sarna, Nahum M., 259
Sartre, Jean-Paul, 102–3, 139, 140, 156
Saussure, Ferdinande, 44, 152, 195–96
Schiller, Friedrich, 140
Schlegel, Friedrich, 215
Schneider, Laurel C., 206–12
scholarship, 47–48, 69, 109, 115–

16, 117, 120, 123, 126–27, 180–81, 186, 188, 213–19, 227–32, 243, 246, 247
Schor, Naomi, 132–33
Schudson, Michael, 263
Schulte-Sasse, Jochen, 218
Schüssler Fiorenza, Elisabeth, 112, 127, 176–78, 180, 216, 224, 229, 230, 263
Schwartz, Regina, 228, 261
Sedgwick, Eve Kosofsky, 206, 210–11
Segal, Lynne, 234–35, 237
Segovia, Fernando F., 17, 113, 115–16, 184–85, 186, 216, 230–31
Seidman, Steven, 235, 237, 238
Sellin, Ernst, 265–66
Serres, Michel, 63
sexuality, 30–31, 52, 96, 99–105, 113, 114, 115, 119, 131–37, 151–52, 196–97, 206–12, 233–38, 243, 251–60
Shannon, David, 216
Shell, Marc, 170–71
Sherburne, Donald W., 203
Sherwood, Yvonne, 69–75
Shils, Edward, 122
Shirato, Tony, 44
sign, signifier, signified, 6, 9–10, 16, 33–34, 36–37, 49, 56–59, 63–68, 69–70, 76, 107–8, 109–10, 128–29, 141–42, 146–47, 151–52, 157–59, 163, 167–73, 174, 177, 190, 192, 206, 207
Simmons, Christina, 235
Simon, Sherry, 235, 257
Singer, Beth J., 268–69
Smith, Abraham, 181, 216, 257–58
Smith, Sidonie, 16
Smith-Christopher, Daniel, 113
Smyth, Damian Barry, 266–67
Snitow, Ann, 237
Snowden, Frank M., Jr., 215–16
Soja, Edward W., 241–43
Southwick, Stephen M., 261